Women's Work

For all of the women in my family.

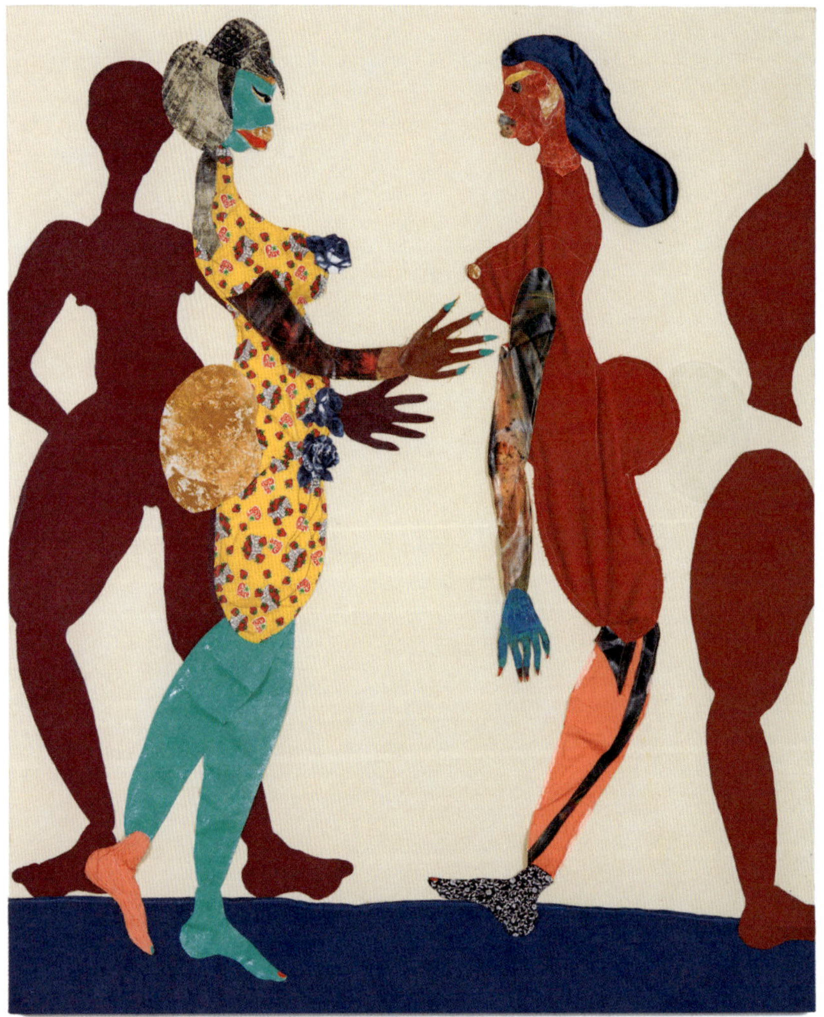

Tschabalala Self, *Out of Body*, 2015 (see page 199).

Ferren Gipson

Women's Work

From feminine arts to feminist art

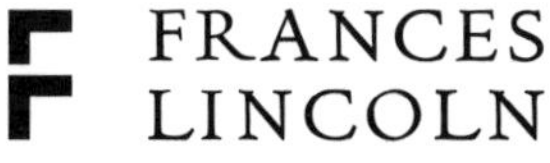

FRANCES LINCOLN

Contents

Introduction 7

The Women of Gee's Bend 12
Maria Martinez 18
Elsa Schiaparelli 22
Anni Albers 28
Lucie Rie 34
Lenore Tawney 38
Dorothea Tanning 44
Louise Bourgeois 50
Rut Bryk 56
Monir Shahroudy Farmanfarmaian 62
Miriam Schapiro 68
Yayoi Kusama 74
Faith Ringgold 80
Magdalena Abakanowicz 86
Olga de Amaral 92
Sheila Hicks 98
Eva Hesse 104
Marva Lee Pitchford-Jolly 110
Judy Chicago 114

Judith Scott 120
Annette Messager 126
Isabelle de Borchgrave 132
Dindga McCannon 136
Cecilia Vicuña 142
Mrinalini Mukherjee 148
Polly Apfelbaum 154
Sarah Lucas 160
Yin Xiuzhen 166
Billie Zangewa 172
Otobong Nkanga 178
Alexandra Kehayoglou 184
Sarah Zapata 190
Tschabalala Self 196
Hannah Hill 202

More artists to explore 210
Bibliography 212
Index 216
Picture credits 220
Acknowledgements 222

Introduction

'At first, I felt proud when someone said, "Your work looks like a man did it." Then I realized that was stupid.'

– Annette Messager, in *The New York Times*, 2007

This is a book celebrating work by women in mediums that have historically been labelled 'women's work'. *And just what is that phrase supposed to mean?*, you may ask. Excellent question. We know that people of any gender can (and do) carry out any type of work, but it is true that women across many cultures have historically done much of the weaving, sewing and spinning in their communities for centuries. In some societies, such as some indigenous cultures of the Americas, women were also the exclusive producers of ceramic objects. Even all the way back in the Stone Age, it was likely to have been women makers who sculpted and fired some of the oldest surviving ceramic figurines. Over thousands of years, these essential skills – which provided clothing, vessels to cook and store food and more – came to be closely associated with the activities of women.

Today, we can acquire most necessities without having to make them or seek out an expert, so it has become easy to take for granted that creating textiles and ceramics requires an incredible amount of skill – not to mention the added difficultly of making these items beautiful. This convenience is a result of the Industrial Revolution, when machines allowed for the easier and cheaper production of goods. But for as long as there have been people who wish to automate processes, there have been creative people who have reacted against that industrialization to preserve artisanal techniques. The Arts and Crafts movement of the late nineteenth and early twentieth centuries is an excellent example, wherein artists championed traditional craftsmanship and produced ornate textiles, furniture, ceramics and architectural designs. It was a movement that centred on several art forms that women had traditionally been working in for centuries, yet somehow, exceptional designers like May Morris (1862–1938) and sisters Margaret Macdonald (1864–1933) and Frances Macdonald (1873–1921), have not always received due acknowledgement for their contributions.

Ah, yes, I mentioned 'crafts'. This is another loaded term that is sometimes used to distinguish textiles and ceramics from 'fine' or 'high' art. The idea behind this distinction is that because these mediums can be used to produce functional objects, they cannot be viewed in a purely aesthetic way. Moreover, as mediums like quilting or sewing have traditionally been categorized as domestic feminine pursuits, they have not always been taken seriously within a male-dominated art world. These attitudes have meant that modern and contemporary artists who have worked in these mediums have had to persevere to overcome the narrow perceptions of their field.

Using the medium of sculpture as an example, we can track how traditional approaches to art have changed over time and how women artists have had a direct impact on that development. For centuries of Western art history, sculpture largely consisted of idealistic classical figures carved from marble, grand statements of power hewn from stone, symbols of religious devotion chiselled from wood and other such three-dimensional works. During the twentieth century, the scope of sculpture in modern Western art expanded as artists created more abstracted forms, and groups like the Dadaists and Surrealists introduced new materials and found objects.

Méret Oppenheim's 1936 Surrealist piece *Object (Le Déjeuner en fourrure)* is an example of the new radical possibilities in sculpture that emerged in the early part of the century. She purchased a teacup, saucer and spoon from a department store and covered each item in gazelle fur. In popular culture, a tea set could be associated with femininity and refinement – perhaps a beverage sipped by the same kind of elegant women who wear furs – but Oppenheim combined these objects and turned them into something shocking. The softness of the fur feels pleasant to the hand, but applied to a cup and touching the mouth, the feeling would be repulsive. This interplay of contrasting elements embodies the spirit of Surrealism and can also be considered an early example of soft sculpture.

'Soft sculptures' are three-dimensional artworks that incorporate fabric, plastics, rubber, fibres and other cloth-like materials. They may be stuffed, draped, sewn or hung. The origins of these types of works are often traced back to 1957, when Claes Oldenburg stuffed a women's stocking with newspaper and hung it on a wall. At the time it was made, it was an untitled work, but this playful piece is now called Sausage. After creating Sausage, Oldenburg redirected his attention to drawing until, from 1961, he revisited the idea. From then, he caused a commotion on the New York art scene with stuffed and sewn sculptures of everyday objects, many of which were sewn by his wife Patty Mucha in the early days.

Around the time Oldenburg returned to soft sculpture, his studio was in the same building as Yayoi Kusama and Eva Hesse – two future giants of the medium, and both featured in this book. In 1962, Kusama showed her first soft sculpture, *Accumulation No. 1*, of an armchair covered in stuffed phalluses. Oldenburg and Kusama were friends as well as studio neighbours, and Kusama has asserted that Oldenburg was inspired by the work she'd been doing on *Accumulation No. 1* in developing his own stuffed works.

Since the 1960s, more artists – particularly women – have worked in soft sculpture, helping to expand the definition and possibilities within sculpture, more broadly. This includes artists like Sarah Lucas, who created stuffed objects, as well as Magdalena Abakanowicz, who made stunning weavings that occupy three-dimensional space. By intentionally utilizing soft, 'feminine' materials to create works in what was long viewed as the hard, 'male' medium of sculpture, women artists have subverted patriarchal norms and visualized new perspectives in art. The same can be said for other women artists who looked to ceramics and other textile mediums as modern forms of artistic expression.

Many of the artists in the pages to follow shook off stale views of their chosen medium by using innovative methods and unconventional materials.

Artists such as Lucie Rie and Anni Albers blurred the perceived line between fine art and design, while others like Mrinalini Mukherjee and Lenore Tawney pushed the technical boundaries of traditional art to create something entirely new. These artists also understood the storytelling potential of their work, and we can observe the power of engaging with different histories and identities in the works of artists like Faith Ringgold and Sarah Zapata.

In an article titled 'Feminism in Art, With Respect', published in the 11 June 2000 issue of *The New York Times*, artist Miriam Schapiro is quoted as saying,

'I hate elitism, and elitism in art through the centuries was handed down by men. We were never seen as makers of art. For thousands of years, weaving, ceramics, sewing were believed to be what untutored women made with their hands. But that was our art.'

The history of 'women's work' has meant that mediums like textiles and ceramics have served as particularly potent tools to engage with feminist issues in modern and contemporary art. These mediums are fortified with a special capacity to express women's stories and diverse perspectives through their historical associations with the feminine. For that reason, they are the perfect means of dismantling stereotypes, tapping into different experiences of womanhood and disrupting historically male spaces.

The artworks in this book are 'women's work' in the most literal sense of having been produced by women and in representing mediums that have historically fallen under the umbrella of that label, but one must place their tongue *firmly* in cheek with regard to the term's antiquated use in defining socially 'appropriate' activities for ladies. Women can and should do whatever-the-hell kinds of work they want.

A Book as a Quilt

This book includes the artworks and stories of thirty-three individuals and one collective who have worked across ceramics, textiles and soft sculpture. I set out consciously to profile a selection of women from different backgrounds, whose lives and works represent a range of artistic, political and social perspectives. Together, their individual stories provide an overview of how the mediums in which they worked developed critically and technically from the twentieth century onwards. Through my research and writing, I was struck by this gestalt and how much it reminds me of quilting. Each artist's story is like one unique block, coming together to form a larger quilt. I thought this would be a perfect metaphor to guide us through this exploration of women's work as it relates to modern and contemporary art.

In quilting, blocks are individual units that are sewn together to form the wider design – they can be solid or formed of different colours and materials. Within this quilt of women's work, each artist has her own block (or chapter) where you can discover how her practice has contributed to the story of textile and ceramic art in the 20th and 21st centuries. Blocks are arranged chronologically by the artist's birth year, which is helpful for seeing how themes and techniques developed, as well as showing how some artists' stories intersect, but feel free to dive in and out of blocks in any order you choose.

Many of the artists featured have worked in mediums outside of the remit of this book, and those works are not discussed at length, if at all. You will also find that there are many women who have worked in these mediums who are not featured. This book does not aim to be a comprehensive history of modern and contemporary women's work, but rather seeks to provide a cross-section of the story from the perspectives of a group of diverse and incredibly talented women working across textiles, fibre art and ceramics.

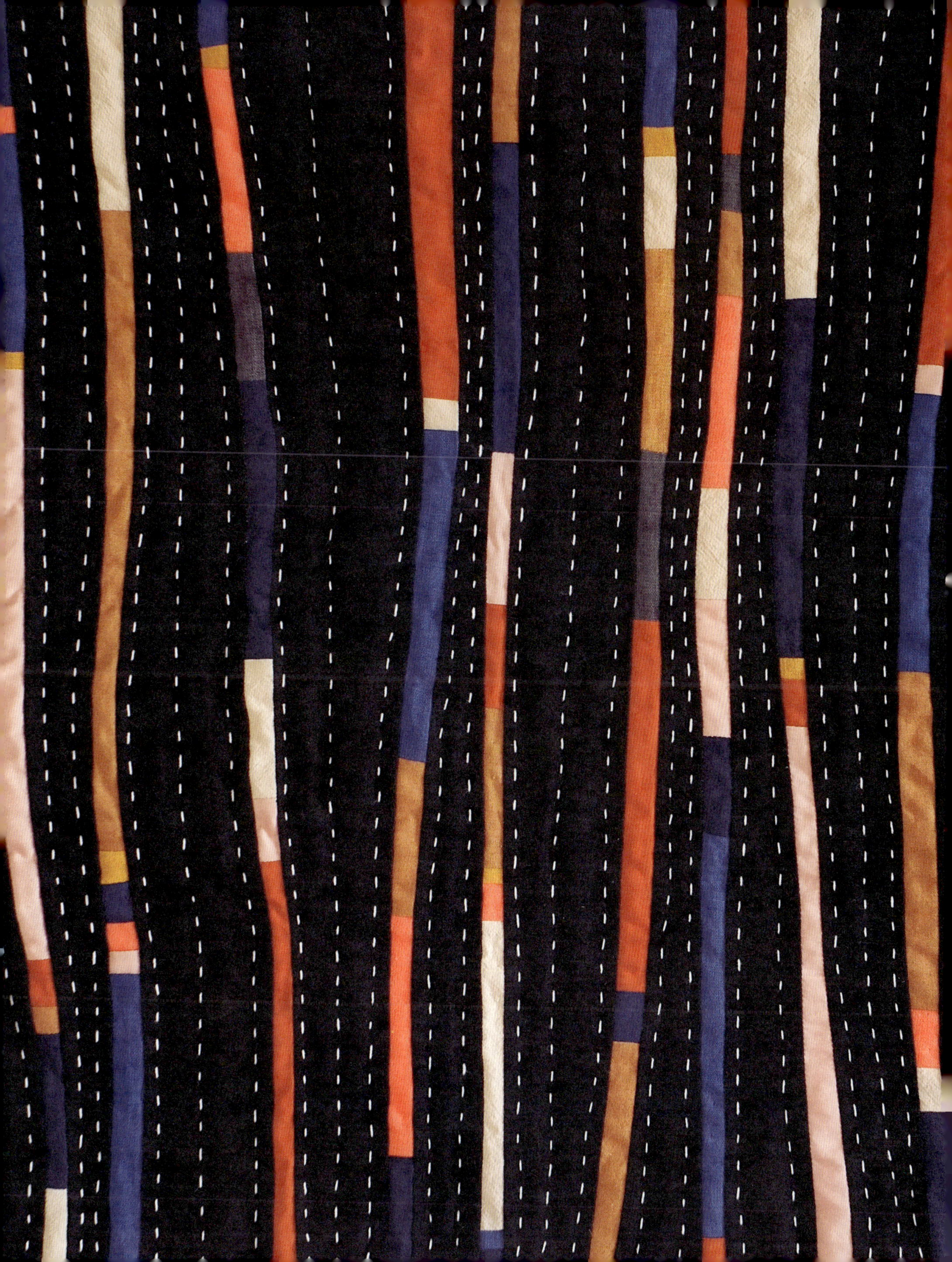

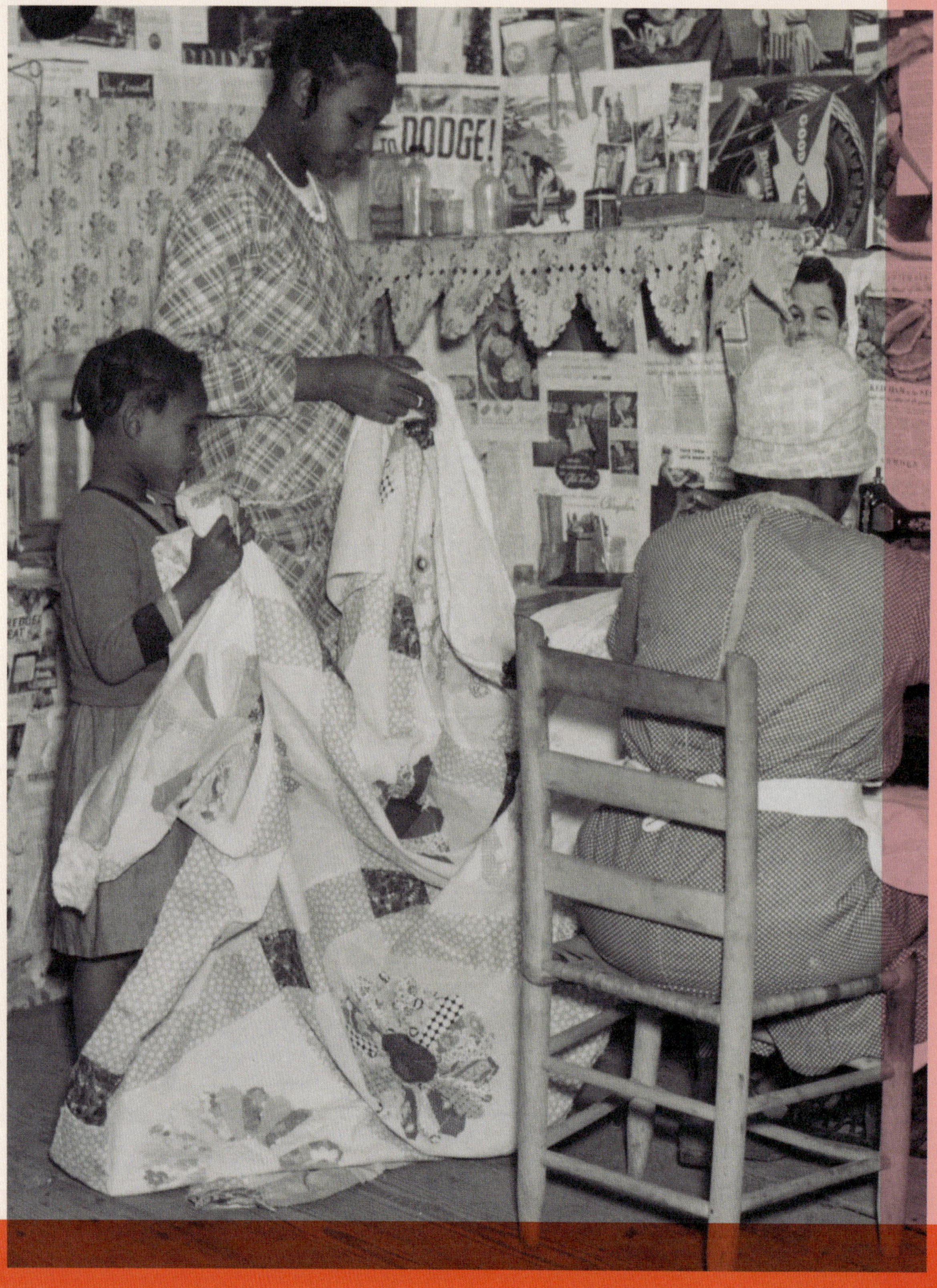

The Women of Gee's Bend

Quilting

Quilts tell a story through the patterns they display, the materials from which they're composed and the traditions they carry forward. Over two centuries, the women of Gee's Bend, Alabama have perfected their own quilting customs and their boldly modern designs are imbued with the legacy of Black artistic traditions and a story that resonates with many Black communities in post-Civil War America.

In central Alabama, there is a tight-knit community of less than 800 people, surrounded on three sides by the winding Alabama River. It's tucked away and rural – there's not even a traffic light to break up a drive along any of its quiet country roads. To find the town on a map, you would need to look for the name Boykin, but it is better known as Gee's Bend. This name traces back to a slave owner named Joseph Gee, who purchased the land in 1816 and brought eighteen enslaved Black people with him from North Carolina to set up a cotton plantation. The plantation was later purchased by the Pettway family in 1845 and some freed families continued to work the land as sharecroppers after emancipation. The present population is predominantly Black, with many residents descended from the enslaved families who were brought to the area centuries ago.

The story of Gee's Bend's quilts has a very practical origin: keeping warm. Up to the 1930s, many houses in the area were designed in what's known as a 'shotgun' layout. They get this descriptive name because one could stand at the front door of the narrow home and fire a bullet that would pass through every room of the house before exiting out the back door. The design is great for keeping cool in the summer, but less effective for staying warm in the winter months – not to mention the draughty wooden windows and floors. Quilts provided a

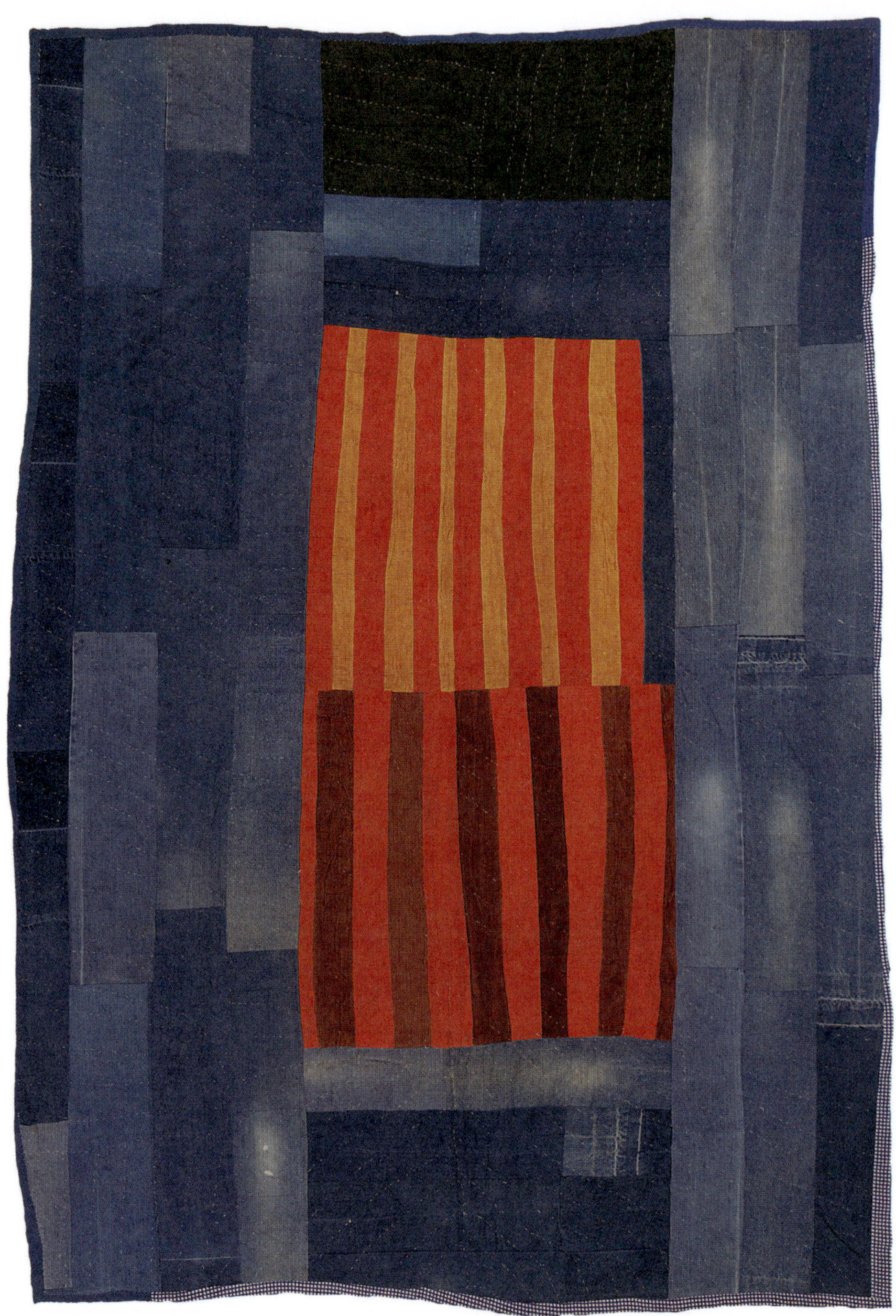

Annie Mae Young, *Work-clothes Quilt with Centre Medallion of Strips*, 1976. Denim, corduroy, synthetic blend (britches legs with pockets). 274.2 × 195.6 cm (108 × 77 in).

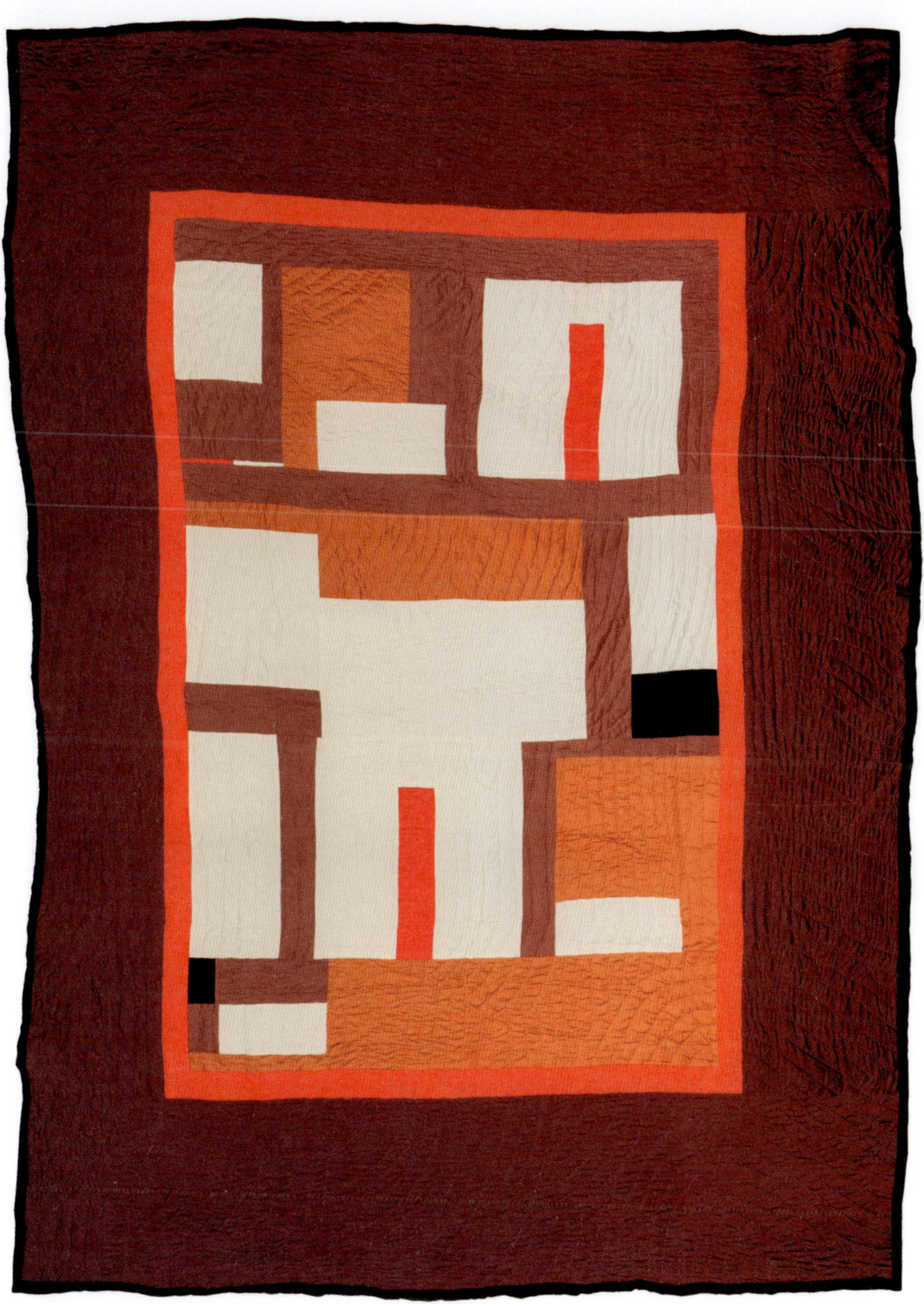

Louisiana P Bendolph, *My Way*, 2000.
Cotton and cotton blend.
238.8 × 218.4 cm (94 × 86 in).

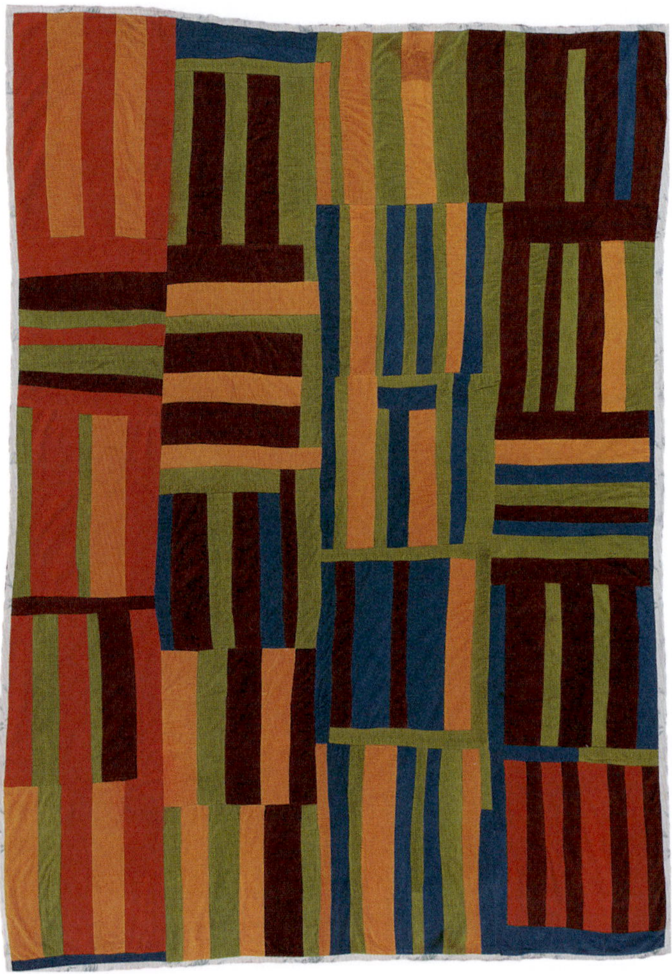

Willie 'Ma Willie' Abrams, *'Roman Stripes' Variation*, c.1975.
Cotton and cotton blend.
238.8 × 218.4 cm (94 × 86 in).

versatile way to wrap up warm in bed at night, but they could also be laid on the ground or hung on the walls to block a breeze.

Since the nineteenth century, quilters in Gee's Bend have repurposed scraps of fabric and old clothes into elaborate abstract designs. The quilts are mainly produced by the women in the community and there is a learning process the younger girls go through to inherit the skill. As small groups of women work on quilts, the little

ones assist by threading the needles. From there, they graduate to making the occasional stitch (which may be cut out and redone if necessary). Mary Margaret Pettway, an educator and third-generation Gee's Bend quilter, began learning in this way from around the age of four and was making her own quilts tops by eleven.

She says, 'A lot of them, to me, are memory quilts. They're not designed as such, but they're memory quilts because you can see your old dress

Since the nineteenth century, quilters in Gee's Bend have repurposed scraps of fabric and old clothes into elaborate, abstract designs.

in a quilt. You think back to the first day of school or your old shirts. You see it and it brings back great memories.'

Stylistically, quilts by Gee's Bend artists are abstract and geometric, with many falling under the category of 'my way' quilts. This is a term the women use for improvisational quilts they create without the constraint of a set pattern or colours. The results are unique compositions with a modern aesthetic comparable to the geometric paintings of Paul Klee or the bold designs of Saul Bass. Even within their improvisational approach, there are some general patterns that are popular amongst the group. The 'housetop' is a favourite design, so named because of the way strips are sewn to the top of a rectangular strip (like a roof) before sewing other pieces around the bottom and sides to create concentric rectangles. This design can be repeated many times across the quilt or can make up the entire composition. In a 1976 quilt by Annie Mae Young (1928–2013), she used strips of old work cloths to create a fiery core of red and yellow stripes surrounded by a modified take on the stepped housetop design. It's a perfect example of how, even when referring to established patterns, the artists could make quilts 'their way'.

After many decades of quilting, the women of Gee's Bend began to draw notice for their work from outside of their community. Their first big exposure came in the 1960s, when some of the artists participated in the Freedom Quilting Bee, a collective of Black women quilters based in nearby Rehoboth, Alabama. The group was formed in 1966 as a way for the women to make and sell quilts to earn extra income, but they also participated in voting rights activism, such as the famous march from Selma to Montgomery, Alabama. Their noble work came at great personal sacrifice: the sheriff retaliated by closing the ferry that helped easily connect the Gee's Bend community to other towns. Despite this challenge, some artists continued to collaborate with the Freedom Quilting Bee.

In 1972, the department store Sears made a deal with the Freedom Quilting Bee collective for the group to sew a line of corduroy pillow covers. They didn't have the opportunity to create these pillows 'their way', but the women were left with a sizeable amount of leftover fabric in very Seventies' shades of avocado, orange and mustard. The quilters took these pieces home to create richly coloured designs with the heavyweight material. A 1975 example by Willie 'Ma Willie' Abrams (1897–1987) demonstrates her take on the traditional Roman stripes quilt pattern. Rather than keeping to a grid of equally sized blocks, she twists and turns stripes at irregular intervals. The lines of the stripes are also inconsistent and wavy in places, adding to the visual interest of the piece and drawing the viewer's eye from one block to the next. The fact that the lines on many of the quilts have a slight wiggle or curve reveals the hand of the artist in a way that a straight line would not, and it gives each piece a unique and expressive quality.

National recognition for Gee's Bend artists came in the 1990s, when a photograph of Annie Mae Young's blue and orange quilt was published in the book *A Communion of the Spirits: African American Quilters, Preservers, and Their Stories* by Roland Freeman. Some years later, collector William Arnett came across this image and visited Gee's Bend. In 2002, he curated an exhibition at the Museum of Fine Arts in Houston featuring quilts by forty-two of the artists. From there, the artists' incredible quilts have garnered greater and continued acclaim as they've exhibited domestically and internationally.

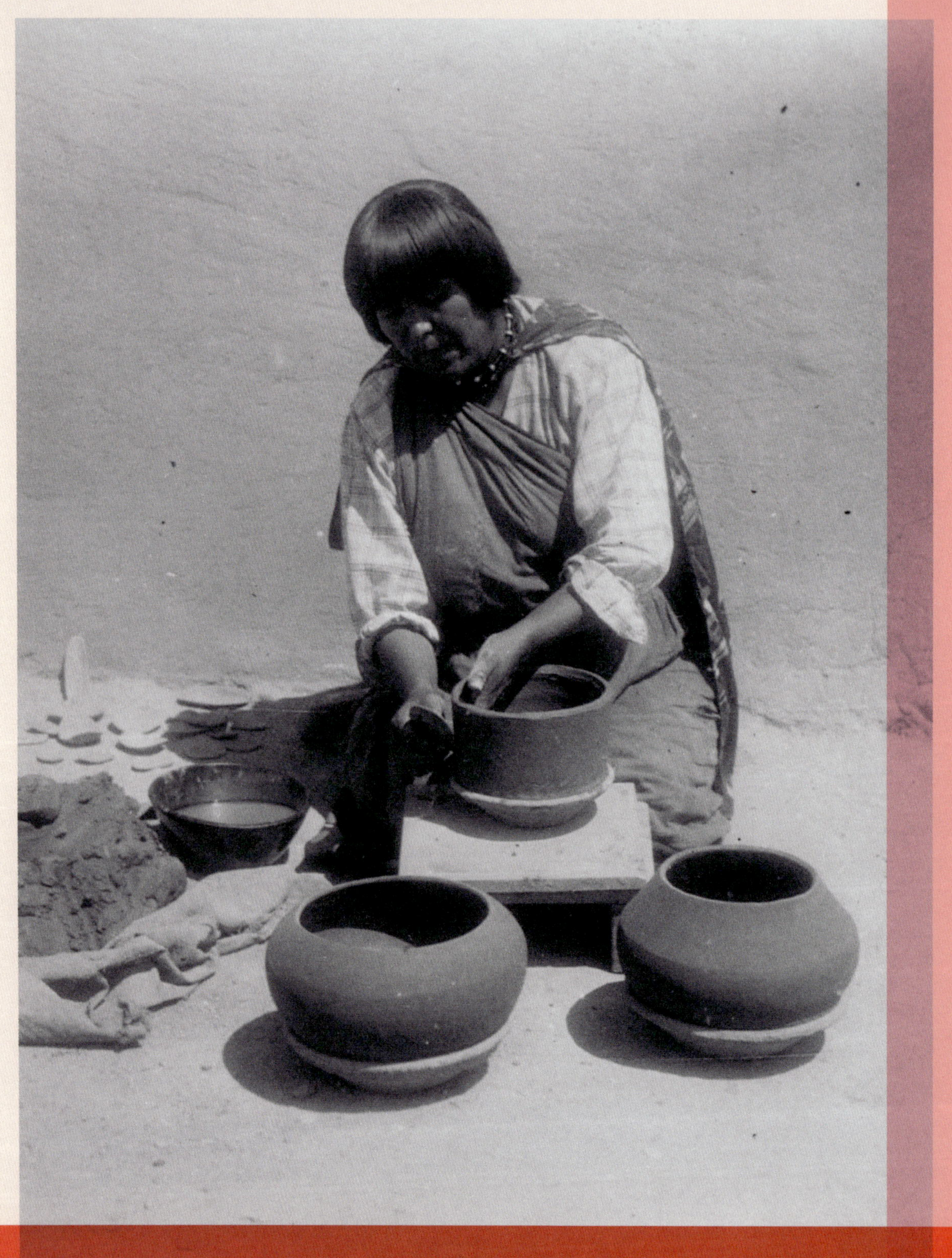

Maria Martinez

(1887–1980)

Ceramics

The sleek black pottery of Maria Martinez is the embodiment of timelessness. Her curved vessels decorated in black-on-black geometric designs hark back to the ancient pottery of her Pueblo Native American ancestors, but also deliver a modern perspective by producing sumptuous vessels as purely aesthetic objects. The distinct blackware aesthetic she developed had a transformative effect on her life, the lives of those around her and, more broadly, perceptions of ceramics as a fine art medium.

Martinez – born Maria Montoya – lived the entirety of her life at the pueblo (a Native American settlement, particularly one by the Pueblo people) in San Ildefonso in New Mexico. Growing up, she and her sisters watched her aunt and grandmother make pots with the other women in their community, using traditional methods. The pottery-making process was often divided so that each person had a specific role, such as painting or firing the wares. After years of watching, Martinez learned to shape pieces by hand and paint dynamic geometric, animal and floral designs. By the time she reached the age of thirteen, it was apparent that she had a special talent for ceramics.

For more than a thousand years, Puebloan pottery was divided into two main use categories: functional and ceremonial. Practical pottery used to prepare and store food was often done in a rough grey design known as greyware (easy to remember). Ceremonial vessels were more decorative by comparison and might include designs in shades of cream, red, brown and yellow. At the time Martinez was growing up, black designs on red clay were the most common style. The wares have always had strong aesthetic merits but they were generally utilitarian in purpose. In the late 1800s, as railroad lines moved west, the Hispanic and Native communities who used these ceramics were able to find cheaper metal or mass-produced alternatives. Thus, the practical need for Pueblo-made pottery, which was time-consuming to make, declined.

In 1904, Maria married Julian Martinez, who became her artistic partner until he died in 1943. Maria shaped the pottery, Julian painted the designs, and they each fired the vessels. Together they established an international reputation as expert ceramicists through exhibiting their skills and wares at world fairs in St Louis (1904), San Diego (1915), Chicago (1933) and San Francisco (1939). Off the back of their growing reputation, they were asked to assist on a Pueblo archaeological site. It was here that the pair encountered sherds of ancient black Pueblo pottery that inspired them to develop their iconic blackware style.

Martinez summoned all her pottery knowledge to work out how to recreate the elegant black effect. She also studied pottery by makers in Santa Clara Pueblo who still produced polished blackware. After extensive experimentation, she found a successful method that involved using special paints and trapping smoke around vessels using cow manure to create contrasting matte and gloss blacks – a less than fragrant technique, to be sure. While she was inspired by ancient techniques and designs, her wares were not reproductions. She and her husband integrated styles from the past alongside new symbolism and methods to create a modern and different aesthetic.

A vessel dated between 1919 and 1920 offers an example of the pair's work after years of perfecting their technique. The bowl has a wide matte black belly with a glossy black design. It depicts the deity Awanyu, a Pueblo water guardian. He's often represented as a snake-like figure with horns. His body is curvy and mimics waving water, while a zig-zag arrow symbolizing lightning shoots forth from his mouth. The deity appears on Pueblo pottery and wall paintings in Arizona and New Mexico

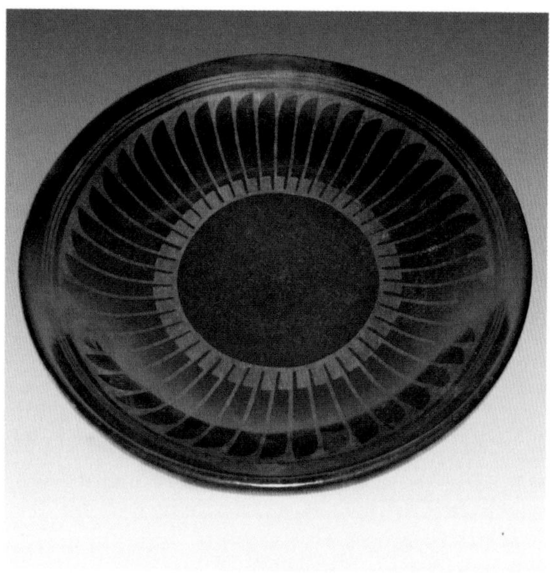

Maria Martinez and Santana Roybal Martinez, *Feather Bowl*, 1948. Polished black matt ware. 5.2 × 37.8 cm (2 × 14⅞ in).

and embodies the importance of water and rain to Native cultures of these desert areas.

By the 1920s, Martinez's designs were established as desirable art pieces, rather than functional objects. Non-Native audiences collected her work and the sales of these pieces helped support the San Ildefonso community. She shared her knowledge with other women in her pueblo and neighbouring pueblos so that they could also generate income from pottery sales. When her husband died, she worked with her sons and her daughter-in-law, Santana Martinez, to continue producing wares. Collaborating with Santana, in 1948 she created a plate which shows how they sometimes drew inspiration from other cultures for some of their designs. The design depicts a ring of glossy black feathers against a matte black background. The blade-like feathers are a motif found in earlier pottery by the Mimbres culture of the North American southwest.

Martinez was an instrumental figure in repositioning traditional ceramics as art objects.

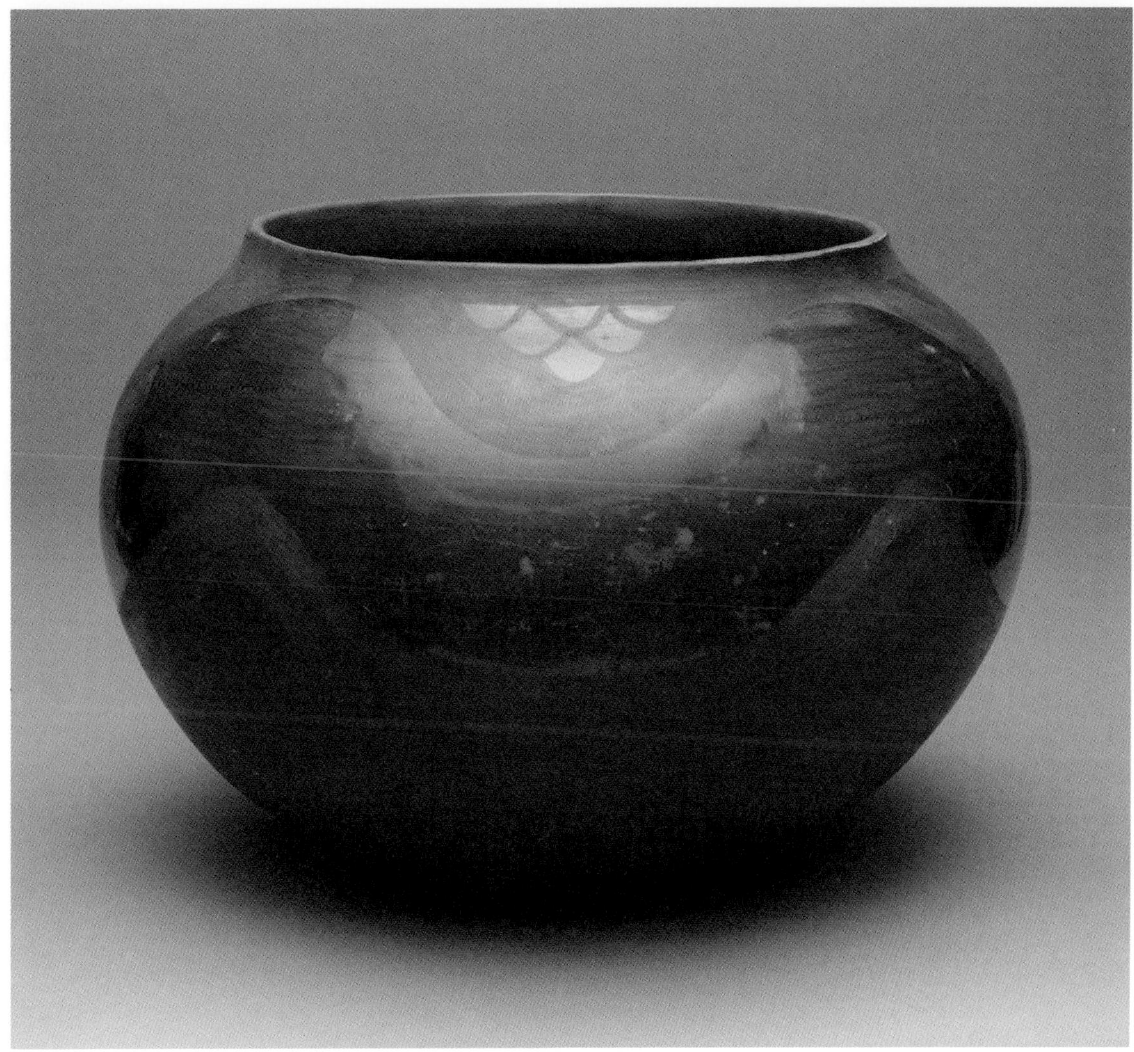

Maria Martinez with Julian Martinez, *Black-on-Black Jar*, 1919–20.
Clay and slip. 29 × 35 cm (11⁷/₁₆ × 13¾ in).

In 1973, she received a grant from the National Endowment for the Arts to establish a pottery workshop. Her ingenuity and fresh perspective on Pueblo pottery helped revitalize an endangered art form and empower other potters in pueblo communities to earn income through their art. It's no wonder that Martinez was invited to the White House four times (by four different presidents) and received multiple awards, including honorary doctorates from New Mexico State University and the University of Colorado. Although she came to be one of the greatest potters of her lifetime, she was known to be humble and generous, repeatedly stating that God gave her gifts to use for her people.

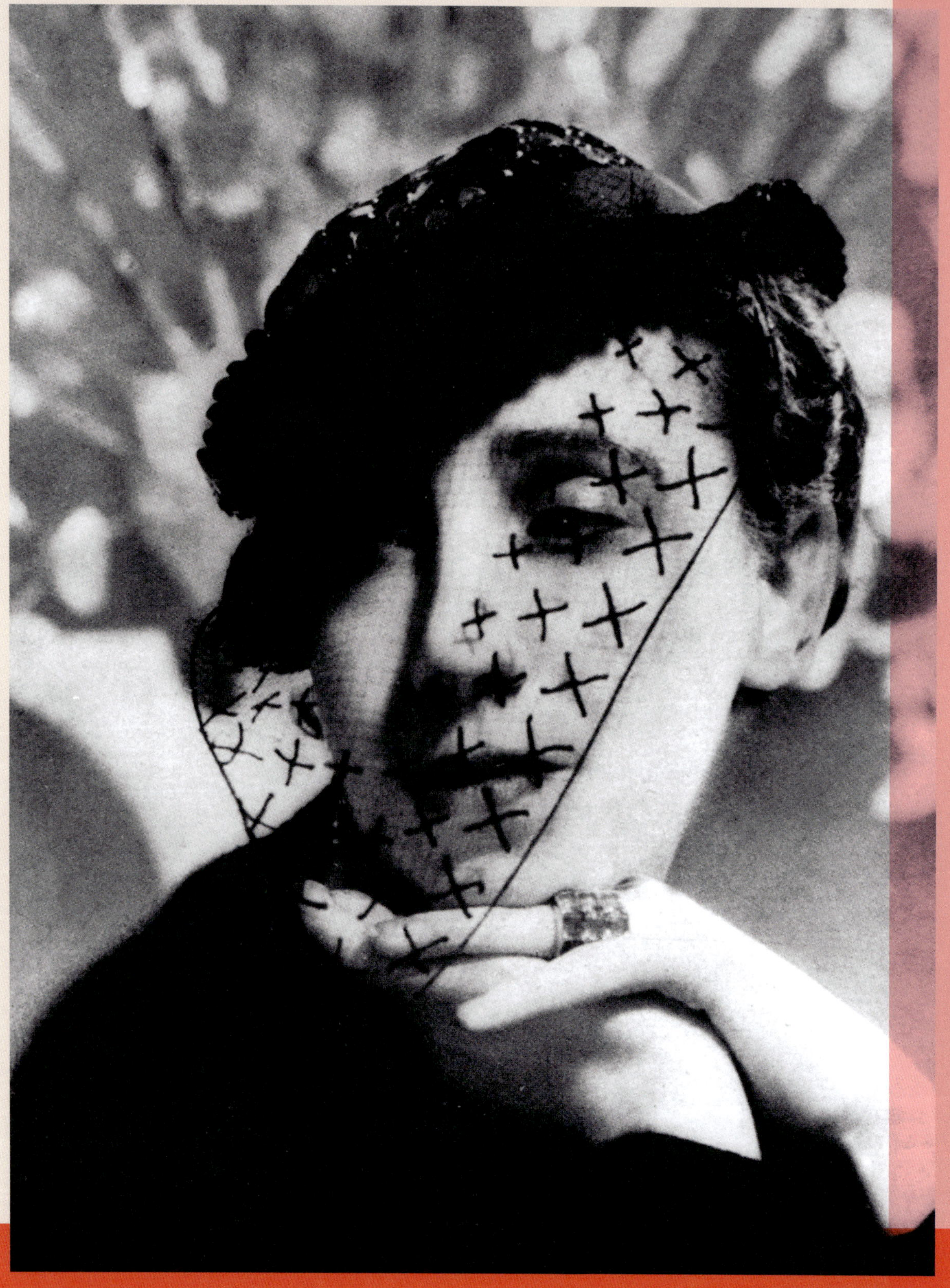

Elsa Schiaparelli

(1890–1973)

Wearable art

Before Lady Gaga wore her infamous 'Meat Dress' and even before Hollywood starlets began attending the annual Met Gala donning boundary-pushing abstract fashions, there was Elsa Schiaparelli. Her rival and contemporary Coco Chanel called her 'that Italian artist who is making clothes', intending it as an insult, but today it reads much more like a succinct description of Schiaparelli's innovative practice. If Chanel thought Schiaparelli could be discouraged by remarks such as that, she clearly didn't grasp the artist's rebellious spirit and willingness to be 'shocking'.

From the moment of her birth, Schiaparelli defied her parent's expectations. The couple had hoped so much that their second child would be a boy, that they hadn't even considered girls' names – yet there she was. The given name Elsa was a last-minute decision at her christening that she would later discard in favour of the nickname 'Schiap'. Her family, who lived in Palazzo Corsini (a palace!) in Rome, was wealthy and exceptionally intellectual. Her father was a scholar specializing in the history of the Islamic world, her uncle was an astronomer and her cousin an Egyptologist. Young Schiaparelli's exposure to these fields stimulated her interests in mythology and mysticism and instilled in her a grand sense of adventure. Her interest in beauty can be traced, in part, to her mother, who constantly called her ugly. Ever the defiant child, she began to imagine whimsical ways of proving her mother wrong. This led to one occasion when she stuffed her ears, nose and mouth with seeds in the hope of sprouting flowers.

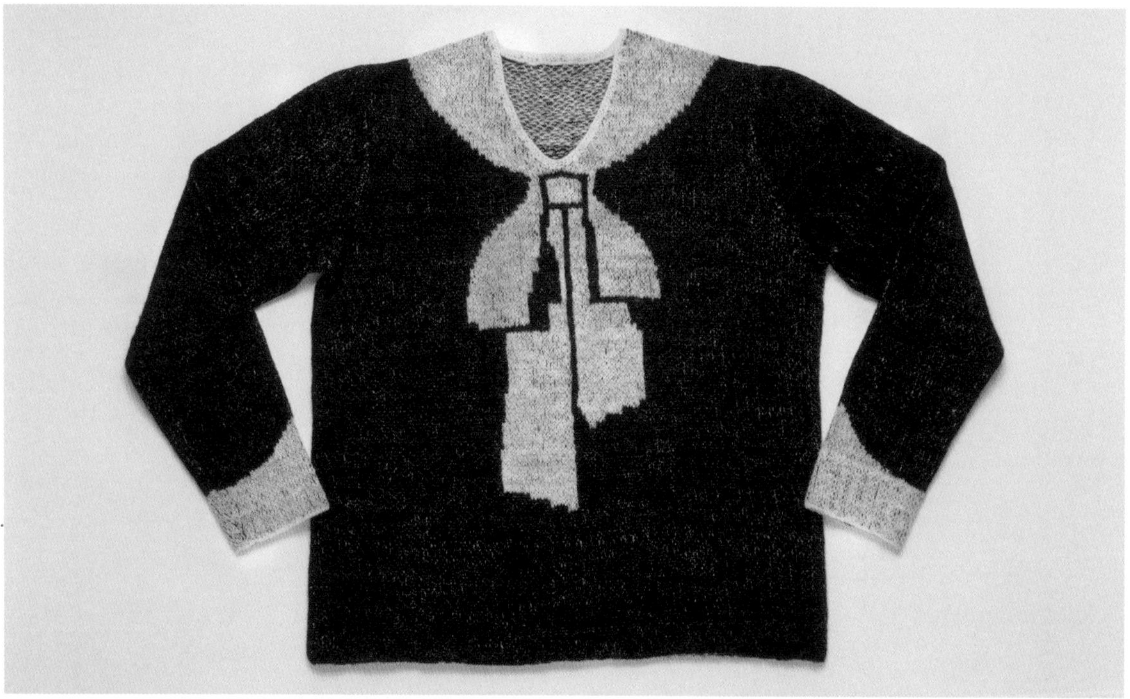

Woman's Sweater, 1927.
Hand-knitted wool.

When Schiaparelli was twenty-two, her parents tried to betroth her to a wealthy Russian suitor. She rejected the proposal and swiftly made plans to move far away to London to work as a nanny. On her journey to England, she made a brief but significant stop in Paris. During her ten-day stay, she discovered that it was a city in which she'd like to live. She even had her first practice at being a couturier when she hastily draped and pinned a gown together to attend a ball. Once she was settled in London, she took in the sights and attended lectures. It was in one such lecture that she met her future husband, Wilhem de Kerlor, who captivated her with talk about magic and philosophy. The pair were quickly married and eventually settled in New York.

Their relationship deteriorated over time and after the birth of their first child, de Kerlor abandoned his family, leaving Schiaparelli in need of money. She worked several odd jobs while socializing with interesting art characters like Marcel Duchamp and Man Ray, whom she met through her good friend Gabrièle Buffet-Picabia, an art critic and the wife of Dadaist Francis Picabia. Many of these friends eventually moved to Paris and, in 1922, Schiaparelli followed. She didn't have much money, but back on European soil, she was able to leverage her family's connections to move within affluent social circles.

Over time, Schiaparelli felt the urge to creatively express herself and, after discarding painting and sculpture as options, decided to pursue fashion. In her biography she made it clear that she viewed dress design as an 'art' rather than a 'profession'. Her first major success was a black sweater she designed in 1927 with a white trompe-l'oeil effect bow. Years after

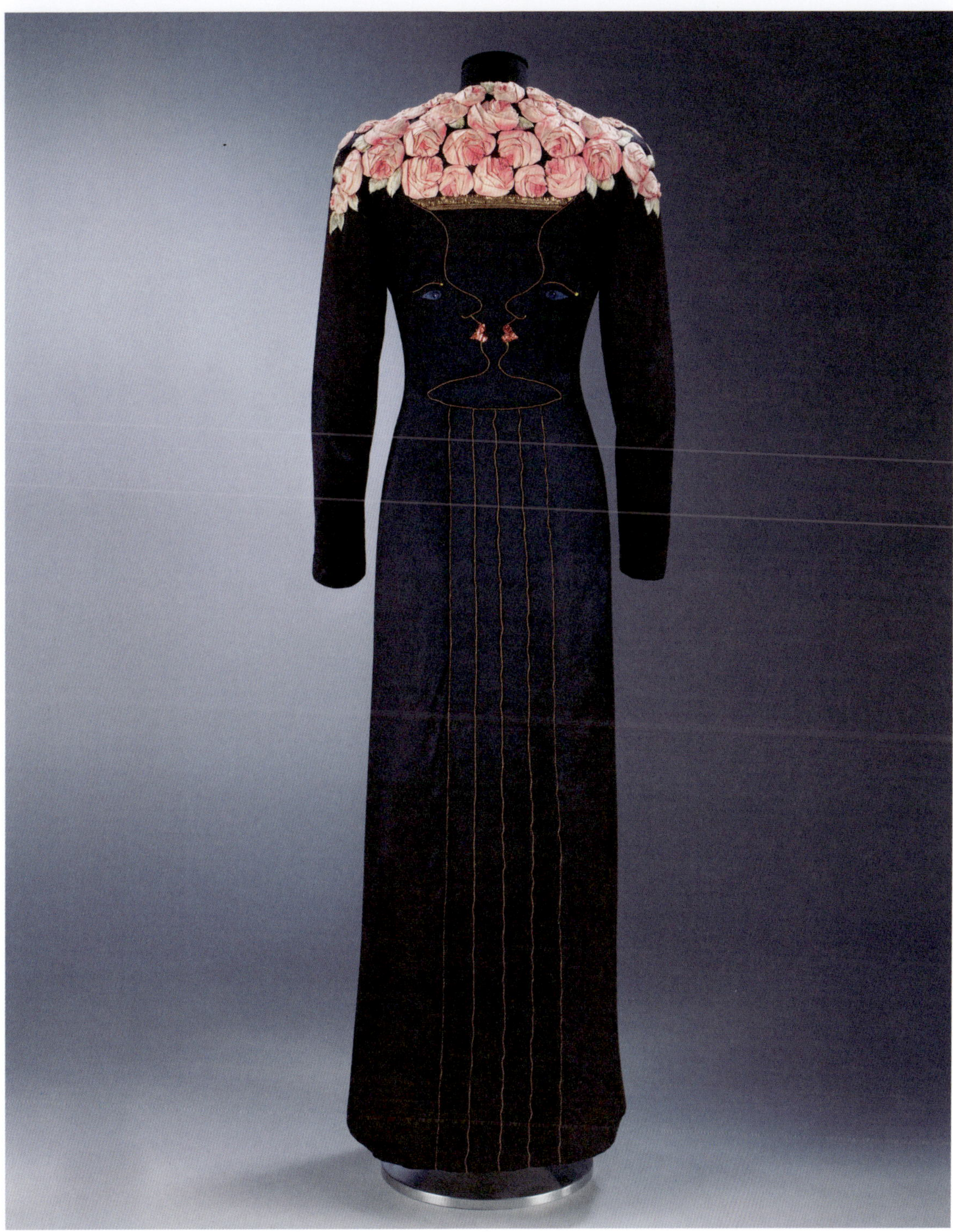

Elsa Schiaparelli and Jean Cocteau, *Evening Coat,* 1937.
Silk jersey, with gold thread, silk embroidery and applied decoration in silk.

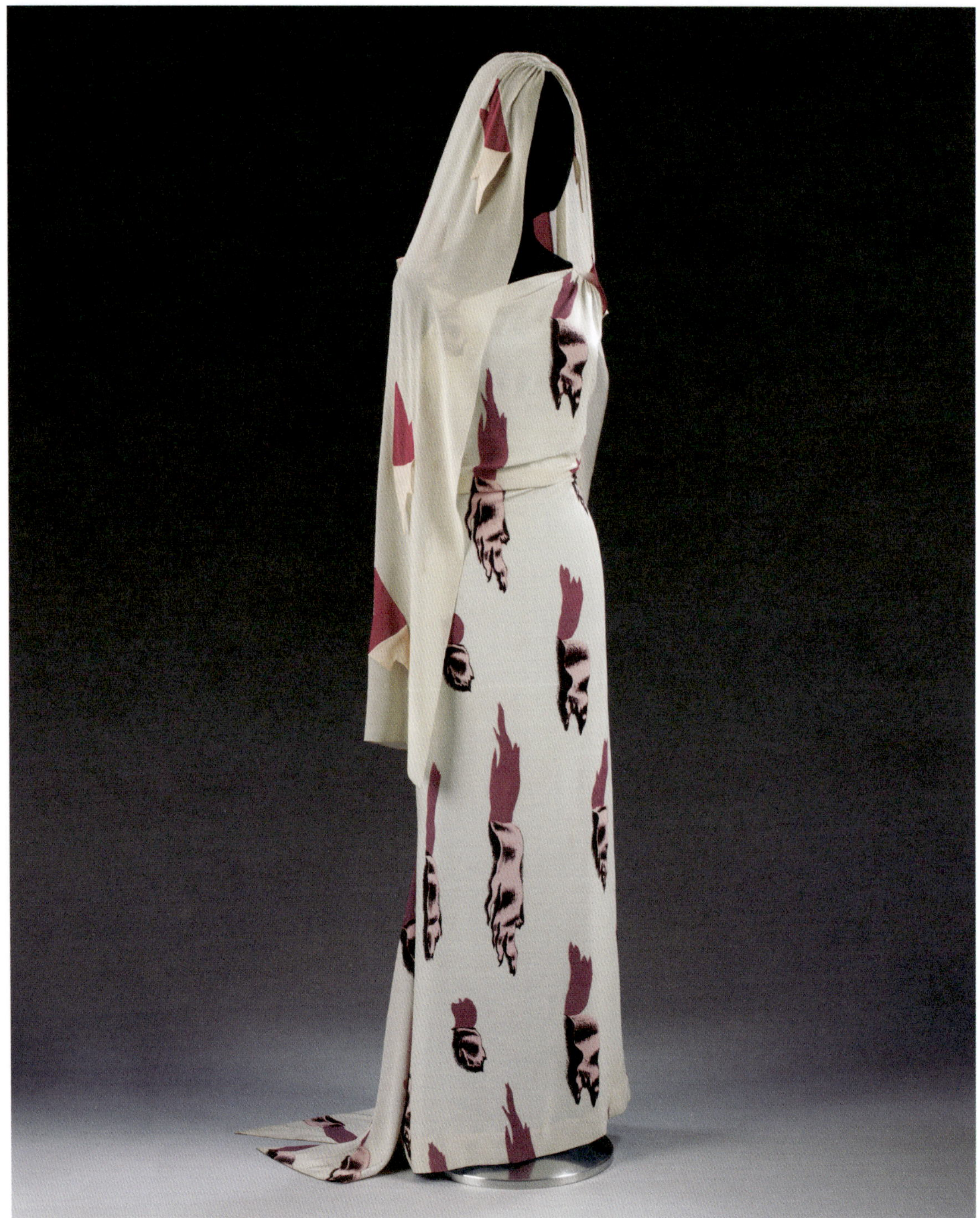

The Tears Dress, 1938.
Viscose-rayon and silk blend fabric printed with trompe l'oeil print.

Schiaparelli's designs had a light-heartedness that drew negative critique from fashion gatekeepers but earned her the respect of artists like Salvador Dalí and Hollywood starlets like Mae West.

it was made, the sweater has been labelled Surrealist – probably due in part to her later associations with the Surrealists, as well as the whimsical trick of the eye in the design. Unable to knit herself, she had a couple, who ran a small factory, knit it for her. After wearing the sweater to a luncheon, she was inundated with requests for reproductions by the society women in attendance. A business was born.

Schiaparelli's designs throughout the 1920s reflect the changing needs of modern women. She designed the wrap dress – an invention often misattributed Diane von Furstenberg – which allowed women to easily dress themselves without assistance and developed a 'divided skirt' (today we might call it a skort) worn by tennis player Lili de Alvarez at Wimbledon. Her designs had a light-heartedness that drew negative critique from fashion gatekeepers but earned her the respect of artists like Salvador Dalí and Hollywood starlets like Mae West. Her work can be seen in its most artistic form when she leaned into her imaginative inclinations, and experimented with unusual materials in the 1930s.

Soon, Schiaparelll was collaborating with other artists on her work. In 1936, she worked with Méret Oppenheim to create a fur-covered bracelet – a design that Oppenheim explored further in her famous *Object (Le Déjeuner en fourrure)* sculpture of a furry tea set later that year. The bracelet was part of a collection that also included a ring covered in – you guessed it – fur. Just a couple years later, Schiaparelli collaborated with artist Jean Cocteau to design a floor-length evening coat that is understated at the front, but full of whimsy at the back. The upper back and shoulders are draped in pink roses and the thin gold outline of two faces – perhaps about to kiss – underneath. Cocteau sketched the design for the coat during a phase in which he was exploring double images in his work. The concept of doppelgängers and twins were popular theme for many Surrealists at this time.

Schiaparelli's most famous artist collaborations are undoubtedly the pieces she created in partnership with Dalí. Together they created the Lobster Dress in 1937, a white A-line gown with a lobster by Dalí painted on the skirt. He thought of the crustaceans as symbols of sexuality and was making several lobster-themed works at the time, including his famous phone. The dress was worn by none other than Wallis Simpson ahead of her scandalous wedding to Edward VIII.

Perhaps a little more surreal, and a nod to Schiaparelli's beginnings with her mock bow sweater, is Schiaparelli and Dalí's Tears Dress collaboration. The floor-length white gown is covered in printed trompe-l'oeil rips and accompanied by a sheer veil with magenta tears incorporated into the design and white strips hanging down. The ensemble looks as if someone has torn at the clothes and flesh of a bride. The piece was part of her 1938 'Circus Collection', which was unveiled in an outrageous fashion show complete with acrobats, horses and elephants.

Schiaparelli was provocative, daring and, yes, shocking to some. She leaned into these traits by naming a perfume and her signature shade of bright pink *Shocking*. She even titled her memoir *Shocking Life*. Her fashions ranged from the artistic and extreme to ready-to-wear garments fit for the everyday. Sure, not everyone could pull off wearing her shoe-shaped hat (another Dalí collaboration), but bold explorations like these by Schiaparelli helped push women's fashion into a modern and exciting new era.

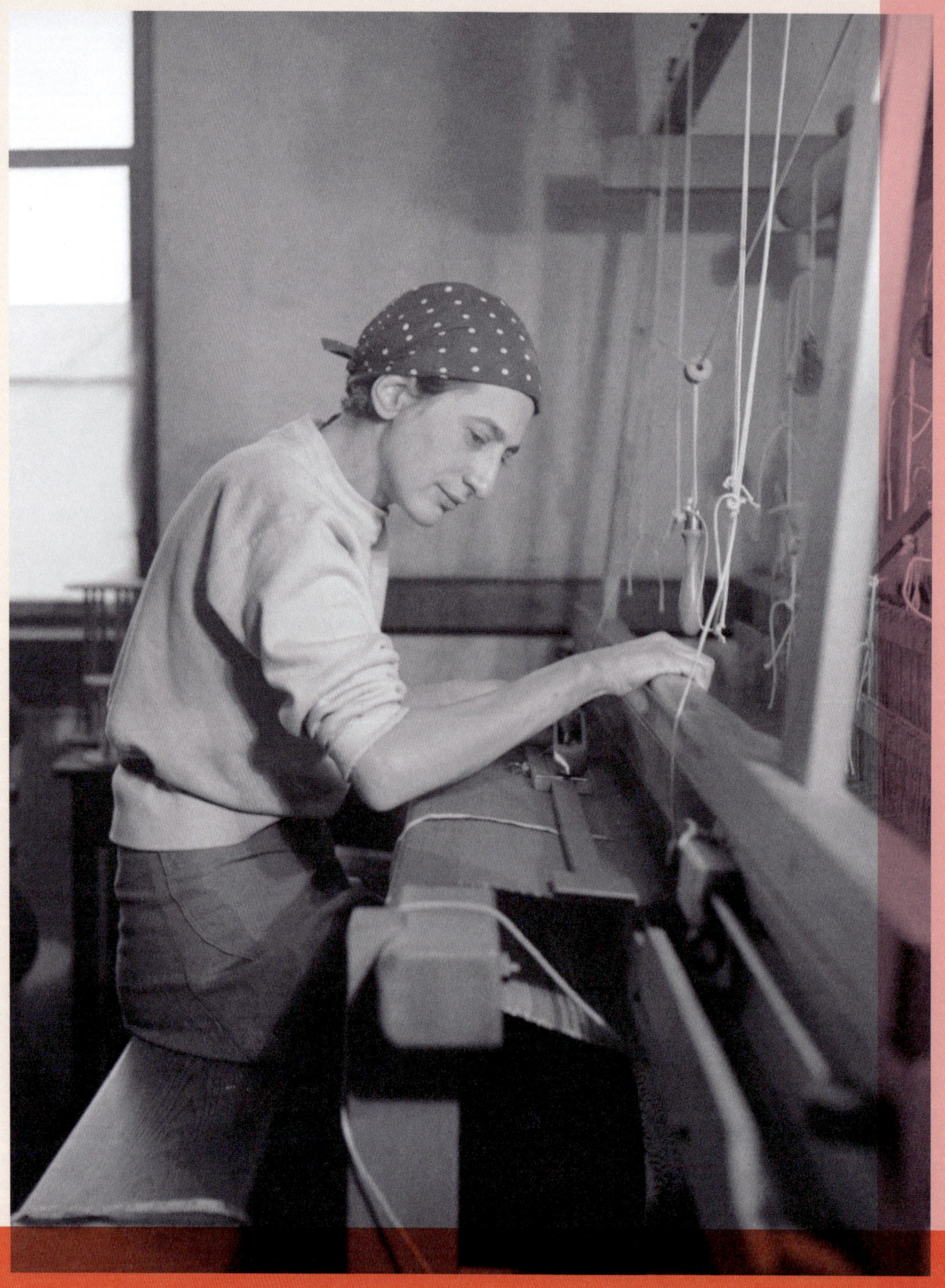

Anni Albers

(1899–1994)

Weaving

It wasn't Anni Albers' first choice to study weaving at the Bauhaus but thank goodness she did. She took an innovative approach to the medium by treating it as a form of fine art expression rather than a functional craft. Albers hung her weavings on the wall, to be regarded at eye level, and her mastery of form and colour shone. Through her own work and the education of others, she became a trailblazing force within the development of modern art.

Albers – born Annelise Fleischmann – grew up in an affluent household, where the main expectation from the women in her family was that they should marry well. Albers had different goals for herself. Although her parents held traditional aspirations for their daughter, they supported her in her interests of drawing and painting. To some parents, this might mean buying a few art supplies, but the Fleischamanns went so far as to take their teenaged daughter to study under the Impressionist painter Martin Brandenburg. She later painted a portrait of her mother and took the work to the painter Oskar Kokoschka in the hopes of studying with him. After seeing the painting, he responded by asking, 'Why do you paint?' And thus, she was rebuffed from pursuing a painting career.

Fortunately, Albers was not dissuaded from art altogether. In 1920, she enrolled in the *Kunstgewerbeschule* (School of Arts and Crafts) in Hamburg, but found the programme wanting. After two short months, she left. After discovering a leaflet for the then fledgling Bauhaus art school, Albers applied twice before she was finally accepted. She left behind her life of comfort for a tiny room in Berlin, where she didn't have access to bathing facilities more than once a week.

The Bauhaus is legendary within the history of art and design. The German art school was only in existence between 1919 and 1933 before it was shut down by the Nazi party, but in that time many giants of modern aesthetics passed through its doors as both teachers and students. This included Wassily Kandinsky, Paul Klee and Ludwig Mies van der Rohe, among others. The Bauhaus was known for advocating a design approach that combined form and function. After all, an item with a practical purpose should not be precluded from looking good. To this end, the school instructed in fine art disciplines, such as painting and sculpture, as well as more design-based disciplines, like architecture and weaving.

The Bauhaus was innovative in many ways, and it was also one of the few formal art schools at the time to accept female students. Even so, women were steered to what were considered the 'feminine' arts of weaving, bookbinding or ceramics. After taking the requisite introductory course, Albers grudgingly settled on weaving. She studied under Gunta Stölzl, who was the only woman master at the school and an alumna of the Bauhaus weaving workshop herself. There, she learned techniques in dyeing and weaving, and created her first wall hangings.

Already, this act of hanging her weavings subverted the more usual applications of textiles (rugs, fabrics, garments, etc.) to use the medium in the more 'fine art' context of wall art. *Black White Yellow* was first woven in 1926 and later recreated by Albers' former teacher, Stölzl, in 1965. It embodies her signature aesthetic of colourful grids and linear forms. The rectangular shapes in this wall hanging appear to mimic the weaving method itself, where bars of colour disappear behind each other and re-emerge in brilliant pops of yellow and subdued greys.

During her time at the Bauhaus, she met and married fellow artist Josef Albers, who was eleven years her senior. Throughout their lives together, the pair were equally yoked with talent and artistic verve. In 1933, when the couple were offered positions to teach at the new experimental art school Black

Albers did such a thorough job of carving a path for herself as a textile artist that she challenged longstanding ideas of 'craft' versus 'fine art' more broadly.

Mountain College, in the United States, they seized the opportunity. As Albers was a Jewish woman in an increasingly unsafe Nazi Germany, the offer to start a new life in the mountains of North Carolina couldn't have come at a better time.

At Black Mountain College, Albers once again found herself immersed in an environment buzzing with artistic innovation, and she worked as an assistant professor of art, instructing on weaving. Her students benefitted from her modern approach to textiles, incorporating abstract designs and unusual materials, such as straw and plastic. She exhibited her weavings throughout the United States at this time, and eventually came to call her works 'pictorial weavings'. This label, emphasizing pictures, made it clear that she was an artist (as opposed to a craftswoman) and her chosen medium was textiles, just as another artist might use paints or marble. This was quite a leap from the Bauhaus' more practical approach to textiles.

Albers made a major step in building the bridge between 'fine art' and 'craft' when, in 1949, she became the first textile artist to have a solo exhibition at the Museum of Modern Art in New York. The press release for the exhibition called her 'one of the most imaginative and daring modern weavers working in the United States'. The show included tapestries, drapery and upholstered pieces woven with experimental materials, such as black cellophane, wood strips, corn and more.

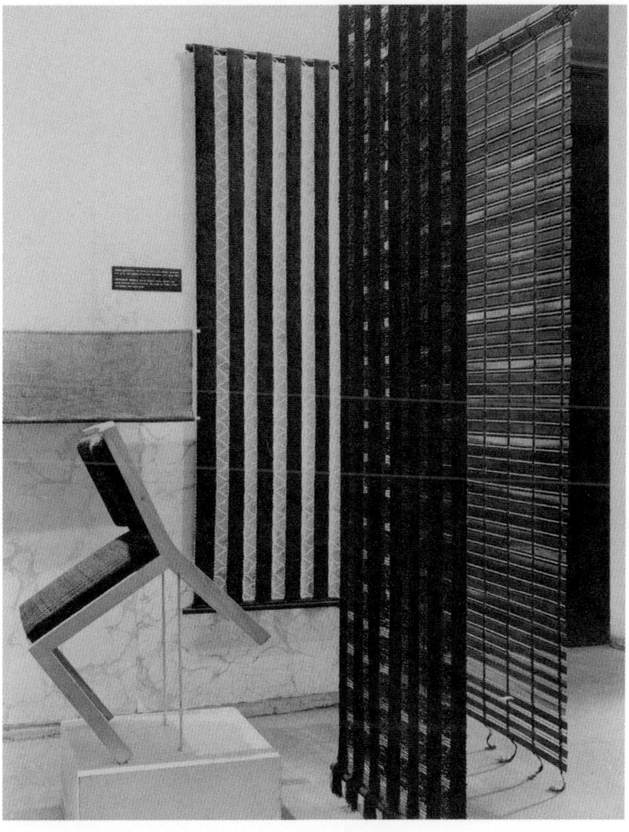

Installation view of the exhibition 'Anni Albers Textiles'.
MoMA, NY, September 14, 1949 through November 6, 1949.
New York, Museum of Modern Art (MoMA). Gelatin-silver print,
19 × 24.1 cm (7½ x 9½ in).

After forty years of weaving, Albers began experimenting with printmaking in 1963. She first tried lithography by chance with her husband as he was teaching in a lithographic workshop. She was able to use the medium to experiment with patternmaking in a new way. In a bold untitled work from 1969, Albers tessellates electric shades of blue and red and this work could easily sit alongside the mind-bending Op Art works of Bridget Riley painted around the same time. From the 1970s onwards, printmaking replaced weaving in Albers' heart, and became her main form of artistic expression.

Throughout her long life, Albers worked with the tools and mediums available to her to assert her artistic perspective. She did such a thorough job of carving a path for herself as a textile artist that she challenged longstanding ideas of 'craft' versus 'fine art' more broadly. She is often given the specific honorific of one of the most influential textile artists of the twentieth century, but her determined creativity helped shake the foundations of what types of works could be considered in fine art discussions. It is much better that she should be counted among the most influential artists of the twentieth century, textile or otherwise.

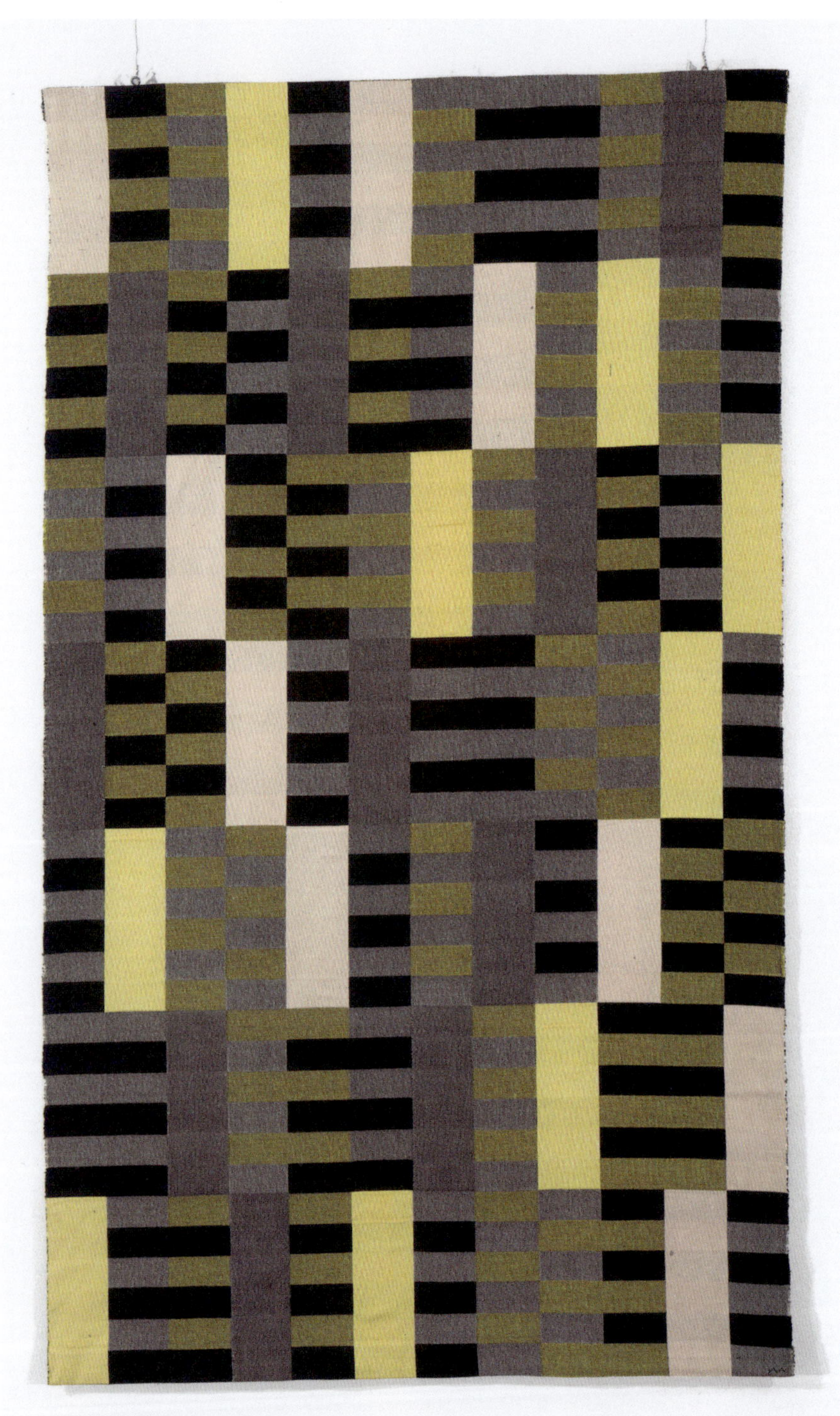

Wall hanging, 1926.
Mercerized cotton, silk.
203.2 × 120.7 cm (80 × 47½ in).

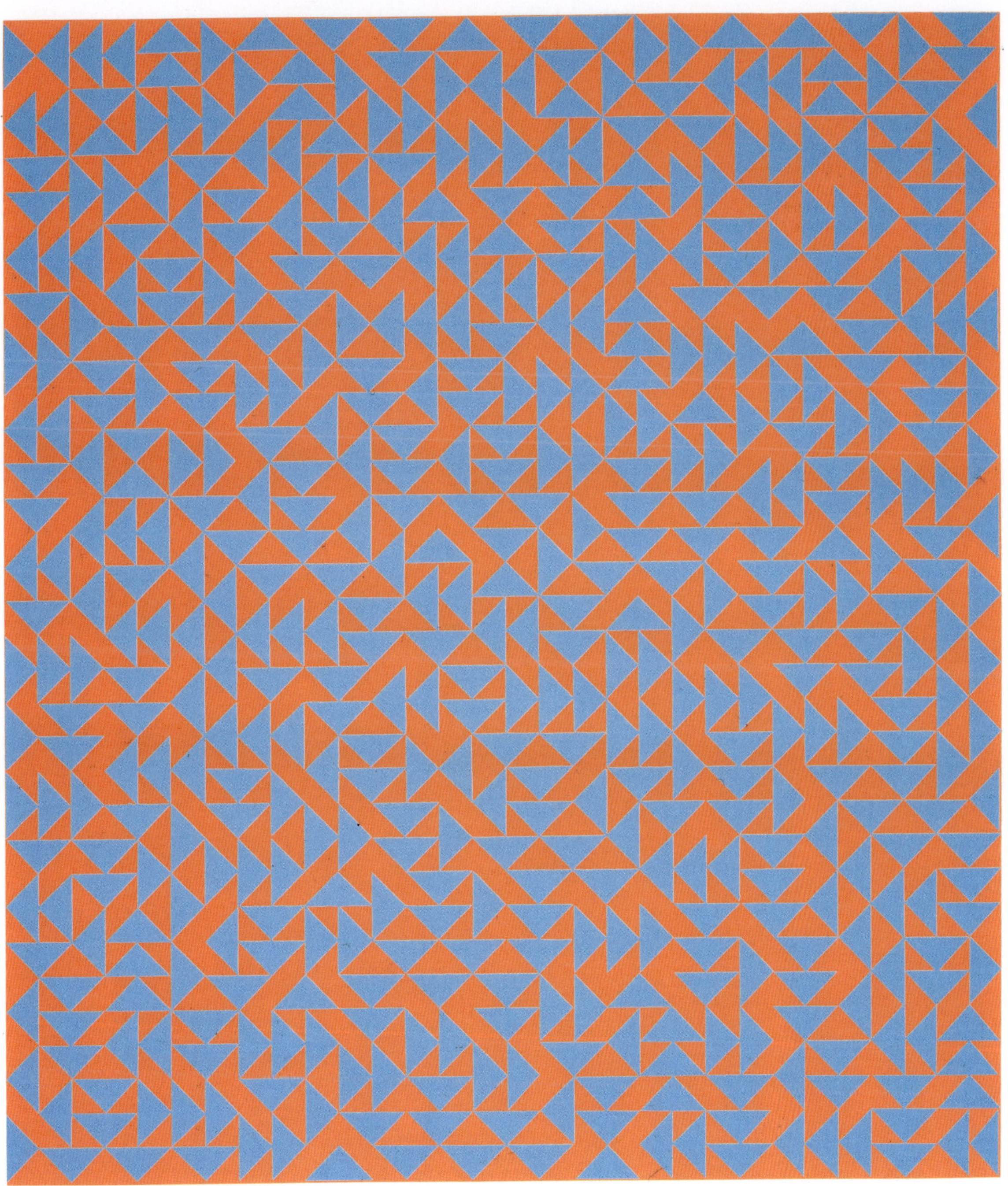

Untitled, 1969.
Serigraph on paper.
61 × 57.3 cm (24 in × 22½ in).

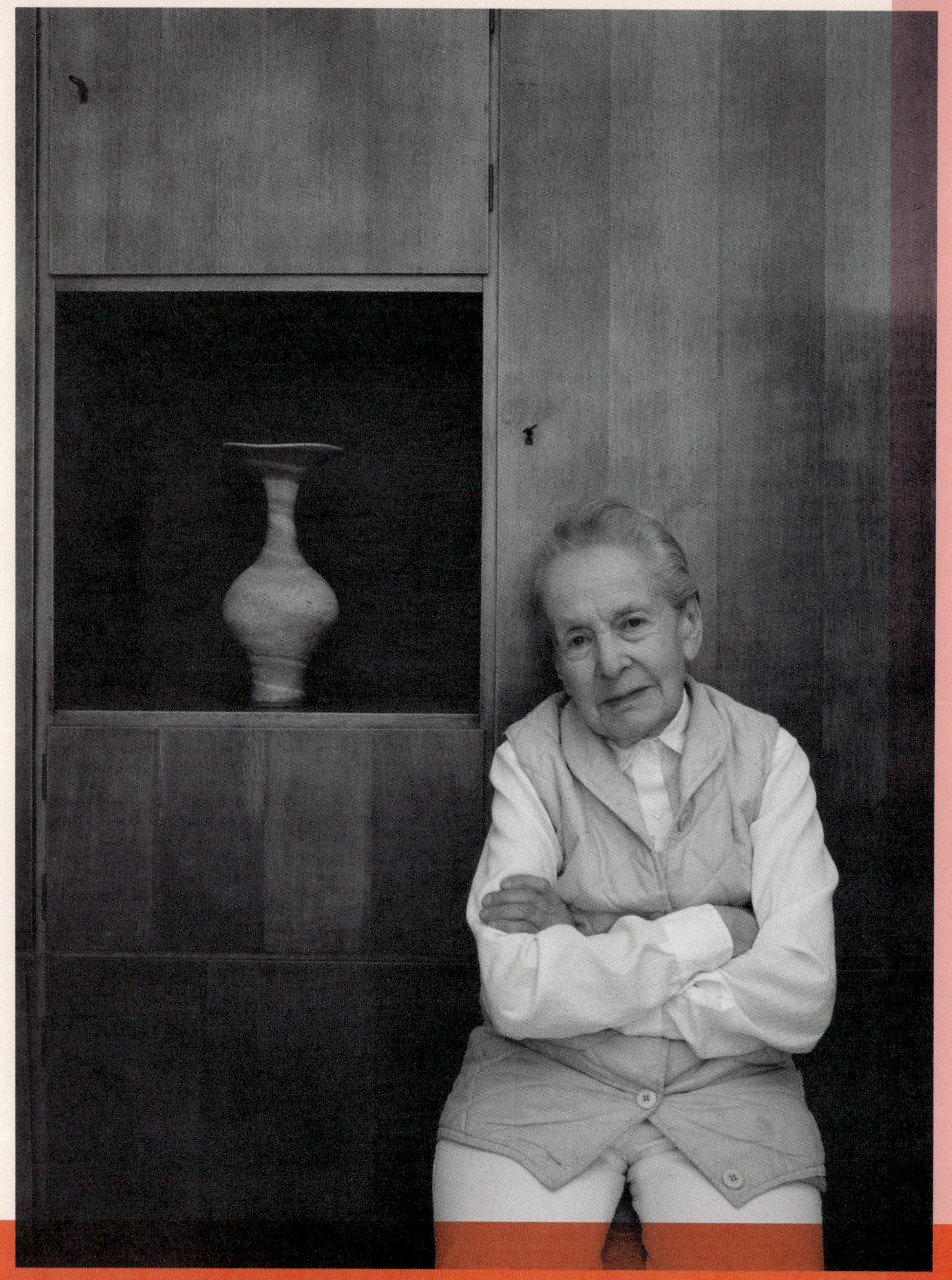

Lucie Rie

(1902–1995)

Ceramics

Lucie Rie is a formidable figure of the twentieth-century studio pottery movement. This was a time when modern potters were creating stunning decorative wares and asserting the merits of ceramics in a fine art context. Rie stood out because of her unique aesthetic point of view, which was informed by her education and the ornamental ceramic traditions of mainland Europe.

Rie – born Lucie Gomperz – grew up in Vienna, the youngest of three children. She was surrounded by progressive ideas. Her father was a respected ear, nose and throat doctor and consultant to the pioneering neurologist Sigmund Freud – the pair were friendly enough that Freud sometimes visited the family's home. As if the occasional chat with Freud wasn't fascinating enough, a young Rie was also exposed to edgy Viennese modernist design in the waiting room of her father's office. Her parents were liberal, educated and interested in the arts, and they cultivated these same qualities in their children. It's no wonder that Rie developed an aspiration to become an artist and enrolled at the Vienna *Kunstgewerbeschule* (School of Arts and Crafts) in 1922.

During her studies, she discovered a passion for ceramics. She learned practical skills, like how to throw pottery using a wheel and the chemistry required for different glazes and effects, while slowly honing her aesthetic. Initially, Rie was intrigued by Classical pottery – particularly the Roman pieces she'd seen in her uncle's collection. It was after studying with the architect and designer, Josef Hoffmann, that she was exposed to the Vienna Secession style, which was formative in the decorative and architectural direction her work would take. She went on to develop a style of thin and elegant vessels with a delicate luxury that clearly stems from the same visual lineage as Viennese Modernism.

Rie established a studio in Vienna in 1925, and by 1935 she was producing pieces that were innovative enough to win a gold medal at the Brussels International Exhibition. In 1937, she won silver at the Paris International Exhibition. Unusually for the time, Rie viewed ceramics as a medium by which she could express her artistic creativity. She didn't shy away from more traditional shapes and vessels, but she asserted her aesthetic at every stage of design and moulding. This was a very modern approach to an art form that – at this time – was largely employed to create objects for domestic use.

In 1938, the Nazis were occupying much of Europe. As a Jewish woman, Rie was forced to flee Vienna for her safety, and she set up a new life in London. To earn an income during the Second World War, she took a job with fellow Viennese émigré Fritz Lampl. His company, Orplid, produced small figurines, buttons and luxury items, and he employed some of his friends in the Jewish community to help make glass buttons.

Button-making turned out to be another medium with which Rie could exercise her considerable creativity. Extant examples of her colourful buttons show a mix of twisted knots, dimpled geometric shapes and ornate organic forms like shells and mushrooms. Many larger button factories had been requisitioned for the war effort, so her new skill provided an excellent business opportunity. She soon began to make stoneware buttons out of her home studio near Hyde Park and, at one point, her studio was producing as many as 6,000 buttons per month. To meet the demand, she employed six studio assistants, including then ceramics novice Hans Coper. The pair developed a mutually beneficial professional relationship, wherein Rie taught Coper how to throw pottery and Coper helped Rie rekindle her passion for making pots. They worked in close collaboration until 1960, when Coper established his own studio.

During this period, Rie produced domestic wares, such as bowls and tea sets for high-end retailers like Liberty department store in

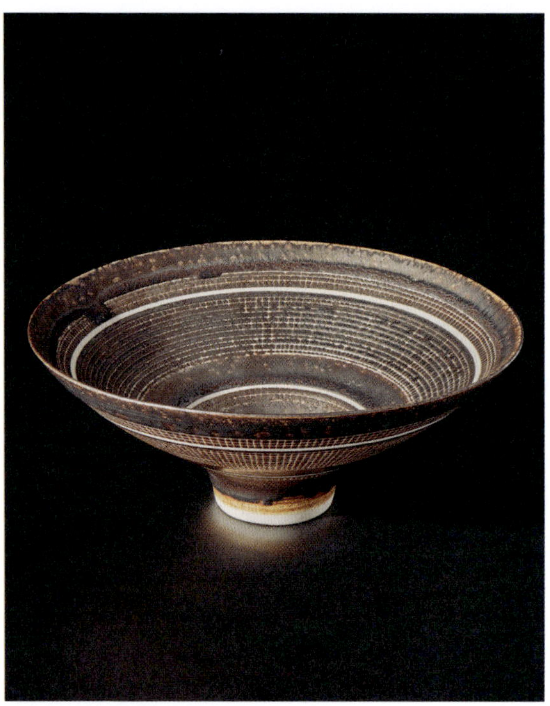

Footed bowl, c.1960.
Porcelain, maganese glaze with fine sgraffito grid design repeated inside and out.
8 × 20.8cm (3⅛ × 8¼in).

London. Many of her pieces are recognizable by their distinctive wide mouths that slink in seductively at the neck or balance on a narrow foot at the base. Another trademark quality of her wares is the fine line work, sometimes accented with touches of gold. This effect was achieved with the sgraffito ('*sgra-fee-toe*') pottery technique. This is a process by which a potter applies a layer (or layers) of colour to an unfired piece and scratches areas of these layers away to create a design. This technique saw a resurgence during the Vienna Secession in the early part of the twentieth century, and Rie's use of it in her work is a clear carryover from her Vienna days. In a footed bowl from 1960 it's apparent how effective sgraffito is at achieving thin, elegant lines. The bands of vertical lines draw a viewer's eye up from the small foot to the wider mouth, while also conveying an impression of something delicate and

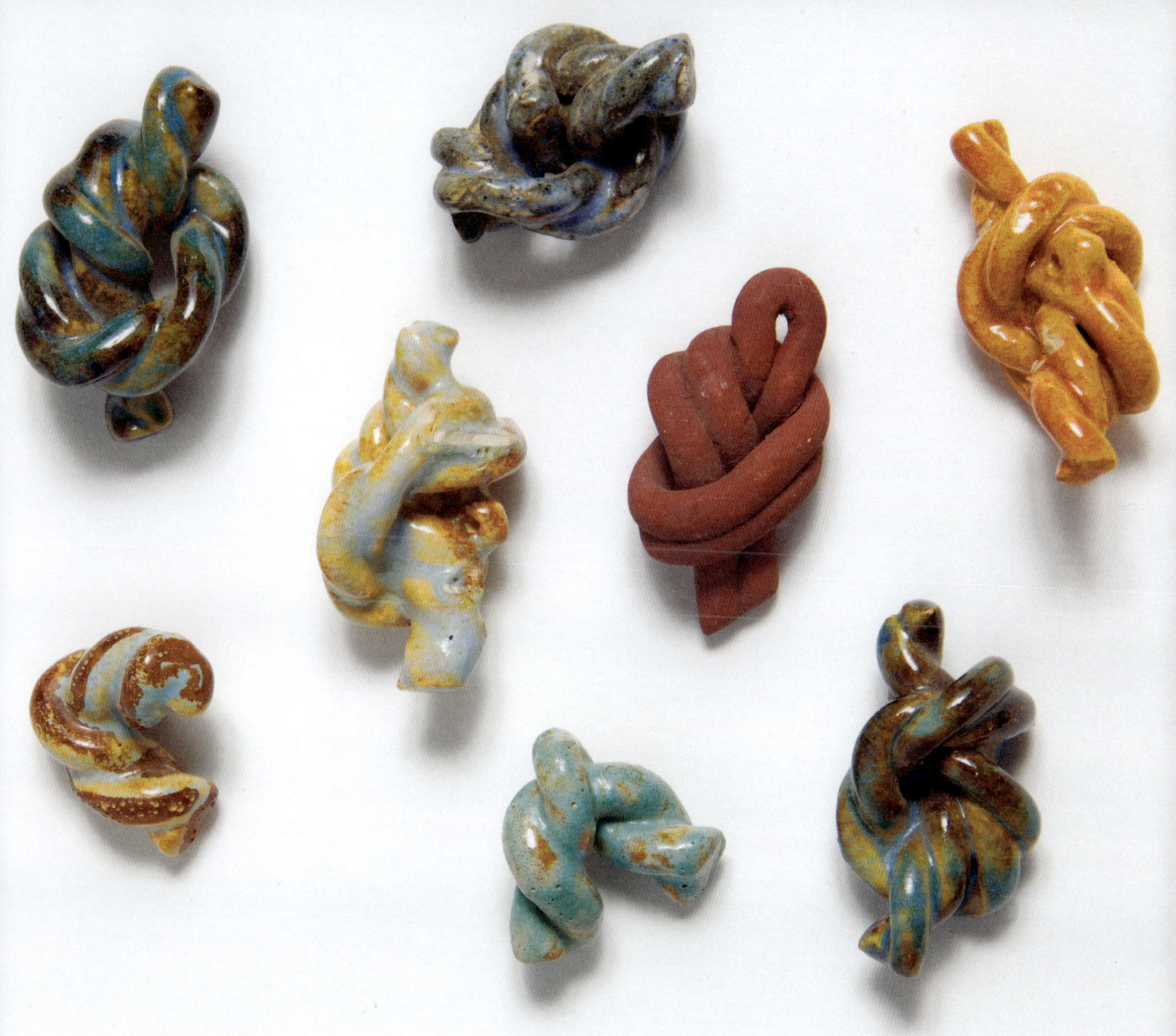

Twisted rope buttons.
Some stoneware, some earthenware.
Dimensions variable.

precious. The surface decorations on her works often serve to accentuate the shape of the vessels in this way.

From 1960 to 1971, Rie taught at the Camberwell School of Art in London. It was during this time that her career gained long overdue recognition. The Arts Council Gallery held a retrospective of her work in 1967, she was honoured with an OBE in 1968 and was awarded an honorary doctorate from the Royal College of Art in 1969. Since then, she has been celebrated in a number of varied and interesting ways, including on a commemorative stamp, being given the honorific title of Dame and having a portion of her studio reconstructed in the Victoria and Albert Museum in 2009. All are fitting accolades for a woman who was instrumental in helping to reframe the way historians and critics look at ceramics as aesthetic objects.

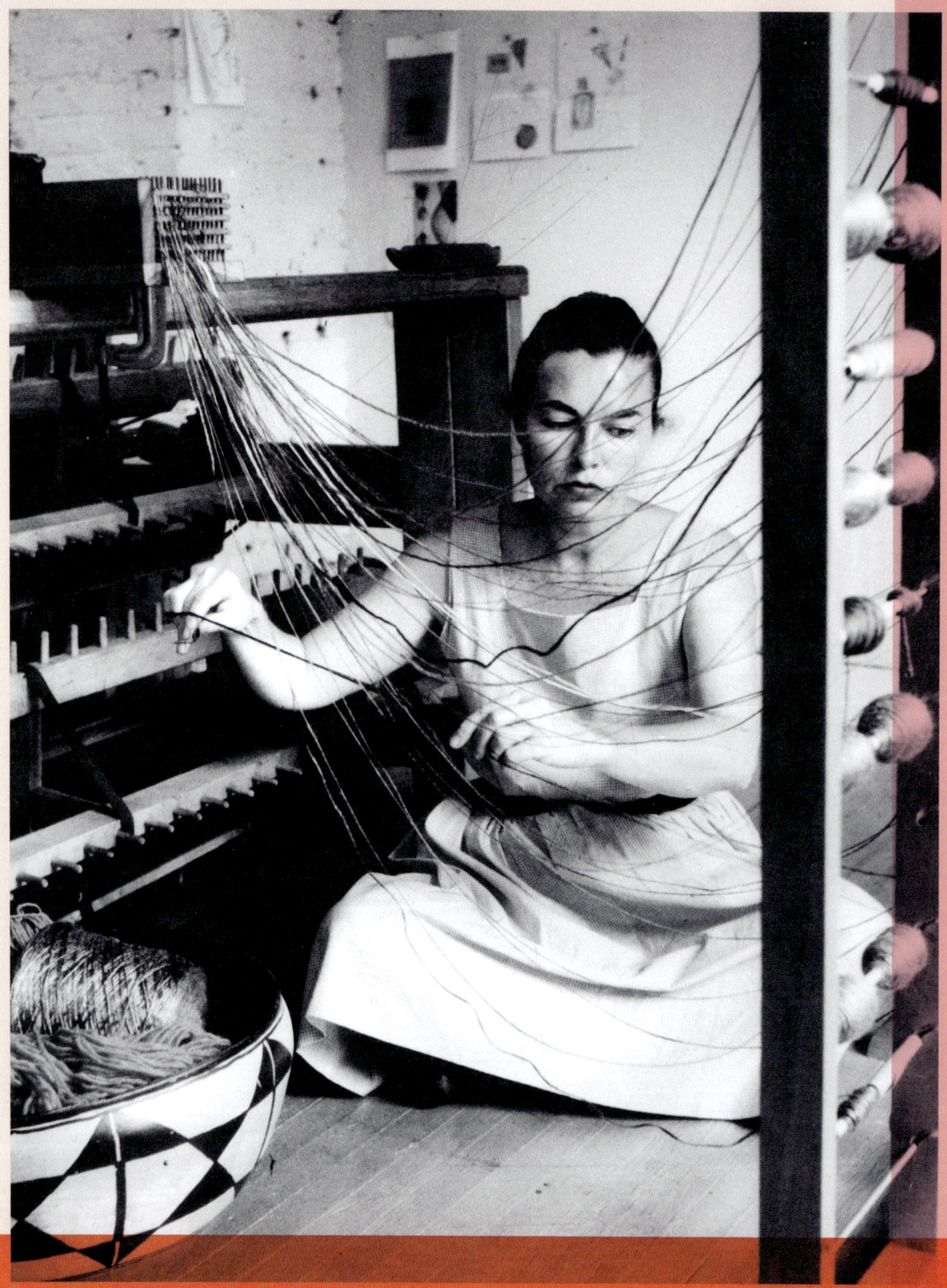

Lenore Tawney

(1907–2007)

Weaving, Fibre art

Sculpture and weaving collide in the ingenious work of Lenore Tawney. She didn't formally train in a weaving programme, instead choosing to dip in and out of workshops to learn the techniques that piqued her interest. Rather than being an impediment, this arguably gave Tawney an unencumbered freedom to merge different methods of working and eventually think completely outside of the loom.

At the tender age of five, little Leonora Gallagher knew her own mind well enough to decide she wanted to change her first name to Lenore – she couldn't be bothered with all those extra letters. She and her four siblings were raised in the lakeside town of Lorain, Ohio. During high school she worked in a men's suit factory, but as there wasn't much opportunity waiting for her after graduation, she chose to follow one of her brothers to live in Chicago at the age of twenty. Even though neither she nor anyone in her family had ever shown a particular interest in art, she soon began taking evening classes at the Art Institute of Chicago while working as a court proofreader during the day.

In 1941, she married psychologist George Tawney, but he died of an illness eighteen months later, at which time Tawney moved to Urbana, Illinois, to be closer to her husband's family. For a year-and-a-half, she studied art therapy at the University of Illinois, where her father-in-law was a professor. She enjoyed the lessons in painting and drawing but was less keen on the medical aspects of the subject. Having to spend time in hospitals was especially difficult, as this brought forth memories of her final two months with her husband. She decided to focus on the art rather than the therapy, and back to Chicago she went.

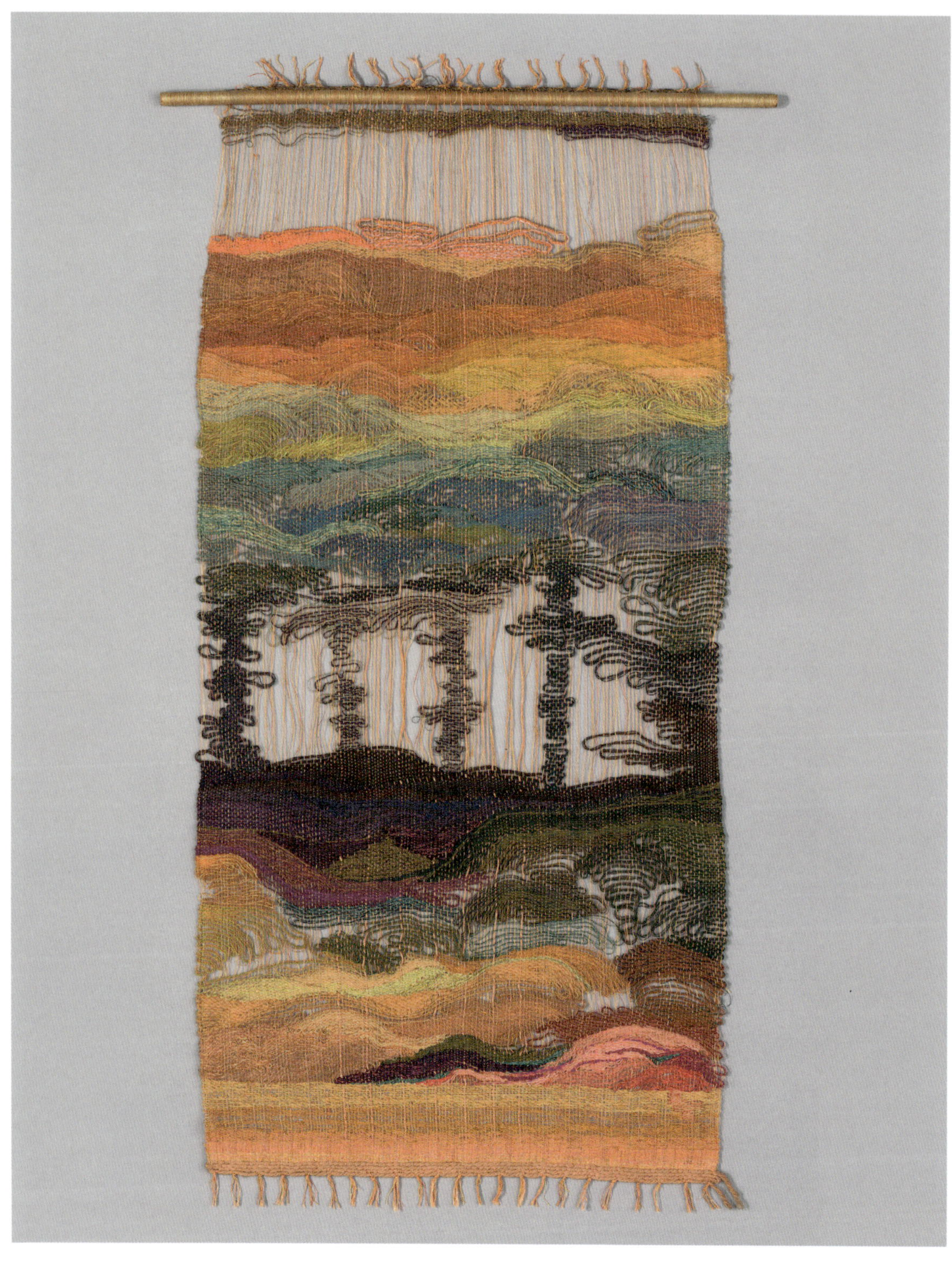

Landscape, 1958. Silk, cotton, bast fibers (probably linen) and rayon, plain weave with
discontinuous wefts and exposed warps; knotted warp fringe over wooden pole
wrapped with linen, plain weave. 142.6 × 66.5 cm (56⅛ × 26¼ in).

Tawney introduced the concept of considered negative space to her weaving. This aesthetic choice renders a weaving decidedly less functional and asserts its position as an art object.

From 1946 to 1947, she attended the Chicago Institute of Design, which brought about the first big spark in her artistic development. The school had a buzzing atmosphere guided by the vision of the former Bauhaus professor László Moholy-Nagy. In fact, the school was originally named the New Bauhaus and was modelled after the same philosophy of form meeting function as the original German school. Tawney's confidence in her drawing abilities grew and she fell in love with sculpture before deciding she couldn't commit herself to the medium with the fervour she thought it required. At this point, she gave weaving a try. She bought a second-hand loom and was taught the basics by a friend – possibly Marli Ehrman, the Bauhaus weaving artist who taught at the institute.

Over the next few years, Tawney took a hiatus from art to travel around Europe and North Africa. When she returned to the US, she once again sat down at her loom. Then in 1954, she attended a six-week tapestry workshop with the Finnish textile artist Martta Taipale at the Penland School of Crafts in North Carolina. This experience inspired her to explore ways of incorporating drawing into her weavings. Her early efforts were relatively straightforward pictorial works, but within a few years she was creating abstracted designs with elegant linework and open unwoven space. She called this style 'open warp' weaving.

A stunning wall hanging from 1958 titled *Landscape* depicts a forest scene with tree trunks made of green fibres zigging and zagging upwards into the canopy above. The rolling green treetops give way to blazing yellow and orange hues, which could be interpreted as a mountainous terrain or a fiery sunset. These colours are echoed below in the brown, gold and pink hues on the forest floor. In between the trees and above the warmer colour fields, Tawney left the weaving open, giving the work a quality akin to a low relief sculpture. In a similar way to how Barbara Hepworth utilized negative space in her sculptures to make it an active visual element of her works, Tawney introduced the concept of considered negative space to her weaving. This aesthetic choice renders a weaving decidedly less functional and asserts its position as an art object.

When she was in her early fifties, Tawney's art career picked up steam. She'd moved to New York in 1957 and rented a studio in a vibrant artist community that included Chryssa, Robert Indiana, Agnes Martin,and other notable names. In 1961, she spent some time studying Peruvian gauze weaving and also designed what she called an 'open reed' for her loom that enabled her to deviate from a traditional rectilinear shape. Each of these developments brought about a new phase in her work, wherein she brought the knotting and braiding techniques she learned to life in innovative new shapes. Interestingly, some of the artists within her circle, such as Jasper Johns and Ellsworth Kelly, were working on shaking off the confines of rectangular canvases around the same time. Her 'Woven Forms' series shows how the open reed allowed Tawney to pinch and expand the shapes of her wall hangings in a new way. Actually, 'wall hanging' was becoming a decreasingly suitable label for these works as Tawney brought them away from the wall and out into the room for viewing in the round as sculptural pieces.

Tawney's practice initially developed at a time when fibre art was a burgeoning and thrilling new art form, but as excitement around the medium declined in the 1970s, she had fewer solo exhibitions. This period also coincided with her spiritual growth

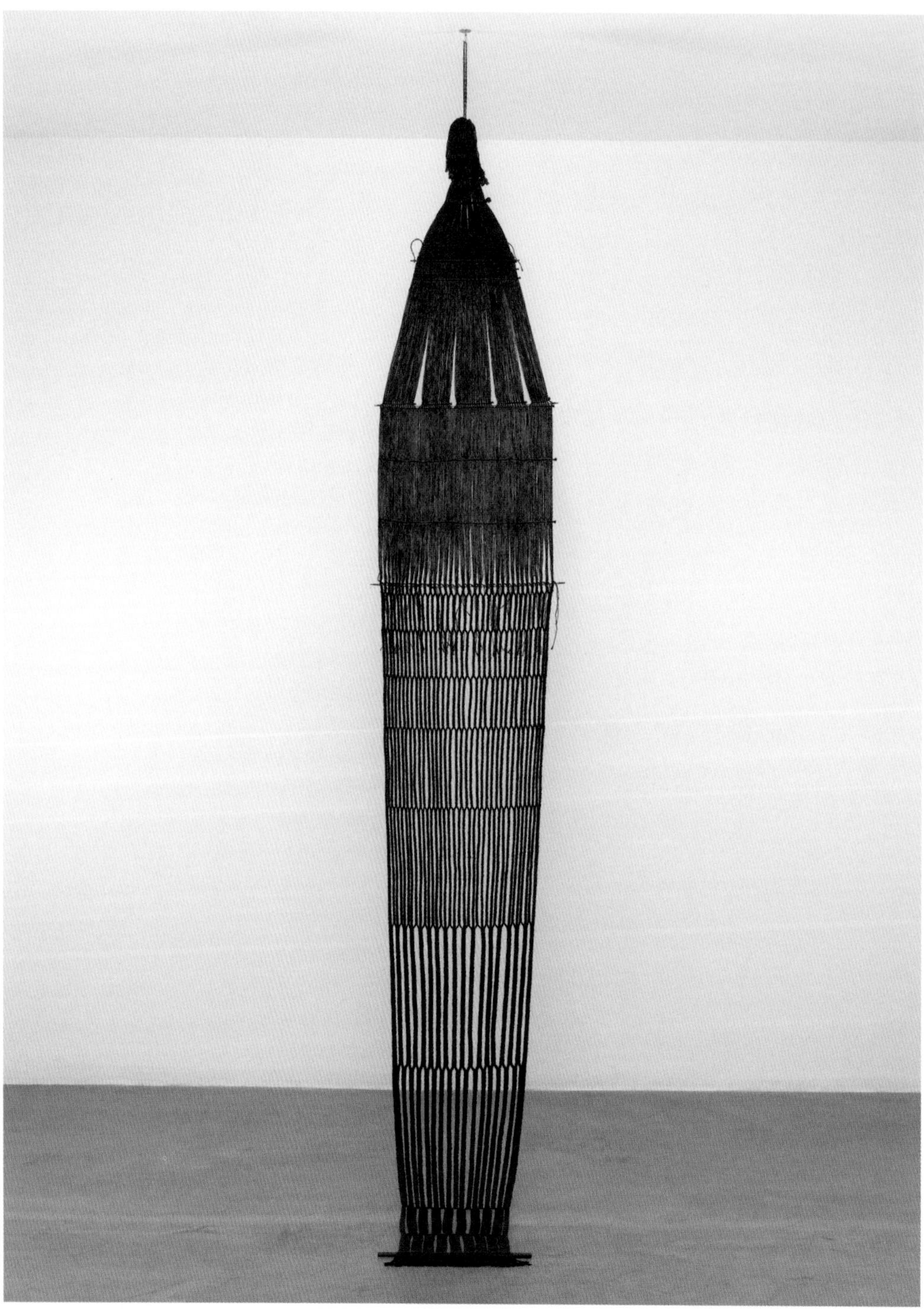

Dark River Wall Hanging, 1961.
Linen and wool. 416.6 × 57.2 cm (164 × 22½in).

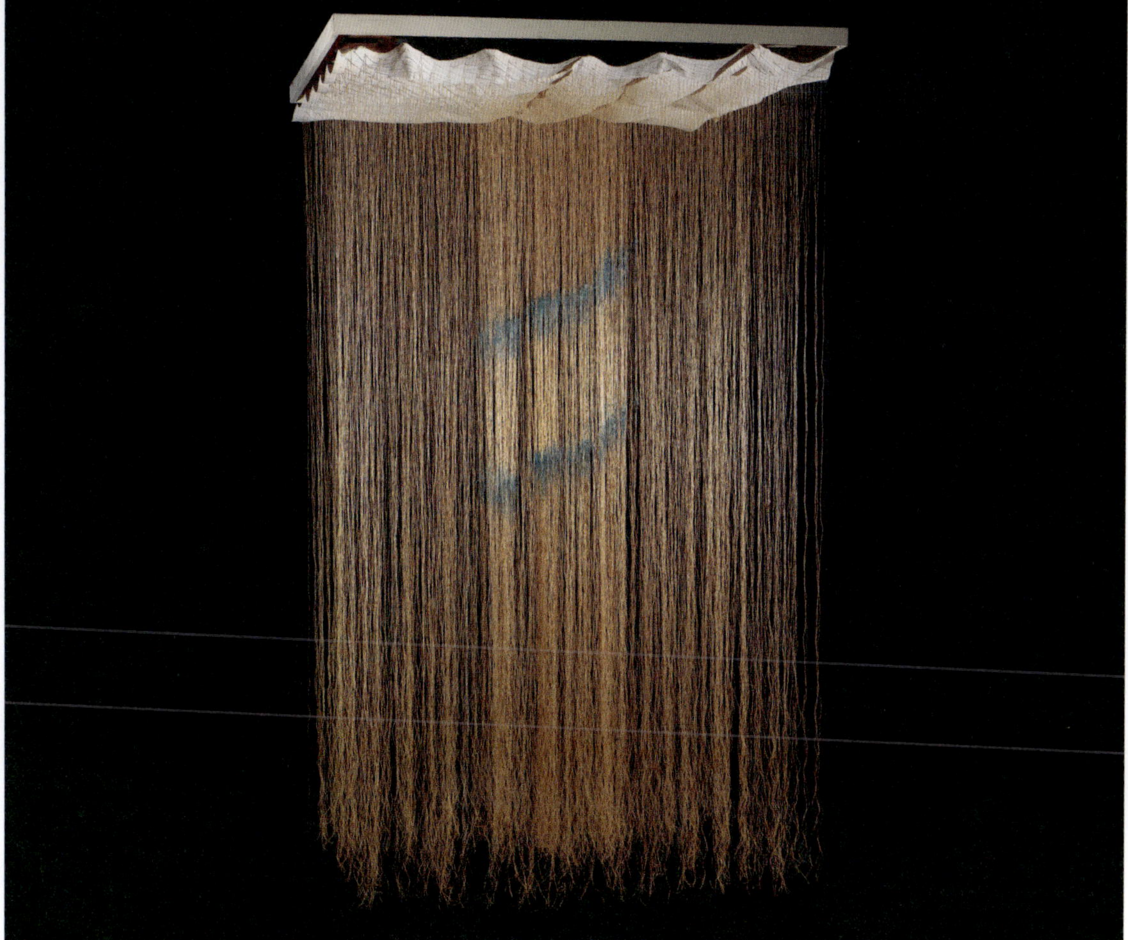

Box of Falling Stars, 1984.
Cotton canvas, linen thread, acrylic paint, and ink.
Approx. 274.3 × 172.7 × 177.8 cm (108 × 68 × 70 in).

and engagement in eastern philosophies. She ensured that her studio was a serene and meditative space, and photos show Tawney sitting peacefully on the floor with her weavings hanging around her. During this time, she created a series of works she referred to as 'shields' and 'masks' inspired by the arts of African and indigenous American cultures. They are smaller in scale than her previous weavings and incorporate feathers, shells and other found materials. Tawney viewed these pieces as having a protective or ritualistic function.

After first experimenting with negative space, followed by the shape of her weavings, it makes sense that the trajectory of her explorations eventually led her to abandon the use of a loom altogether. In the later stage of her career, she created large fibre works for her 'Cloud' series in which long lengths of thread hang from horizontal canvas material like lashings of rain. If the 'Woven Forms' series moved Tawney's work further towards sculpture, then these are a firm step into the realm of installations. They are minimalist embodiments of gestalt that shift the vibe of a room. As a cloud takes shape through the accumulation of tiny water droplets, the *Cloud* sculptures are given grand form through the gridded arrangement of thousands of threads.

Tawney's inventiveness built upon traditional weaving to make way for the fibre art movement that followed. She occupies a space between the two while unabashedly embracing craft and fine art techniques. She continued to work until her death at the age of one hundred, and her works can be found in collections around the world.

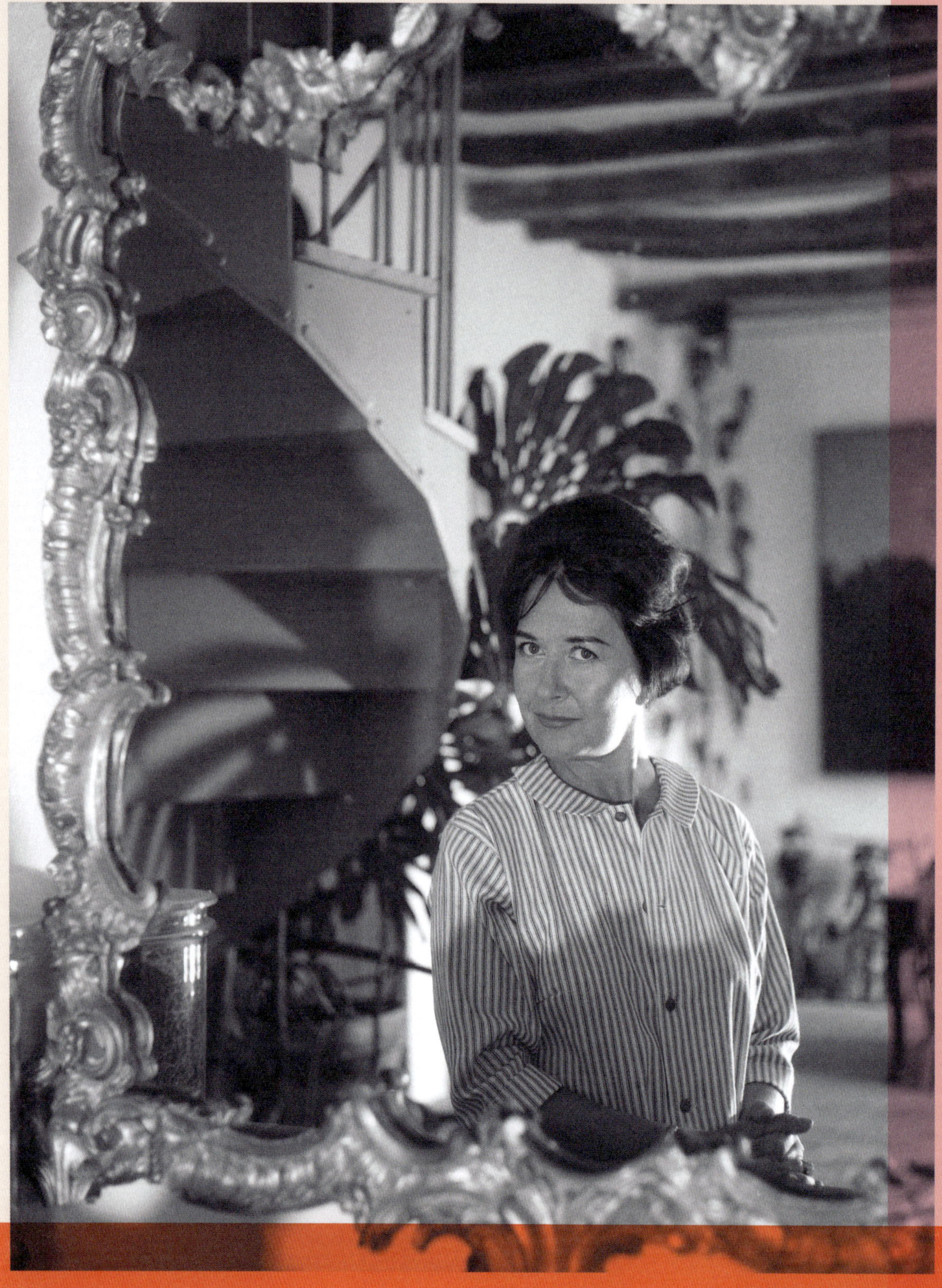

Dorothea Tanning

(1910–2012)

Soft sculpture, Wearable art

Many of Dorothea Tanning's works depict women's bodies and experiences in haunting and unconventional ways. The fantastical paintings of her early career are captivating, but so too are the soft sculptures she created in the 1970s – each one as curiously unsettling as any of her early Surrealist dreamscapes. She wilfully eschewed conventional sculptural materials in favour of the plush, transient materials of cloth and wool. The result is a collection of sculptures that embody the power that can lay behind 'softness'.

Tanning grew up in the middle-American town of Galesburg, Illinois, alongside her two sisters. In her memoir, she describes a gentle, nurturing mother and a father surrounded by female relatives, including visiting aunts and cousins. She had an interest in drawing and painting from a young age, but the hobbies her traditional parents once found adorable for a small child seemed worryingly 'bohemian' to them. They were given quite the surprise when a fifteen-year-old Tanning painted a nude woman with leaves growing out of her hair.

After graduating high school, Tanning worked in her local public library, where she developed a love for Gothic literature. The dark and fantastical scenes from these books would later influence the surreal themes in her paintings. Around the same time, she attended Knox College in her hometown, but the school didn't have an art programme, so she left after two years to study painting at the Chicago Academy of Art. While there she took life drawing classes and faithfully sketched the nude figures perched before her. She soon discovered that the department steered students towards the modernist style of Picasso, in which she had little interest,

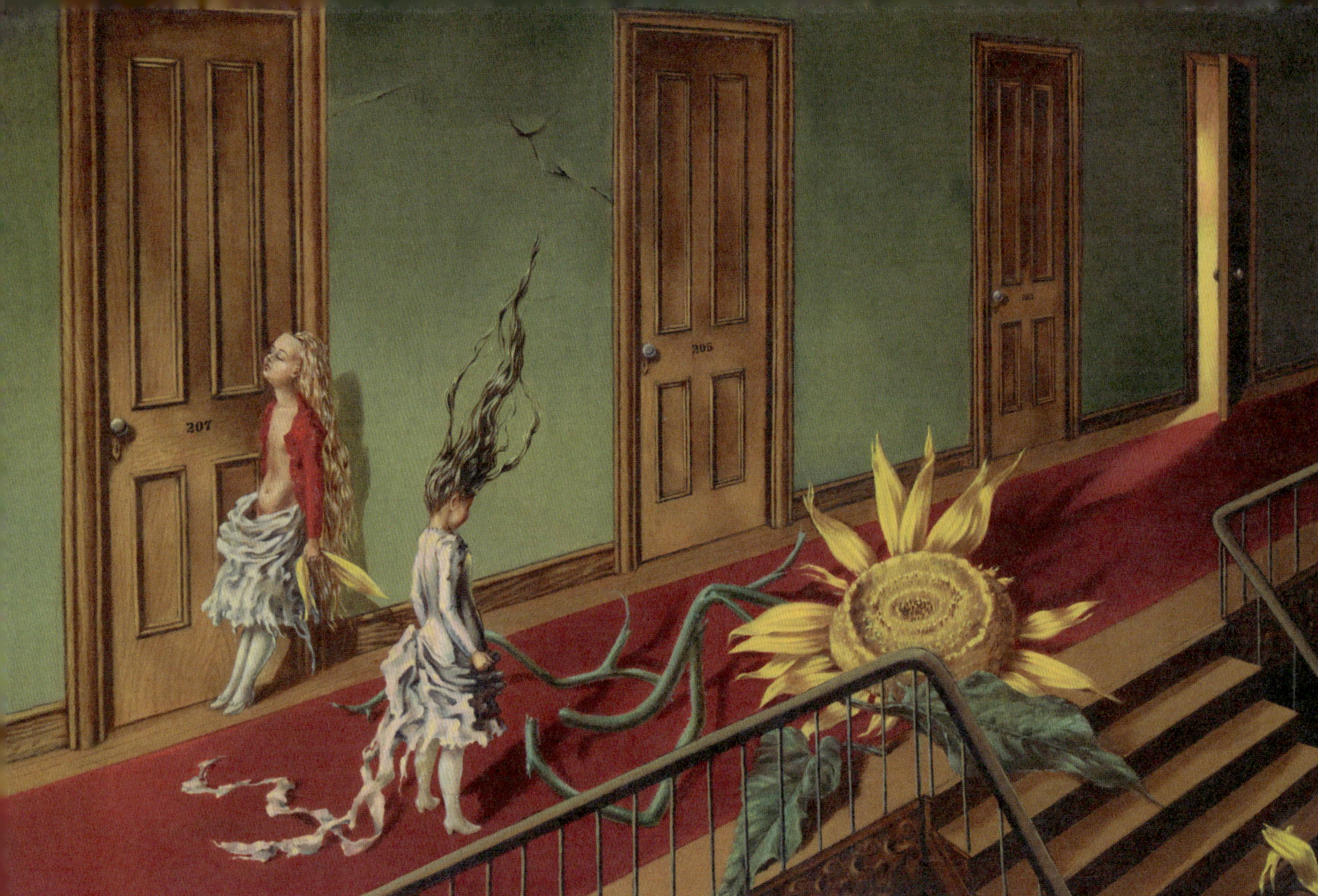

Eine Kleine Nachtmusik, 1943.
Oil on canvas. 41 × 9.5 cm (16⅛ × 24in).

so after only three weeks, she left. The rest of her artistic development came through self-teaching.

After a stint in Chicago, Tanning moved to New York City. She worked as an advertising illustrator and painted in her free time. Then in 1936, she discovered a modernist style more to her taste – Surrealism – at the *Fantastic Art, Dada, Surrealism* exhibition at the Museum of Modern Art. The artworks she saw there opened her mind to possibilities for her own practice and her work took on a more fanciful quality. Her burgeoning style eventually came to the attention of the art dealer Julien Levy, who signed her to his gallery. Levy was a great supporter of the Surrealists and his gallery had previously shown the works of such giants of the movement as Salvador Dalí and Frida Kahlo.

Surrealism had mainly been growing in Europe up to this time, but the horrors of the Second World War brought many of the artists to New York. Through her connection to Levy, Tanning was introduced to the European Surrealists she'd come to admire. Most notably, in 1942, she met her future (second) husband, Max Ernst. (She'd previously been married to writer Homer Shannon for a year, in 1941.) When Ernst's wife at the time, the formidable art collector Peggy Guggenheim, was organizing an exhibition of women artists at her Art of This Century gallery, she sent him to see if any gems could be found in Tanning's studio. The story goes that the couple fell in love that day over a game of chess. He moved in with her a week later.

The following year, Tanning completed one of her best-known paintings, *Eine Kleine Nachtmusik*, named after a Mozart composition. Two figures stand in a dreamlike trance at the top of the stairs as a giant sunflower snakes its way across the hall.

A life-size doll leans sleepily against a door frame as a little girl faces the flower, hair standing on end. The setting is a hotel hallway lined with numbered doors, and one stands eerily ajar. The painting stirs suspense around what curious events might be taking place. Tanning explained in her memoir that the flower is a symbol of the challenges youth encounter, and the wider image is about life's many confrontations and unknowns.

During Tanning's Surrealist period, she and Ernst lived in Sedona, Arizona, where they painted and entertained artist friends, including Man Ray, Lee Miller, Kay Sage and others. She also explored other mediums during this time. After meeting choreographer and co-founder of the New York City Ballet George Balanchine, Tanning designed sets and costumes for several of his ballets, including *The Night Shadow*. One costume sketch for the character 'A Guest' exemplifies the fantastical whimsy Tanning brought to her stage designs. The character is shown in a pink gown with the head of stag. For an added touch of glamour, the stag's antlers are jewelled. The elegantly dressed women of her paintings and earlier fashion ad illustrations were now three-dimensional, leaping across the stage in fanciful combinations of man and nature. She later designed costumes for choreographer John Cranko and director Jean-Louis Barrault as well.

In 1949, Tanning and Ernst moved to France, and by the mid-1950s she was exploring more abstracted and prismatic forms in her work. Many of her paintings appeared fragmented, as if depicted through a broken mirror. A further development came in 1969, when she began to experiment with soft sculptures over a five-year period. She was initially inspired by a synaesthetic experience she had at a concert listening to Karlheinz Stockhausen's composition *Hymnen*. The sounds made her think of organic shapes and soft forms, and she was compelled to bring these visions to life in soft forms wrapped in tweed and wool.

The resulting creations were oddly humanoid shapes that Tanning thought of as 'living sculptures'.

While some critics remarked that it was a shame the works were not made of more traditional, long-lasting sculptural materials, Tanning was unbothered by the impermanence of cloth and saw this as one of the sculptures' more interesting qualities. She also stated in a 1976 interview with Monique Lévi-Strauss in *American Fabrics and Fashions* that soft sculptures celebrate the triumphs of 'cloth as a material for high purpose' and 'softness over hardness'.

Her soft sculptures were an extension of the themes and images in her abstract figural work from the same period, with each depicting contorted nude female figures, but they are also a return to Surrealism. Although they are soft, many are menacing, including Boschian faces with no

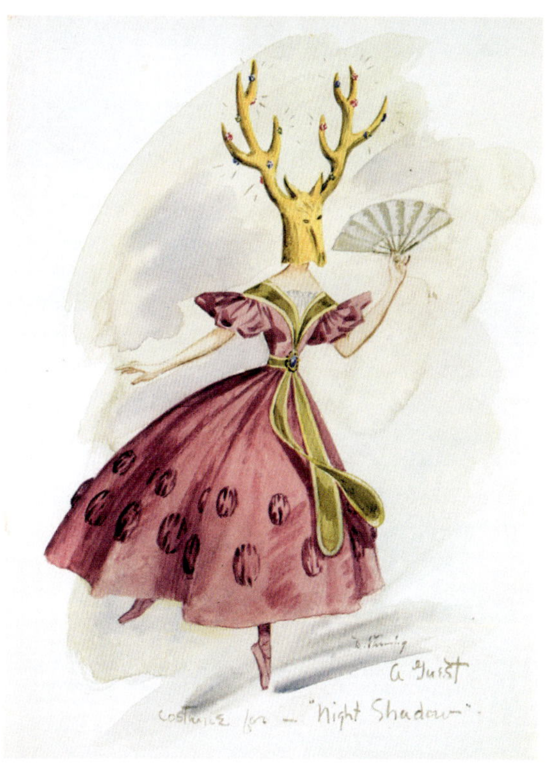

A Guest, costume design for *The Night Shadow*, a ballet by George Balalchine, 1945. Watercolor and wash on paper. 35.3 × 25cm (13⅞ × 9⅞in).

48

eyes and bodies with confusingly intertwined limbs. The connection to her earlier Surrealist work is especially clear between *Eine Kleine Nachtmusik* and her installation *Hôtel du Pavot, Chambre 202* (1970-73). The installation displays supple humanoid soft sculptures twisting, bursting from the furniture, and being pulled into walls. As in *Eine Kleine Nachtmusik*, Tanning transports the viewer to a hotel scene, but this time we are inside one of the rooms. The open door reveals that the room is number 202, which is tantilizingly close to the door numbers visible in *Eine Kleine Nachtmusik*. If we imagine that the two works share a universe, one can easily see how this installation takes the viewer inside the lit room in the earlier painting (or another room within the hotel).

The themes of children and music are also carried between the two works. *Hôtel du Pavot, Chambre 202* is inspired by a creepy song Tanning recalled from childhood about the death by suicide of Kitty Cane, a Chicagoan mobster's wife, in room 202 of a hotel. The song mentions talking walls, and in Tanning's room, this idea comes through in walls appearing to harbour nefarious living beings. The women of the Surrealist movement were often not given their just dues but Tanning never needed the affirmation of critics. In a 1987 letter, she described *Hôtel du Pavot, Chambre 202* as 'the surrealist work par excellence – and probably the last'.

Indeed, when Tanning died at the age of 101, she was the last living artist of the original Surrealist cohort. Although she is most frequently discussed in the context of her Surrealist paintings, her innovative exploration of soft sculptures laid significant visual groundwork for other great explorers of the medium, such as Louise Bourgeois (see page 50) and Sarah Lucas (see page 160), decades later. Rather than existing as permanent monuments, her soft sculptures have a lifespan and will continue to slowly transform over the years to come.

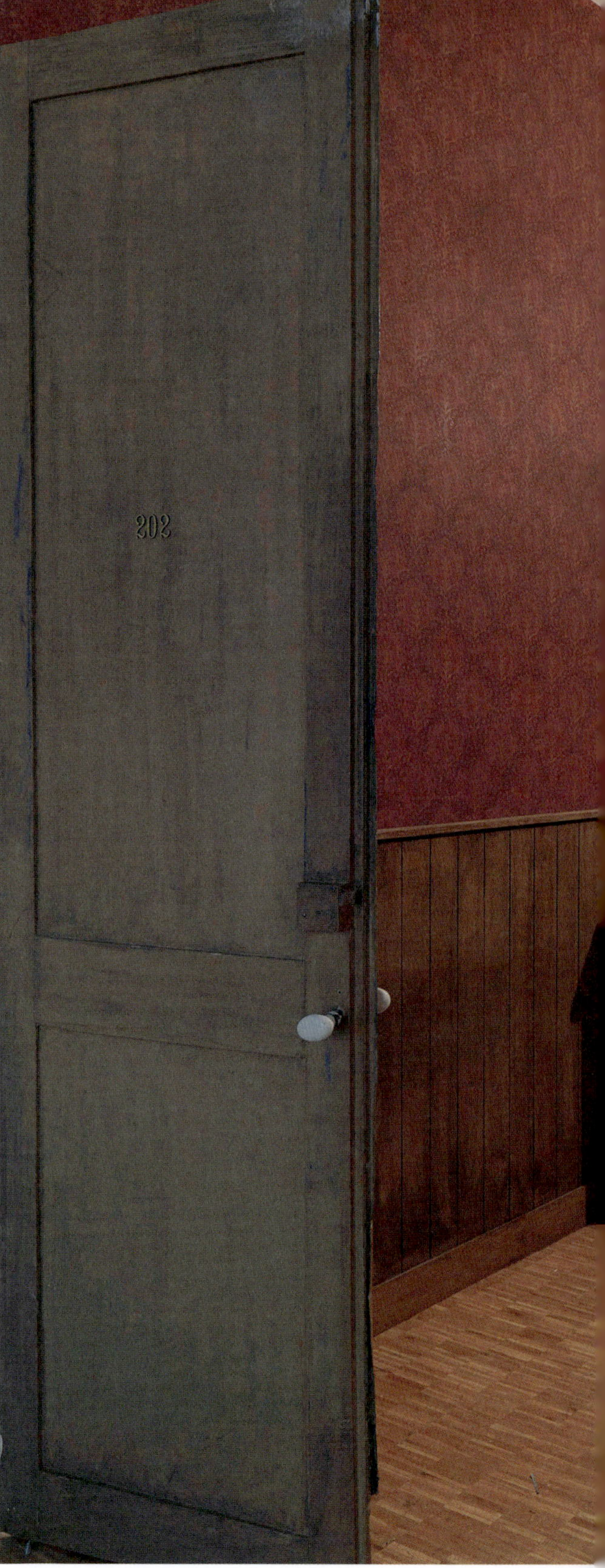

Hôtel du Pavot, Chambre 202, 1970–73.
Fabric, wool, synthetic fur, cardboard and ping-pong balls.
340 × 310 × 470 cm (133 ⅞ × 122 ⅛ × 185 in).

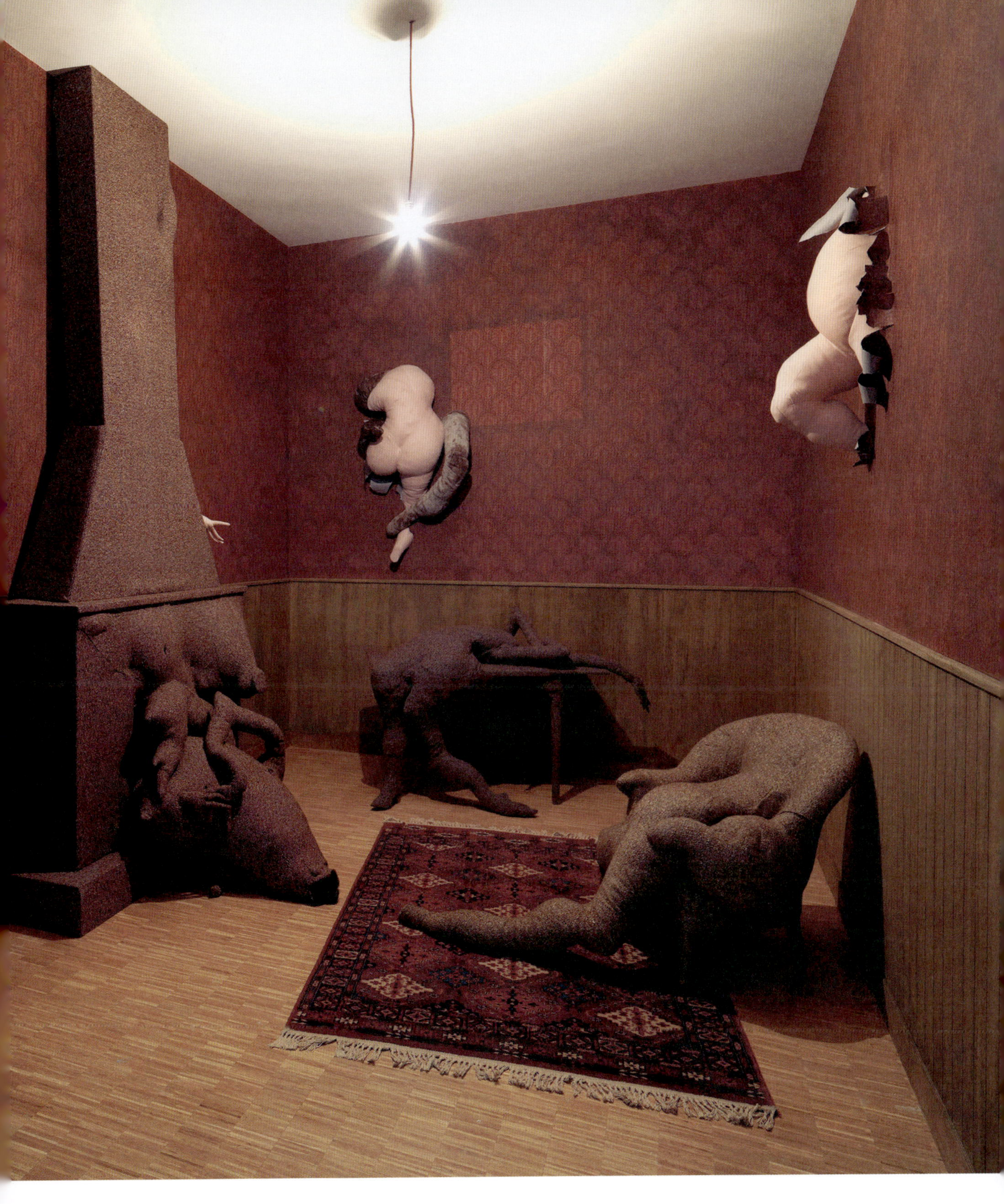

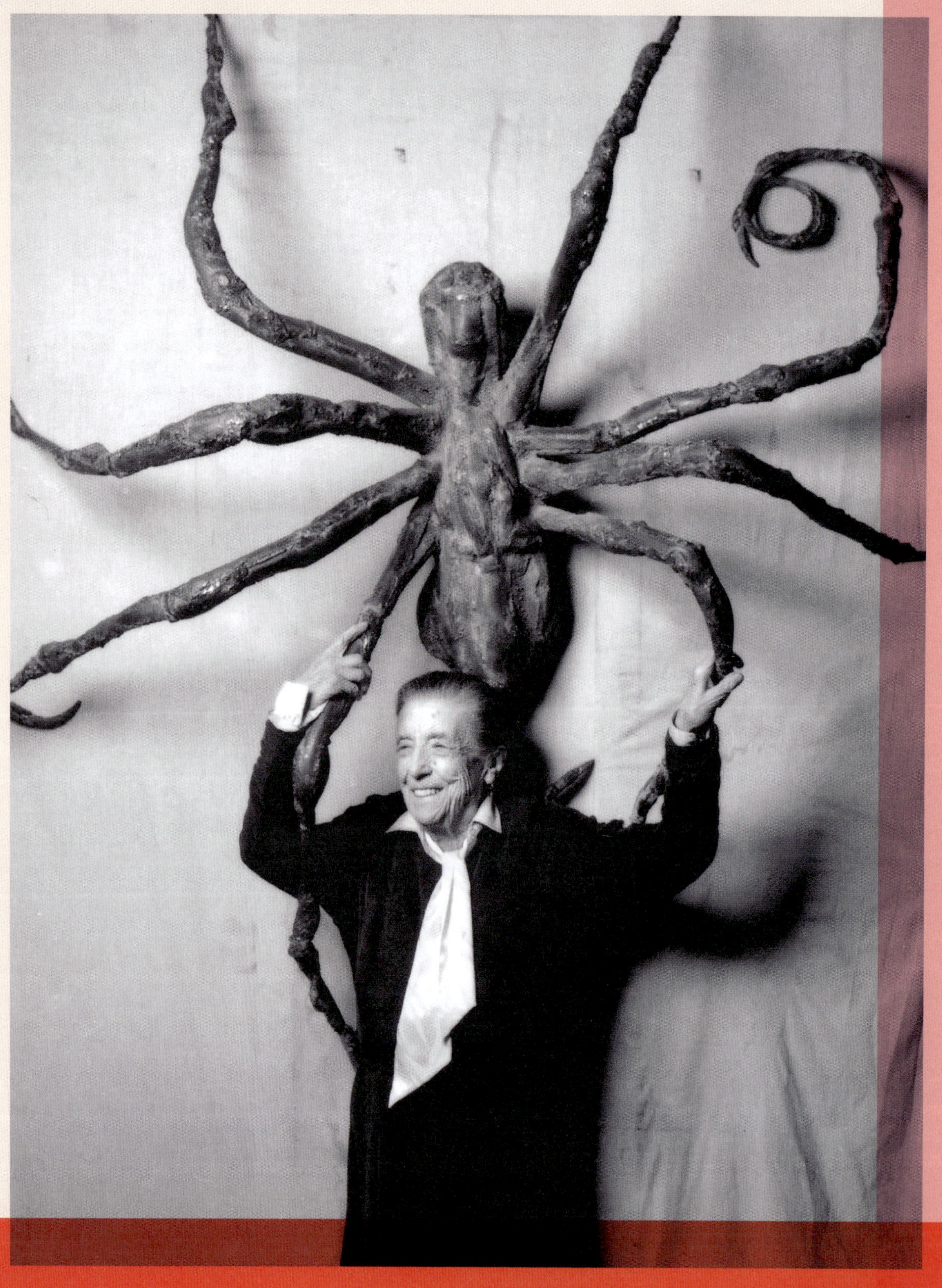

Louise Bourgeois

(1911–2010)

Soft sculpture, Weaving

Louise Bourgeois could do it all. Although she is best known for her sculptures and installations, she utilized a range of mediums, including painting, drawing, textiles and printmaking within her art practice. Bourgeois' fabric and soft sculpture work, created in the later stages of her career, explore themes of sexuality, the body and autobiographical themes from her childhood.

On Christmas Day 1911, the Bourgeois family received a gift – the birth of their daughter, Louise. Throughout Bourgeois' childhood, the family owned a gallery selling and restoring antique tapestries, thus, the young Bourgeois was exposed to the art of weaving from an early age. She even contributed to the family business by occasionally drawing missing areas from designs – she was especially good at sketching feet. She described her mother as sensible and affectionate, but she was often ill and in need of Bourgeois' care. Her father, on the other hand, was passionate, but unfortunately directed that passion towards temperamental outbursts and extramarital affairs, including one with Bourgeois' beloved English tutor. She recalled arguments at the dinner table between her parents, when she would distract herself by making sculptures out of bread. The effects of these opposing traits in her parents stayed with Bourgeois and manifested themselves in her work repeatedly.

Drawing on her mother's practical nature, Bourgeois first went to the Sorbonne, in Paris, to study mathematics in 1930. Two years later, her mother died and she switched her studies to art, attending the École du Louvre, École des Beaux-Arts. At one point, she also worked in the atelier of Cubist artist Fernand Léger, who after seeing Bourgeois' drawings, promptly declared that she should be a sculptor.

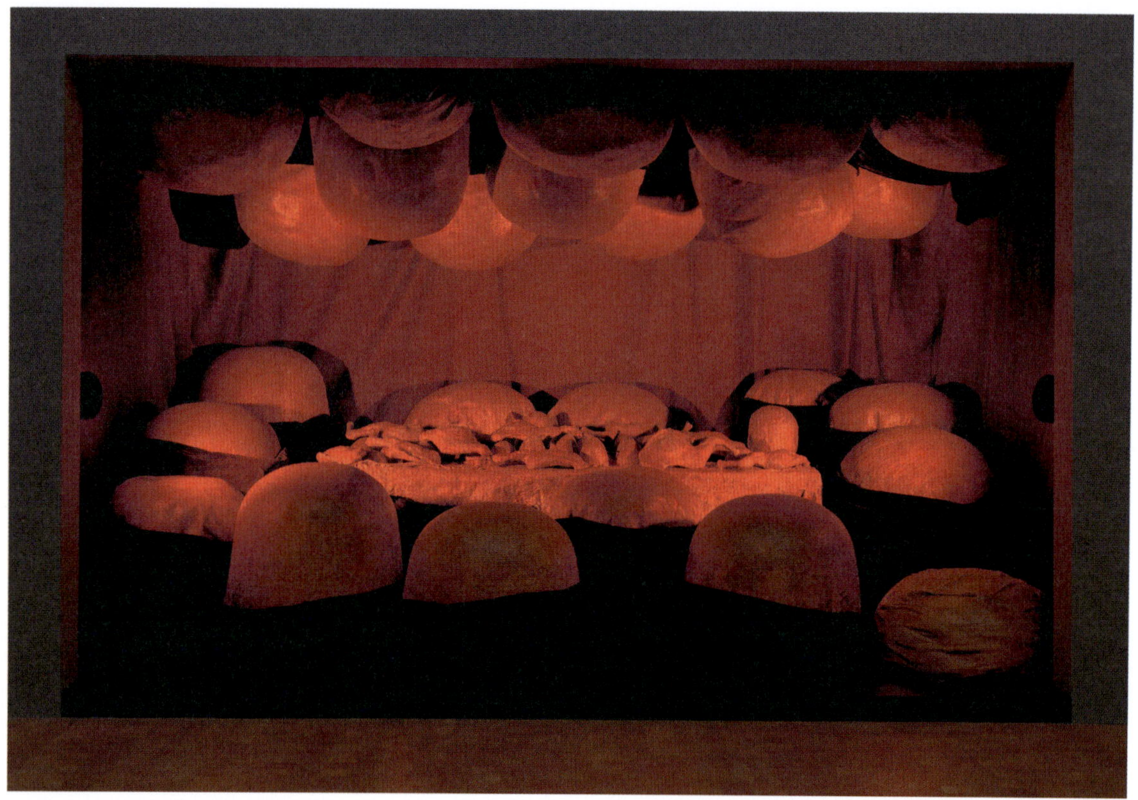

The Destruction of the Father, 1974.
Plaster, latex, wood, fabric and red light.
237.8 × 362.3 × 248.6 cm (93½ x 142½ x 97½ in).

Despite his assessment, she continued to produce early works in the mediums of painting and printmaking and when she completed her studies, she returned home to open a print shop next to her family's tapestry gallery. It was here that she met her husband Robert Goldwater, an American art historian, and the couple moved to the United States soon after.

From the 1940s, Bourgeois began working in sculpture, using the more traditional materials of wood and bronze, and creating a series of work depicting the human anatomy. These pieces often included interpretations of sexual body parts, such as breasts and genitals, and even fused parts together in unusual and provocative ways. She

combined penises and breasts or might represent one set of genitals in a way that resembled others – for example, her sculpture *Tits* (1967) depicts two conjoined breasts that look like testicles. She enjoyed the ambiguity of this imagery and the way they juxtaposed contrasting elements.

Her first major work to incorporate softer materials was the 1974 installation *Destruction of the Father*. In this piece, viewers get insight into the trauma she experienced as a child due to her father's behaviour. She creates a bizarre dining scene, with flesh-coloured mounds hanging from the ceiling and protruding from the floor. These breast-like forms are covered in latex, as are the smaller shapes presented on a table, which

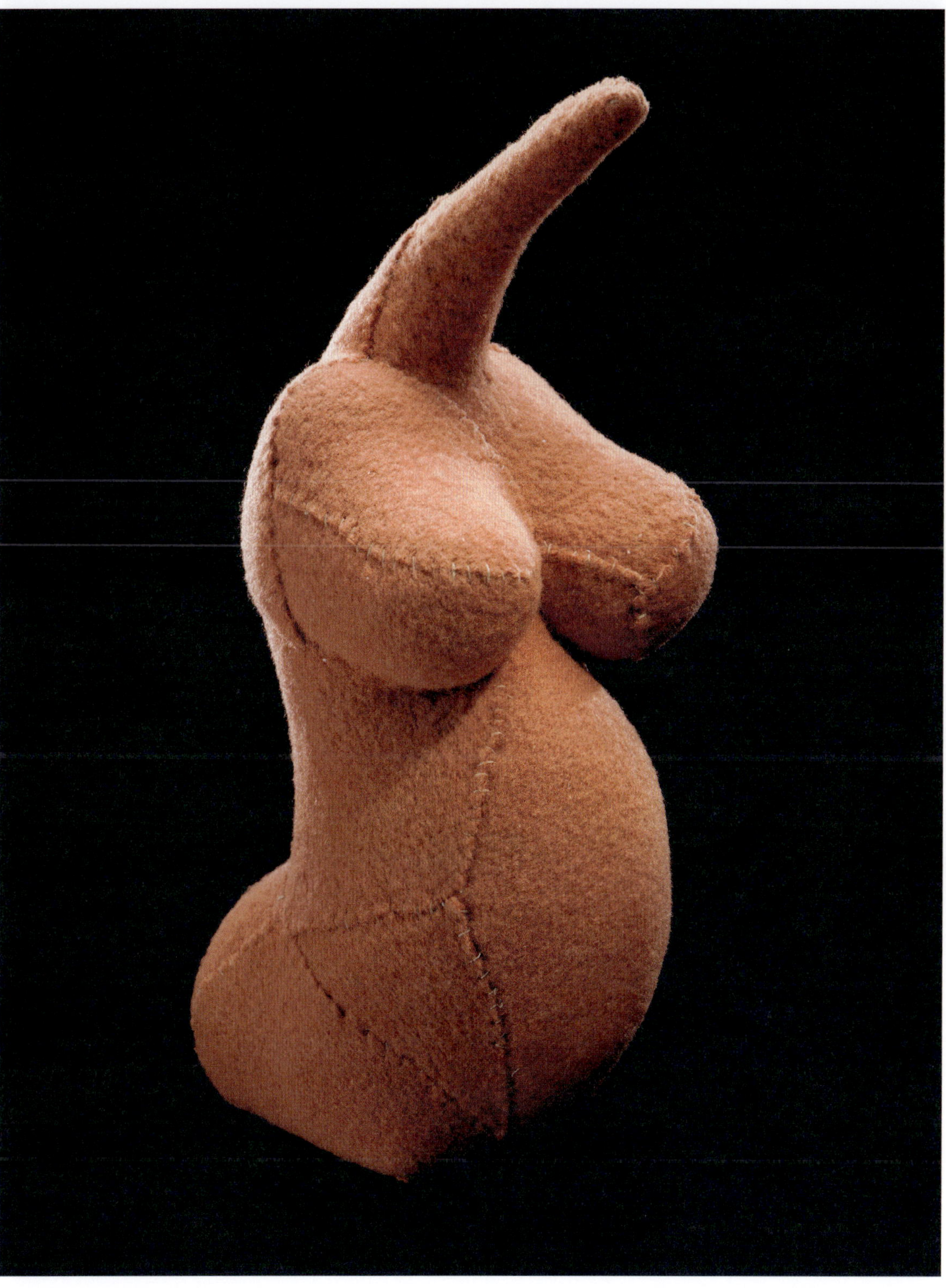

Fragile Goddess, 2002.
Fabric. 31.7 × 12.7 × 15.2 cm (12½ × 5 × 6in).

itself is draped in a skin-like tablecloth. The scene is lit with a red light that feels all the more sinister once we consider the story unfolding in the work. Bourgeois explained that it relates to the fantasy of a family becoming fed up with their horrible father, cutting him into pieces, and having him for dinner. Yikes.

From the 1990s, then in her eighties, Bourgeois began to concentrate on themes relating to weaving and her mother. Her work is, at times, tinged with feelings of sadness or fear, but it's without the anger present in pieces like *Destruction of the Father*. This was the period when she began her well-known series of spider sculptures. The 1997 *Spider (Cell)* depicts a large steel spider standing over a cylindrical cage, or 'cell'. The chain link cell walls evoke the image of a web, with the spider penetrating the top. Tapestry panels are contained within, but it is unclear whether the spider is protecting or preying on the contents of the cell. Bourgeois said that spiders, who are nature's weavers, reminded her of her mother, who was a weaver and who she described in an ode as being 'as useful as a spider'.

Bourgeois' exploration of soft sculptures increased in the latter stages of her career, and this phase is sometimes called her 'Old Age' style. The bodies and parts that she'd once created from hard materials like stone or bronze were now stitched and stuffed fabric works. The materials bring to mind children's toys, which are frivolous and prone to wear, but her subject matter is decidedly adult and sculptural. In some cases, such as in her 2002 sculpture *Fragile Goddess*, her works are soft reinterpretations of earlier works that she originally produced in bronze. This was a direct challenge to the elevation of traditional sculptural materials above soft materials, which had long been discounted as 'domestic' or diminished because they are less hard-wearing.

Fragile Goddess depicts a nude female figure with large breasts, a curved stomach and a pert bottom. It simultaneously recalls images of pre-historic Venus sculptures and ancient Classical

Across her eight-decade career, Bourgeois masterfully walked the line between contrasting ideas. Her works are soft, but sculptural; gendered and androgynous; the work she created in her old age recalls memories from her childhood.

sculptures of goddesses that have lost arms over the centuries. Like some of Bourgeois' earlier sculptures, the shape alludes to both male and female forms. A woman's curvy figure is immediately apparent, but the long neck terminating at the breasts is also phallic. The stitching on the work zig-zags across the figure's body, as if it had been broken and pieced back together and connects back to Bourgeois' memories of the women in her family's workshop repairing tapestries, which fostered her associations between needlework with repair in a psychological and physical sense.

At the same time as Bourgeois was working in soft sculpture, she produced a series of fabric 'drawings' from old clothes and other textiles she'd saved over the years. Many of these personal items bear signs of their previous life through stains and wear, and by weaving and sewing these materials together, she essentially created a collection of abstract self-portraits. Sitting at her kitchen table in the last decade of her life, Bourgeois used a skill that is often employed in a domestic setting to give household textiles (clothing, sheets, napkins, etc.) new life as fine art. It is a quietly radical series that shouldn't be overlooked within her wider oeuvre.

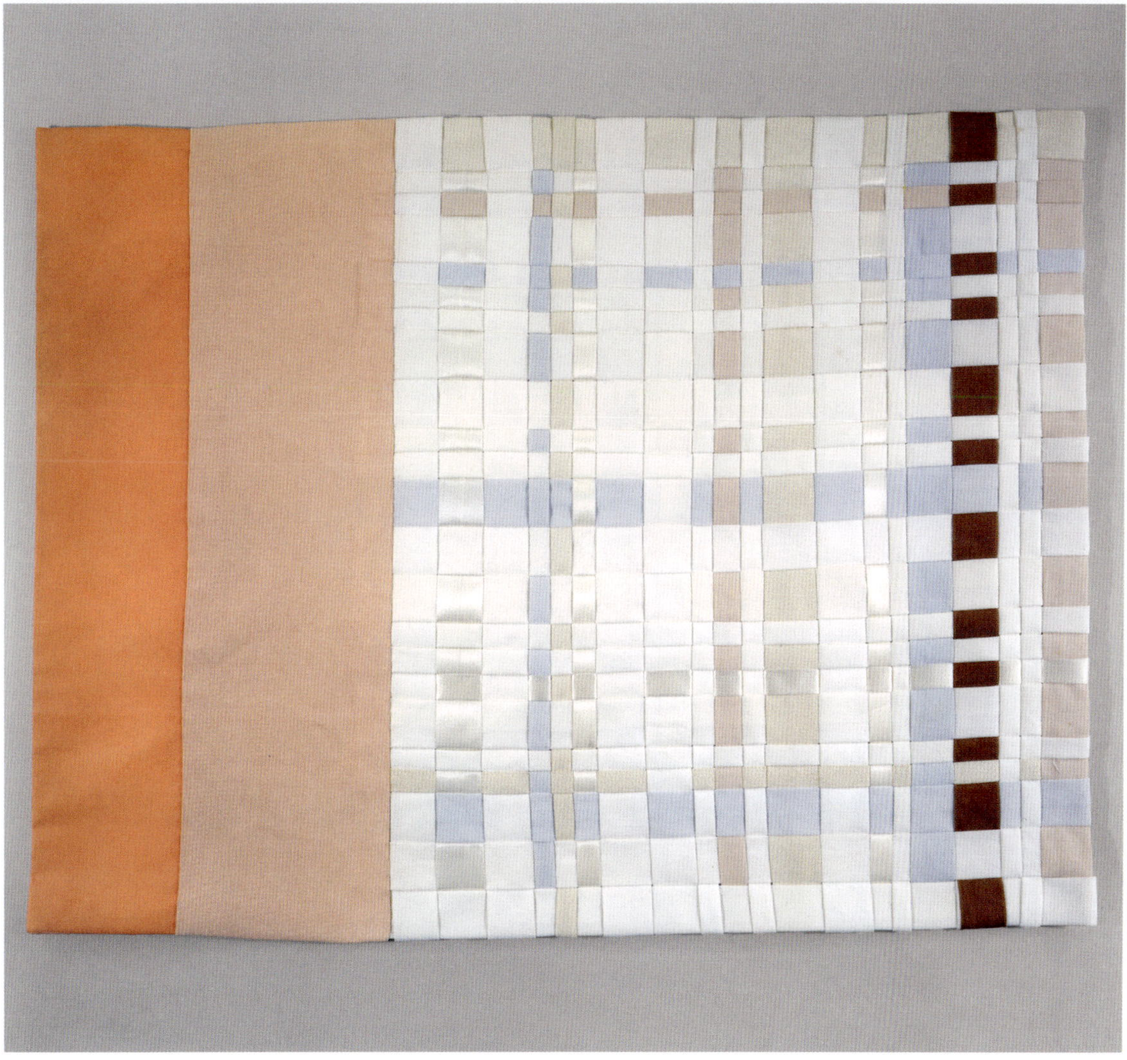

Untitled, 2003.
Woven fabric. 43.8 × 58.4 cm (17¼ x 23in).

Across her eight-decade career, Bourgeois masterfully walked the line between contrasting ideas. Her works are soft, but sculptural; gendered and androgynous; the work she created in her old age recalls memories from her childhood.

International success came later in life for Bourgeois, with her first retrospective taking place at the Museum of Modern Art when she was seventy-one-years old. Fortunately, she continued working for another twenty-seven years and was able to see her work exhibited at major institutions around the world.

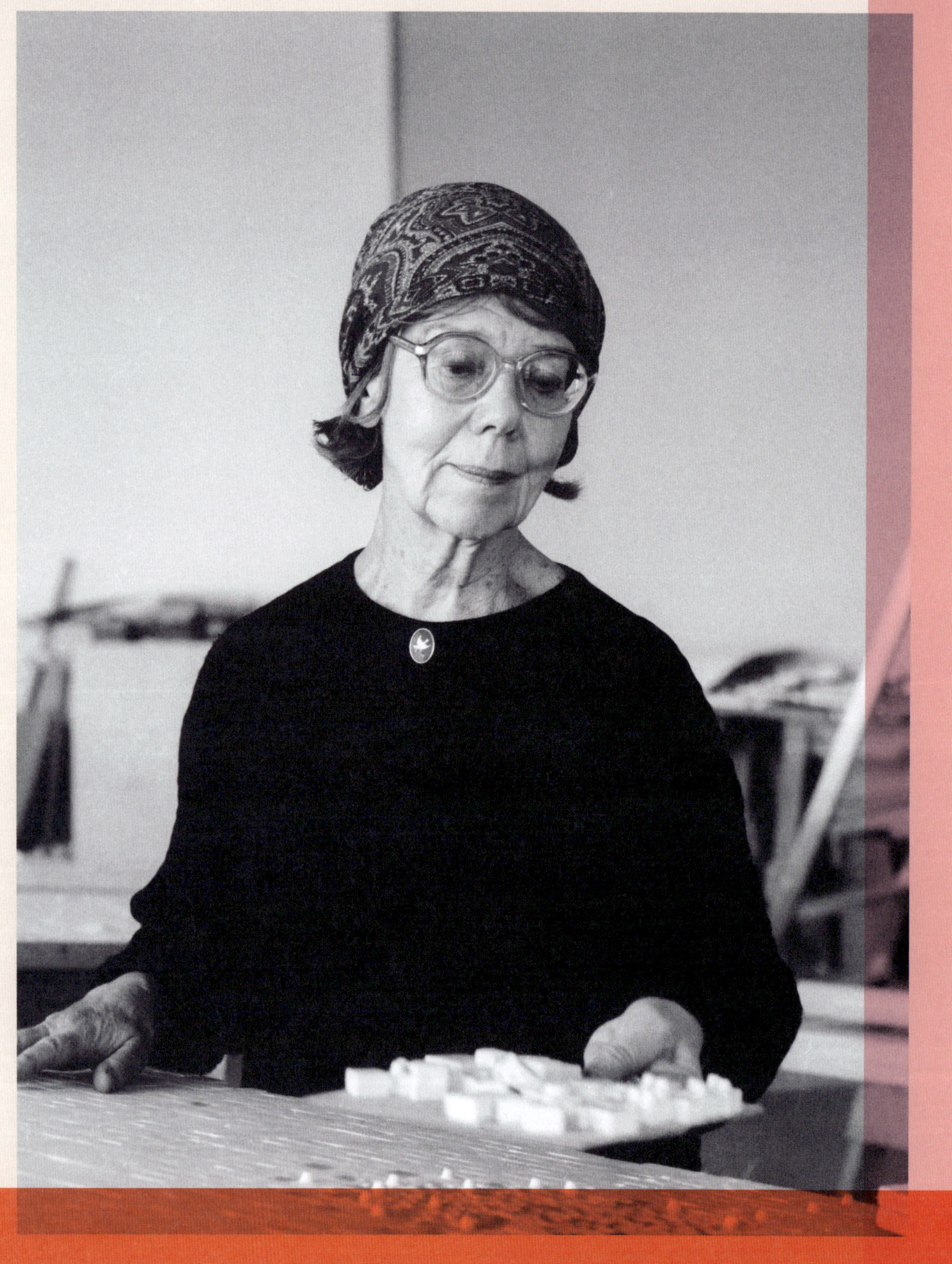

Rut Bryk

(1916–1999)

Ceramics, Textile design

The lines between 'art', 'craft' and 'design' can be tricky to distinguish and, every now and then, an artist comes along who obliterates those delineations altogether. Rut Bryk's artistic vision permeated all her creative endeavours, from printmaking to textile design to ceramic installations. Her innovative approach to the materiality of ceramics and its use as a painterly and sculptural medium in the mid-twentieth century brought a completely fresh view to modern Finnish ceramics.

Bryk was born in Stockholm, where she and her family lived until they moved to Finland during her high school years. Aspects of her childhood sound picturesque. Her father was an entomologist specializing in butterflies and the family passed summer vacations in scenic Finnish villages. In 1936, Bryk enrolled in the Central School of Industrial Crafts in Helsinki to study graphic art and printmaking. She also took an interest in textile design at this time, drawing notice to her designs whenever she entered school competitions. She experimented with hand-printing fabrics using linocuts, weaving tapestries using her mother's old looms and collaborating with the design organization Friends of Finnish Handicrafts to design embroidery and other textiles.

In 1942, a couple of years after finishing her studies, Bryk got a job in the art department of the ceramics company Arabia. Working alongside the ceramicist Birger Kaipiainen, she learned how to scratch designs into ceramic objects using the sgraffito technique. Her early works are clearly informed by her previous graphic training, depicting figurative images of animals, people and plants. Her childhood was also a source of inspiration. Some of her tile designs show houses in similar styles to what she encountered on her early holidays in the Finnish countryside, and she also produced several pieces featuring butterflies, which are undoubtedly an influence from her father. This phase of her work is often referred to as 'naive' – perhaps due to her use of flat, bright colours, simply rendered forms and narrative themes.

Interestingly, her style at this time was consistent across mediums – from greeting cards to ceramic plate designs – which shows that she approached each as vehicles for artistic expression even though she was first introduced to ceramics in a commercial context. In fact, some of her ceramic designs were inspired in part by painters like Paul Klee and Marc Chagall. A piece titled *Venice Palace* utilizes outlines and flat graphic fields to depict three people looking out from the windows of an aged grey building. The style and use of colour are very reminiscent of Klee's Bauhaus period, and what could be more Bauhaus than Bryk creating works that bridge painting (form) and ceramics (function)? The lines and shapes are irregular, as is the scale of the figures and architectural features. Bryk's elastic approach to scale in this work allowed her to show greater detail in select areas. Where her ceramics have a leg up over painting is that they are not bound by conventional rectangular surfaces as painters are with a canvas (although artists like Frank Stella later play with canvas shapes). For Bryk's figurative ceramics, her 'canvases' are sometimes shaped like the things she is representing, unbound by unnecessary negative space. So, in the example of *Venice Palace*, which is shaped like a building, the viewer need only concern themselves with the palace and its inhabitants.

In 1951, Bryk won the top prize at the Milan Triennial for her tile designs, garnering recognition for her talents on the global art stage. This kickstarted a period of international travel, which saw her visit and exhibit across Europe, India, Mexico and the United States. By the late 1960s, her many travel experiences coalesced into new ideas within her art practice. She began to make larger scale pieces, including huge ceramic works

Some of Bryk's fabric designs were sold by the metre and others could be purchased as towels, bedding, tablecloths and other domestic goods. Bryk also incorporated some of the textiles in her ceramic exhibitions, once again displaying her ability to comfortably walk the divide between commercial and fine art objects.

with geometric patterns inspired by traditional art styles she'd encountered in Europe and India. A piece named after the city of Jaipur shows tessellated tiles with black and white half-moon geometric designs that evoke the awe-inspiring tile work from the city for which it's named. Fittingly, Bryk would later design a 32 sqm piece for the Finnish Embassy in New Delhi in 1985.

Architects increasingly wanted to work with Bryk to integrate her artworks within the design of spaces. This enabled her to expand the size of her pieces even further and thoughtfully plan them in a site-specific manner. Examples of these works can be found in Helsinki's City Hall, the Bank of Finland in Helsinki and in the official residence for the President of Finland. Some works fill entire walls, with varying depths of tiles that create interest through changing textures, light and shadows. In works like *Singing of a Migratory Bird*,

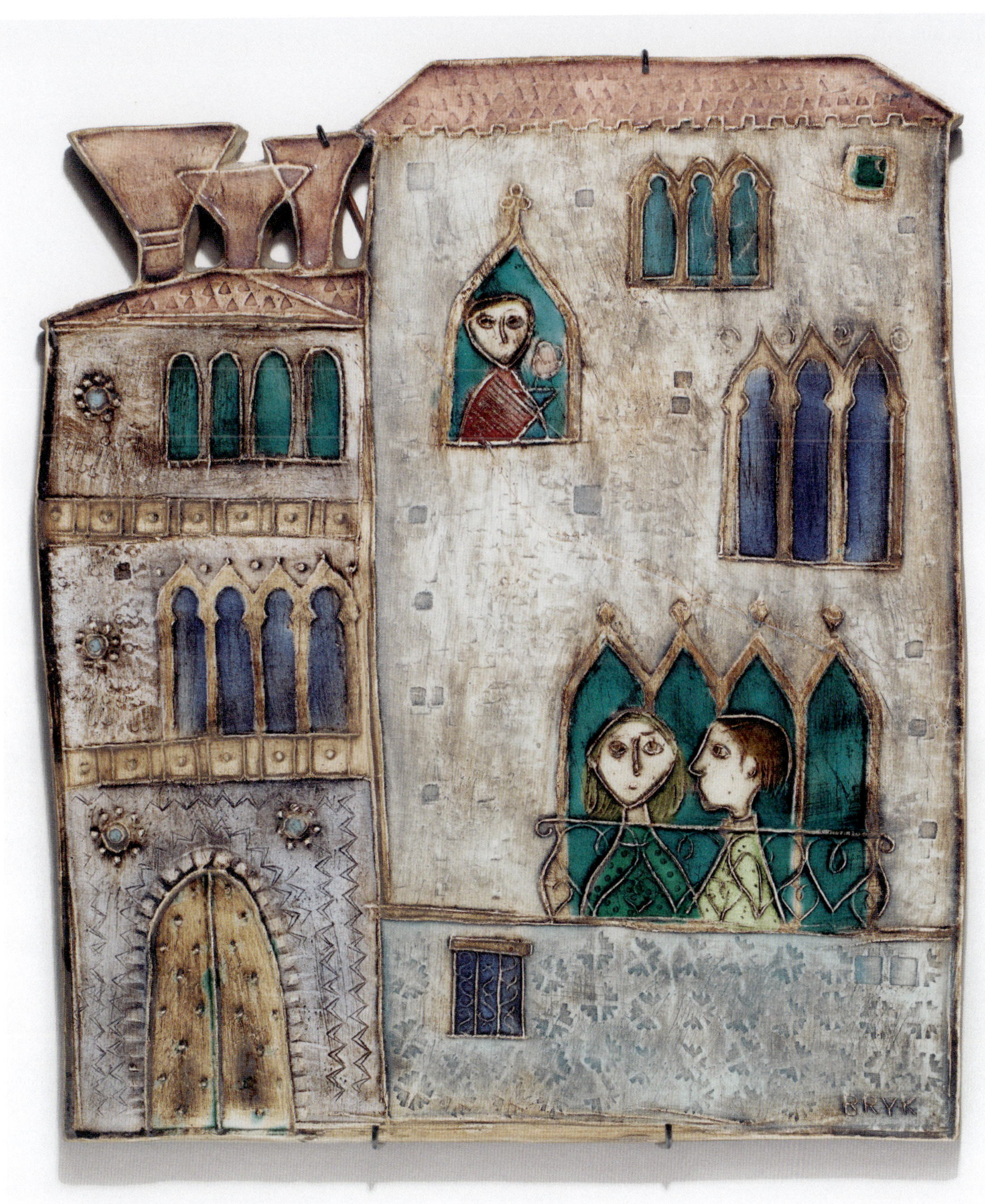

Venetian palace: figures in a window, 1955.
Faience, glaze. 47.6 × 41.9 × 3.2cm (18¾ × 16½ × 1¼in).

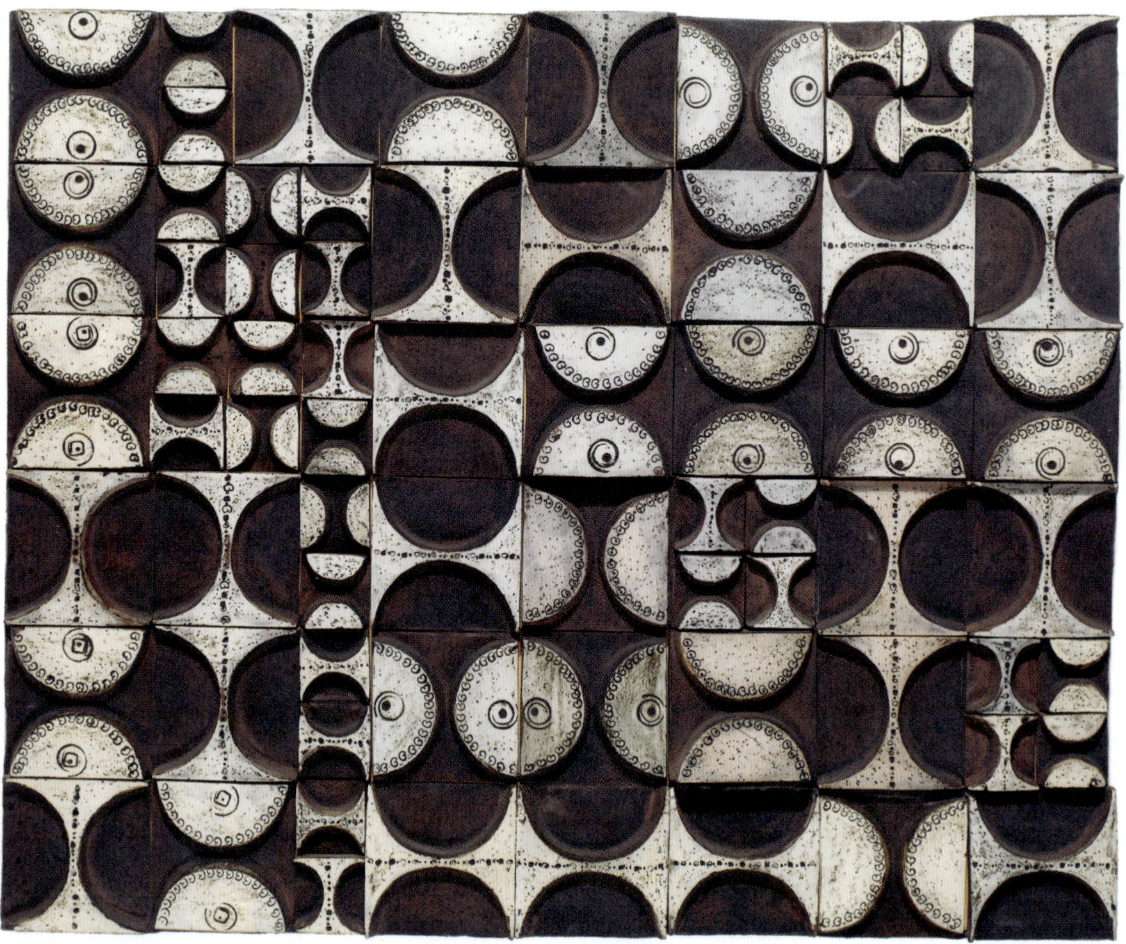

Jaipur, 1967.
Faience, wood panel, glue.
35.3 × 43.6 × 4cm (13⅞ × 17⅛ × 1½in).

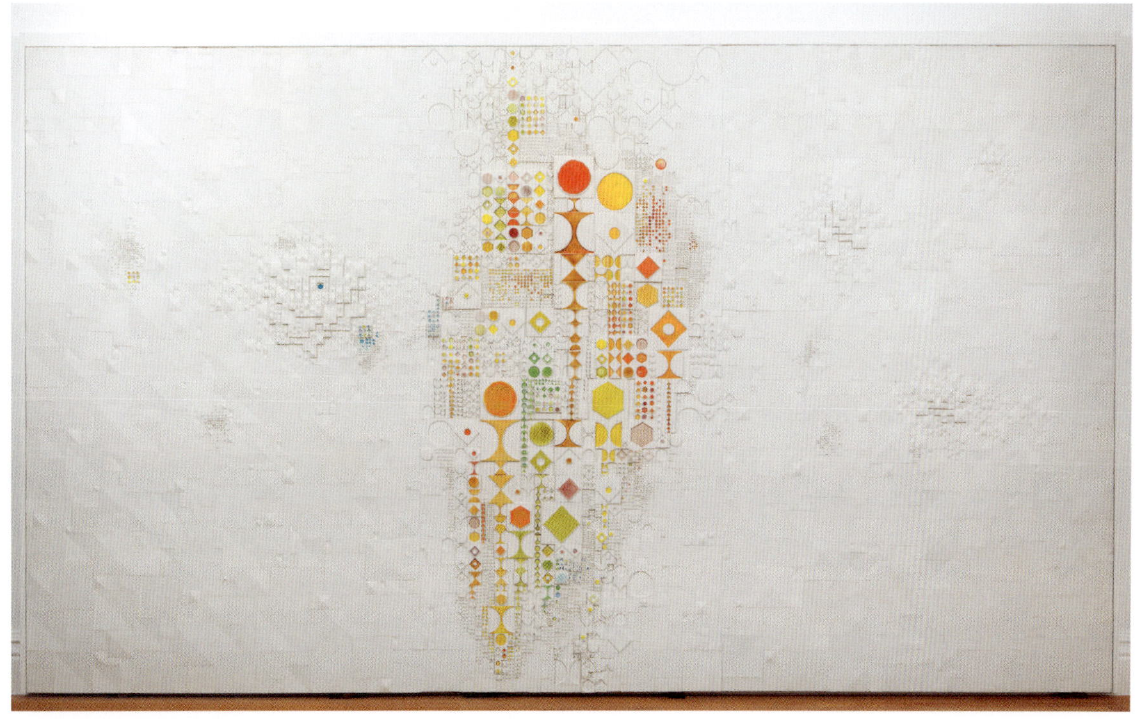

Singing of a Migratory Bird, 1974.
Faience, glaze.
262 × 472cm (103⅛ × 185¾in).

the tiles appear to bubble up from the white wall and converge in a fissure of yellow and orange. The tiles are all rigid geometric or prismatic shapes, but there's an organic – even topographical – look to the composition.

The 1960s also saw Bryk return to textile design. She created the *Seita* collection for the cotton manufacturing company Vaasan Puuvilla-Finlayson. The designs were simple and the palette was inspired by the colours of fields she'd seen in Lapland, including fabrics in solid jewel tones or bold striped patterns. Some of Bryk's fabric designs were sold by the metre and others could be purchased as towels, bedding, tablecloths and other domestic goods. Bryk incorporated some of the textiles in her ceramic exhibitions, once again displaying her ability to comfortably walk the divide between commercial and fine art objects.

Bryk was celebrated with numerous awards during her life, including the Pro Finlandia medal in 1962 and an honorary doctorate from the University of Helsinki in 1994. She built a formidable legacy and receives continued praise as one of the most influential figures of modern Finnish ceramic art.

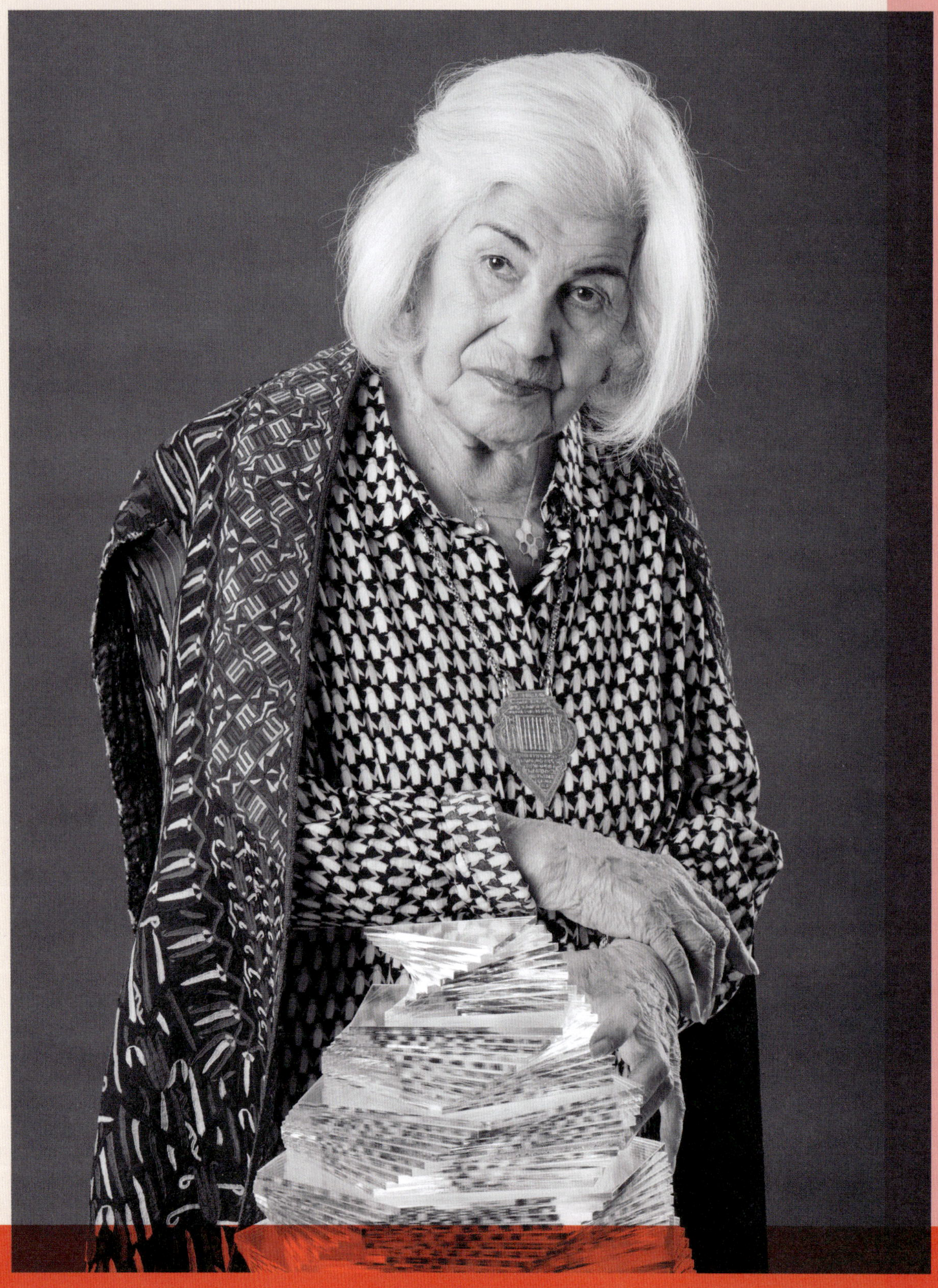

Monir Shahroudy Farmanfarmaian

(c.1922–2019)

Mosaics

Monir Sharoudy Farmanfarmaian's works create an incredible bridge between traditional and modern Iranian aesthetics. Her complex geometric mirror mosaics could sit as comfortably alongside centuries-old Islamic art forms as they could with the structured minimalism coming out of New York in the 1960s and 1970s. The development of her art practice reflects her incredible life, which was filled with unexpected challenges and serendipitous encounters.

Farmanfarmaian was born Monir Shahroudy in the northern Iranian city of Qazvin. Her family was highly respected within its community: her mother, Fatemeh, was descended from Ottoman aristocracy, and her father, Bagher, established Qazvin's first school for girls. Her parents ran an intellectual and progressive household that encouraged education and free thinking, and they also exposed Farmanfarmaian to the arts from a young age. Her father sometimes designed intricate carpets inspired by gardens and nature, the family's house was filled with paintings and beautifully crafted furnishings, and Farmanfarmaian enjoyed passing the time doing drawing and needlework.

In 1932, her father was elected to Parliament and the family moved to the capital city of Tehran. During high school, Farmanfarmalan started taking private drawing lessons and practised her skills by copying postcards of Western masterpieces. She went on to enrol in the Fine Arts College at the University of Tehran, where she was introduced to the works of the Impressionists and Post-Impressionists by one of her teachers. She became enamoured with the idea of studying in Paris, but the Second World War made that dream impossible. Instead, in 1944,

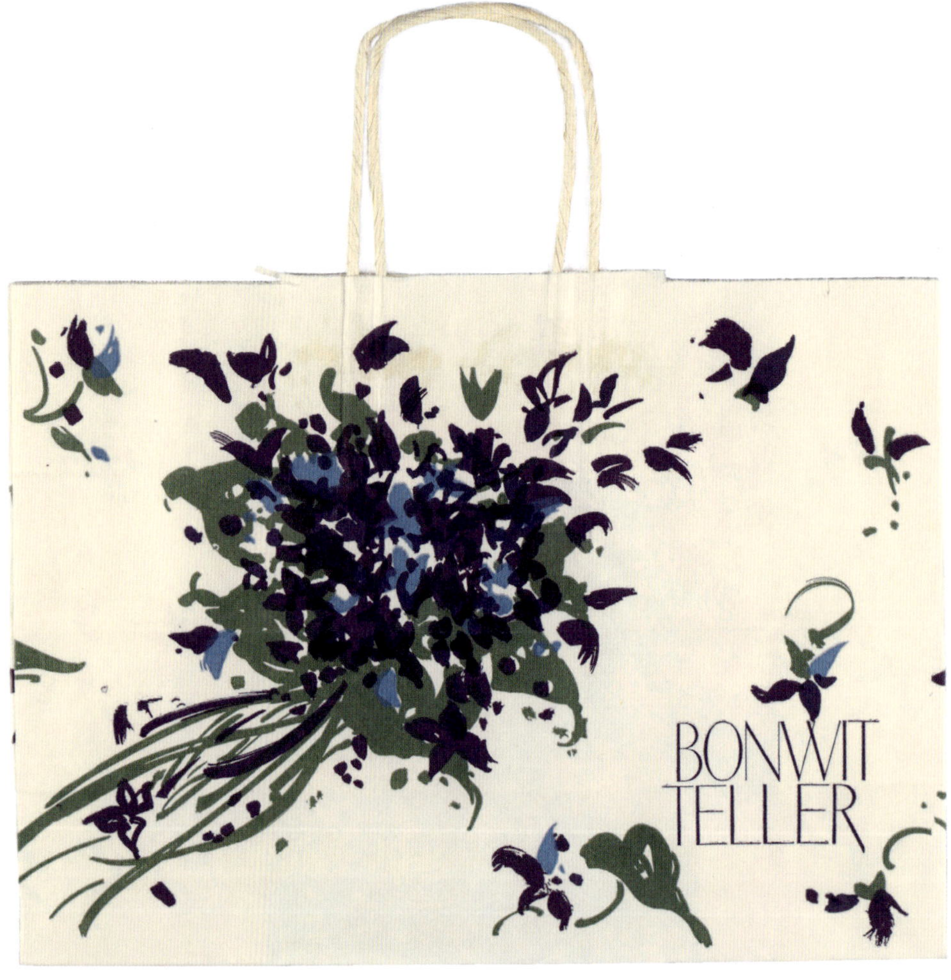

Shopping Bag, Bonwit Teller, designed c.1960 by J. Hyde Crawford with illustration by Monir Shahroudy Farmanfarmaian.
Paper, white rafia handles. 29.2 × 40.6 cm (11½ × 16 in).

she embarked on a remarkable journey wherein, with the help of a friend with CIA connections, she sailed to India and then on to Los Angeles on a US warship. From LA, she made the trek across the United States to the growing art hub of New York City.

Farmanfarmaian excitedly took in the art the city had on offer. She visited galleries and museums and attended summer art courses at Cornell University. She then followed this up by studying fashion illustration at Parsons New School for Design between 1946 and 1949. It wasn't long before she fell in with the 'it' art crowd. She rubbed

shoulders with cutting edge artists like Willem de Kooning, Louise Nevelson and Joan Mitchell at The Club, a series of private informal gatherings of painters and sculptors that took place in Lower Manhattan studio spaces.

After finishing school, she worked various freelance illustration jobs with publications like *Glamour* and *Vogue*, before taking a permanent position doing fashion layouts for the luxury department store Bonwit Teller. One of her colleagues was none other than Andy Warhol, who she said was particularly good at assisting her with shoe illustrations.

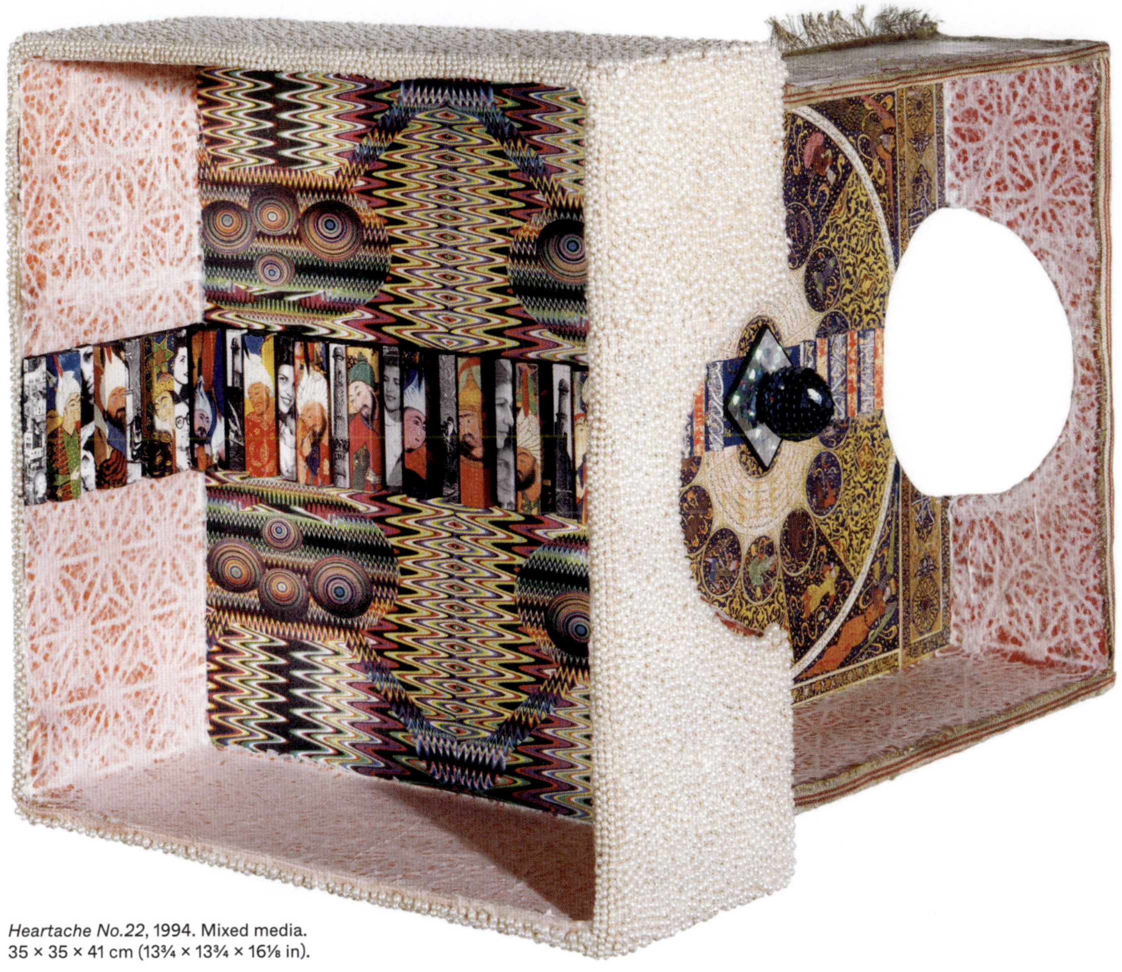

Heartache No.22, 1994. Mixed media.
35 × 35 × 41 cm (13¾ × 13¾ × 16⅛ in).

In 1957, she married the prominent Iranian lawyer Abolbashar Farmanfarmaian and returned to Tehran. Back home, she travelled around the country visiting heritage sites and developing a deeper appreciation for the traditional Iranian art forms she encountered. Then in 1958, she exhibited a group of floral monotypes at the Venice Biennale, earning a gold medal. Much of her early work depicted fluid floral imagery in a style more in line with Safavid-era still lifes than the geometric works for which she would later become known. Indeed, before she worked with Bonwit Teller, the company had purchased one of her illustrations of Persian violets to use on their iconic shopping bags and other branded materials.

The change in Farmanfarmaian's art practice was brought about by a visit to the Shah Cheragh mosque in Shiraz in 1966. For hours, she was transfixed by the glittering mirror mosaics covering the walls and ceiling, and she determined to explore this captivating visual within her own work. She sketched geometric patterns and worked with craftsmen to have the shapes expertly cut from glass and high-quality mirror. These were arranged in dazzling patterns reminiscent of the sacred geometry found in Islamic architecture

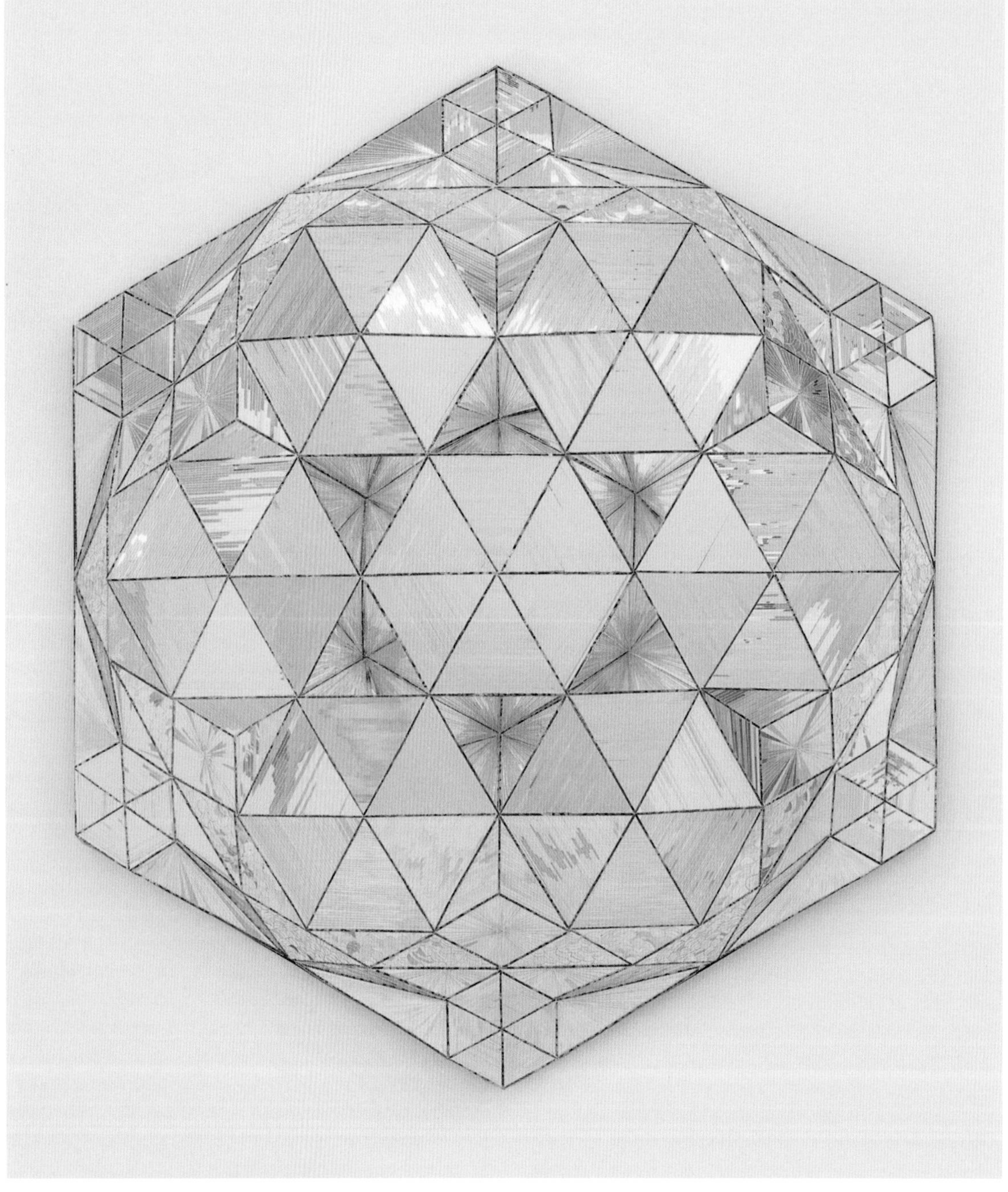

Third Family Hexagon, 2011. Reverse painted glass, mirrored glass and plaster. 122 × 122 cm (48⅛ × 48⅛ in).

Farmanfarmaian's artistic focus largely turned to textiles, collages and what she called 'Heartache boxes'. These assemblages exhibit the complex patterning of her mirror work, but also incorporate textiles and personal effects, such as photographs and prints.

and design, which traditionally include a mixture of circles, squares, stars and floral shapes interlocking and overlapping in a symmetrical layout. Of course, Farmanfarmaian introduced her own modern perspective to this tradition. Her works are contained artworks affixed to a backing board rather than large-scale architectural transfigurations. In early examples of these works, she sometimes incorporated her paintings behind some of the glass tiles as well. This clean, geometric style was very much in line with abstract minimalist explorations happening in the United States around the same time, and Farmanfarmaian even became good friends with Frank Stella after his visit to Tehran in 1974.

In 1979, Farmanfarmaian and her family took a trip to New York that turned into an unplanned exile from their home country. Due to the start of the Iranian revolution, they were forced to settle in the city for a period that stretched into more than twenty years. She received commissions for her mirror work in the 1980s, but she didn't have access to the thin mirrors and expert glass craftsmen with whom she'd previously partnered. For this reason, her artistic focus largely turned to

textiles, collages and what she called 'Heartache boxes'. These assemblages exhibit the complex patterning of her mirror work, but also incorporate textiles and personal effects, such as photographs and prints. The bulk of the boxes were made after the death of her husband, and the works were a way for Farmanfarmaian to engage with the many forms of loss she'd experienced in her life – the loss of her home, the loss of her early artworks, the loss of her belongings and then the loss of her husband. There's an altar-like quality to the works that connects them to the subtle spirituality of her mirror mosaics as well.

In 2005, Farmanfarmaian permanently returned home to Iran. From then on, she began to produce her mirror mosaics once again. Many of these works experiment with three-dimensionality, where the tiles are lifted and tilted within geometric orientations. This allows the light to refract and reflect in different ways. In both traditional mirror mosaics and in Farmanfarmaian's modern interpretations, one of the objectives of the designs is to convey the sense that the surfaces are emanating light rather than simply reflecting it, giving the designs a grand or spiritual presence. This is amplified in Farmanfarmaian's later mirror works by the faceted surface design, which adds a layer of dynamism to the already dazzling effect.

In 2015, Farmanfarmaian became the first Iranian artist to have a solo exhibition at the Guggenheim Museum in New York. Then in 2018, with the opening of the Monir Museum, she became the first woman artist in Iran to have a museum solely dedicated to her art. It was a beautiful celebration of her homecoming after having spent so many years in exile, and after decades of loss she was finally able to step into the light of her own brilliant work.

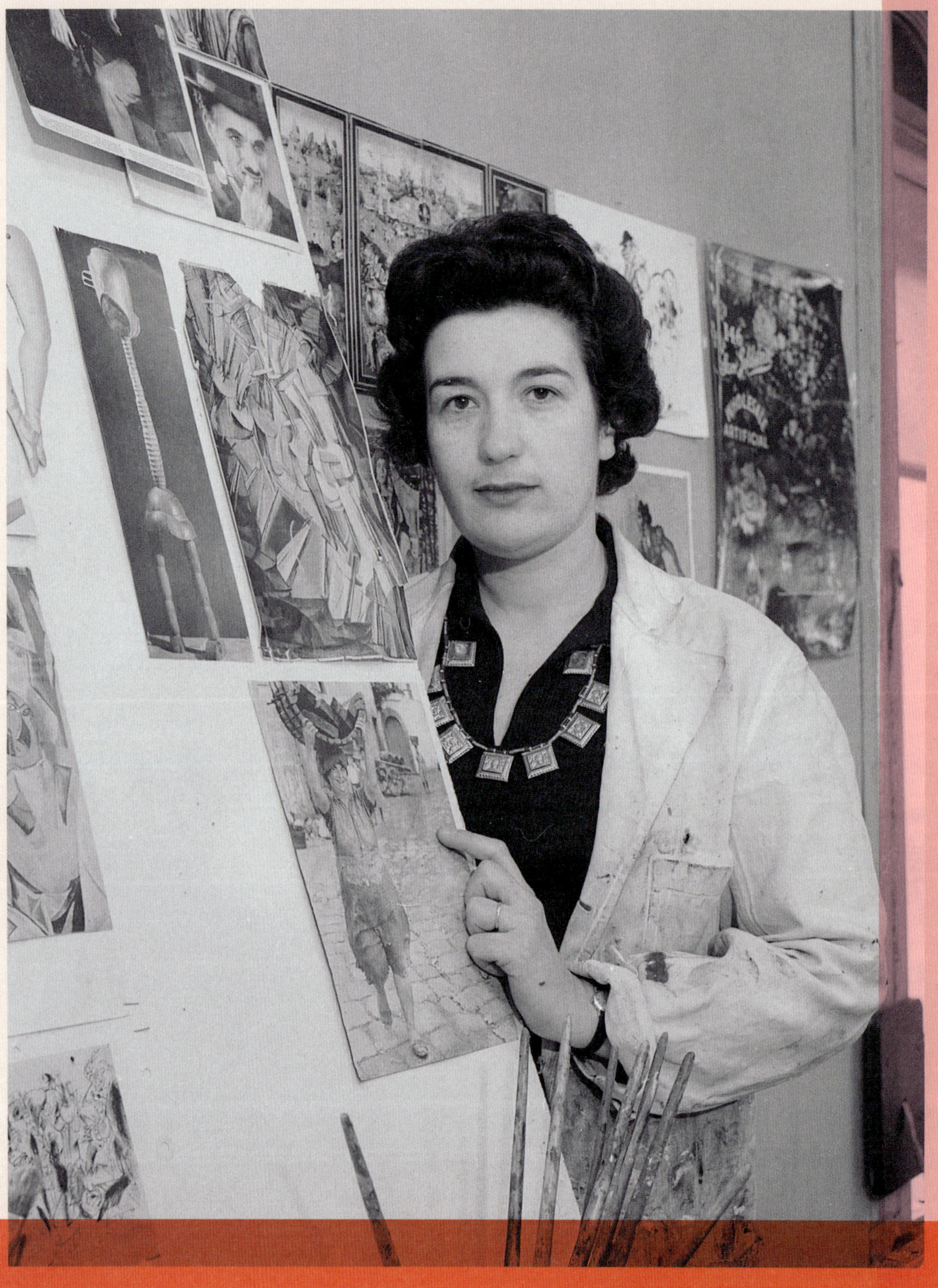

Miriam Schapiro

(1923–2015)

Quilting, Textile art

Miriam Schapiro understood the socio-political history of craft and decorative arts, and brazenly embraced these art traditions in a modern and radically feminist way. She rejected the idea that because some mediums had traditionally been utilized by women in domestic spaces, that they were any less artistically valid. Not only did she choose to work in these mediums, she engaged with subjects relating to femininity and womanhood – effectively doubling down on the feminine energy within her work through both medium and content.

Schapiro was born on a wet and chilly November day in Toronto, Canada. Her mother had come to the city to be with family for the birth while her father was studying at the Beaux-Arts Institute of Design in New York. She is descended on both sides from Russian Jewish grandparents who emigrated to North America in the early twentieth century and – fun fact – her paternal grandfather invented the first moveable dolls' eyes used in the United States. During the Great Depression, the small family of three settled in Brooklyn permanently.

Schapiro's father was an artist and worked as an industrial designer, so when she showed an early interest in drawing at the age of six, he was very encouraging. During her high school years, she attended extracurricular art courses at the Museum of Modern Art and through the Works Progress Administration (WPA) programme – she was all of fourteen when she attended the WPA's nude drawing classes for adults. After graduating high school, she briefly attended Hunter College in New York before transferring to the University of Iowa. There, she studied a combination of painting, printmaking and art history, earning a BA, MA and

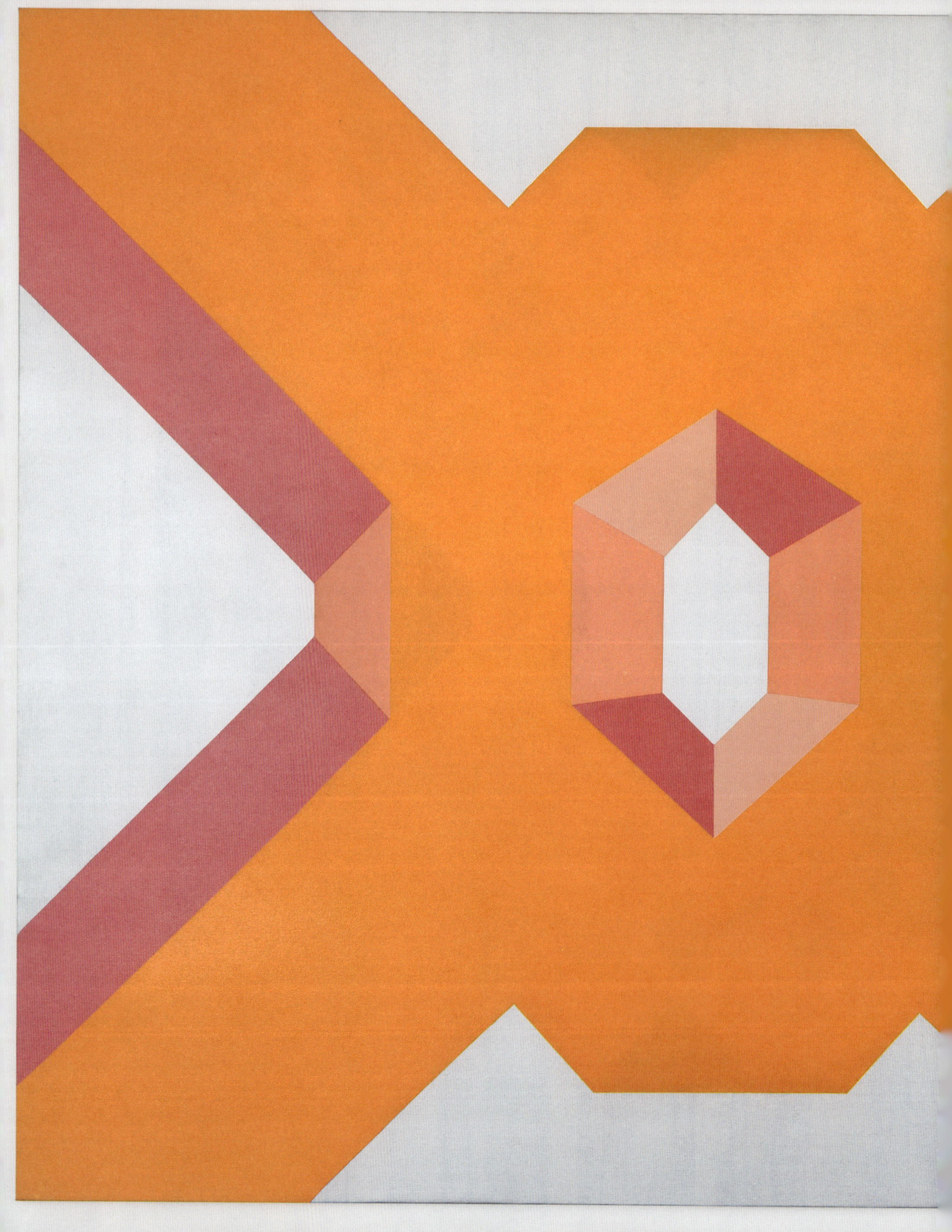

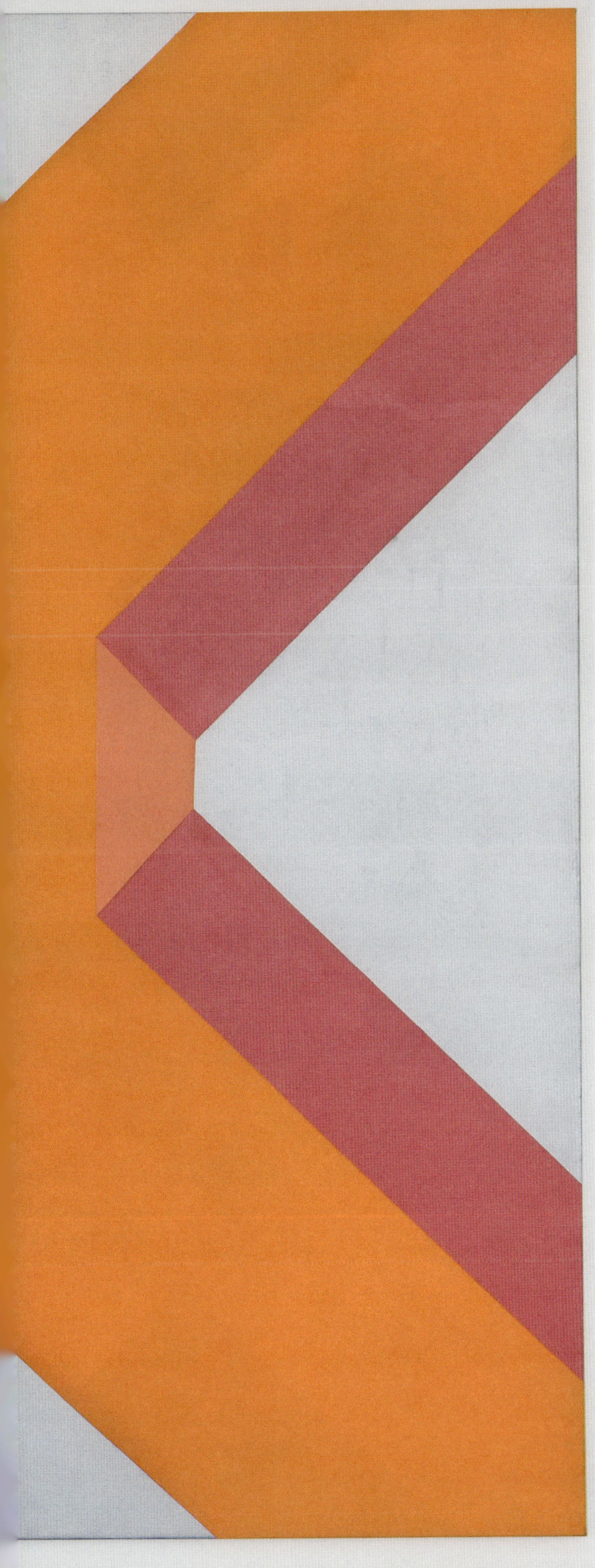

MFA. She also worked as a printmaking assistant for her teacher, Mauricio Lasansky, and assisted him in forming the Iowa Print Group at the university.

In Iowa, she met and married fellow artist Paul Brach. After graduating, Brach took a teaching position at the University of Missouri, and the couple relocated for his job in 1950. During this period, Schapiro worked as a rabbi's assistant and children's art teacher. In 1951, they moved again to New York City, where their live–work studio was situated in a hub of creativity and the couple fell in with the Abstract Expressionist crowd. Schapiro continued teaching art to children for a stretch, but by 1955, she was working as a full-time artist.

Schapiro's work throughout the 1950s was part of the second generation of Abstract Expressionists, but in the 1960s, she created a series of comparatively more representational 'shrine' paintings. The themes of these works explored her experiences navigating the roles of artist, wife and new mother. At this time, she worked out of a room in the centre of the house, and juggled responsibilities as she passed between rooms. This multiplicity comes through in her paintings of stacked window-like scenes depicting aspects of life as a woman artist. The series coincided with the developing second wave of feminism, wherein women around the world were challenging traditional gender roles and oppressive ideas around women's sexuality. These works were an early version of some of the feminist concepts she would develop in her later work.

Schapiro moved to California in 1967, where she and her husband both took positions working at the University of California, San Diego. Initially, she worked on cutting edge computer art in collaboration with physicist David Nalibof, using the computer to plot out complex designs and then transferring them to canvas to paint. This placed her at the forefront of artists experimenting with the then emerging medium. Once again, these works were artistic expressions of feminist ideas.

Big Ox, 1967. Acrylic on canvas.
229 × 274 cm (90 × 108 in).

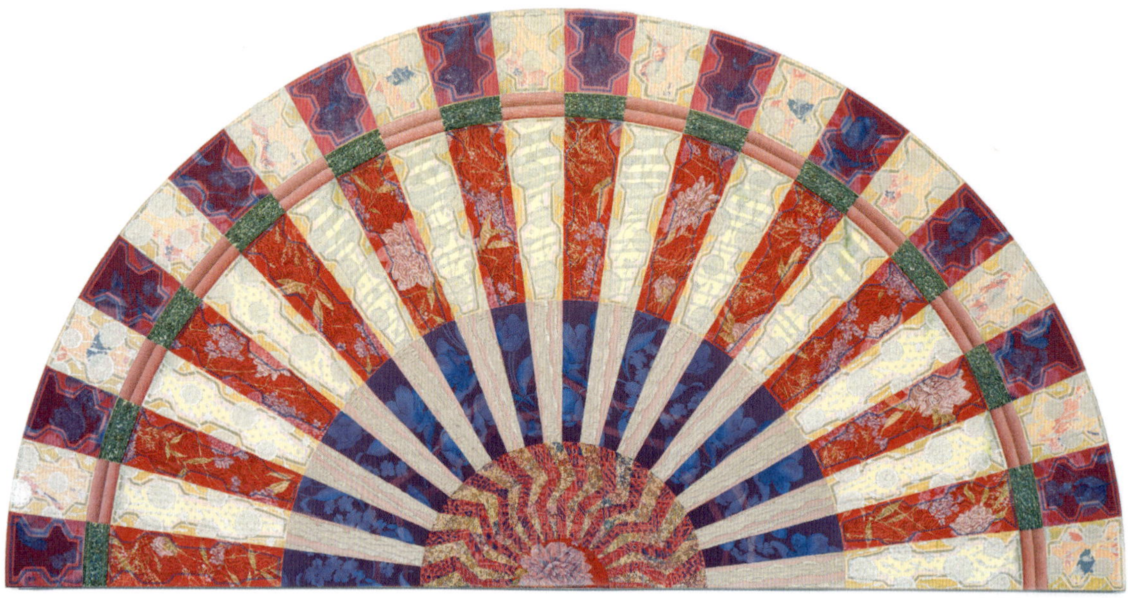

Barcelona Fan, 1979.
Fabric and acrylic on canvas.
182.9 × 365.8 cm (72 × 144 in).

Schapiro employed a technology from what was, at the time, a predominantly male field to create minimalist geometric forms, – but she was subverting these 'male' tools to make work about women's issues. In her 1967 painting *Big Ox*, she created a hard-edge symmetrical design centred around the letters 'O' and 'X' in feminine shades of orange and pink. It seems like a straightforward minimalist piece, but in actuality, she used the letters to create an abstracted image of the vaginal opening and four limbs extending outwards. This was a radical theme for a woman artist to allude to at this time. A 2016 exhibition of her work at the National Academy Museum quoted Schapiro in a wall text saying that, 'the piece was so powerful to me that when I was finished, I turned it to the wall for six months until I dared approach it again.'

After meeting fellow artist Judy Chicago (see page 114) in 1970, the pair bonded over a shared mission of supporting other women artists in their practice. Together they established the Feminist Art Program at the California Institute of the Arts and collaborated on the first feminist art exhibition *Womanhouse* (1972). Schapiro's contribution to the house-turned-exhibition space was *The Dollhouse* (1972), which incorporated found objects like toys and fabrics to create a miniature house, exploring similar themes to her earlier shrine paintings.

In the years that followed, she became increasingly interested in using fabrics in her work. She was attracted to their look and feel, but also to the history of textiles as an undervalued form of women's labour and artistic expression – particularly as so many women were denied access to other mediums for so many centuries.

Working with a combination of paint and fabrics, Schapiro began creating collages that she termed 'femmages'. In an addendum to an oral interview for the Archives of American Art, Smithsonian Institution, she describes these pieces as 'contributing to post-Modernism by challenging Modernism … through the combining of formal art with artefacts from women's culture'. This disruptive approach placed her at centre of the Pattern and Decoration (P&D) movement in

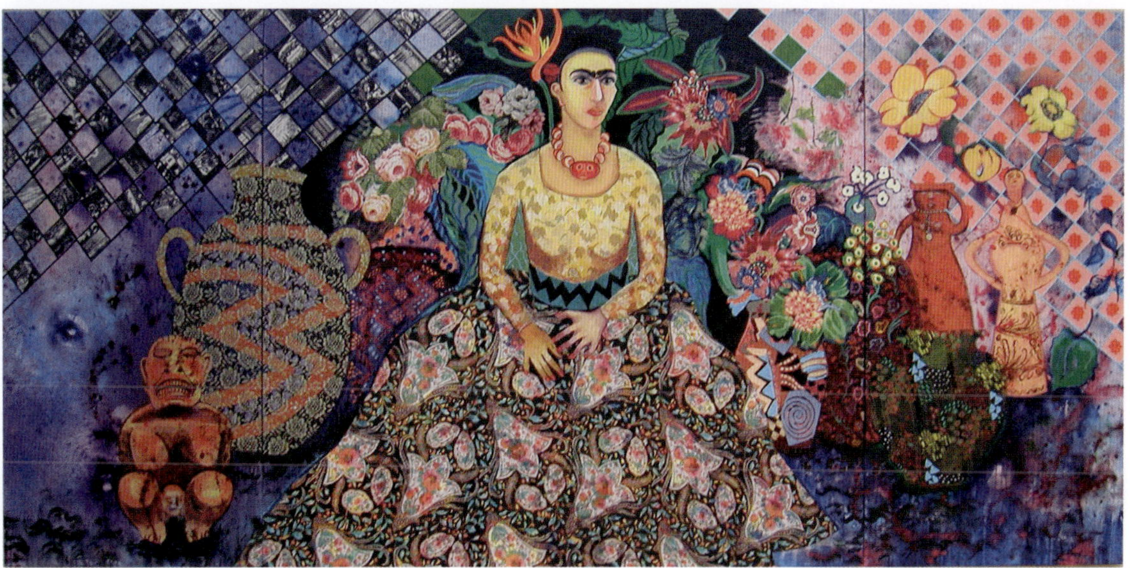

Conservatory (Portrait of Frida Kahlo), 1988.
Acrylic and mixed media on canvas.
189.2 × 386 cm (72 × 152 in).

which artists worked to bridge the divide between decorative and fine arts. Some femmages took the form of large fans, an accessory that has been associated with women in many cultures. A coded fan language was even used by some society women in eighteenth- and nineteenth-century Europe. It's fitting that Schapiro used fans as part of her own 'lexicon of imagery' (her term) to express her feminist perspective. Other images within this visual language include aprons, houses and hearts.

From 1975, Schapiro was back living in New York and had a studio space of her own for the first time. She continued to create P&D works, but her imagery became more figurative. One catalyst for this change was that she was a member of the College Art Association and helped form a Women's Caucus within the organization to champion the work of women artists and scholars. This mission influenced her decision to create a series of figurative femmages celebrating the contributions of historical women artists. Schapiro called these works 'collaborations', and they typically include references to a woman artist in the centre, surrounded by a quilt-like collage of fabrics and other materials that incorporate that artist's work. In *Conservatory (Portrait of Frida Kahlo)* (1988), she paints the Surrealist painter Frida Kahlo on a throne of flowers and draped in brilliant floral fabrics. To either side is a patchwork of imagery taken from Kahlo's iconic works. Schapiro also combines her facial features with Kahlo's, to hint at seeing some of herself in the artist or descending from her legacy.

There's a running theme across Schapiro's story of boldly taking up space. Physically, artistically, historically, domestically – how can women find and take up a space of their own? Throughout her career, Schapiro investigated this question and made great strides to bring other women artists on that journey with her. Schapiro's work reflects her personal relationship with feminism and was instrumental in claiming space for herself and other women artists to explore their diverse experiences of womanhood through art.

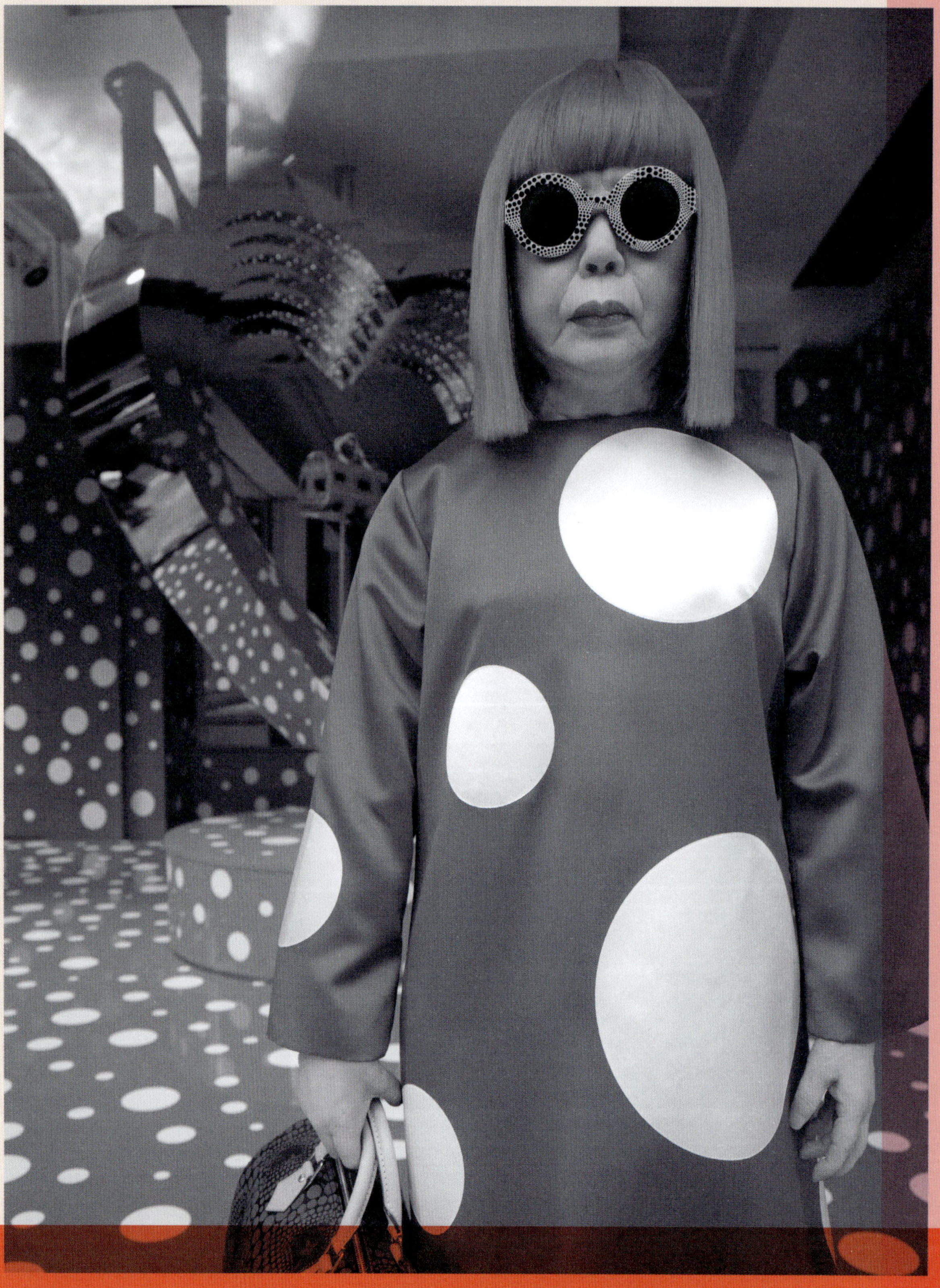

Yayoi Kusama

(b.1929)

Soft sculpture

The avant-garde work of Yayoi Kusama conjures imagery of dots. Lots of dots. The foundations for her bold aesthetic were laid at an early age when she experienced aural and visual hallucinations of spots and aura. From around the age of ten, she harnessed these imaginings into oil and watercolour paintings of dots and nets – as an adult, this concept grew to include immersive installations, paintings and ground-breaking soft sculptures.

Kusama was born in Nagano, Japan, into a well-to-do family of seedling merchants. Her relationship with her parents was formative, but grim. Her mother was abusive, her father a womaniser. He was known to hang around with geisha and Kusama witnessed him having affairs with numerous women. This planted the seeds for Kusama's distaste for sex and the male sex organ, both of which would play out in some of her later artworks. She describes her parents as being conservative, traditional and unsupportive of her artistic inclinations, but she persevered in drawing whenever she could as a child.

On her family's farm, Kusama was surrounded by plants and describes having visions of flowers moving and speaking to her like an infinite sea of animated dots. On one trip to the farm with her grandfather, she saw her first pumpkin and imagined that the gourd was speaking to her – from that moment, she became enamoured with the fruit. Inspired by these experiences, the drawings from her youth began to include the dot and pumpkin motifs for which she would later become so well-known.

After the Second World War, during which time she sewed parachutes for the army, Kusama studied traditional Japanese painting

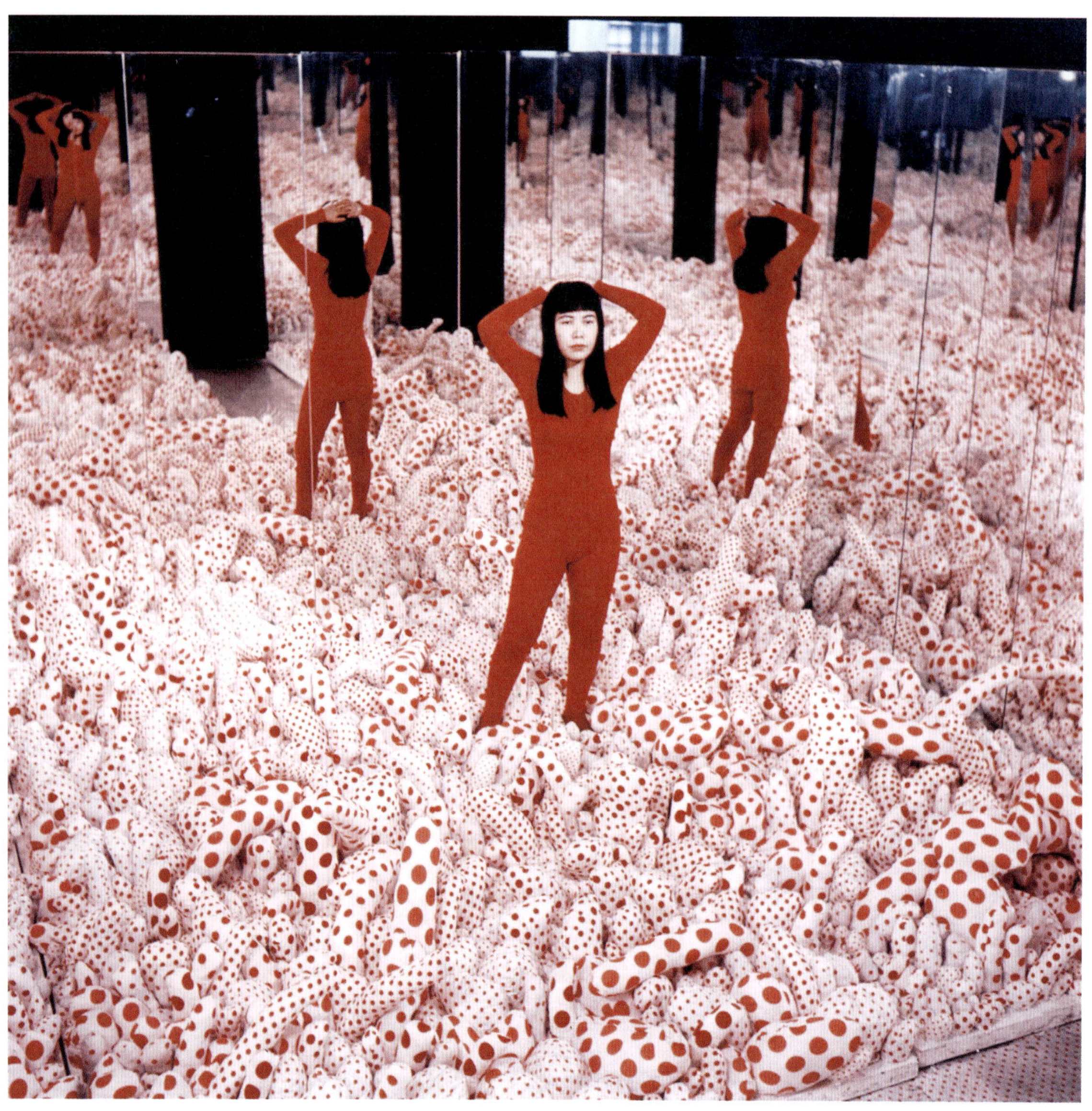

Infinity Mirror Room – Phalli's Field, 1965.
Mixed Media.

Above: A selection of Kusama's soft sculptures on display
at The Whitney Museum of American Art, New York, 2012.
Below: *Accumulation No. 1*, 1962.
Sewn stuffed fabric, paint and chairfringe.
94 × 99.1 × 109.2 cm (37 × 39 × 43in).

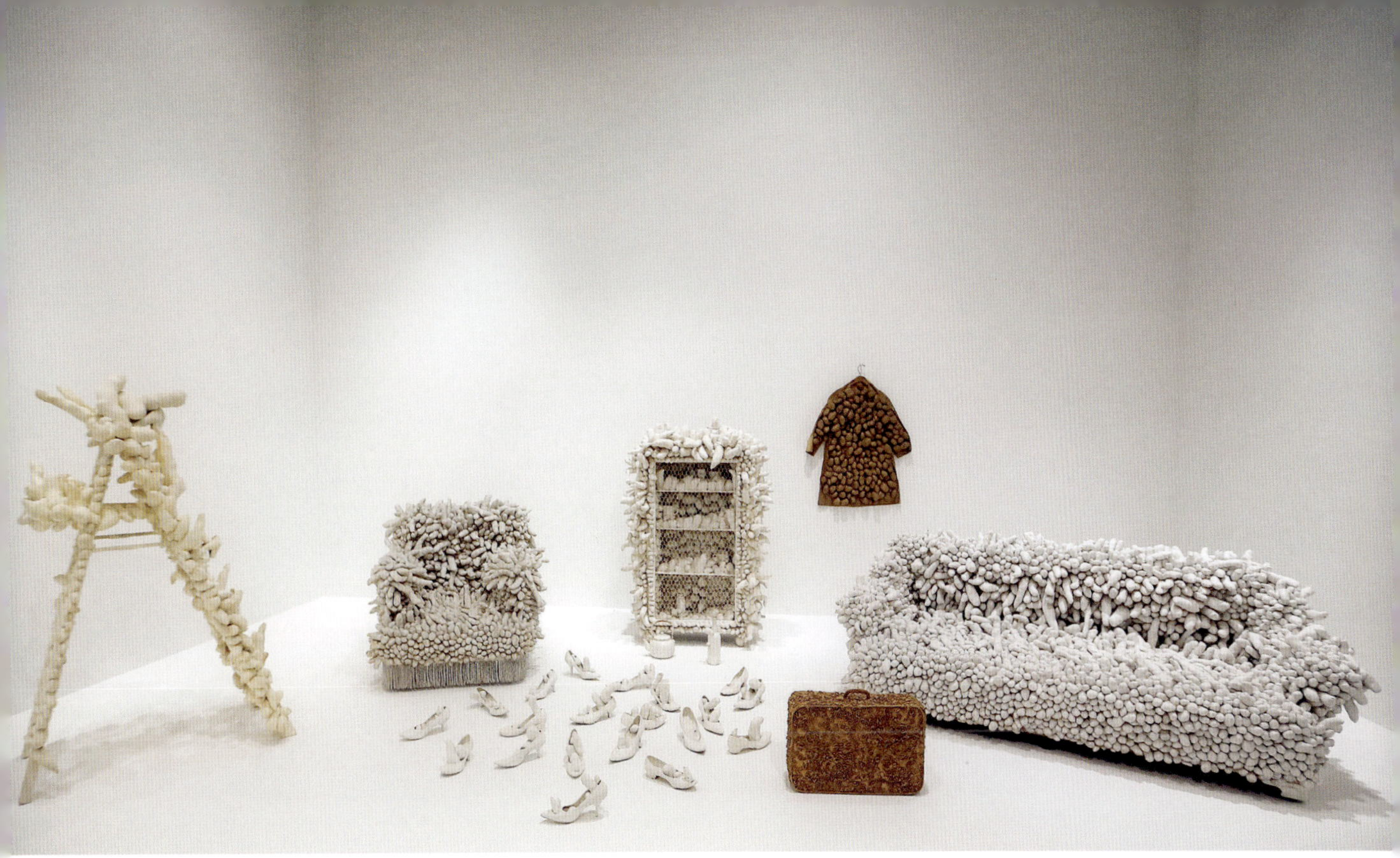

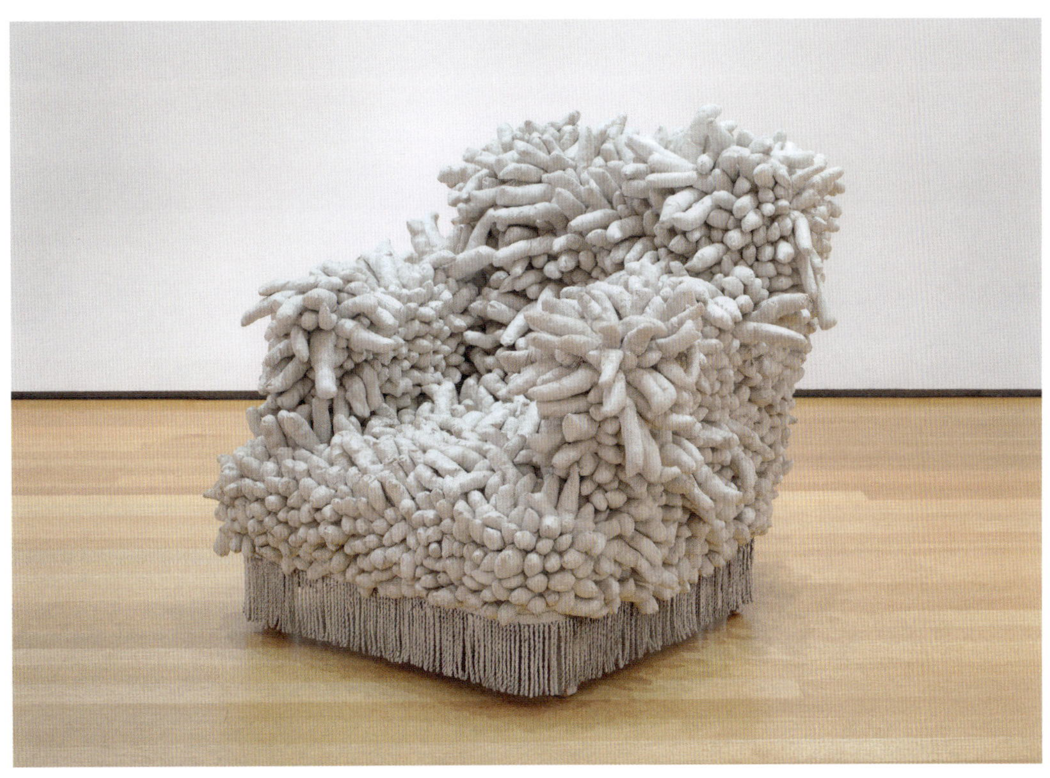

(*nihonga*) at Kyoto Municipal School of Arts and Crafts. After graduating in 1949, she spent much of the 1950s finding her artistic voice. She produced thousands of paintings, which help established her early career and enabled her to exhibit in Japan and the United States; she later destroyed many of these works when she moved to the United States in 1957. Her first stop was Seattle, where she held an exhibition at Zoë Dusanne Gallery, but she was drawn to the buzzing art scene in New York City.

Kusama lived and worked in New York from 1958 to 1973. During this stint, she was part a circle of avant-garde artists, including Eva Hesse (see page 104), Donald Judd and Andy Warhol, who were all admirers of her work. Not long after her arrival, she began to experiment with her first soft sculptures. She exhibited the first of these sculptures, *Accumulation No. 1*, in a 1962 group exhibition at the Green Gallery. This show has now come to be viewed as the first group Pop Art exhibition. Kusama's sculpture consists of an armchair covered in layers of painted hand-sewn stuffed penises. In the years that followed, she covered other furniture, rooms and even a boat in these stuffed phalluses. These works contrast domestic objects and techniques, which are often associated with the feminine, with the masculine visual of a penis. The idea of sitting on such a chair is deeply erotic, but ironically stems from Kusama's dislike of sex. The trauma of witnessing her father's promiscuity left a lasting impression on her that developed into an obsession. She hoped to steep herself in the image of penises as a way of numbing herself to the anxieties they invoked. She calls this process 'obliteration'.

The repetition of forms in *Accumulation No. 1* also relates to Kusama's interest in creating infinite spaces and patterns. In 1965, she hit upon an idea to create spaces that truly felt as though they went on forever with her mirror rooms. The first of these immersive installations was *Infinity Mirror Room – Phalli's Field*. The walls of the installation were lined with mirrors and the floor was covered in more of her stuffed phalluses – this time covered with spots! She then took photographs of herself within the space,

Kusama wasn't given the same level of recognition as her male counterparts. This was particularly frustrating for her, as she repeatedly saw these same men praised for employing her ideas.

which bring the effect of the room to life. In seeing a person in the space, viewers can imagine how it would feel to stand among a sea of dots that bend and curve around hundreds of tiny tubular forms. Further still, the work offers a simulation of what her hallucinations might have felt like as a child when she visualized flowers turning into a vast field of dots.

Her ideas were innovative, exciting and had a major influence on the direction of modern art but she wasn't given the same level of recognition as her male counterparts. This was particularly frustrating for her, as she repeatedly saw these same men praised for employing her ideas. She has cited Oldenburg's soft sculptures, Warhol's use of repetitive images and Lucas Samaras's mirror installation as ideas inspired by her own creations, and instances such as these triggered periods of great frustration and depression for Kusama. The death of her closest friend Joseph Cornell also took a toll on her and, in 1973, she ultimately returned to Japan due to her physical condition.

Back in her home country, art became a form of therapy for Kusama when she took up permanent residency in a Tokyo hospital. She focused on writing and painting, but her career was considerably quieter than it had been in New York. In the 1980s, another motif from her childhood resurfaced in her work. She once again began drawing and creating pumpkins,

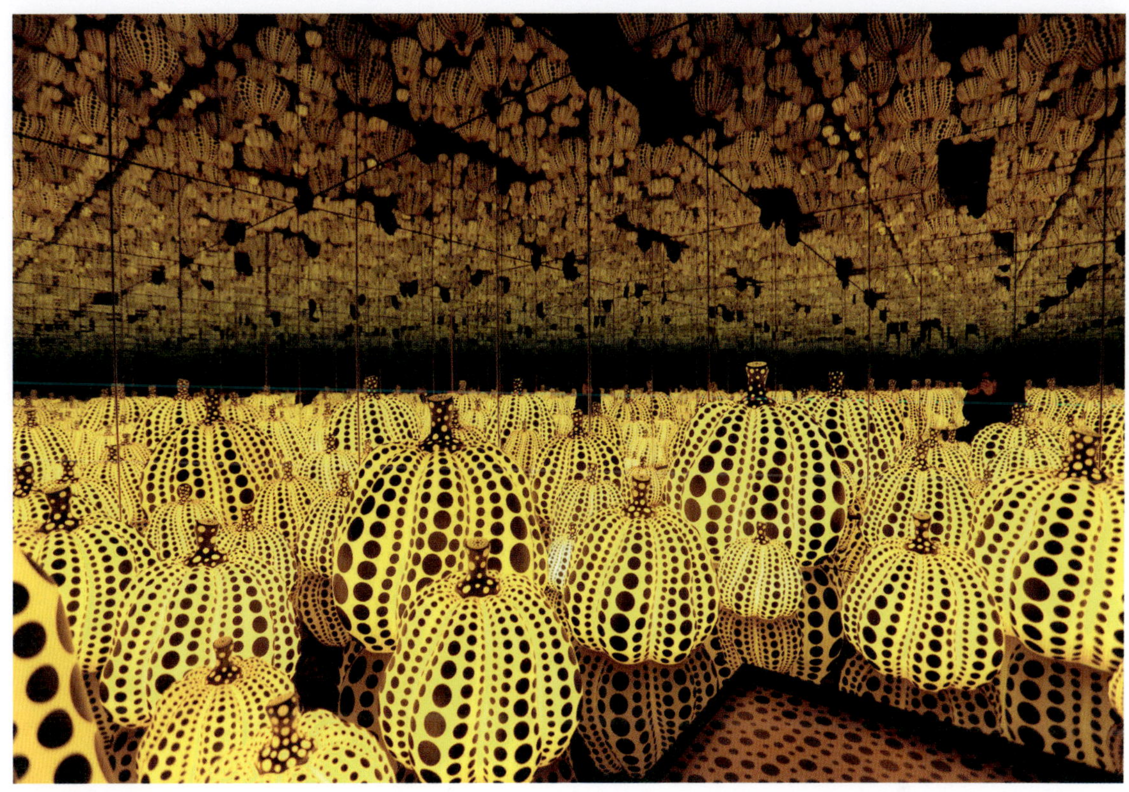

All the Eternal Love I Have for the Pumpkins, 2016.
Mixed Media. 292.4 × 415 × 415 cm (115⅛ × 163⅜ × 163⅜in).

an activity she had found so calming as a child. Her dotted gourds are typically bottom-heavy in form and have a wobbly, supple appearance; sometimes the dots vary in size, emphasizing the dips and curves of the surface. Kusama's pumpkins have taken the form of hard and soft sculptures, paintings and products. In 1993, she made a grand return to the world art stage when she became the first solo artist to represent Japan at the Venice Biennale with an installation filled with pumpkins.

Kusama has employed her eye-catching aesthetic across painting, performance art, sculpture and product collaborations with luxury brands such as Louis Vuitton and Marc Jacobs. From the 1990s, she has had several major solo exhibitions, including shows at Tate Modern, in London, and the Museum of Modern Art, in New York. She also opened the Yayoi Kusama Museum in Tokyo. Although she may have struggled to find due praise in the early part of her career, Yayoi Kusama has now deservedly become one of the top-selling women artists in the world, taking her rightful place as a giant within the canon of art history.

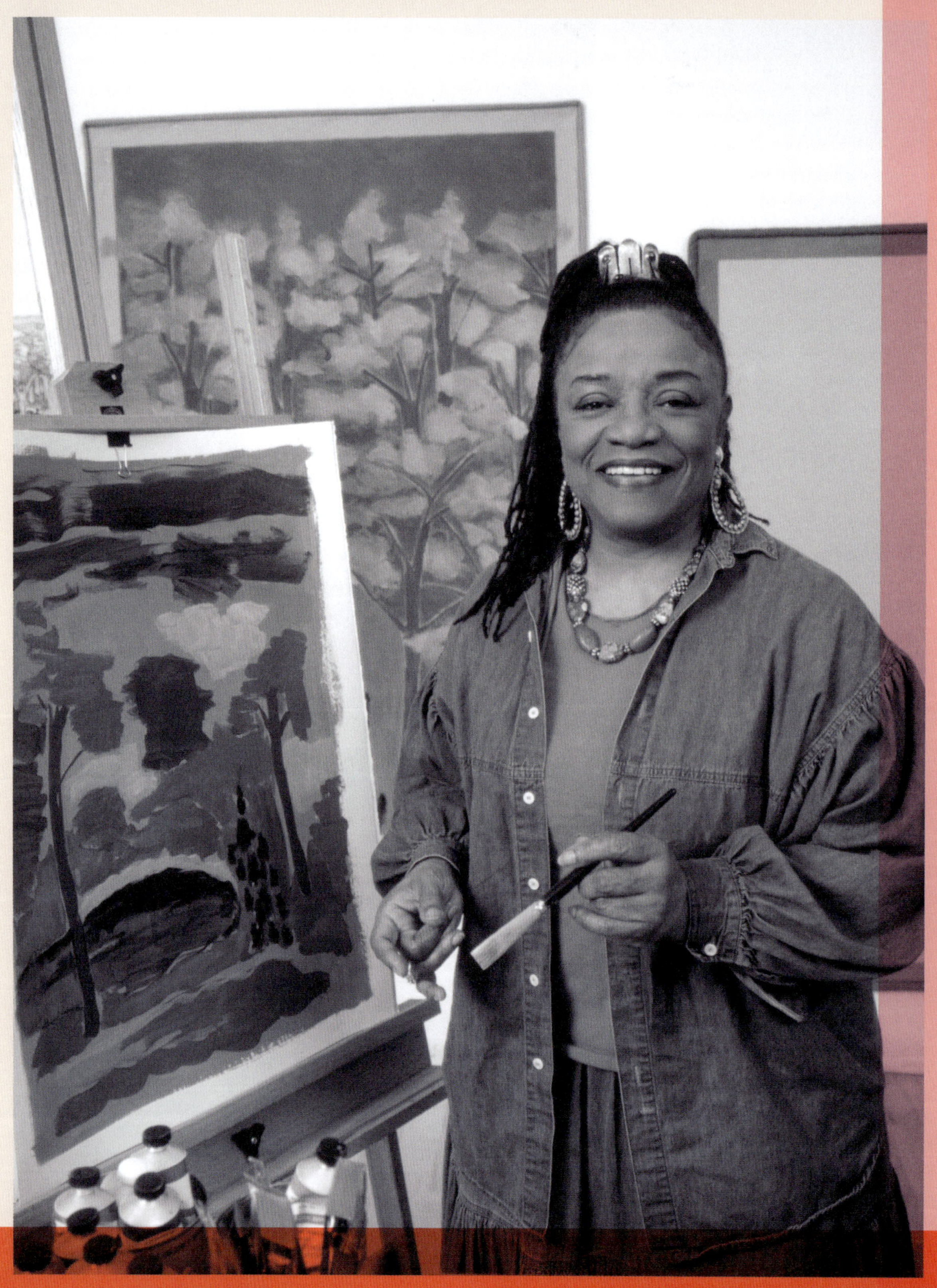

Faith Ringgold

(b.1930)

Quilting, Soft sculpture

When Faith Ringgold first began to paint on fabric, critics didn't know what to make of it. They tried to define her work within terms they understood – wall hangings, banners, textiles – but she was drawing on imagery and traditions outside their notions of 'fine art'. Ringgold's quilt and textile artworks unite painting with the traditional mediums of various cultures to share narratives that are real and imagined – all while centering the stories of Black women, from early feminist icons to the women in her own family.

Before her mother, Willi, or even the doctor could adequately prepare, Ringgold made her grand entrance into the world in New York's Harlem Hospital. Her mother didn't even have a name ready – Faith, the nurse suggested. Faith Willi Jones. She grew up in a bustling house, including two siblings and a steady stream of visiting family and friends. When she was just two, she had her first asthma attack, and this led to restrictions on the types of activities she was allowed to do and even the foods she could eat as a young child. No fried food, no ice cream from the ice cream truck, and no going to kindergarten. Instead, she passed the time making art, reading or going on excursions to museums or the theatre with her mother. They would also sew together, with her mother handing her scrap fabrics to make mix-matched creations. Finally by the first grade, Ringgold was allowed to attend school with other children.

During the Second World War, her mother worked sewing army jackets and began making clothes for friends on the side, eventually becoming a full-fledged designer. This afforded the family the ability to move to the more affluent Black neighbourhood of Sugar Hill in Harlem, with residents including prominent celebrities like Duke Ellington, Sarah Vaughan and Willie Mays. Her mother's sewing skills would later prove very useful when she helped Ringgold with her early art quilts.

Ringgold and her siblings were raised to understand the opportunities that a good education could afford them. Her mother worked hard to send the kids to integrated schools, where the educational standards were higher, although that meant that they had to navigate racial aggressions from teachers and classmates. It was understood within her family that she would go to college, just like her sister had before her, and in 1948, Ringgold graduated high school and enrolled in City College, which was only ten blocks from her house.

Her intention was to major in art, but at this time, women were not allowed in the college's School of Liberal Arts. Undeterred, she found a workaround by studying art within the School of Education. There, she was met with the highly competitive spirit of her classmates and a mixture of support and discouragement from her teachers. Her drawing teacher publicly laughed at her work, while her oil painting teacher, Robert Gwathmey, made an effort to connect with and encourage her. Each experience motivated her in its own way to succeed. She graduated in 1955.

By this time, Ringgold was a mother of two and soon to be divorced from her first husband. She got a job as an art teacher with the New York City public schools and returned to City College to obtain her master's in art, graduating in 1959. Up to this point, her paintings included portraits of loved ones and impressionistic landscapes. In the summer of 1961, she took a trip to Europe with her mother and daughters to see what artistic inspiration the continent might bring. After sailing over on the luxurious *SS Liberté*, the ladies made their first stop in Paris before making their way over to Italy. She took her girls to see the *Mona Lisa* at the Louvre and the Rembrandt paintings on display at the Uffizzi Gallery. They reached Rome before the unexpected news of her brother's death necessitated they return home.

In the 1960s, America was changing. The Civil Rights Movement was gaining momentum and Ringgold was reading the writings of great minds like James Baldwin. Over time, her work became more connected with Black issues and her style leaned more towards Cubism and Expressionism. Her 1967 painting, *American People Series #20: Die,* embodies the many changes and influences her work underwent at this time. The layers of paint are thinner and the colours are flatter than her earlier works. The representation of catastrophic racial fighting taking place overtop the long grey background is as much a nod to Pablo Picasso's *Guernica* as it is to Jacob Lawrence's Harlem-inspired style of 'Dynamic Cubism'. Additionally, by the 1970s, another movement was underway: feminism. Ringgold became as motivated by the women's movement as she was for racial justice, and she started to explore how her art could also reflect intersectional feminist perspectives.

A major shift in her practice came during a 1972 trip to Europe, where Ringgold saw an exhibition of Tibetan *thangkas* (colourful Buddhist paintings on silk) at the Rijksmuseum in Amsterdam. This inspired her to paint her own interpretation of *thangkas* when she returned home, beginning with a collection called 'Feminist Series'. These were also inspired by classical Chinese landscape paintings depicting symbolic flowers and scenery overlaid with poetic political text. The *thangkas* showed vivid landscapes with gold text running down vertically as the characters do on some Chinese landscape paintings. The words were all taken from quotes by Black women like Sojourner Truth, Harriet Tubman and Shirley Chisholm, who had championed feminist ideas since the time of slavery in America. Ringgold held these women up as beacons at a time when Black women were being discouraged from participating in the feminist movement as though one can only focus on one issue at a time.

Ringgold made several other *thangka* series during the 1970s and also created soft sculptures of masks and human figures, with her mother helping her to sew costumes for some of the more complex

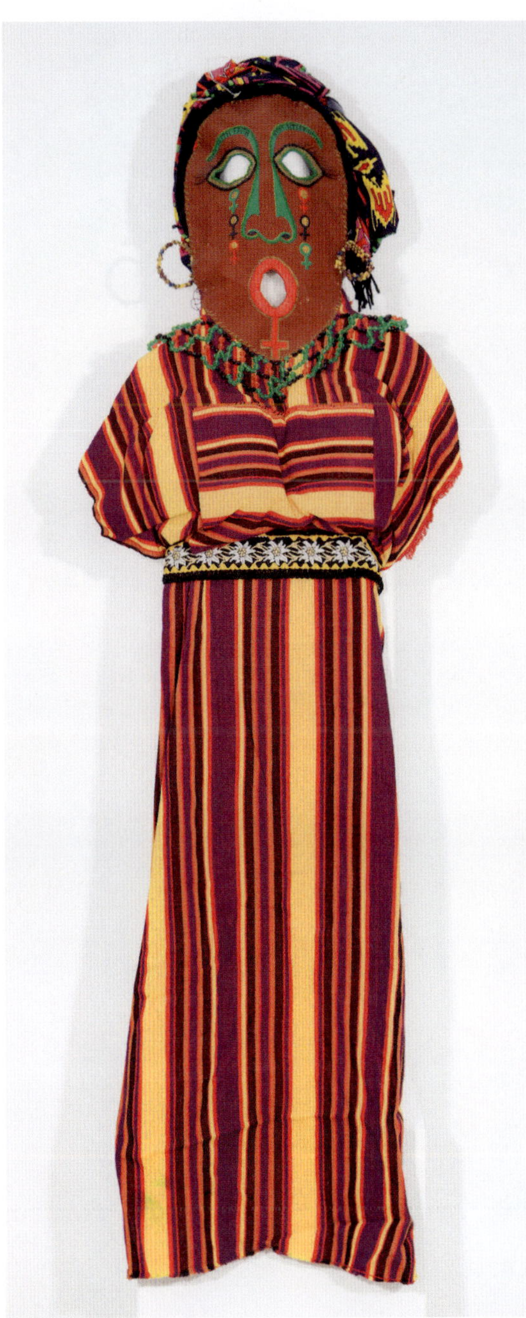

Faith (The Family of Women), 1973.
Mixed media.
165.1 × 48.3 × 22.9 cm (65 × 19 × 9 in).

pieces. The designs were inspired by ceremonial African masks and the figurative sculptures were informed by a mixture of celebrities and people she knew. Her early sculptures, such as one of basketball player Wilt Chamberlain, were created with a rudimentary rope armature, but her later sculptures were stuffed and sewn underneath their costumes (and they were anatomically correct, if you know what I mean). These textile works and her use of the masks in performance art to tell stories were a big step in the direction of creating the story quilts, for which she is so well known.

Ringgold made her first quilt, *Echoes of Harlem*, in 1980 with the assistance of her mother. Like the *thangkas*, she painted images onto fabric, but she also stitched many patches together in a style that draws on Black American quilting traditions. Some are composed of many central patches telling a story across panels, while others have one large-scale narrative painting in the centre surrounded by a colourful patchwork border.

Around the time she created her first art quilt, she was also struggling to find support publishing her autobiography. This frustration led her to the idea of using her art quilts as a storytelling medium – hence, the name 'story quilts'. Her first was *Who's Afraid of Aunt Jemima* (1983), which creates a fictional backstory for the pancake brand character across a grid of painted and written text panels. Ringgold takes the Aunt Jemima image away from toxic Mammy stereotypes of Black women and rounds out her story as a businesswoman.

Ringgold's later stories were sometimes expanded across several quilts, such as the 1991 series 'The French Collection'. This twelve-part collection provided her with the space to paint elaborate scenes from the life of the fictional character Willia Marie Simone. Willia is an early twentieth-century African American woman who lives an enviable life wherein she moves to Paris to pursue her dreams of being an artist; she is in the thick of the modern art action, posing for Matisse and having dinner with Gertrude Stein. In a very meta scene, the character also sits down to make

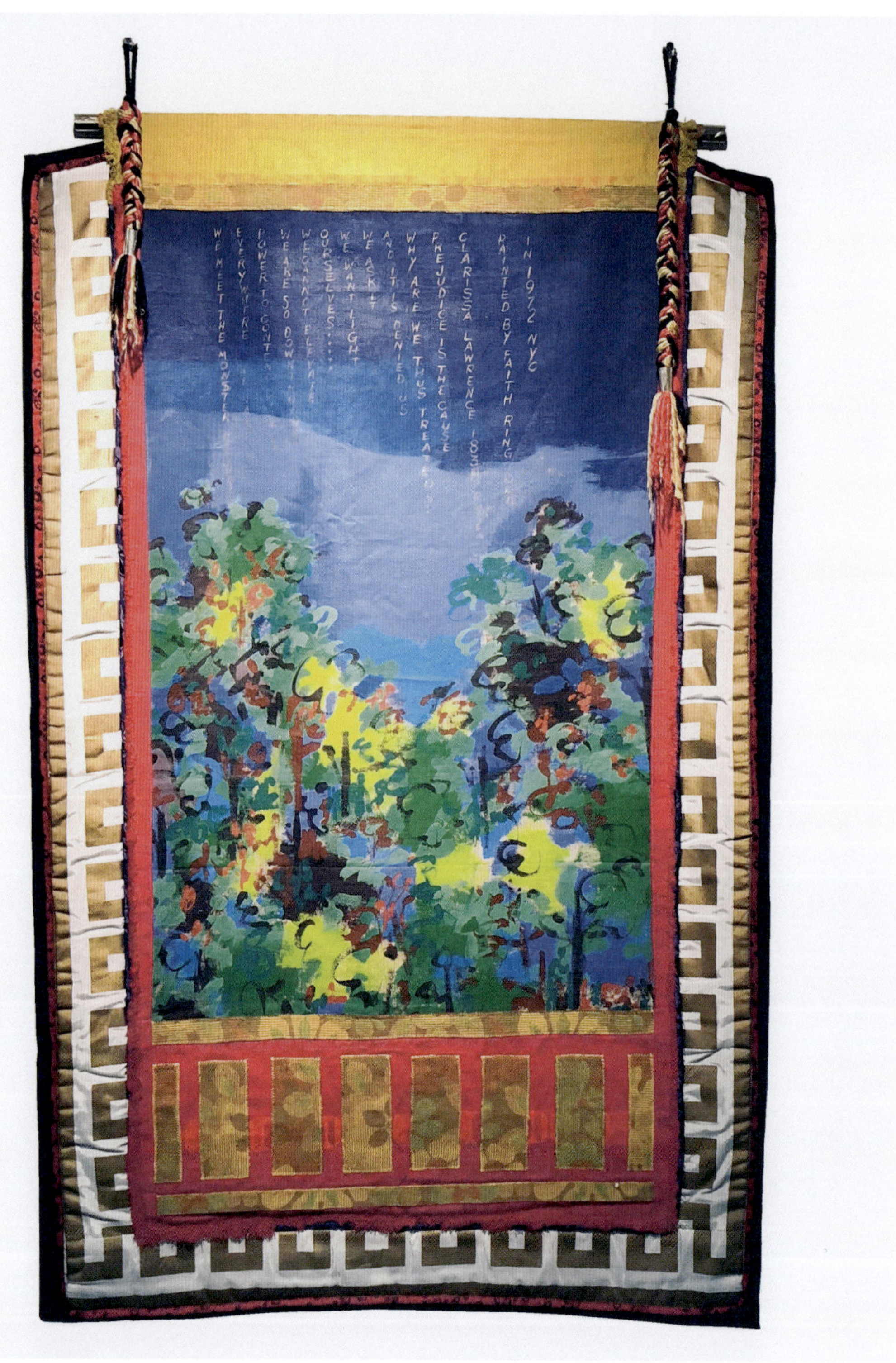

We Meet the Monster (#12 of 20), 1972.
Acrylic on canvas framed in cloth.
127 × 82.6 cm (50 × 32½ in).

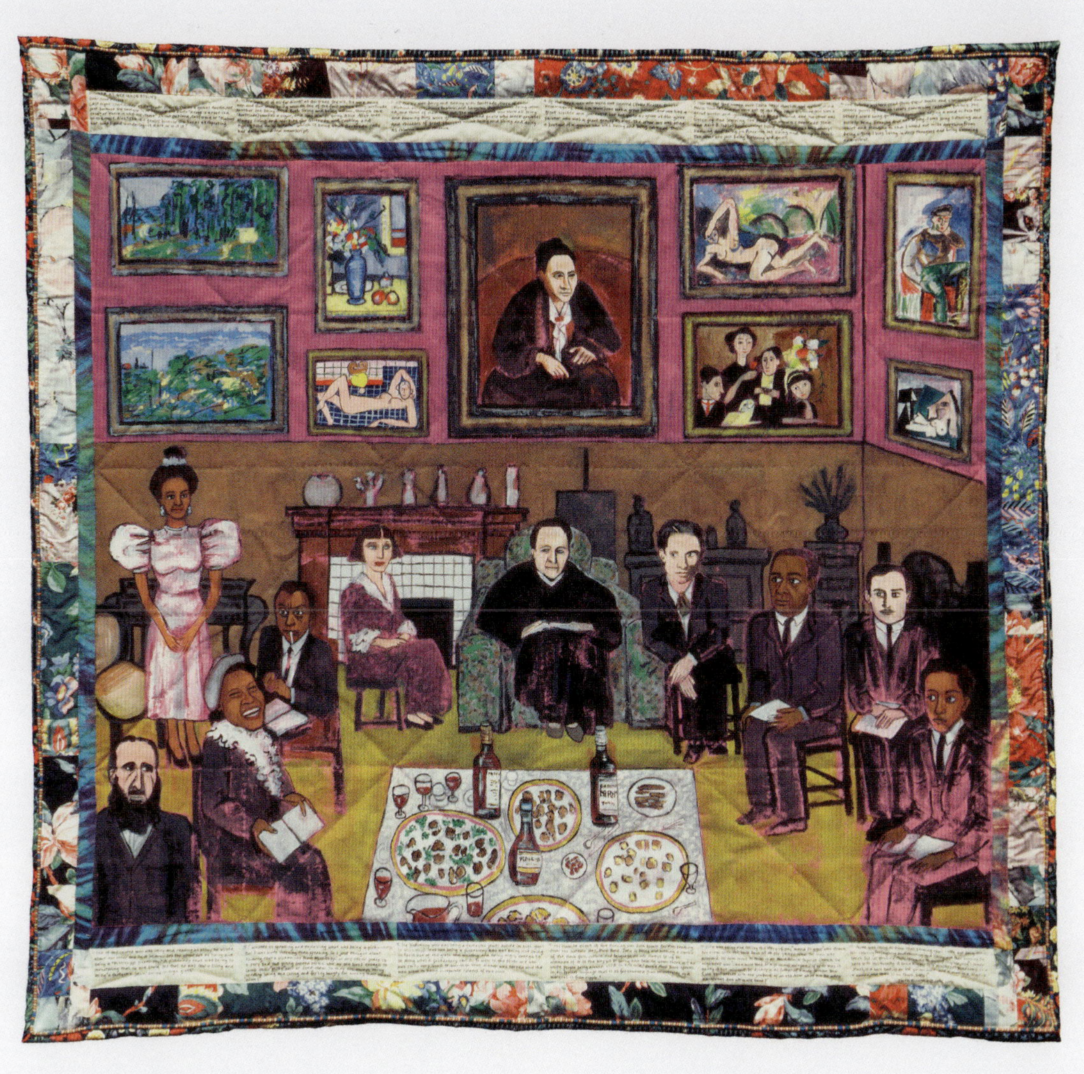

Dinner at Gertrude Stein's (The French Collection, Part II: #9), 1991.
Acrylic on canvas, printed and tie-dyed fabric.
200.7 × 213.4 cm (79 × 84 in).

a quilt with influential Black American women, including Sojourner Truth, Rosa Parks and Mary McLeod Bethune. Some scenes, such as *Dancing at the Louvre*, seem to take a page out of Ringgold's own story, as this quilt shows Willia visiting the *Mona Lisa* with a group of little girls, as she had done with her own daughters. The images from this series include brilliant interpretations of modern art history and masterpieces, with Willia – a Black American woman – at the centre.

Ringgold's art practice and activist work form a beautiful celebration of Black women's societal and cultural contributions. In addition to her artistic output, she has written a children's book about Harriet Tubman, and advocated for better representation of Black women artists in galleries. Ringgold understood the need for intersectional feminism early on, and her career is a triumph in representing the complexities of simultaneously being Black, a woman and a Black woman.

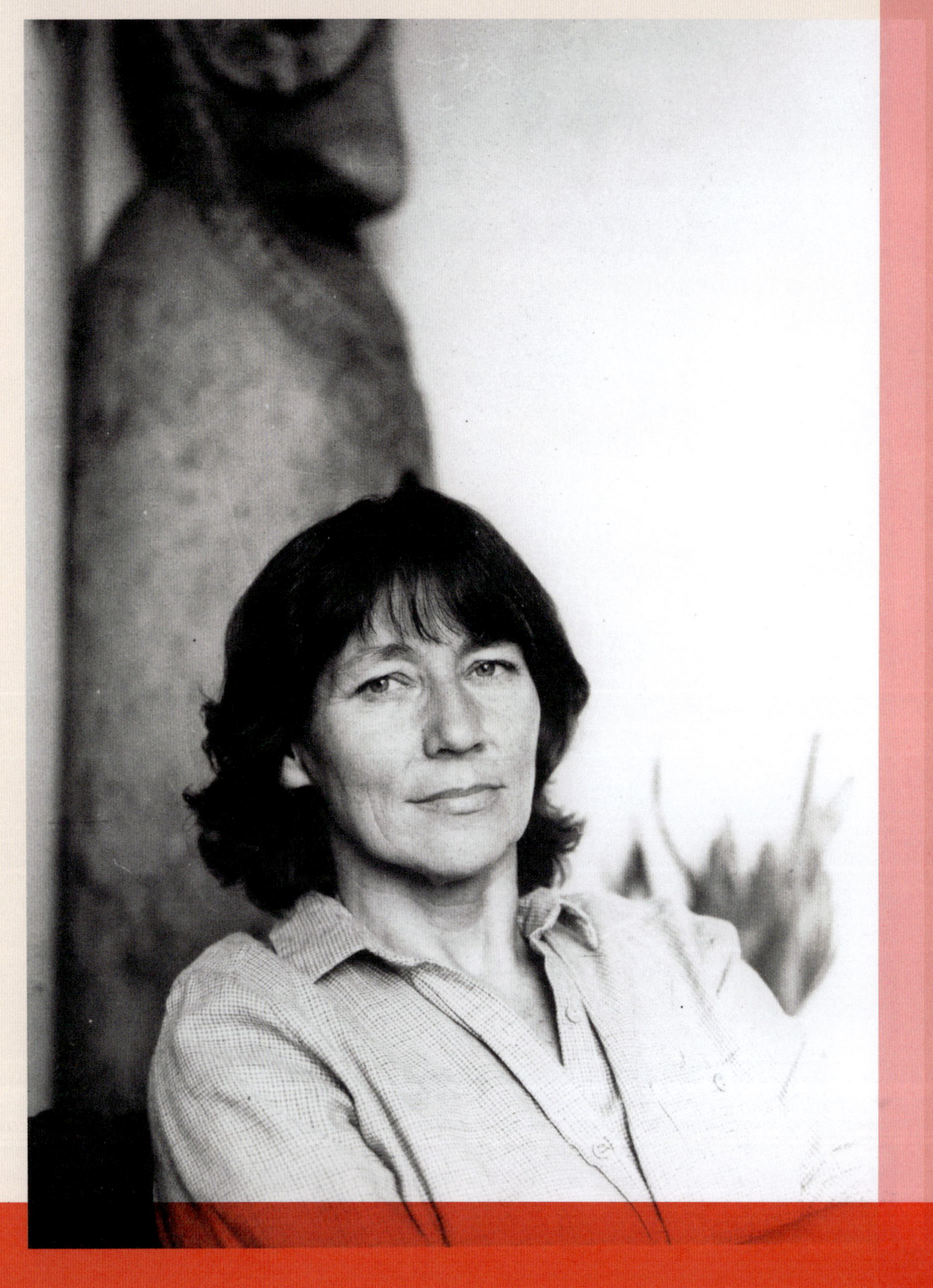

Magdalena Abakanowicz

(1930–2017)

Weaving, Soft sculpture

Magdalena Abakanowicz's work is thoughtful and requires thoughtfulness from the viewer. The longer one looks at her massive woven sculptures, the more there is to see in the details of the weaving and folds – her works continually reveal themselves and raise questions. She has also created pieces that are about thinking and the inner workings of the human brain. Her curiosity for nature and the human condition imbues her work with a captivating, organic quality.

Abakanowicz was the second daughter of an aristocratic family that was hoping for a boy. Her parents' disappointment at her sex developed into a coldness that she coped with by wandering the hallways and grounds of her family's large estate. While playing in the wooded areas, she would spend long periods thinking on her own, reflecting on nature and would sometimes mould little objects from stones and clay. These melancholy moments developed an interest in natural forms and materials that would manifest in her later art practice.

Before Abakanowicz was born, her family had already fled revolutions in Russia to live in Poland. They once again faced unrest when she was nine years old, when the Nazis invaded their adopted home country. Her once quiet home became a hub for resistance fighters and refugees and, in 1943, she witnessed the horror of a German soldier shooting her mother in the arm, severing it below the shoulder. The next year, the family fled their home to Warsaw, where the fourteen-year-old Abakanowicz worked as a nurse's aide, treating the wounded and dying. After the war, Poland became part of the Soviet Bloc and her family suffered further indignities as they were

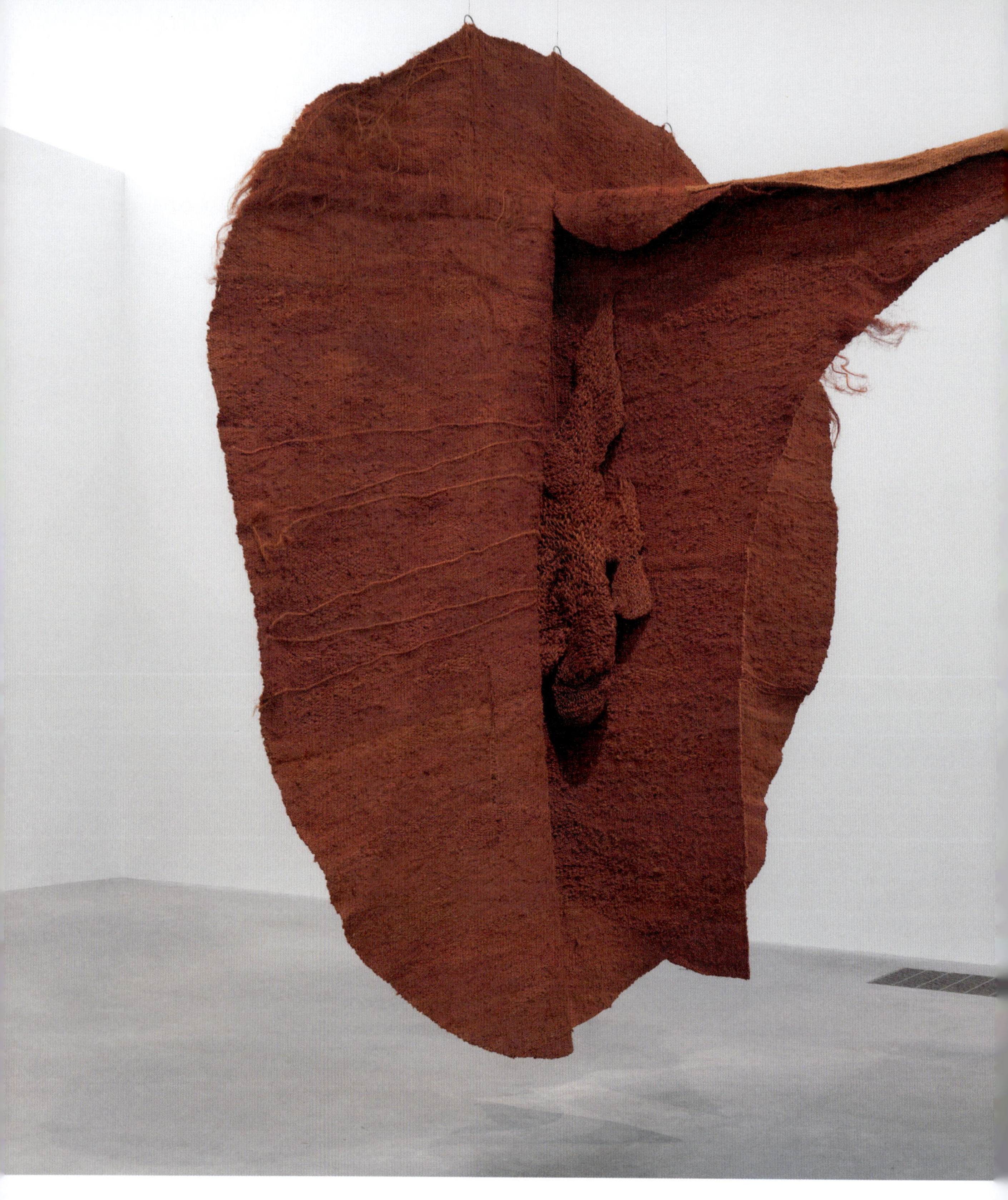

forced to conceal their background from the new communist regime.

Pretending to be a clerk's daughter, Abakanowicz enrolled at the Academy of Fine Arts in Warsaw in 1950. The curriculum was dictated by the government at this time and students had to train in the state approved Socialist Realist style. She hated it. She wanted the freedom to explore her own ideas, not rules specifying that she could paint. At night, she would go into the school's studio and create huge, abstracted paintings on bedsheets that she'd sewn together. She painted animals, insects and other organic forms using large fields of colour, watercolour and gouache that were stylistically similar to the stained canvases Helen Frankenthaler was experimenting with around the same time – each unbeknown to the other. Although she wasn't a fan of the academy, graduating from the programme in 1954 enabled Abakanowicz to join the Artists Union. With this credential, she could establish a studio, exhibit and sell her work.

Abakanowicz put together her first solo exhibition in 1960, consisting of some of her large paintings and some small weavings on rudimentary frames. When officials had a look at the abstract works, the gallery was not permitted to open its doors for the show. Fortunately, the weaver Maria Laszkiewicz peeped through an open window and saw enough to recommend Abakanowicz to exhibit at the first Biennale International de la Tapisserie in Switzerland. For the next seven years, Laszkiewicz allowed Abakanowicz to use the loom in her basement and shared her weaving knowledge with her young mentee. During this time, Abakanowicz vehemently challenged the broad perception within the art community that weaving could not be employed by fine artists. She began to pull her works away from the wall, distancing them from associations with craft and tapestries, instead using metal supports to create increasingly sculptural works from woven materials.

Abakan Red, 1969.
Sisal and metal.
405 × 382 × 400 cm (159½ × 150⅜ × 157½ in).

In 1965, she started her first major series called 'Abakans' (named after herself). They are large-scale woven works that can be hung or folded to stand on their own. From a distance, they are immense organic forms that look vaguely familiar, like an animal or body part you've seen but can't quite pinpoint. Abakan Red could resemble a vulva, but it also looks like a stingray – one can see in these works whatever they choose. Up close, the detail in the tight monochromatic weaving is stunning, with a mix of thin fibres and chunky cords that twist and knot around each other. The work is undeniably sculptural in the dynamic way it occupies three-dimensional space through variation in textures and planes of material extending in multiple directions. It demands the viewer observes the high relief of the weaving up close and looks at the structure in the round. Around this same time, Abakanowicz was also creating her 'Black Garments' works, which are large woven sculptures that resemble headless cloaked giants.

Moving into the 1970s, Abakanowicz became increasingly fascinated with the functions of the brain and how the organ connects humans to their ancestors, other animals and nature. She explored these interests well into the 1980s and also introduced new materials into her practice, including rope, burlap and resin. In 1974, Abakanowicz travelled to London to receive an honorary doctorate from the Royal College of Art and during this trip, she met the neurologist Patrick Wall. She took the opportunity to ask him question after question about the functions of the brain and nervous system. More curious than ever, she returned home to Poland and developed a phase of works called 'Alterations'. Think of this as a sort of superseries or a period that encompassed other related series of works, including 'Heads', 'Embryology', 'Seated Figures' and 'Backs'.

During her 'Alterations' period, Abakanowicz's work was figurative and muted in tone, often keeping to the natural brown colour of her materials. Her 'Heads' are tall (around 3 ft) pods made of sewn burlap or serpentine lengths of rope woven together

Abakanowicz leaned into ambiguity with the wisdom that her work depicts varied and nuanced human experiences.

and bonded with resin. They suggest at the shape of a human head, rather than showing the features of the eyes and nose in explicit detail, and have no body. Some are a mixture of smooth burlap and twisting rope, as if the brains of the head are exposed. These visualize the stressful feeling of being overcome with thoughts and them spilling forth.

Conversely, 'Backs' and 'Seated Figures' depict bodies with no heads. She made plaster moulds of the forms and affixed strips of burlap to the surface. Their posture is slumped and lifeless, conceptually a result of their missing heads. The last of the 'Alterations' series, 'Embryology', are sewn and stuffed burlap forms that are even further pared back in form, with neither heads nor bodies. Their name suggests they are a starting point for life to come, and their rock-like presentation connects to Abakanowicz's longstanding affinity for nature, stemming back to her childhood. She reinforced these connections when she occasionally exhibited works from 'Alterations' series outdoors. It's possible it reminded her of meditative moments in nature as a child.

From the 1980s onwards, Abakanowicz continued to depict human and organic forms, increasingly working with metal materials and engaging with heavier themes of war. All the while, she continued working from her studio in Poland, producing works that people around the world could find their own meanings and subtexts. She leaned into that ambiguity – reflecting on all that she'd been through in her early life – with the wisdom that her work depicts many varied and nuanced human experiences.

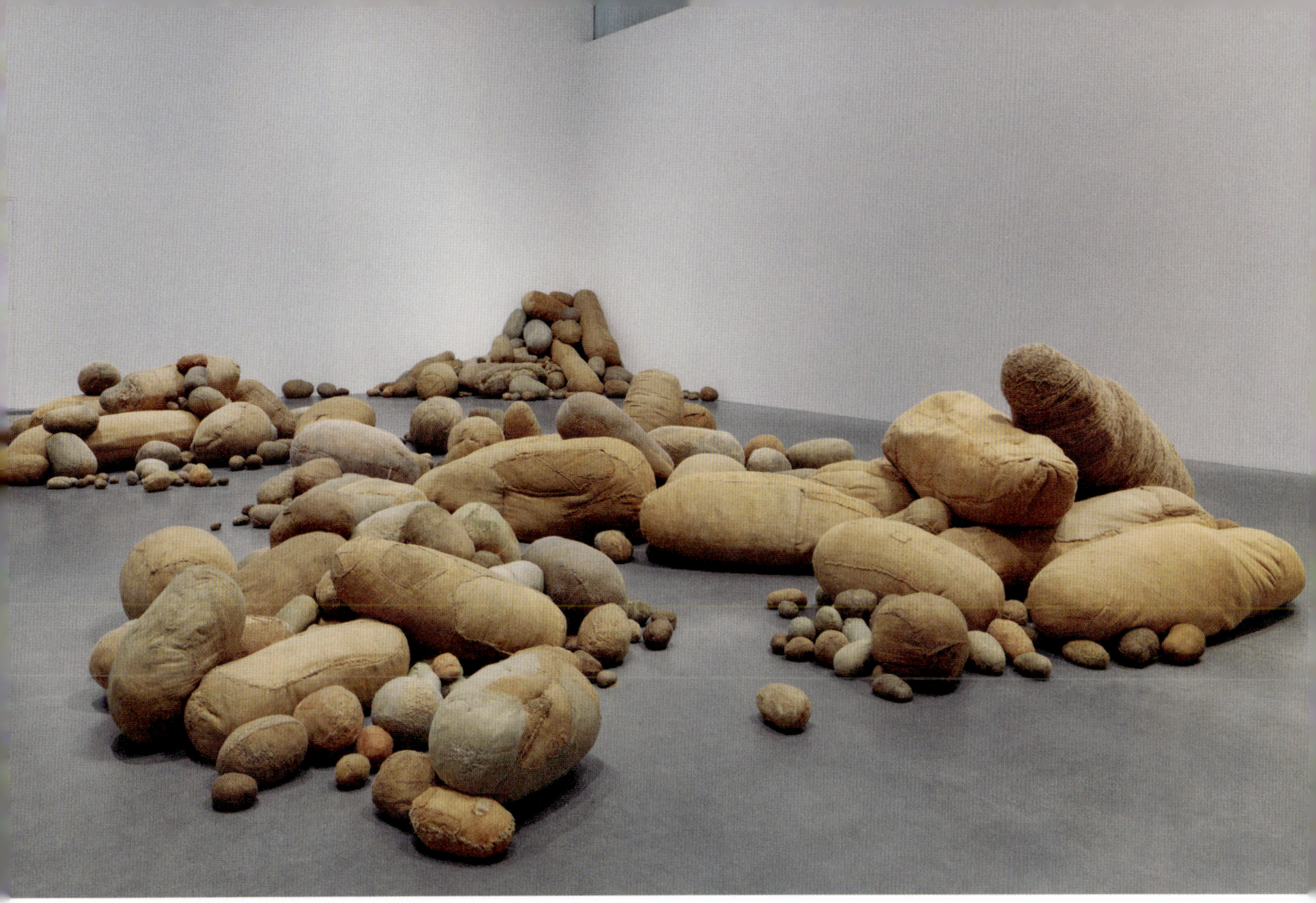

Above: *Embryology*, 1978–80.
Burlap, cotton gauze, hemp rope, nylon and sisal.
Dimensions variable.
Below: *Heads (14 pieces)*, 1973–75.
Burlap and hemp rope. Dimensions variable.

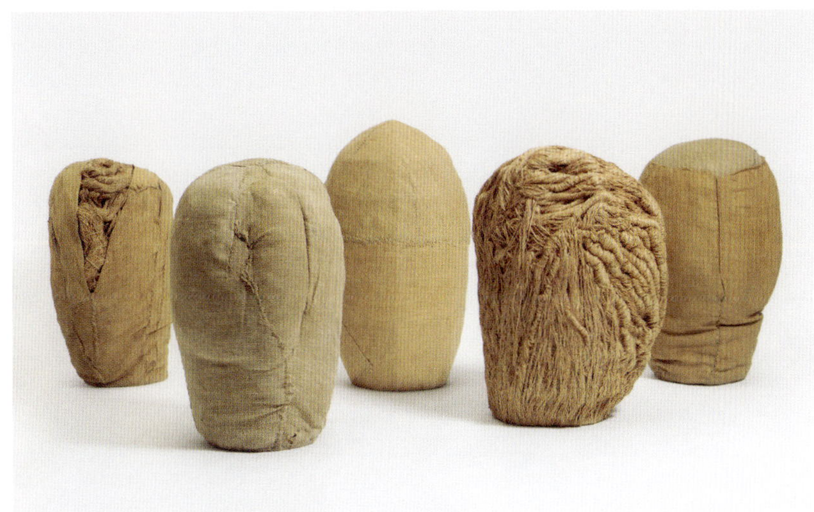

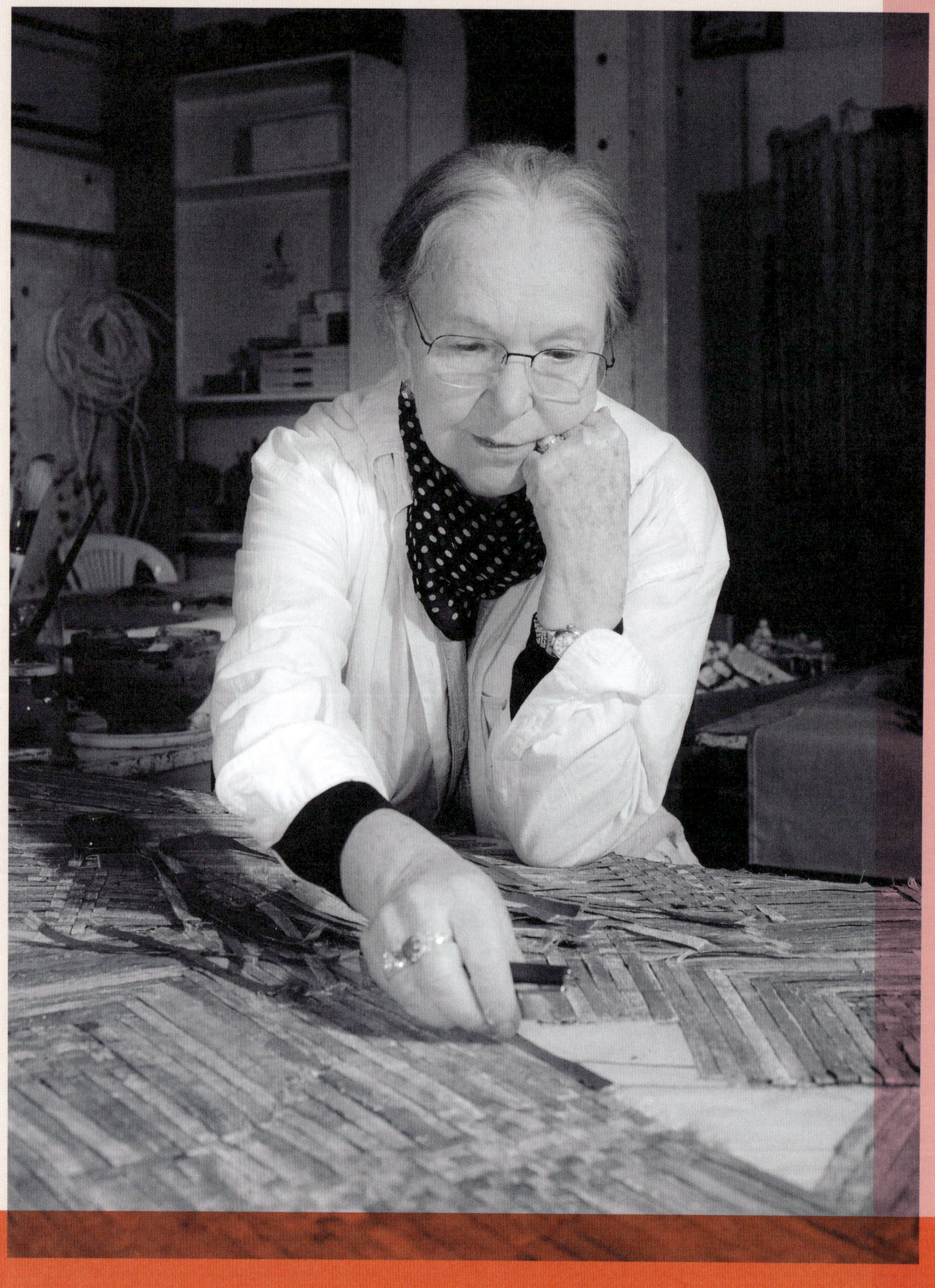

Olga de Amaral

(b.1932)

Fibre art, Weaving, Wearable art

Olga de Amaral has the Midas touch and has been transmuting textiles into luxurious golden wall hangings for decades. Through her use of colour and natural fibres, she taps into the rich histories, cultures and geography of her home country of Colombia. She was among the pioneering figures of the fibre art movement of the 1960s and 1970s and has continued to be one of the most important abstract artists working in Latin America.

Amaral was born Olga Ceballos Vélez in Colombia's capital of Bogotá. She grew up in the city alongside seven siblings, but she has always felt a close connection to her ancestral home in the Antioquia region as well. Amaral and her family often spent time on a large farm there, where she would ride horses, swim and play in nature. It wasn't until she took a drawing class in her final year of high school that she first discovered her love for art and design. After graduating, she fueled this spark by pursuing a degree in architectural design from the Colegio Mayor de Cundinamarca in Bogotá. Her father and brothers were engineers, so the idea of working in architecture felt familiar and secure. She completed the programme after one year and, despite only being nineteen-years old, was asked to stay on working as the director of the Architectural Drawing Faculty the following year.

In 1954, she moved to the United States for the first of two brief stays. She initially stopped off in New York to study English at Columbia University before making her way over to Michigan to do a postgraduate programme in textiles at the Cranbrook Academy of Art. The school was founded in 1932 to be an artist-led institution in a similar vein to the Bauhaus or Black Mountain College. Unlike its counterparts, the school is still extant today, with eleven departments, including a mixture of design and fine arts practices. Notable artists and designers associated with the school include Florence Knoll, Charles Eames and Keith Haring, who did an artist residency there.

Amaral's time in the programme was serene. The decision to focus on fibre was made for her because it was the only department the school allowed her to enter with the credits she'd earned from her previous college. After an adjustment period of teaching herself how to work at a loom, she passed many days peacefully working on her own and experimenting with bold patterns and colours. The programme emphasized commercial and interior textiles, so many of the projects she made during this period include designs for rugs and other soft furnishings. After graduating from Cranbrook in 1955, Amaral returned home to Bogotá and established a studio, employing local artisans to assist her.

With such a thorough grounding in architecture and interior design, Amaral was able to secure commissions from local designers to make woven textiles. She also created a fashion line that included modern interpretations of *mantas guajiras* – a traditional Colombian dress – and would make small tapestries whenever she wanted to flex her creative muscles. In the United States, she'd had access to a breadth of materials, but back home her options were more limited. She, therefore, began to work with materials like horsehair and linen, which were more readily available. Over time, her work drew notice around Colombia and internationally. She was asked to establish a textiles department at the University of the Andes in 1965, but in the end, she found that teaching wasn't for her and she resigned.

Her second stint in America came in 1966, when she moved to New York with her husband and children for a year. The textile designer Jack Lenor Larsen had encountered Amaral's studio back in Bogotá and encouraged her to visit him if she were ever in New York. Taking him up on the invitation, they reconnected and Larsen subsequently

Amaral labelling her work 'presences' captures the awesome experience of standing in front of one of her gleaming gold or silver wall hangings.

exhibited some of her work in his showroom. From there, she was invited to participate in the Museum of Modern Art's epic *Wall Hangings* exhibition that took place in 1969. Among the twenty-eight artists in the show were Anni Albers (see page 28), Magdalena Abakanowicz (see page 86), Sheila Hicks (see page 98) and Lenore Tawney (see page 38). Amaral exhibited *Orange Weaving* (1966), which is stylistically representative of many of her wall hangings from the 1960s. A similar piece from 1965 titled *Entrelazado en rojo y negro* (Interlaced in red and black) shows how she used fabrics as a weaving material by cutting slits and interweaving the different colourful layers through the openings.

During her stay in New York, she met Aileen Osborn Webb, the founder of the World Crafts Council (WCC), and became the organization's Colombian representative. This afforded Amaral opportunities to travel internationally, including one serendipitous trip to London where she met the ceramicist Lucie Rie (see page 35). Amaral visited Rie's home studio with the intention of purchasing a piece, but the one she liked best was broken. Rie explained that she liked to mend broken ceramics with gold, in a similar manner to the Japanese art of *kintsugi*. From that point on, Amaral became fascinated with incorporating gold into her own works. She referred to a later series of works as '*alquimias*' (alchemies) because she used gold leaf to transform natural fibres into gold objects, as if through alchemy.

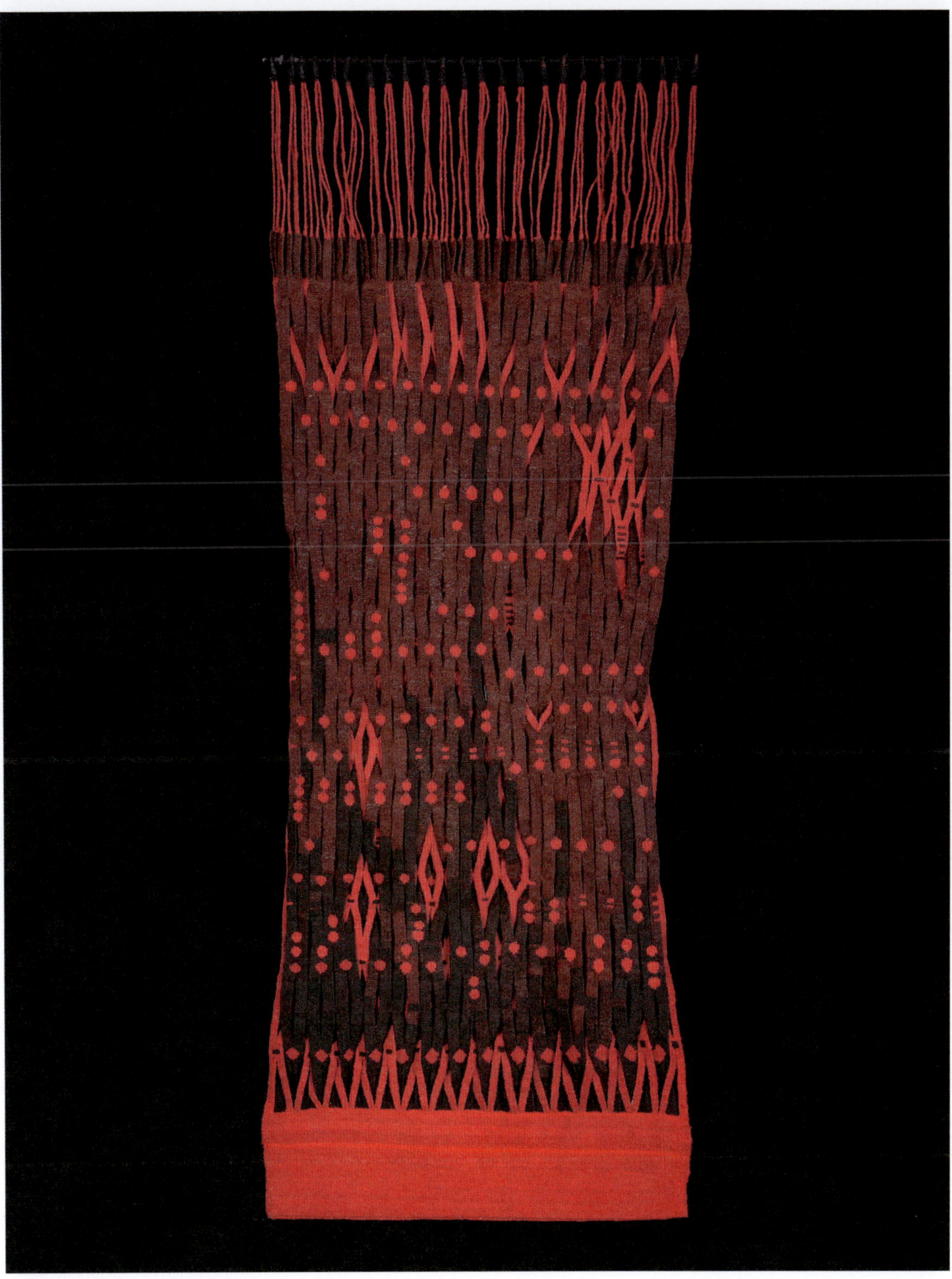

Entrelazado en rojo y negro, 1965.
Wool. 130 × 50 cm (51⅛ × 19½ in).

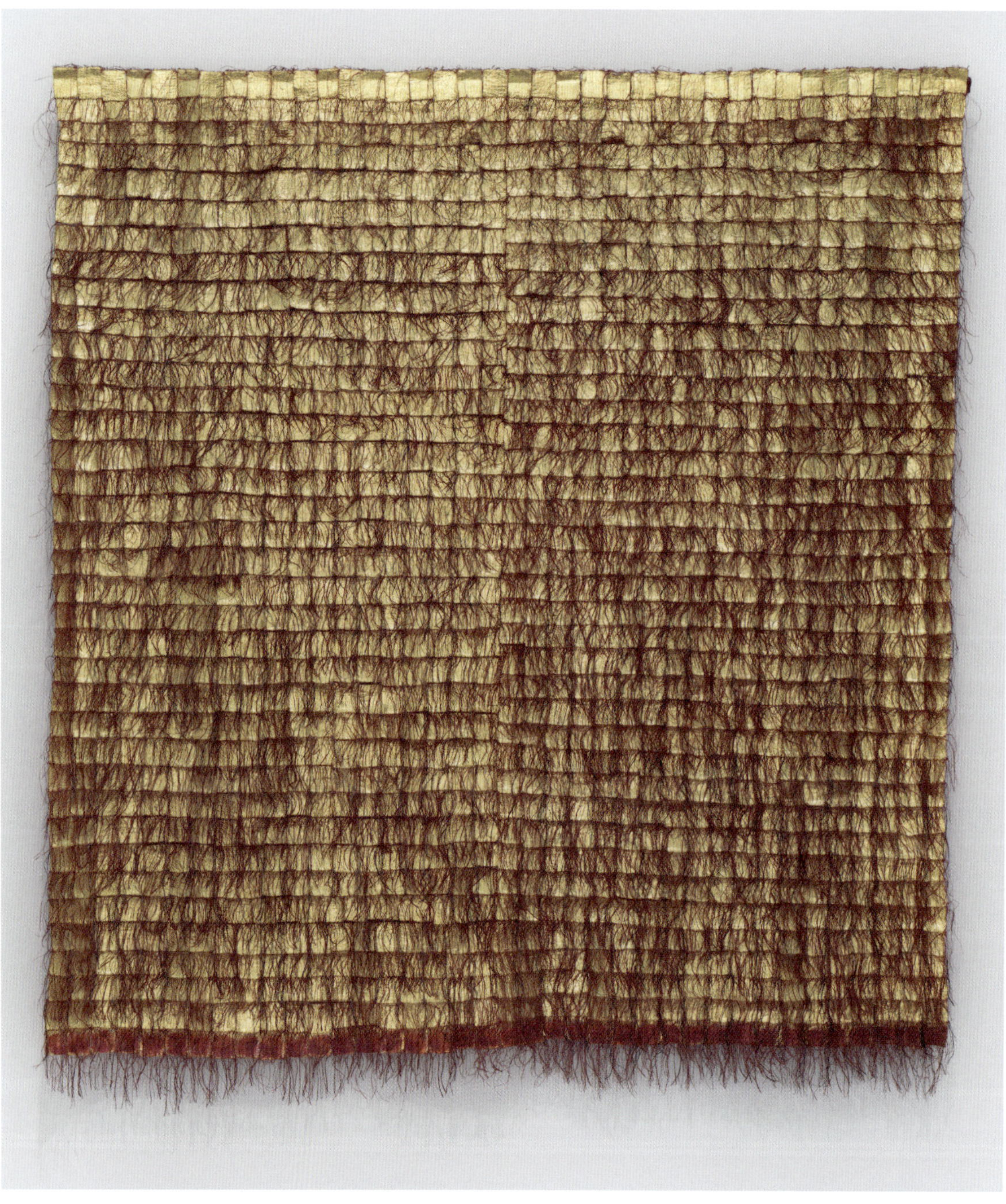

Alchemy 50, 1987.
Canvas, gesso, gold leaf and acrylic paint.
165 × 150 cm (65 × 59 in).

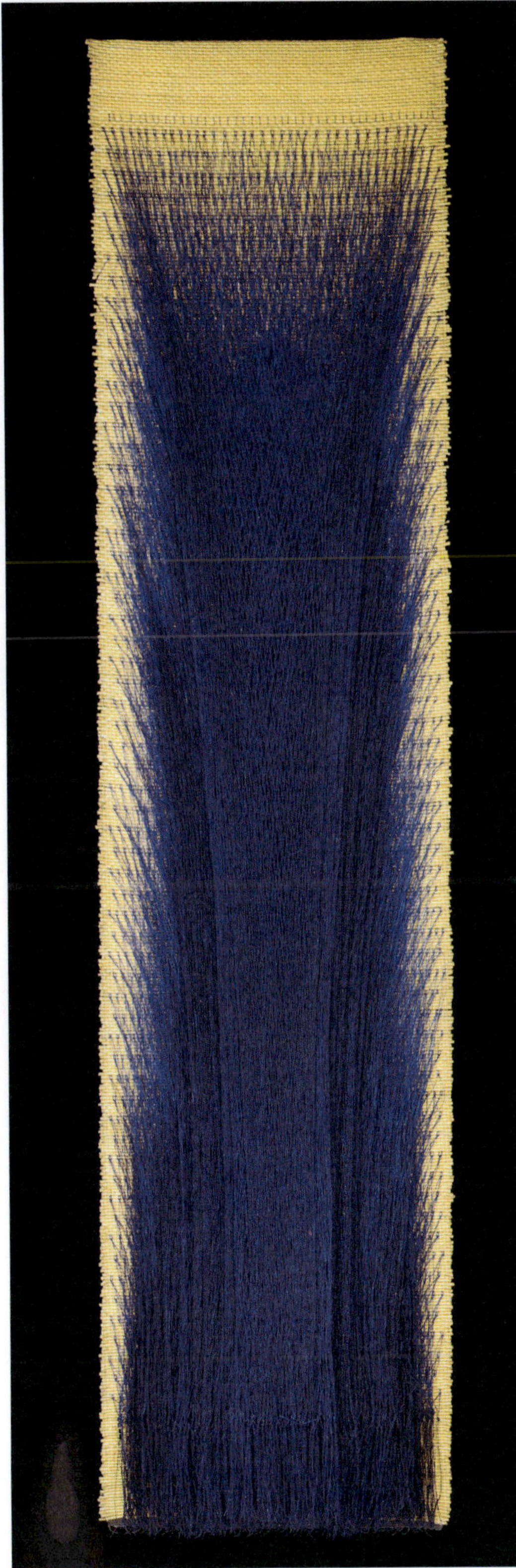

Aside from being visually stunning, gold held a spiritual association that reminded Amaral of the gilded ornamentation she saw in churches growing up. The material also engaged with Colombia's complex histories before and after the arrival of Spanish colonists. Both the indigenous people and the Spanish valued the material in their own ways, but the Spanish lust for gold was so great that it had catastrophic effects on several native civilizations of the Americas. This layered history can be observed in her *alquimias*, which are as much inspired by the tiled roofs on older Colombian homes as they are by glittering Baroque churches.

In the 1970s, Amaral and her family lived in Europe for a period, travelling throughout the continent from their base in Paris. While there, she began to experiment with incorporating canvas and acrylic paints into her work. This provided more flexibility and control with the colours she could achieve. In *Lienzo ceremonial 14* (1989), which is part of her 'Lienzos Ceremoniales' (Ceremonial Cloths) series, she applied blue acrylic paint to threads that emanate from a woven background. The fibres cascade down the surface and deepen in colour from the root to the ends of the threads. This creates a sense of depth that would be more difficult to control through dyeing processes. For Amaral, the rich indigo colour ties to abstract concepts like freedom or dreaming, but also to more tangible things, like water and the mountains in Colombia.

No matter how far Amaral travels, she always finds her way back home to Bogotá, but her work can be found in collections internationally. Critics have struggled to classify Amaral's work, at times labelling it craft, sculpture and even jewellery. She shakes off these conventional labels in favour of her own: 'presences'. Her name for her practice acknowledges its ineffable quality and the awesome experience of standing in front of one of her gleaming gold or silver wall hangings.

Lienzo ceremonial 14, 1989.
Flax and acrylic.
227 × 60 cm (87⅜ × 23½ in).

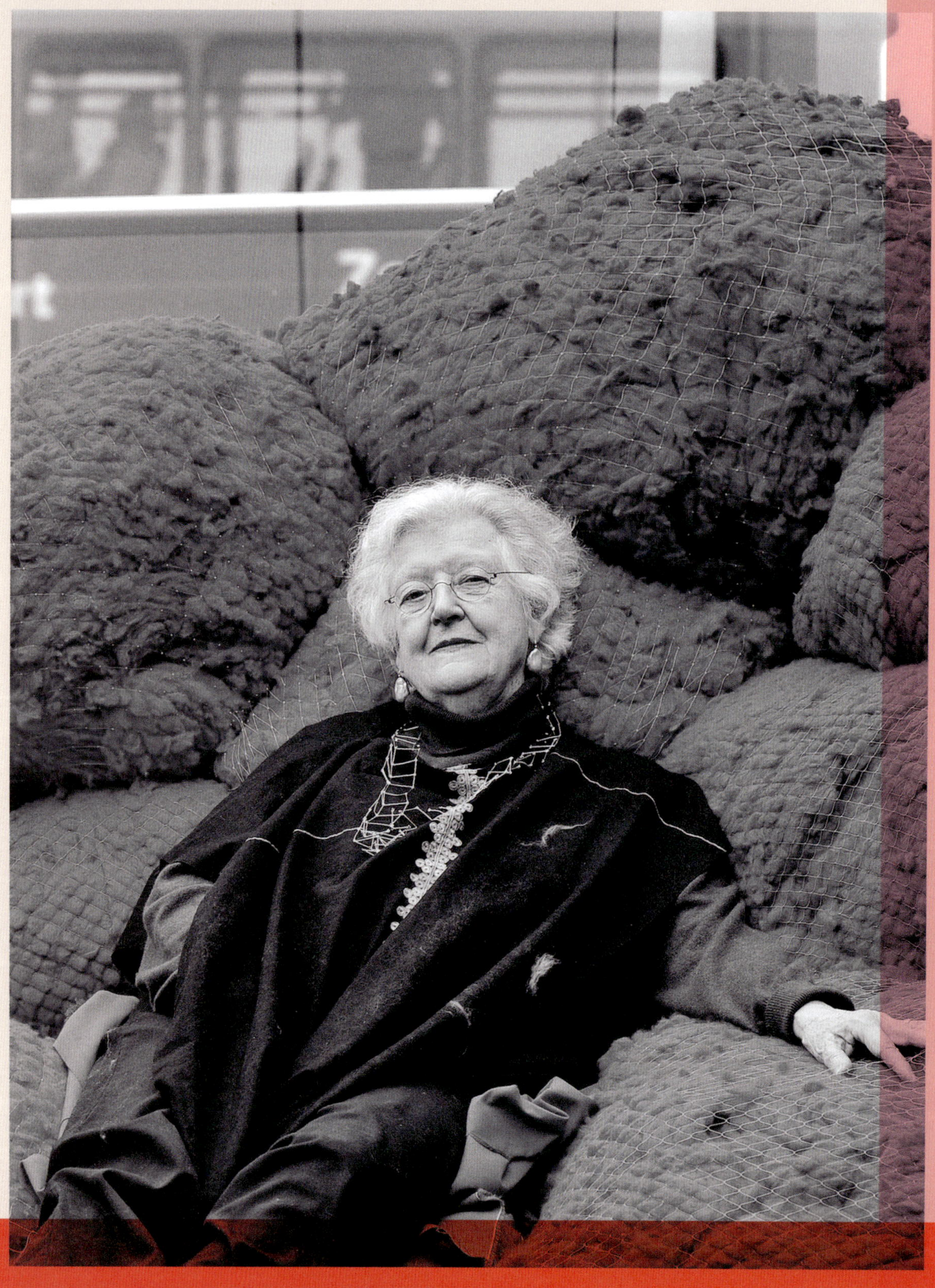

Sheila Hicks

(b.1934)

Weaving, Fibre art,

Soft sculpture

A look at some of Sheila Hicks' bundle installations is enough to make anyone want to take a running jump into the colourful mounds. Hicks's vivid artistic perspective could only be imagined by someone with her unique experiences. Her training, travels and interests intersected to place her at the forefront of the weaving and fibre art movement in the 1960s and 1970s, but her mastery of colour and her category-defying practice asserts her position as an innovator within sculpture and installation art more broadly.

In 1934, when Hicks was born, America was in the midst of the Great Depression, the consequences of which reverberated throughout the nation and particularly in agricultural centres like Hicks' home state of Nebraska. Her father struggled to find work and moved the family around to follow opportunities in a migratory lifestyle that lasted several years. Hicks, her parents and siblings lived out of their car until the Second World War brought about stable employment for her father in Detroit. The family's new home unleashed a new set of problems, however, as Hicks and her brother got involved with street gangs of neighbourhood kids.

To edify her wayward children, Hicks' mother sent her and her brother to weekly art lessons at the Art Institute in Detroit. Her mother would also spend time painting with the children at home and collecting balls of string and tin foil for the war effort. She filled their lives with so many extracurricular activities that they had no time to get in trouble. Towards the end of high school, the family moved once more to Chicago, and Hicks continued taking art classes in school.

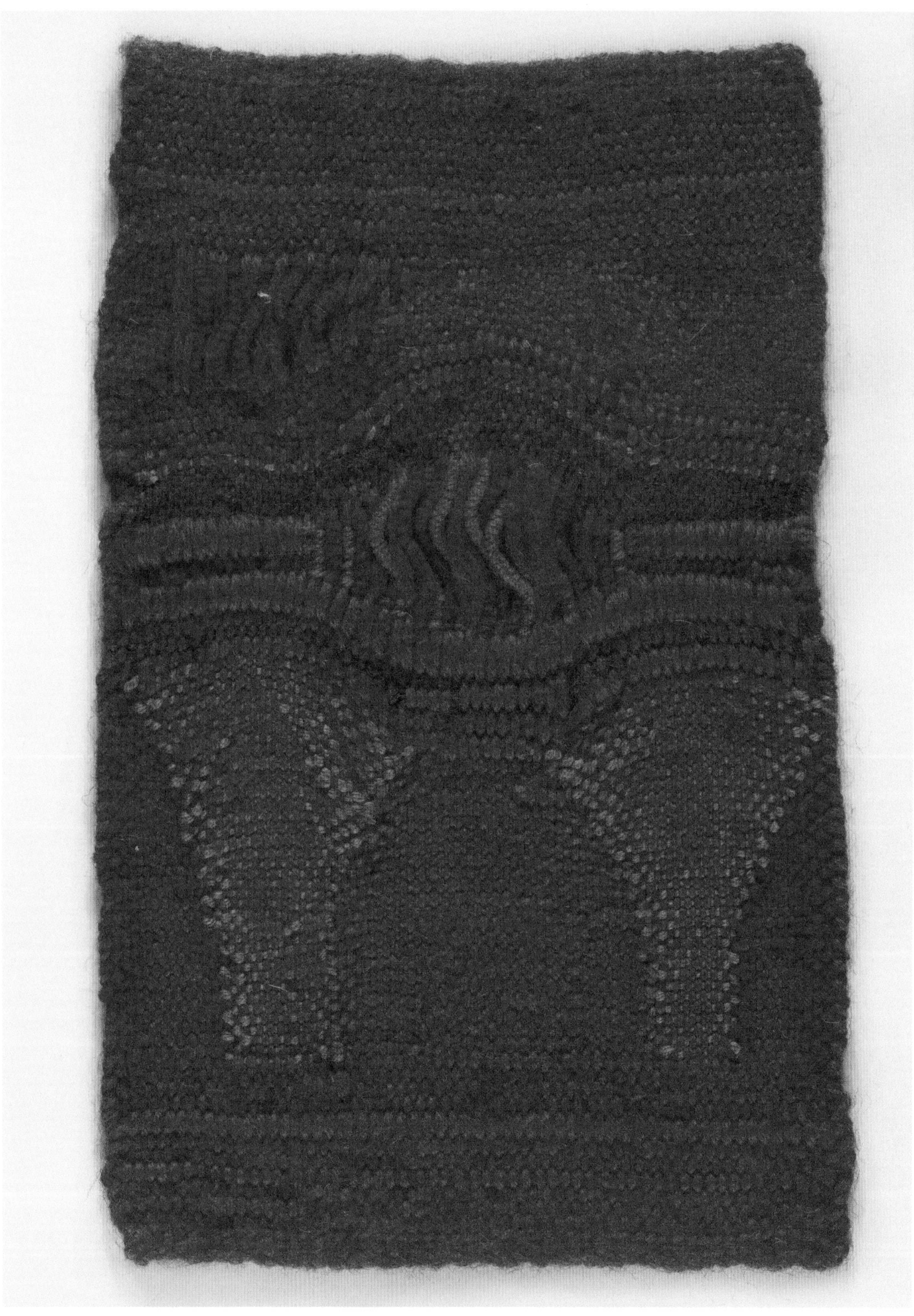

Greta Weaving No. 55, 1961.
Wool. 22.9 × 14.6 cm (9 × 5¾ in).

After graduating, Hicks enrolled in the art department at Syracuse University, where she took courses in drawing, painting and printmaking. Two years into the programme, a friend encouraged her to submit her portfolio in application to Yale. She had a happy-go-lucky life at Syracuse but applied to the prestigious school to see what would come of it. She was accepted and headed off to New Haven the following autumn. The director of the Yale School of Art at the time was Josef Albers. Hicks took studio art and design courses that were in keeping with Albers' Bauhaus ethos, and also took classes in art history and criticism. Most significantly, she was exposed to two subjects that would be especially formative for her future work: through Albers' teachings she obtained a firm grasp of colour theory, and in taking an 'Art of Latin America' class she was introduced to Andean textile arts. Although painting was her primary discipline at the time, she studied textile techniques in private sessions with Anni Albers and during a stint as a Fulbright Scholar in Chile. She received her Bachelor of Fine Arts in 1957 and left Yale with her Master of Fine Arts in 1959.

For the next several years, Hicks lived in Mexico, working on miscellaneous creative projects and studying traditional textile methods. She briefly lived in Paris between 1959 and 1960 on an art grant but returned to Mexico after discovering she was pregnant. Examples of her weavings in the early 1960s are tightly woven with variations in the warp (threads running lengthwise) to create changes in texture. They are monochromatic wool pieces in a flat, rectangular format and were small because they were made on makeshift looms in her small village home. She calls them 'minimes'. They seem fairly conventional at first glance, but the bright colours Hicks used were of her own creation – experiments informed by her time with artisans in Mexico and her earlier studies under Josef Albers. Even though she sold some minimes to the Museum of Modern Art in New York in the early 1960s, she struggled to get gallery recognition. She was also slowly outgrowing the small workshop she'd established

Hicks' weavings in the early 1960s are tightly woven with variations in the warp to create changes in texture. They are monochromatic wool pieces in a flat, rectangular format and were small because they were made on makeshift looms in her small village home. She calls them 'minimes'.

in Mexico. These factors stoked her growing desire to move back to Paris. She secured a contract as a designer for the furniture company Knoll, which provided enough monthly income for her to move to France in 1964.

Ever the nomadic spirit, Hicks travelled the world from her base in Paris, gathering new art techniques along the way from Germany, Morocco and India. The Museum of Modern Art had asked if she could produce some larger-scale works, so it became a sort of quest to find methods to produce big works without compromising their quality and style. At the same time, her work with Knoll helped establish her position within the design community. She showed at the 13th Triennale of Design in Milano, collaborated with architects on installations and was selling works through design shops, like Crate and Barrel. It began to look as though she was stepping firmly into the realm of design, rather than fine art, but it seems that the two had always been interrelated to her anyway.

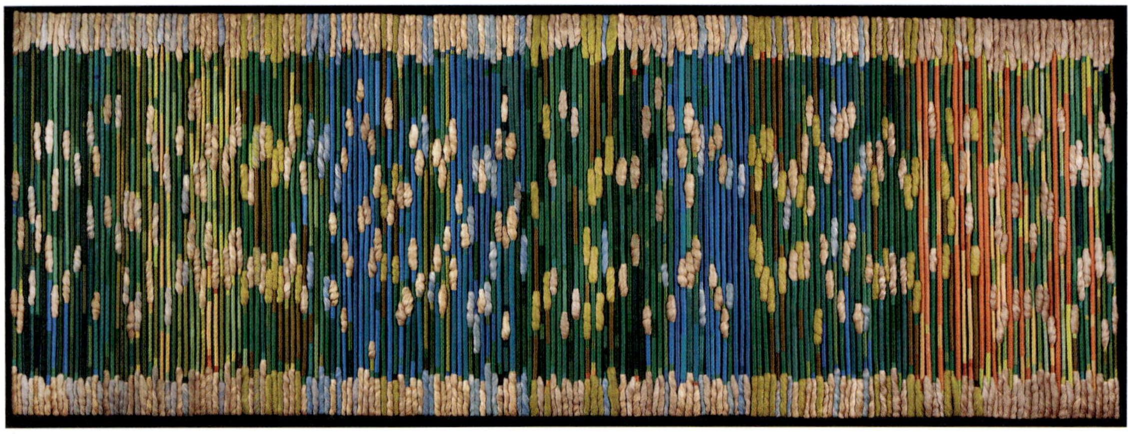

The Silk Rainforest, 1975.
Silk, linen, and cotton.
243.8 × 685.8 × 7.6 cm (96 × 270 × 3 in).

In the 1960s and 1970s, Hicks' work was often grouped in with discussions of tapestries in an effort to label and understand it but she was actually creating something new. She sometimes hung her pieces away from the wall, from the ceiling, or even laid them in heaping piles on the floor – rather unlike a tapestry. She also started to make large works with cotton and linen fibres wrapped in silk and lined up in colourful columns of cords. She calls these 'ponytails'. A piece she was commissioned to make for the AT&T headquarters titled *The Silk Rainforest* (c.1975) showcases Hicks' command of colour theory and her open approach to textile work. Shades of green melt into yellows and blues, broken up by brown twists of linen and cotton. The effect is like looking upon a thicket of assorted plants and trees, with bits of sky breaking though. The cords emulate the appearance of weavings when viewed from a distance, but her process for creating them and their manner of display is something else entirely. It was a nebulous emerging art form that was still taking shape at that time: fibre art.

Hicks' minimes and ponytail works continue to be a staple of her art practice, but her 'bundles' have become some the most recognizable pieces of her oeuvre. These are collections of yarn and fibres that are wrapped together to form a mass. Individual bundles can be multicoloured or monochromatic and shown singularly or in piles. She also refers to them as 'stones' and they can be presented as companions to long tubular forms called 'sticks'. Hicks relates these to the ideas of 'listening stones' and 'talking sticks', the latter of which has origins in Native American, African and Maori cultures as a way of symbolizing authority or facilitating productive conversation. These are mutable forms that can be mixed and displayed in a fresh way each time they're exhibited. Some more playful versions of bundle installations attach them to the base of hanging fibres, as if frozen in the process of falling from the sky with an almighty splat.

Hicks' openness has enabled her to work between disciplines and borders to create architectural weavings and painterly sculptures. Critics continue to ask if her work is tapestry or design, art or craft – and they can keep on asking. She deftly shakes off these labels in favour of free experimentation. That's probably why today, her pieces can be found in art *and* design museums around the world.

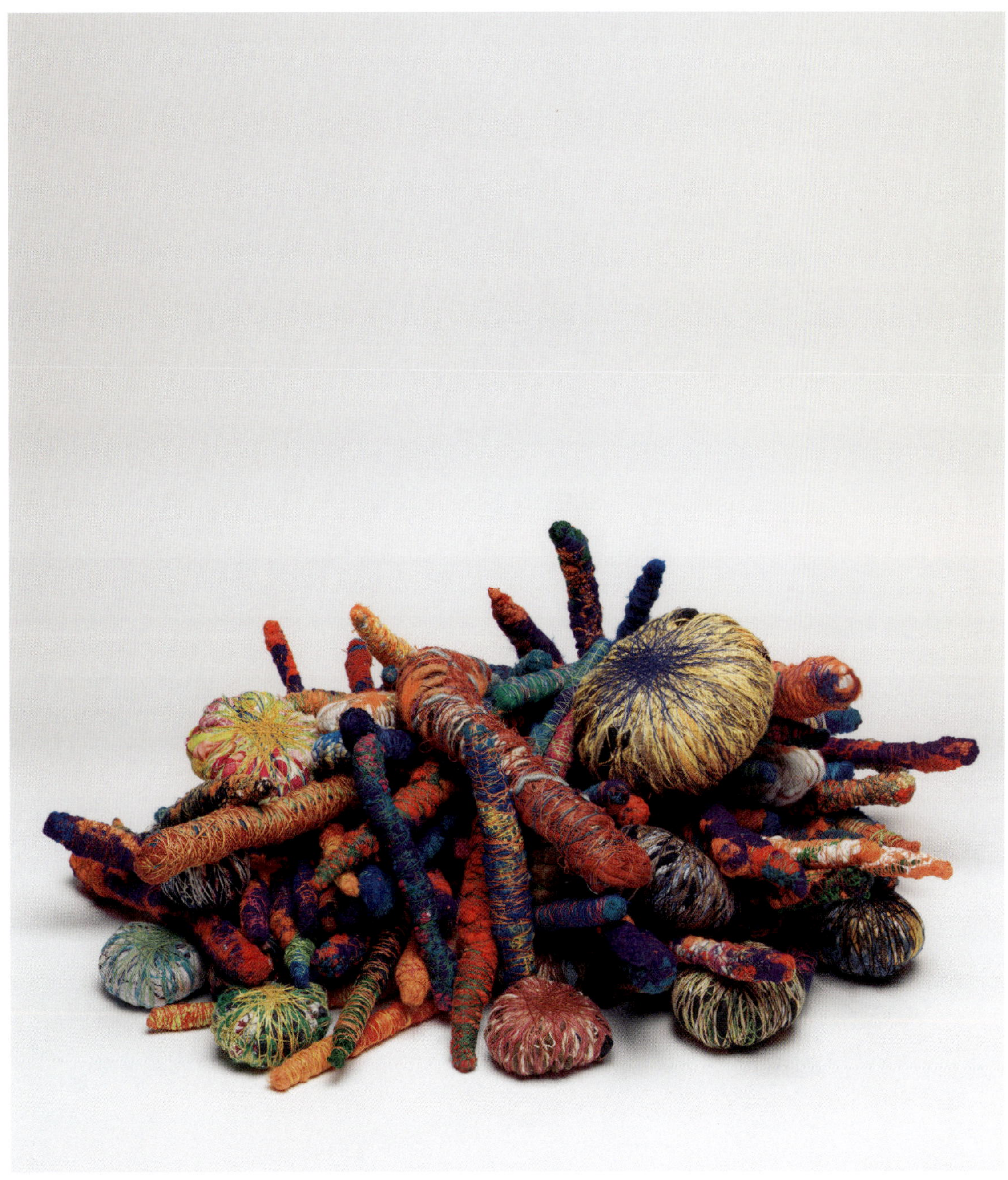

Palitos con Bolas, 2011. Installation of 26 small, handmade
rocks and 97 handmade twigs. Cotton, linen, nylon and silk.
Dimensions variable.

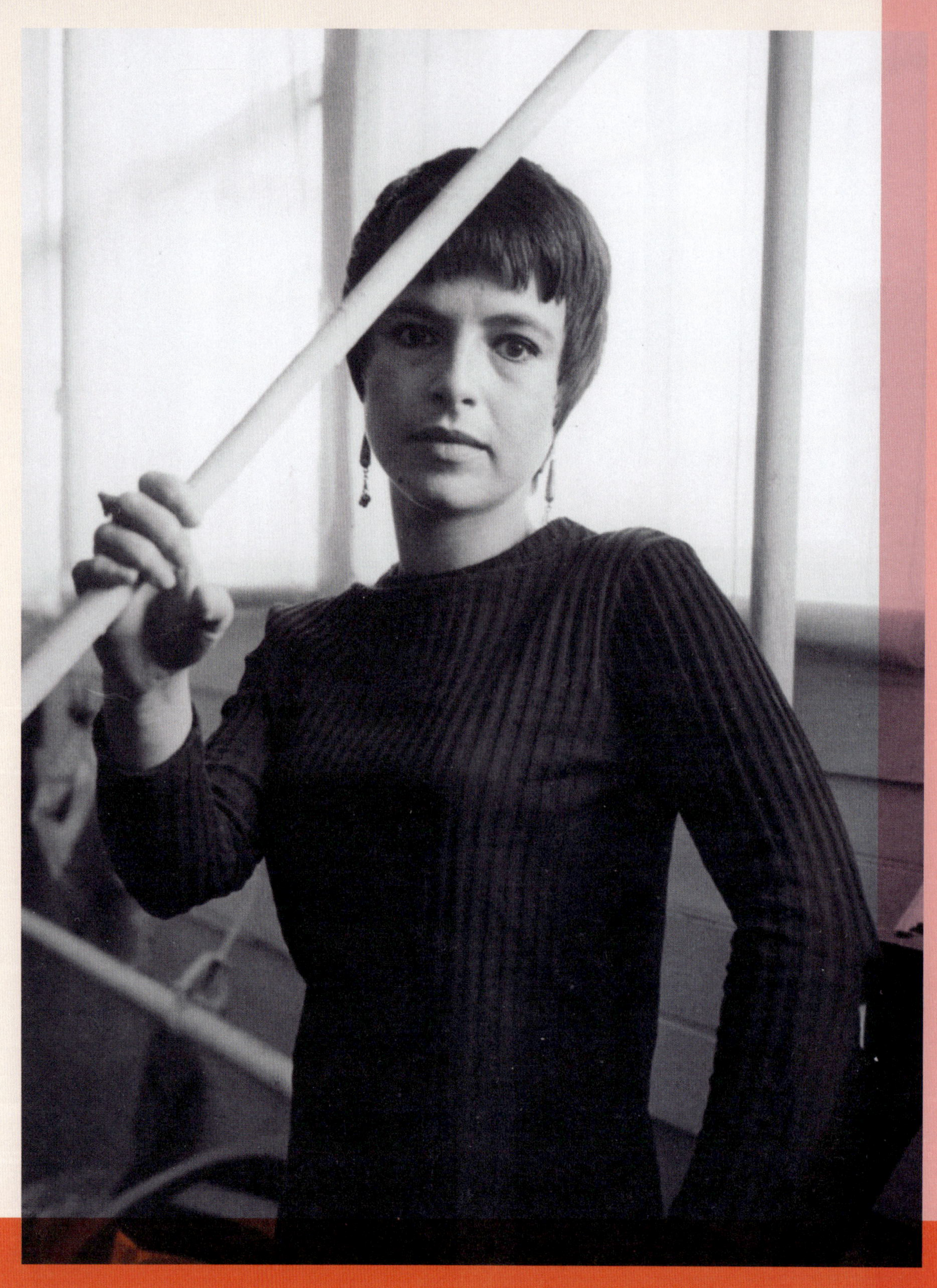

Eva Hesse

(1936–1970)

Soft sculpture, Fibre art

Eva Hesse lived a life filled with extremes. In fact, she found the highs and lows of her life so intense that she said the whole of it had been 'absurd'. Using unconventional and industrial materials, Hesse explored concepts relating to exaggeration and contradictions, which connect back to that idea of absurdity. Her time in this world was cut short by illness, but in her years as an artist she emerged as a ground-breaking sculptor and a forerunner of the post-minimalist aesthetic.

On 7 December 1938, Hesse's parents placed her and her sister on one of the last *Kindertransport* trains rescuing Jewish children out of Nazi Germany. She was two years old. The girls' father kept extensive diaries about their early childhood and wrote of his worry in that moment that they might never be reunited. The sisters stayed in the Netherlands for a few months before their parents were able to collect them, secure visas to England and, eventually, emigrate to the US. They went on to settle in New York City's Washington Heights neighbourhood, where there was a growing community of German Jewish refugees. There, the family reconnected with old friends and adjusted to life in their new home as best as they could while the war in Europe raged on. Hesse's parents eventually divorced in 1945 and her mother, who had long lived with bipolar disorder, died by suicide the following year. It's more tragedy than anyone should have to experience in a lifetime, and Hesse traversed it all by the age of ten.

In a letter written to her father when she was around fourteen, Hesse expressed her desire to become an artist, and he supported her dream by sending her to the School of Industrial Art for high school. At home she felt insecure and anxious, but at school she thrived socially and scholastically. She graduated from the school's window display programme in 1952 and next enrolled in the Pratt Institute, where she studied advertising design. Hesse was interested in Abstract Expressionism at the time, but her painting classes emphasized traditional still lifes. She wasn't into it. She was also very young compared to her classmates, entering the programme at only sixteen. She stayed only three semesters before leaving and was then in need of a job. She marched up to *Seventeen* magazine's offices and landed an internship off the back of her audacity. The following year, the magazine ran a feature on her as a young artist, including images of her work.

Hesse maintained her art skills by going to live drawing sessions at the Art Students League a few times a week and frequenting the Museum of Modern Art. Then in 1957, she enrolled in Cooper Union, which she loved. She earned a certificate in design a couple of years later and secured a scholarship thereafter to attend Yale School of Art. Her studies overlapped with Sheila Hicks' (see page 98) time at the school, and both women spoke on what a tumultuous phase this was for the programme. Josef Albers, who headed the programme, was at odds with other faculty members and that tension trickled down to the students. While there, she performed well within Albers' colour theory focused approach, but once again, she found the programme wasn't in line with her painting aspirations. Nevertheless, this time she stayed and graduated in 1959.

After Yale, Hesse returned home to New York. She worked as a part-time textile designer and set up a studio space in the same building as Yayoi Kusama (see page 74), Claes Oldenburg, Donald Judd and other soon-to-be art darlings. Sol LeWitt also had a studio not too far away and became one of Hesse's close friends and confidants. She was largely working in two-dimensional mediums at this time and her style was expressionistic. She created energetic figurative paintings that are now referred

Hesse worked with a mixture of industrial materials, including steel, fibreglass, rubber and latex, which she experimented with repeatedly.

to as her 'spectre' paintings because of the ghostly vibe of some of the works. By 1963, she had her first solo show at Allan Stone Gallery in New York.

The early 1960s was a period of soul-searching for Hesse, wherein she was trying to uncover her unique artistic perspective. Some of her drawings were beginning to explore the grid motif that would appear in her later sculptural work, but she was not yet in what one may consider her mature period. In 1964, she reluctantly moved back to Germany with her husband at the time, Tom Doyle, who had an art residency near Düsseldorf. The couple lived in an abandoned textile factory and Hesse continued to work and exhibit. The building contained old parts and materials from its previous life as a factory and, perhaps inspired by the playful and abstract sculpture scene in Germany, Hesse decided to experiment with these leftovers. In 1965, she created her first sculptural piece, *Ringaround Rosie*, made with cloth-covered electrical wire and papier-mâché on a masonite board. In a letter to Sol LeWitt, she wrote that the image simultaneously reminded her of a penis and breasts. She carried on experimenting with unconventional materials and by the time she returned home to New York later that year, she was a sculptor.

In the years that followed, Hesse worked with a mixture of industrial materials, including steel, fibreglass, rubber and latex, which she experimented with repeatedly. Her affinity for latex has likely become a small nightmare for collectors and

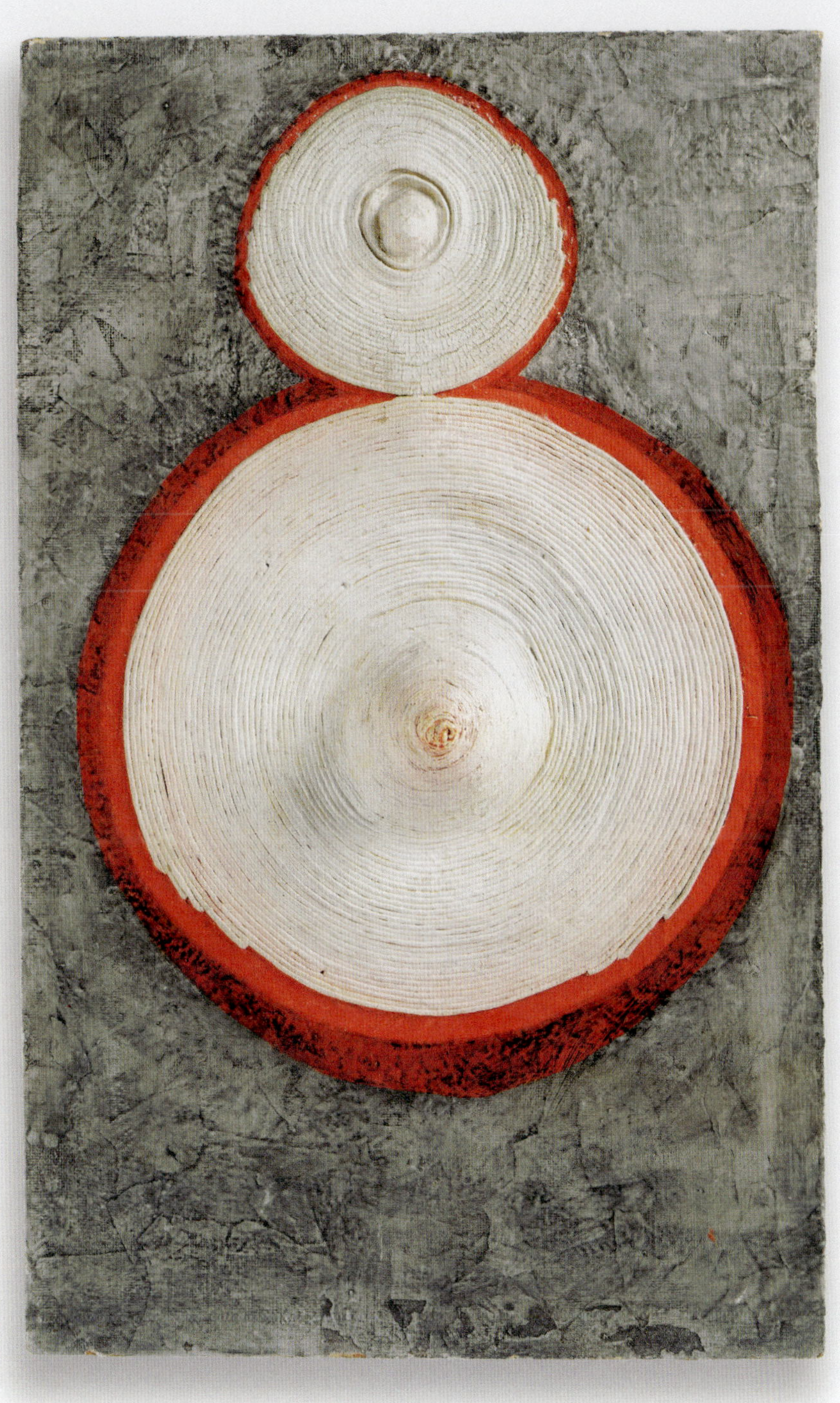

Ringaround Arosie, 1965.
Varnish, graphite, ink, enamel, cloth-covered wire, papier-caché,
unknown modeling compound, Masonite and wood.
67½ × 42½ × 11½ cm (26½ × 16¾ × 4½ in).

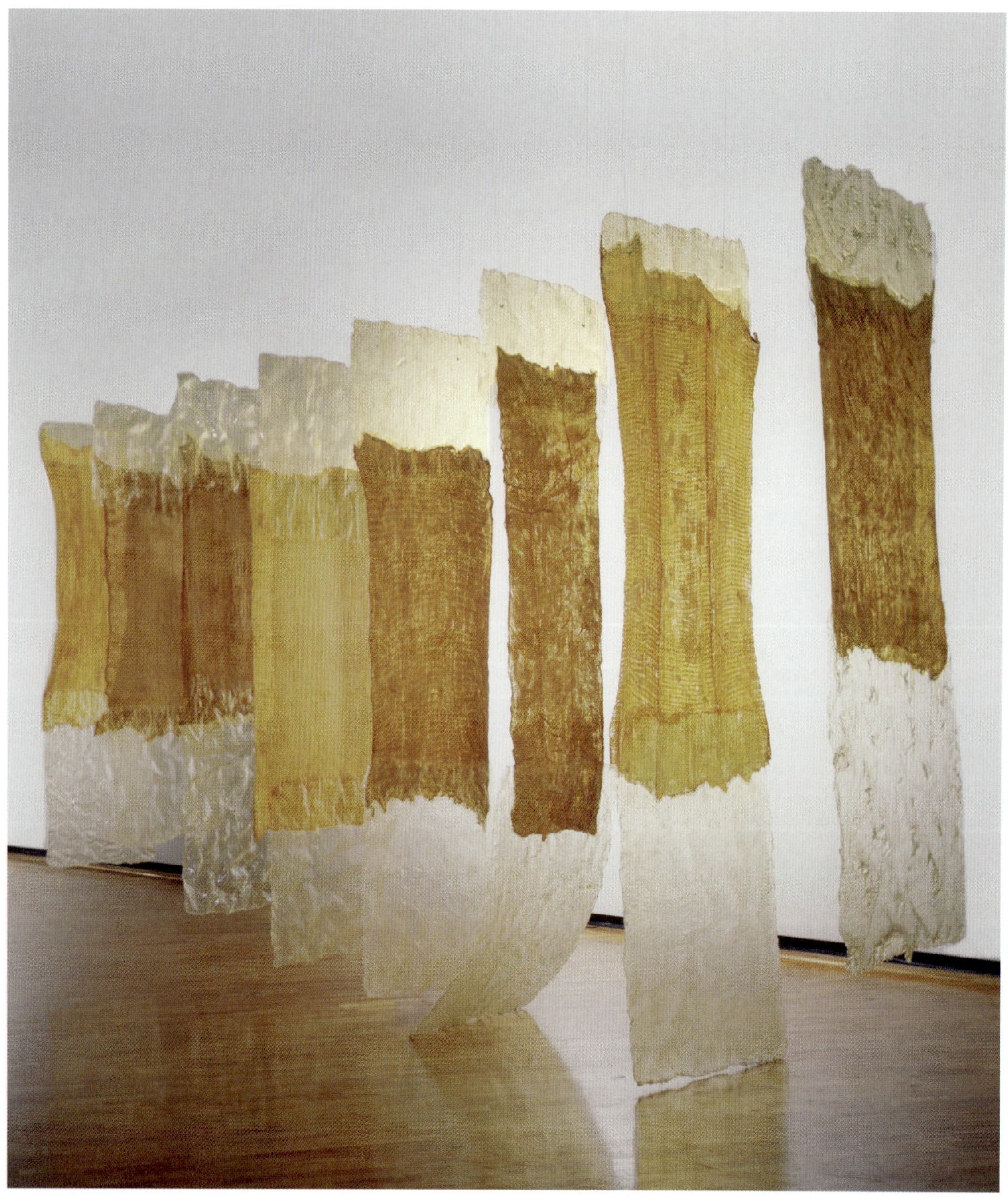

Contingent, 1969.
Fiberglass, polyester resin, latex and cheesecloth.
8 units, 350 × 630 × 109 cm (138 × 248 × 43 in), variable.

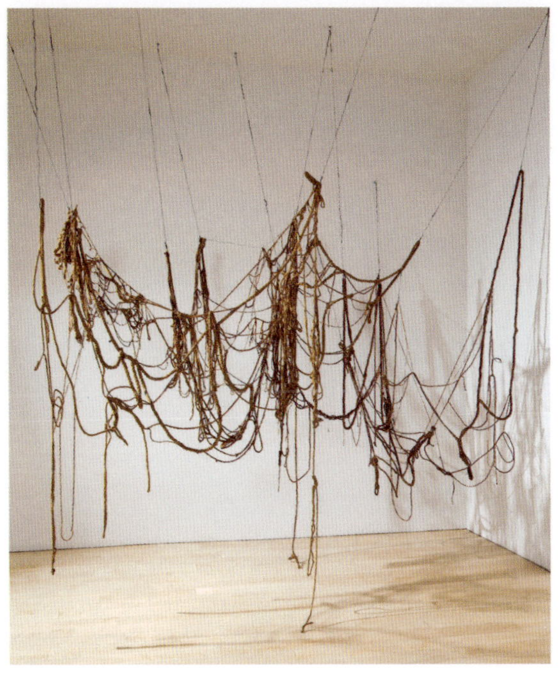

No title, 1969–70.
Latex, rope, string and wire. Dimensions variable.

conservators, as this material degrades over time. Hesse knew this when she created the sculptures, but her love for the material was too great not to use it. In 1968, she showed a latex piece titled *Area* in the *Soft and Apparently Soft Sculpture* exhibition, which also featured pieces by Louise Bourgeois (see page 50) and Yayoi Kusama (see page 74).

Latex material and its tan hue have a skin-like appearance that gives her works an organic quality. This resemblance to skin is particularly clear in her 1969 installation *Contingent*, which looks like a collection of animal hides. In this piece, Hesse suspends latex-coated cheesecloths from subtle strings, as if they are floating in air, at either end of each latex sheet are translucent sections of yellow fibreglass. Light filters through the materials in different ways, encasing the entire installation in a soft, golden glow. Repetition is a design element that appears across many of her works, and in this installation she repeats the banner-like hangings eight times. In a 1970 interview with Cindy Nemser for *Artforum*, Hesse explained that she liked to repeat forms because it exaggerates them and makes them more 'absurd'.

In 1969, Hesse was diagnosed with a brain tumour. She underwent chemotherapy and two operations, but the disease would tragically claim her life the following year at the age of thirty-four. She carried on working as long as she could after the diagnosis, and at one point attended an opening for an exhibition of her sculpture *Expanded Expansion* (1969) at the Whitney Museum of American Art with the use of a wheelchair.

No Title (1969–70) is among the final pieces Hesse worked on and is currently in the Whitney collection. The sculpture resembles a spiderweb, a network of veins or some other such organic mass, hanging from the ceiling from thirteen points. To create the piece, she dipped knotted rope into liquid latex and allowed it to harden. Although the ropes are stiffened, the work is intended to be changeable so that it can be installed in variable ways. At first glance, it appears to be a chaotic cluster, but in actuality it is as planned and modular as any of her gridded sculptures – it's the sort of playful contradiction Hesse liked to explore.

In her interview with Nemser, Hesse said, 'There's not been *one* normal thing in my life – not one – not even my art.' This explains some of her attraction to the absurd. Just as the Dada artists reacted to the trauma of the First World War through their caution-to-the-wind aesthetic, Hesse allowed herself the artistic freedom to react to the extremes of her own life. The rapidity and progress of her development as an artist is remarkable and means that, although she died far too young, the echo of her short career continues to reverberate across the history of art. Her works continue to transform as the materials age or pieces are installed in new configurations, so as her works change we will be presented with repeated opportunities to revisit her sculptures within new contexts.

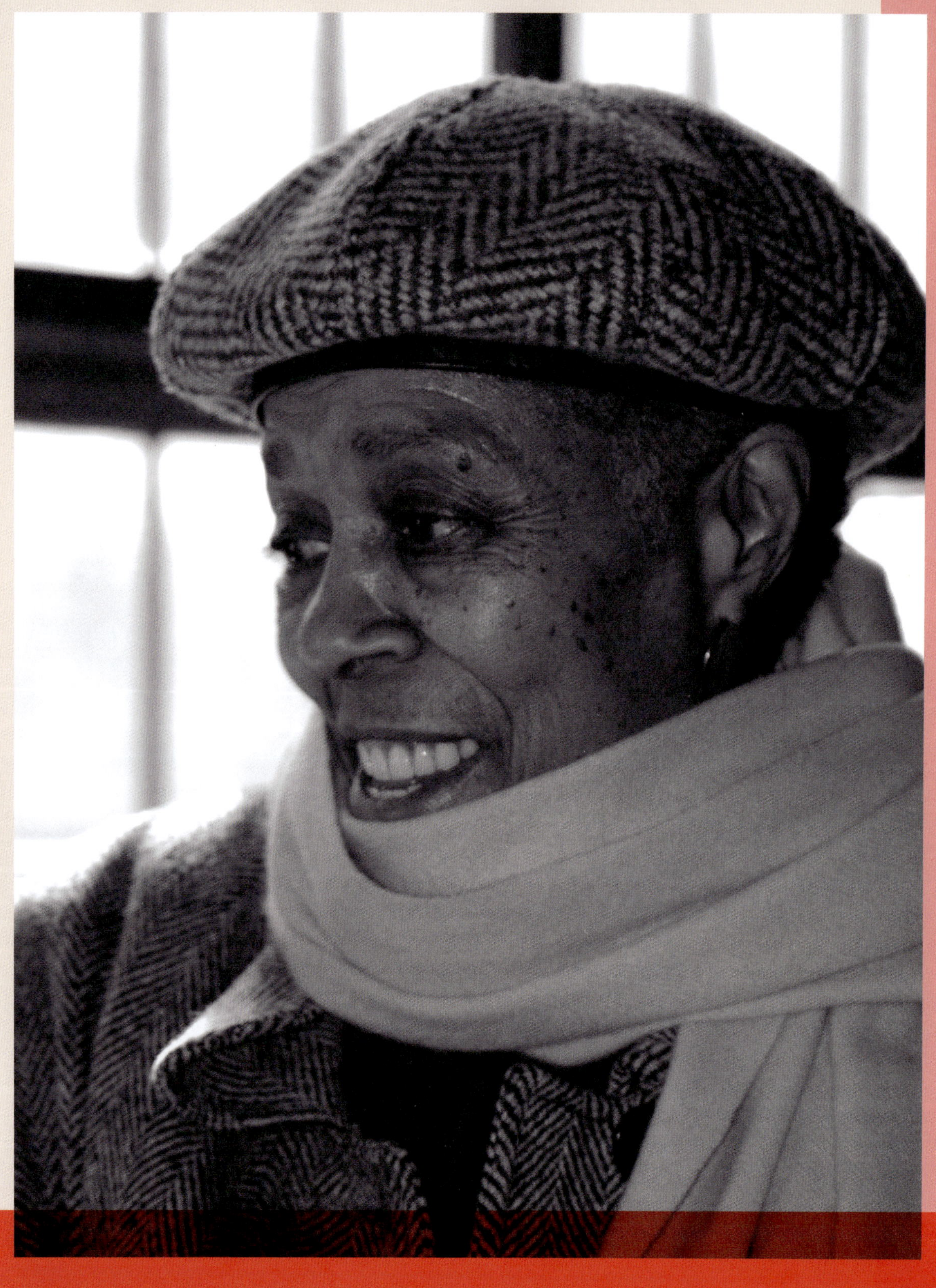

Marva Lee Pitchford-Jolly

(1937–2012)

Ceramics

It is no easy thing to tell a good story. Marva Lee Pitchford-Jolly recalled that her mother was an excellent storyteller when she was growing up, and for years she thought she might like to test her own abilities through writing. Eventually, she discovered that her form of storytelling was visual and she learned to do it in a way that made incredible use of her longstanding love for the feel of clay.

Pitchford-Jolly was born in Crenshaw, Mississippi, as one of a pair of fraternal twins. Although she had seven siblings to play with, she was happiest when playing in the mud on her own. The wet earth on her parent's farm was her first introduction to shaping objects with clay, even if they were only mud pies. She lived for the rainy days that provided her the opportunity to build and sculpt, and people started referring to her lovingly as a little artist. Life changed dramatically when her mother died in 1948, resulting in her father moving north to find work. In 1951, her family moved to Chicago – where there was markedly less mud – and her clay-making interests were set to the side.

She went on to attend Roosevelt University in Chicago, where she earned a BA in Urban Studies in 1961. After college, she spent the first half of her career working in social services and health planning, but throughout all those years, her love for playing in the mud never left her mind. In 1968, she decided to sign up for her first ceramics class at the Hyde Park Neighbourhood Club. One stimulus for finally taking this leap was that she felt it could be a good way to decompress from the social upheavals of the Civil Rights-era. Working from her dining room table, she continued working on ceramics as a hobby at first, and gave many of her early pieces away to friends.

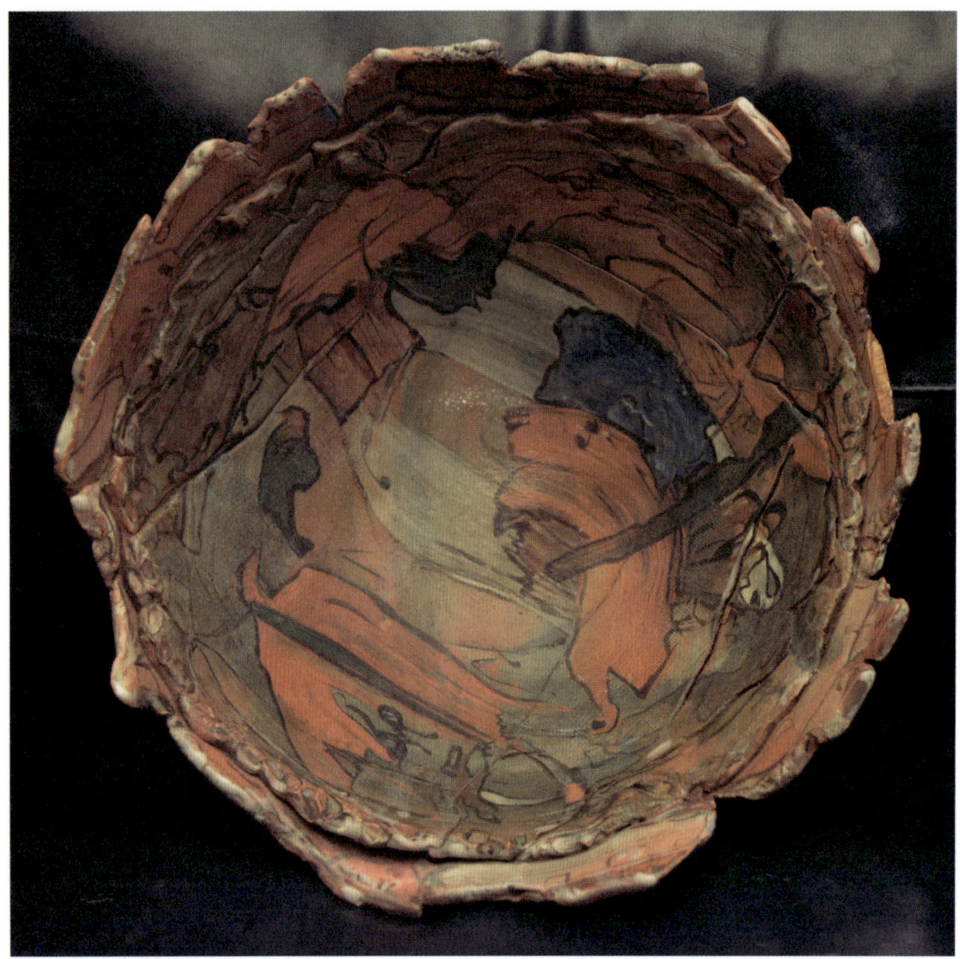

Story Pot, c. 1994.
Clay.

In the early 1980s, funding for healthcare was increasingly scant under the new Reagan administration. The effects of this landed on Pitchford-Jolly's doorstep when she was laid off from her job due to cuts around 1981. One sometimes hears stories about people who turn layoffs into life-changing opportunities, and Pitchford-Jolly was one of those people. She decided to focus on being an artist, and was bolstered in this journey when she was offered a ceramics teaching position at Chicago State University. This allowed her to simultaneously teach and learn about ceramics alongside her students, and the opportunity was particularly useful in improving her knowledge of glaze chemistry.

Many of Pitchford-Jolly's best-known works are vessels of various shapes, ornamented with patterns in the surface of the clay or through painting. She taught herself to draw on clay and said that she felt more adept drawing on pots than paper. Ceramics gave Pitchford-Jolly a platform to tell stories, which she'd long wanted to do with writing, but never had the confidence to do. Soon, she developed the 'Story Pots' series of painted vessels depicting figurative narratives – some personal and some historical. In an interview with the oral history archive, The HistoryMakers, she called these works 'the real stuff', in comparison to some of her other vases and vessels that she said were for 'getting [her] hands together', like an artistic warm-up.

Her early story pots were monochromatic because she was inspired by the autumnal landscapes in the American South. As the grass dries and the leaves drop from the trees, the earth and branches reveal themselves, creating stark lines and colours. In the 1990s, more vibrant palettes entered her repertoire, particularly in what she called 'friendship bowls'. In addition to her love of the countryside, she was motivated by her love of people – which is evidenced by her decades of working in the social sector. Counter to the closed, spherical shape of the story pots, friendship bowls are typically open at the top and some are nearly as shallow as plates. This was her way of visualizing the openness required for friendships, and the varied depth of the bowls shows how some can fall a little flat.

Other examples of Pitchford-Jolly's work include sculptural reliefs of faces emerging from the clay surface. While her pots and bowls are typically painted, her reliefs were often left in the natural hues of the clay. In a portrait titled *My Mama's Light*, she shows her mother's face with her eyes closed and lips slightly parted. The figure's serene expression could indicate that she is sleeping, but the work also resembles a death mask, which have historically been created across many cultures to commemorate the dead. Pitchford-Jolly thought of herself as a 'mama's girl' and her mother is a repeated subject in her pots and reliefs. The artist greatly valued their shared creativity and appreciated how her mother always supported her in playing in the mud as a child. She also valued her mother's love of people and deep friendships – another shared trait between the two women.

The importance of friendships and cultivating human connections in Pitchford-Jolly's life may

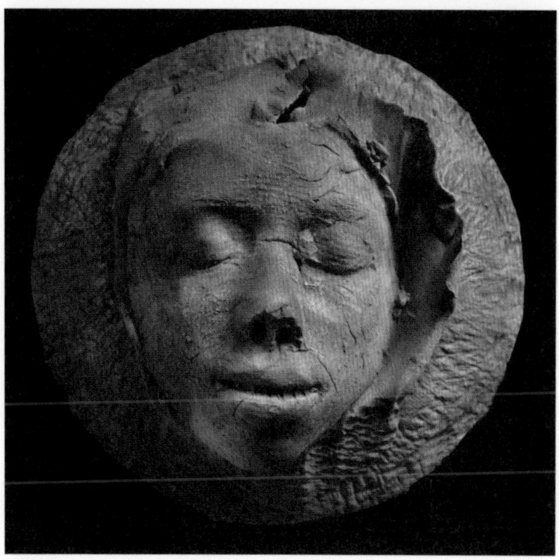

My Mama's Light, c. 1994.
Clay.

be one reason why she often directed her energy outwards to nurture other artists. She travelled to Africa several times, including a six-week stay in Zambia where she did a pottery residency. Back in Chicago, she founded the Mud People's Black Women's Resource Sharing Workshop, a gallery and studio in support of Black women artists. After the closure of the studio, the concept evolved into the Sapphire & Crystals collective, started by Pitchford-Jolly and fellow artist Felicia Grant Preston in 1986. The name was inspired by the women of the group's interest in crystals and spirituality, and a reclamation of the stereotype of 'sassy Black women' embodied by the character Sapphire on the old *Amos 'n' Andy* sitcom.

Pitchford-Jolly's work was deeply personal, but it was also inclusive. She honoured her Southern herltage and celebrated the beauty and spirituality of the Black women in her life. In so doing, she represented stories with which many Black women could relate, and simultaneously empowered other women to do the same for themselves.

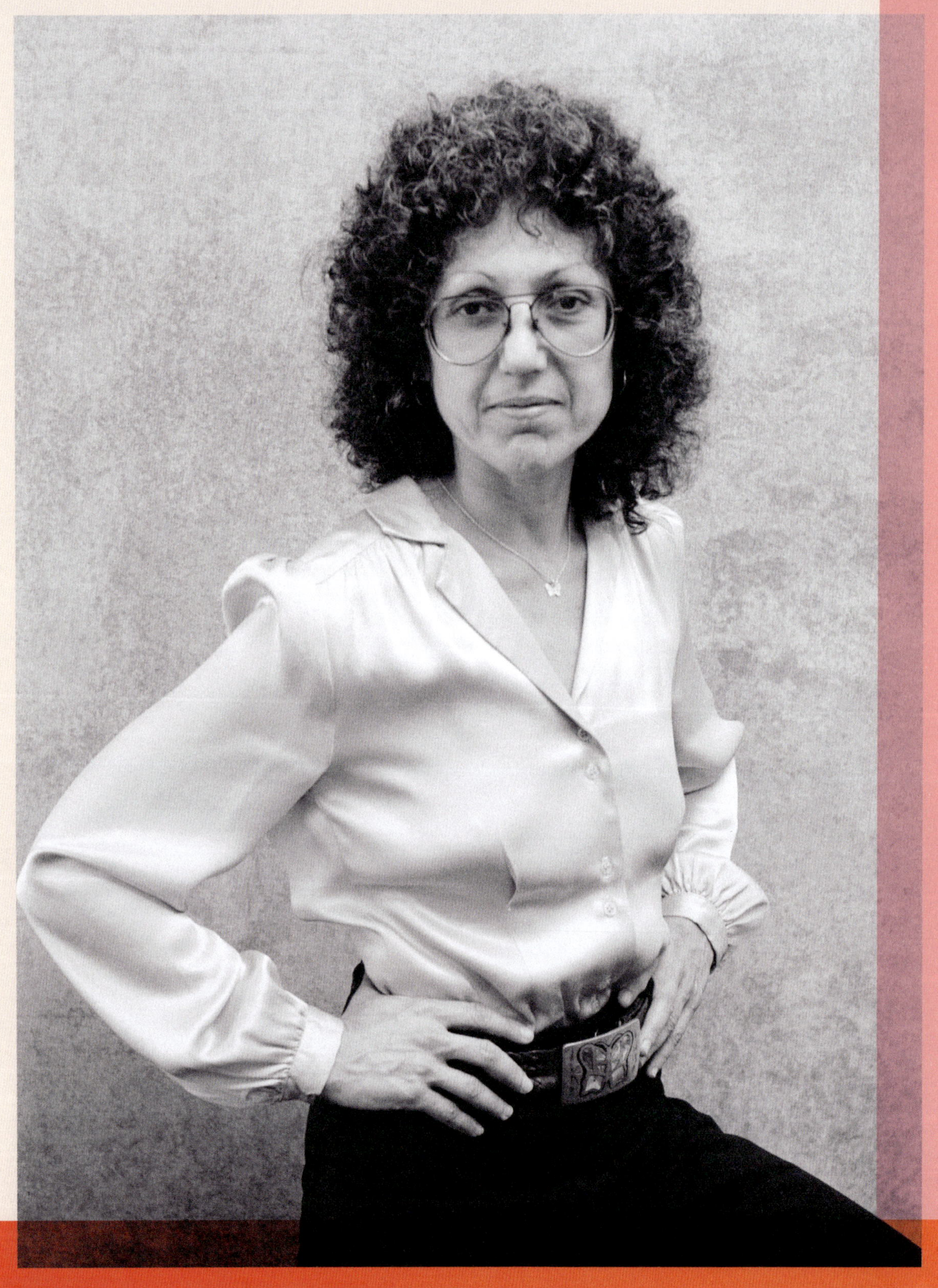

Judy Chicago

(b.1939)

Ceramics, Quilting, Textile art

To put it plainly, Judy Chicago's work is iconic. Her artistic practice developed in tandem with the Feminist movement of the 1960s and 1970s, and she emerged as one of the pioneers of the Feminist Art Movement. Her audacious artworks take the form of paintings, sculptures, textiles, ceramics and more, but they nearly always uplift the stories and experiences of women. She boldly takes up space within male-dominated environments, while also creating space for other women through collaboration and educational outreach.

Chicago was born and raised in – you guessed it – Chicago. She was born Judy Cohen and underwent one name change through marriage before legally restyling her last name as Chicago in 1970. The new surname was inspired by her hometown, but most importantly, it was not tied to a relationship with a man, be he father or spouse.

Chicago grew up in an extremely liberal household. Her father broke with twenty-three generations of family tradition by choosing not to become a rabbi and instead working at the post office in the evenings. During the day, he looked after Chicago and her brother, and was also a politically active Marxist and labour rights organizer. Her mother had been a dancer before taking work as a medical secretary and was inclined to support to her children's artistic interests. As early as pre-school, Chicago's teachers recognized that she had a special talent for art, so her mother placed her in Saturday classes at the Chicago Art Institute from 1945. She continued attending classes at the school for more than a decade, developing skills in still-life drawing, figure painting, and more. Time she spent creating art became especially important to her, when her father died suddenly from surgery complications when she was thirteen.

With an enviable art foundation under her belt, Chicago enrolled in UCLA after high school, majoring in art and minoring in humanities. The campus was buzzing with political activity from students in support of issues ranging from socialism to civil rights. Thinking back on her father's activism, Chicago was happy to lend her skills to causes, including joining her local NAACP chapter. Even within such a liberal school, this was a radical thing for her to do at that time. Her classes were equally stimulating on social issues – for better or worse. In particular, one professor's maddening declaration that women haven't made any significant contributions to history set Chicago down a path to prove him wrong. This quest eventually culminated in *The Dinner Party* installation several years later.

In the early stages of her artistic development, Chicago worked in a minimalist style, in keeping with the trends of the art world at the time. She stayed at UCLA for grad school and worked on a vivid series of paintings and sculptures in geometric patterns and eye-popping colours. She also supplemented her university education by studying at an auto body school to learn spray painting – she was the only woman in a cohort of 250 students. Many of her pieces where entirely abstract and showcased the stunning gradients she could achieve with spray painting, but she also made some stark paintings with phallic and vulval imagery. As her auto body classes would indicate, the car world is often viewed as a masculine space, but in pieces like *Birth Hood* (1965), Chicago juxtaposed this notion against imagery of a painted vulva in 'feminine' shades of pink and purple on the surface of a car bonnet. These contrasting ideas embody her personal experience as a woman navigating the male-dominated art world.

Over time, Chicago felt an increasing desire to engage with ideas surrounding womanhood as a part of her art practice. She was also keen to help other women artists in their development and

began teaching a women-only art course at Fresno State College. This idea grew into the Feminist Art Program that she later taught at the California Institute of the Arts alongside Miriam Shapiro (see page 68). Within her own work, Chicago was still thinking about the undervalued contributions of women throughout history and created the *Great Ladies* series of abstract paintings, named after powerful figures like Queen Victoria and Marie Antionette. She'd also started to learn how to glaze pottery after being inspired by a stunning plate she encountered in an antique store. Between 1974 and 1979, these two interests – women's history and ceramics – coalesced as she worked on her magnum opus, *The Dinner Party*.

Chicago's fantasy dinner party installation plays off of the iconography of *The Last Supper,* but in the place of Jesus and his twelve disciples, she multiplies the table by three and seats a total of thirty-nine historical and mythical women. The three tables are positioned in an equilateral triangle and sit atop a porcelain triangular floor. The floor was intended to have an additional 999 women's names, but one man's name was mistakenly included, making it 998. The settings are lavish, with embroidered table runners, golden eating utensils, and bespoke ceramic place settings in a butterfly/vulval motif tailored to each guest.

Throughout the process of making *The Dinner Party*, Chicago enlisted the help of 400 assistants to make various elements and twenty researchers to help compile names. Figures like Georgia O'Keeffe, Virginia Woolf and Sojourner Truth have bespoke settings at the table, and the names of Frida Kahlo, Joan of Arc and hundreds more are inscribed on the tiled Heritage Floor. Interestingly, and unbeknown to Chicago at the time, British artist Vanessa Bell previously created her own ceramic ode to women with *The Famous Women Dinner Service* (c.1932–34). Bell painted a fifty-plate dinner service that included figures such as Sappho, Cleopatra and Pocahontas.

From the 1980s and into the 1990s, Chicago created several series of complex textile works,

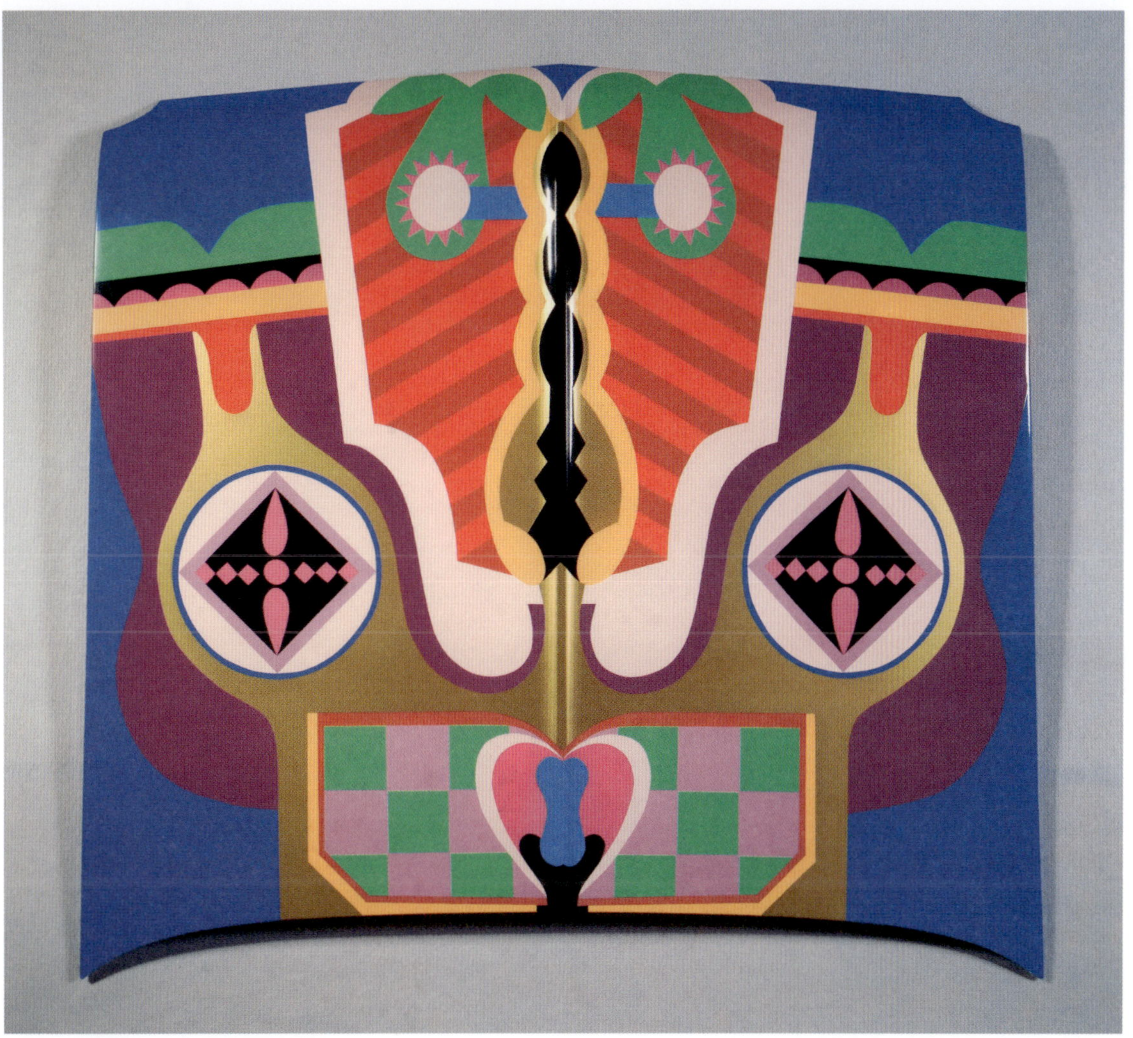

Birth Hood, 1965.
Sprayed automotive lacquer on car hood.
108.9 × 108.9 × 11 cm (42⅞ × 42⅞ × 4⁵/₁₆ in).

working with other women to incorporate a mixture of tapestry, needlepoint, appliqué and quilting techniques. As a later companion piece to *The Dinner Party*, she invited people around the world to create two-foot triangular quilt blocks honouring women of their choosing. The result of this global quilting bee is the *International Honor Quilt* (1980), complete with 539 blocks. Collaborating with other makers in this manner gives Chicago the opportunity to realize large-scale projects, tap into different skillsets and cultivate a community among artists. Chicago partnered with weaver Audrey Cowan to create her epic tapestry *The Fall* (1993),

which confronts the horrors of the Holocaust, and worked with 150 needleworkers over five years to produce her *Birth Project* series, which celebrates the strength and wonder of giving birth.

As a part of the Birth Project, textile artist Jane Gaddie Thompson executed Chicago's lush vision for *Birth Tear* (1982). Embroidering with white and red threads over deep red silk, the artists depict a woman giving birth and the tearing that can occur during the delivery of a child. Her hair flows around her in psychedelic waves, while what appears to be her placenta is off to her side surrounded by a twisting umbilical cord. It's

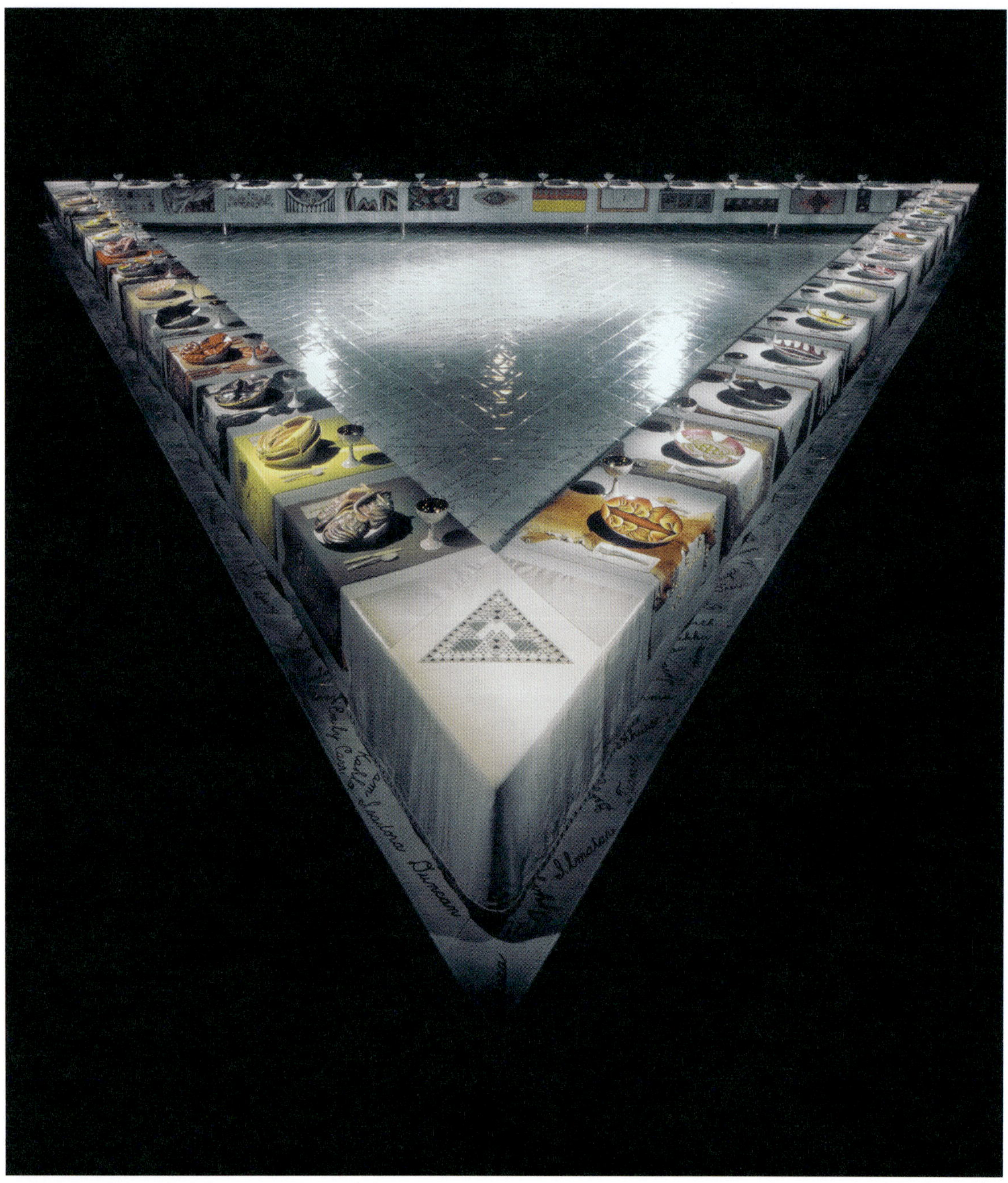

The Dinner Party, 1974–79.
Ceramic, porcelain and textile.
1463 × 1463 cm (576 × 576 in).

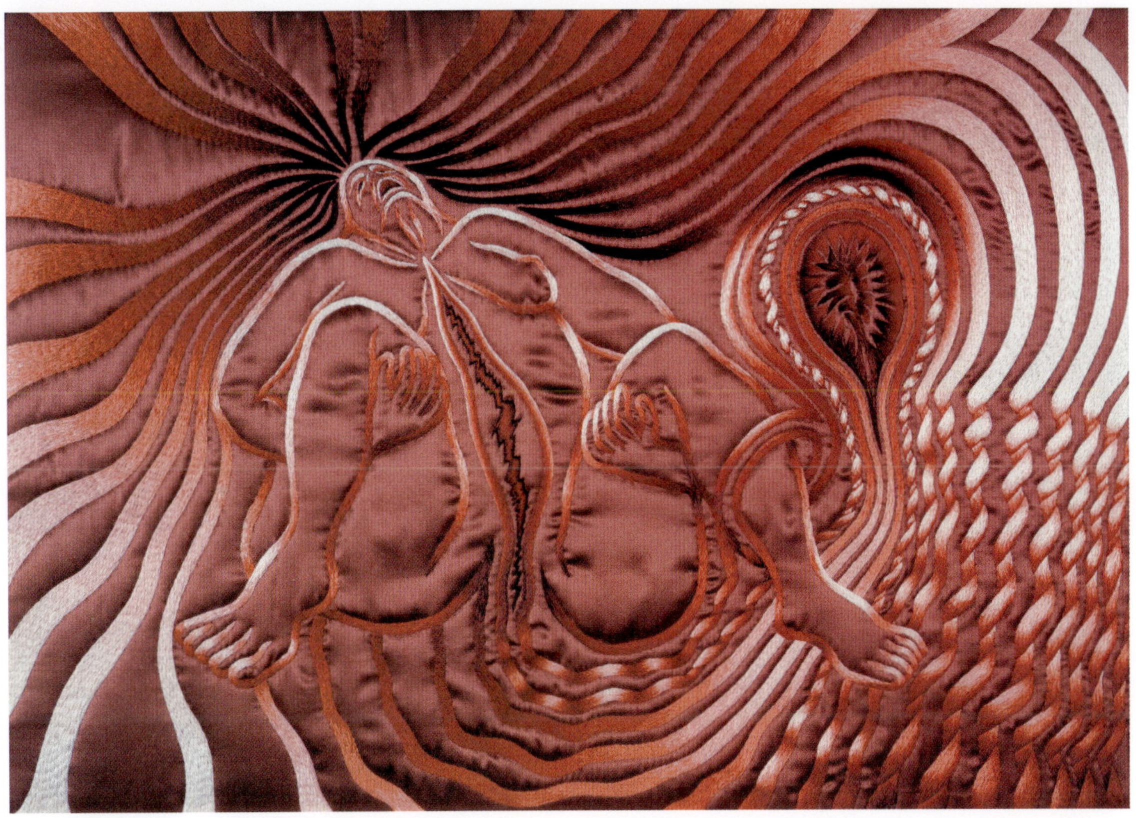

Birth Tear, 1982.
Embroidery on silk.
52.1 × 69.9 cm (20½ × 27½ in).

a powerful image that encapsulates the pain, strength and emotions that can accompany giving birth. Additional works from the series include other versions of *Birth Tear* showing the mother with children, imagery of Woman as the Creator, and woven 'birth garments' depicting the torsos of pregnant women. These works all serve to introduce more birth imagery to the art world, which Chicago felt was woefully underrepresented throughout art history.

Across Chicago's career, she has steadily reached outward to establish studios, workshops and collaborative projects with and for other women. She aims not only to lift women up through the themes in her artworks, but through building relationships and educating others. These collaborations mean that her practice has been able to span textiles, painting, glassware, ceramics and more. Chicago has been an essential voice in the advancement of women within the art world, subverting patriarchal structures through boldly feminist imagery and the use of traditionally 'feminine' art forms.

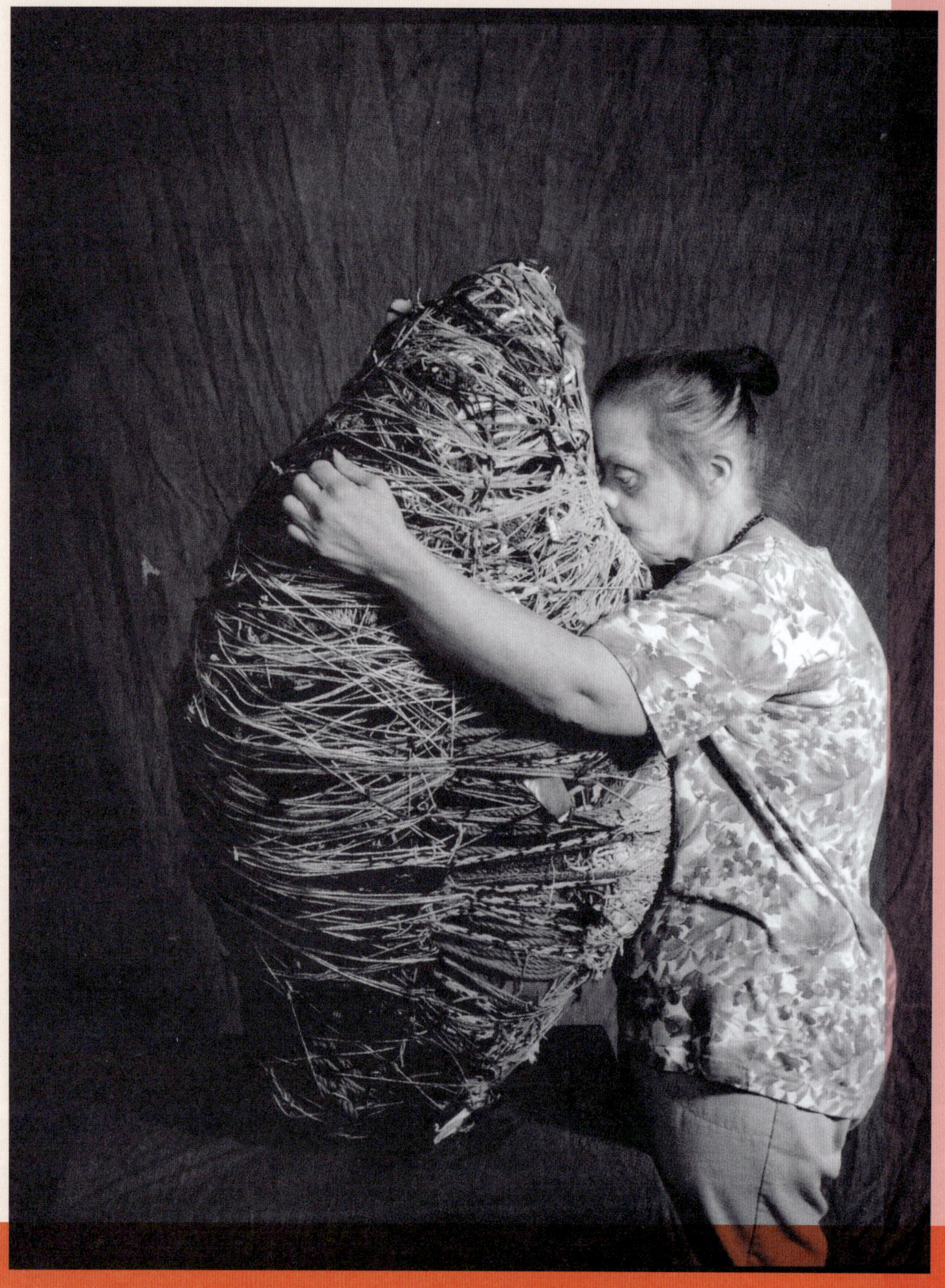

Judith Scott

(1943–2005)

Fibre art, Soft sculpture

For a masterclass in employing form, colour and texture in art, one needn't look further than the fibre sculptures of Judith Scott. With each piece, she encased found objects ranging in scale from twigs to chairs in dizzying layers of yarn and string. Her expressive aesthetic commands a lingering look and connects the viewer back to Scott's transformative process of building up each incredible sculpture.

Scott and her fraternal twin sister grew up in Cincinnati, Ohio, as the youngest of five children. The sisters were incredibly close, constantly playing side-by-side and even sharing a bed. Scott was the only sibling born with Down's Syndrome and had been ill with Scarlet Fever as an infant, resulting in hearing loss. Unfortunately, her family were not aware of this until much later and Scott was subsequently not taught to sign or speak as a child. This also meant that necessary accommodations were not made for her to sit her school's oral entrance test for children with learning disabilities, and her parents were subsequently advised to send her to live in institutional care. One morning, when she was seven years old, her father drove her to the Columbus State Institution while her sister still lay sleeping in their shared bed. Neither girl was aware of the coming change and both were devastated.

Scott was negatively impacted by the abrupt move and did not adjust well to her new home. Within a few years, her family moved her to a smaller institution in Gallipolis, Ohio, where she spent the next three decades. By this time, her sister, Joyce, had moved to California, and visited only sporadically. In 1986, Joyce made the decision to bring Judith to come live nearer to her.

After moving to California, Scott began attending art workshops at Creative Growth Art Centre, a non-profit serving artists with disabilities in Oakland. At the Ohio institution, Scott had not been given the opportunity to do art activities and, for nearly two years of going to Creative Growth, she had little interest in the workshops. She tried painting, woodwork, ceramics and drawing, but none of them sparked her artistic passions. One fateful day in 1989, she attended a session hosted by fibre artist Sylvia Seventy and became slowly engrossed as the minutes of the workshop ticked on. By the end of the class, she'd found her medium. Her first sculpture was a bundle of sticks and cloth sparsely wrapped with twine and adorned with small, coloured beads (see page 125).

Later sculptures from 1989 show that Scott quickly hit a stride, building on the ideas of her first sculpture and developing her aesthetic. These works also share a kinship to drawings she'd created in previous workshops of vigorous spirals and expressive line work filling the page. Her wrapped sculptures have this same energy, revealing layers of colour and lines of thread that dynamically overlap each other. She would sit at a large table five days a week and, using found objects for an armature, create small cocoon-like sculptures wrapped in fabric, yarn and twine. Sometimes her pieces had to be undone, as she'd commandeered the odd set of keys or wallet in service of her craft, but many objects were gladly sacrificed in support of her work. Her process could take anywhere from days to months, and she typically worked on one piece until it was complete before beginning another.

By the 1990s, Scott's sculptures were growing in size and complexity. She never used the same colour scheme twice and her materials varied greatly, depending on the resources available to her. In 1994, she created her only monochrome work out of paper towels after running out of her usual

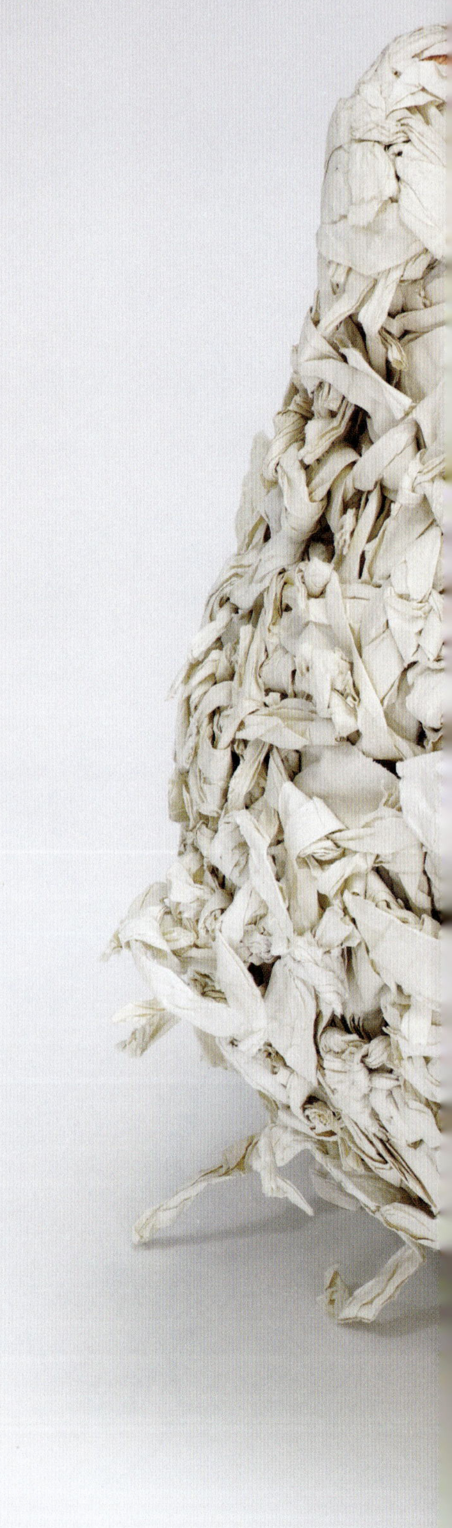

Untitled, 1994. Fiber and found objects.
68.6 × 58.4 × 43.2 cm (27 × 23 × 17 in).

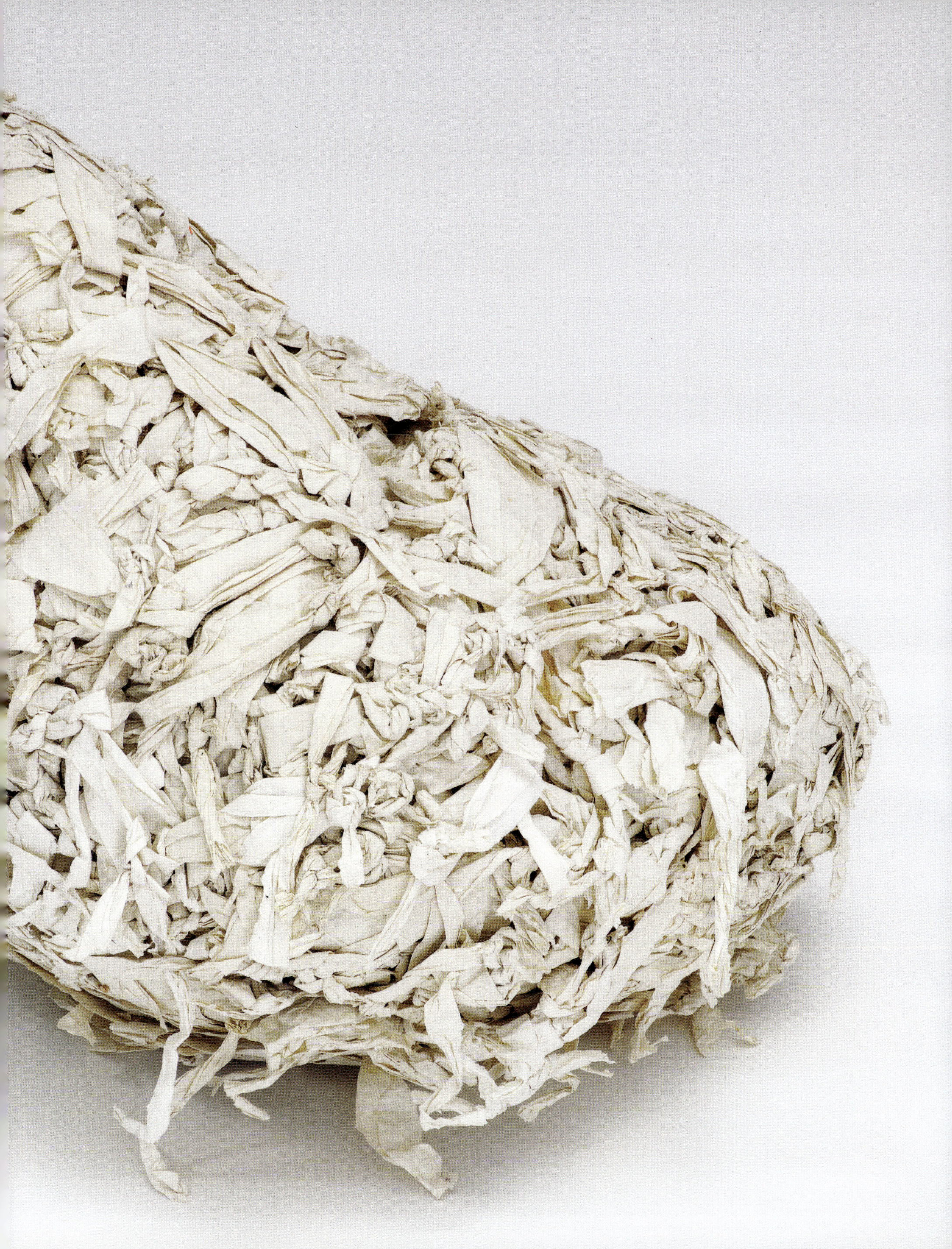

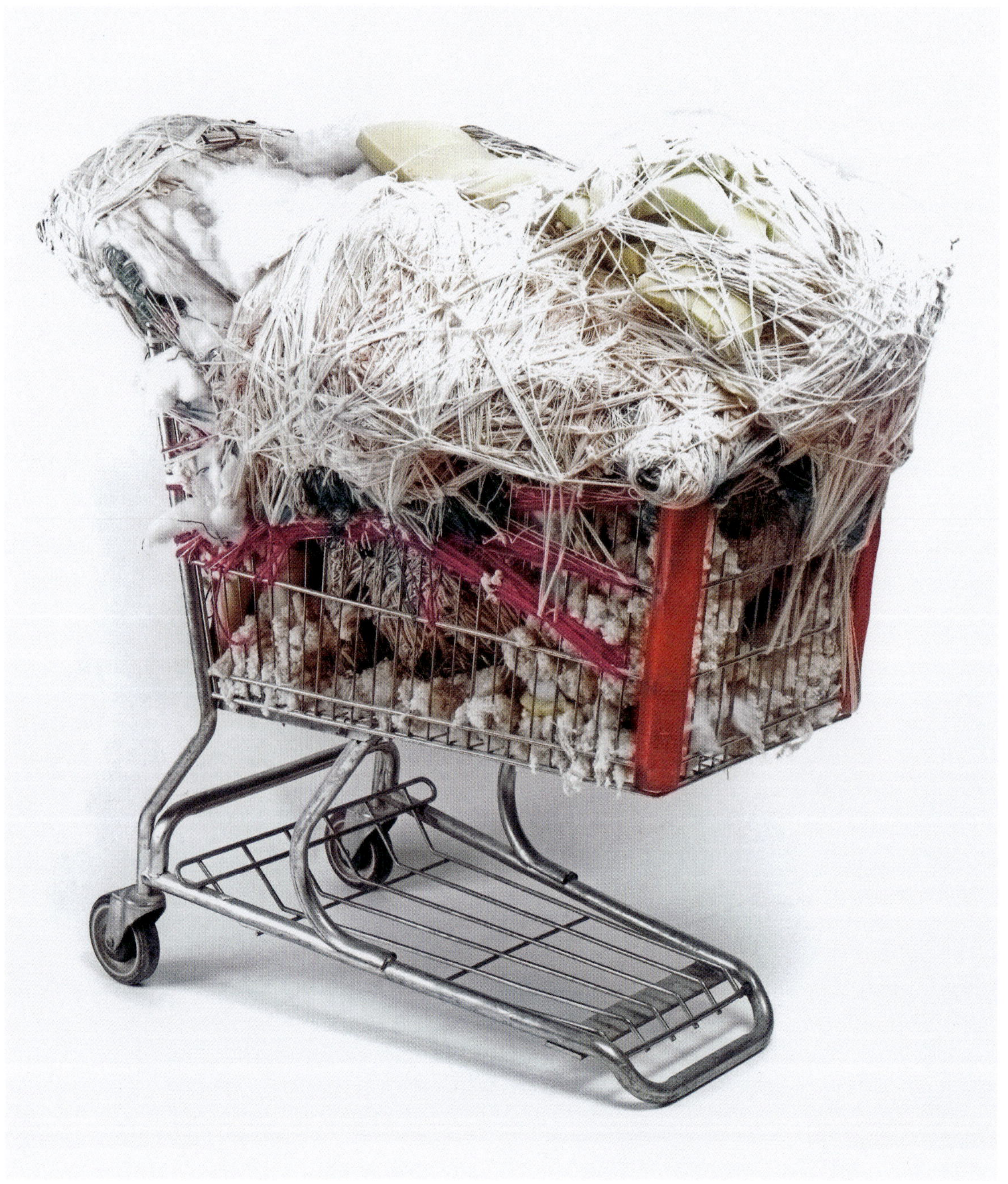

Untitled, 2003–2004.
Fiber and found objects. 109.2 × 119.4 x cm (45 × 47 × 31 in).

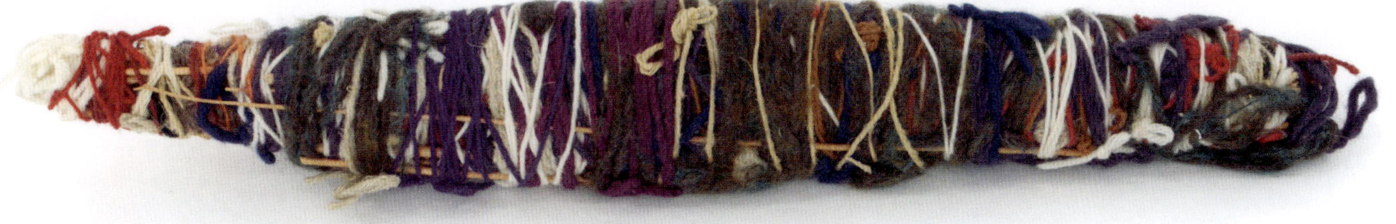

Untitled (JS 62), 1988.
Fiber and found objects.
61 × 10.2 × 10.2 cm (24 × 4 × 4 in).

supplies and noticing the material while washing her hands (see page 123). It's a stunning pod-like mass of pulled and knotted paper towels. The top has straight, smooth sections, while select strips on the bottom are gently peeling away. Considering the delicacy of the material, this sculpture is a feat of patience and dexterity.

Scott's first exhibition took place at Creative Growth in 1999. The show included pieces she hadn't seen in years displayed on pedestals throughout the studio. After finishing a sculpture, Scott would gesture for one of the studio staff to take it away, and some of her works had been kept in storage for as much as a decade by the time of the exhibition. When she was reunited with the pieces in the hours before the opening, she went around the room greeting each one with an assortment of waves, hugs and kisses. The works were met with an equally warm reception by the public later that evening as collectors and the press admired her captivating cocoons. From this point, her reputation quickly gained steam and she began to exhibit around the US and internationally.

In the latter stages of her career, Scott's choice of materials grew even more unconventional, and distinct objects are easily recognizable in several of her works. In one untitled piece she worked on between 2003 and 2004, she used a shopping trolley as a base (opposite). Much of the trolley is unwrapped and it's stuffed nearly beyond capacity with bound masses. The front two wheels have been removed to provide stability, but this also renders the cart useless, much like Duchamp's bicycle-topped stool or Meret Oppenheim's fur-covered cup. During her eighteen-year art career, Scott produced more than 200 fibre sculptures. Although she never communicated any context or intentions around her work, the emotionality of the pieces shines in their expressiveness and her interactions with them. She passed away in her sister's arms from natural causes in 2005, but her career has continued to flower in the years since. Scott's work has been exhibited at 2017 Venice Biennale, in the permanent collections of institutions like the Museum of Modern Art in New York, and in a retrospective exhibition at the Brooklyn Museum.

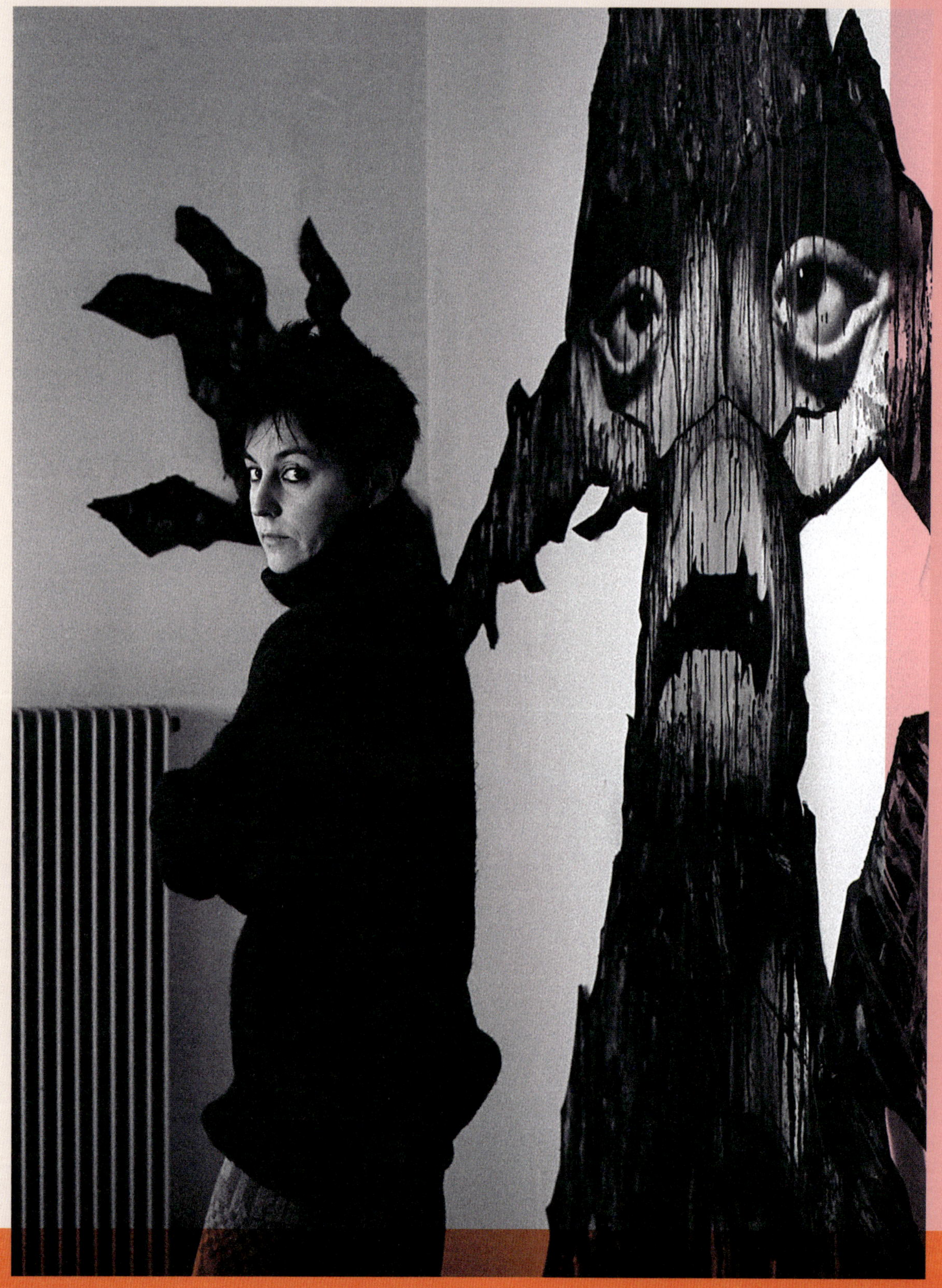

Annette Messager

(b.1943)

Soft sculpture

Annette Messager is a champion of materials and techniques that have long been considered 'outsider' art. This explains, in part, the diversity of media within her practice, spanning soft sculpture, textiles, assemblage and more. Her use of common materials and everyday imagery taps into the power of memory – hers and ours – and fortifies her work with the emotionality of those objects.

Let's transport ourselves to the small seaside town of Berck-sur-Mer in France, where Messager grew up. It was such a pleasant location that, from the nineteenth century, those in need of physical and mental rest took refuge in the many sanatoriums in the town. Recuperating residents often took up painting and writing to pass the time, giving a young Messager the feeling that everyone was an artist in some capacity or another. She may have been more keenly attuned to the art around her because her father was an amateur painter and photographer. He took her on walks to nearby churches to admire their architecture, paintings and stained-glass windows, and he encouraged her when she showed a shared interest in photography.

With the support of her parents, Messager left home to study sculpture at École Nationale Supérieure des Arts Décoratifs, in Paris. During this period, she continued with her photography interests alongside formal sculptural training as well. In a classic 'proud mum' move, her mother entered one of her photos into a competition sponsored by Kodak, and Messager ended up winning an enviable trip around the world, exposing her to art and cultures across Europe and Asia. When she returned to Paris, she found further stimulation in the entertainment

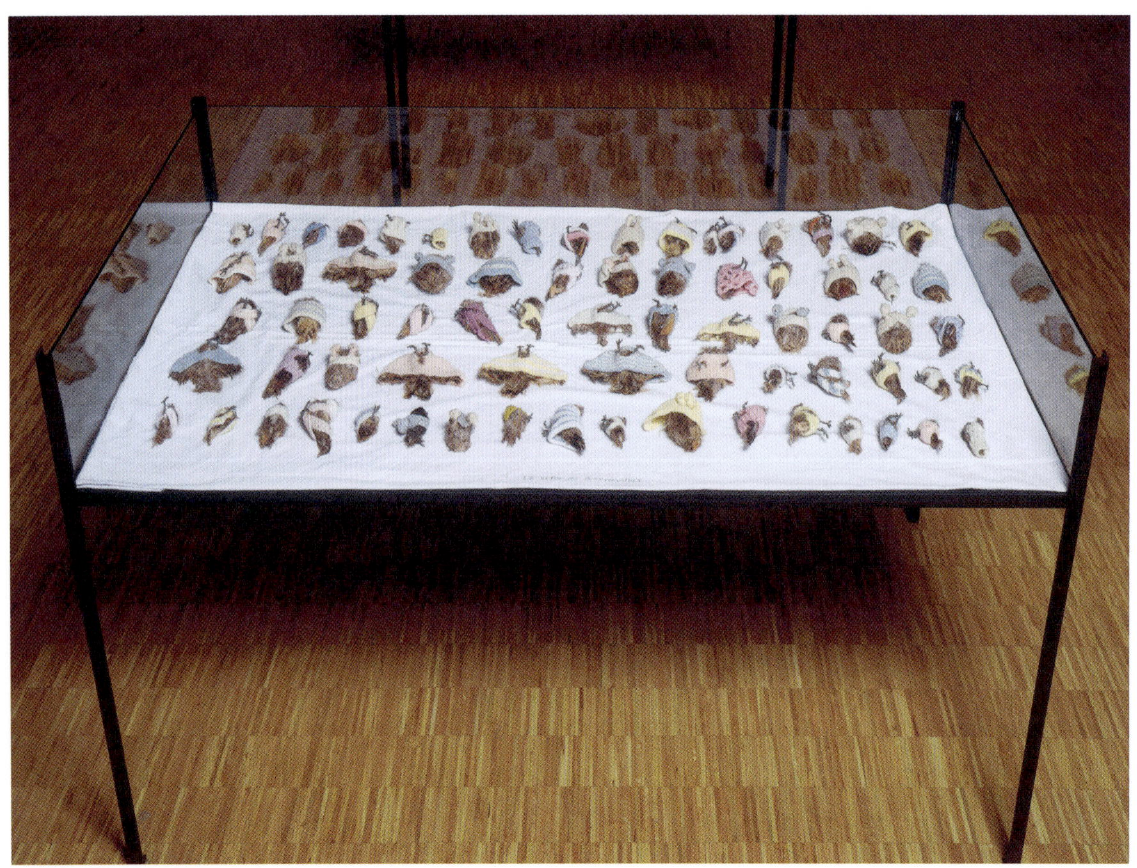

Les Pensionnaires, 1971.
Installation of 14 display cases, 3 murals and a bulb suspended
from a wire. Dimensions variable.

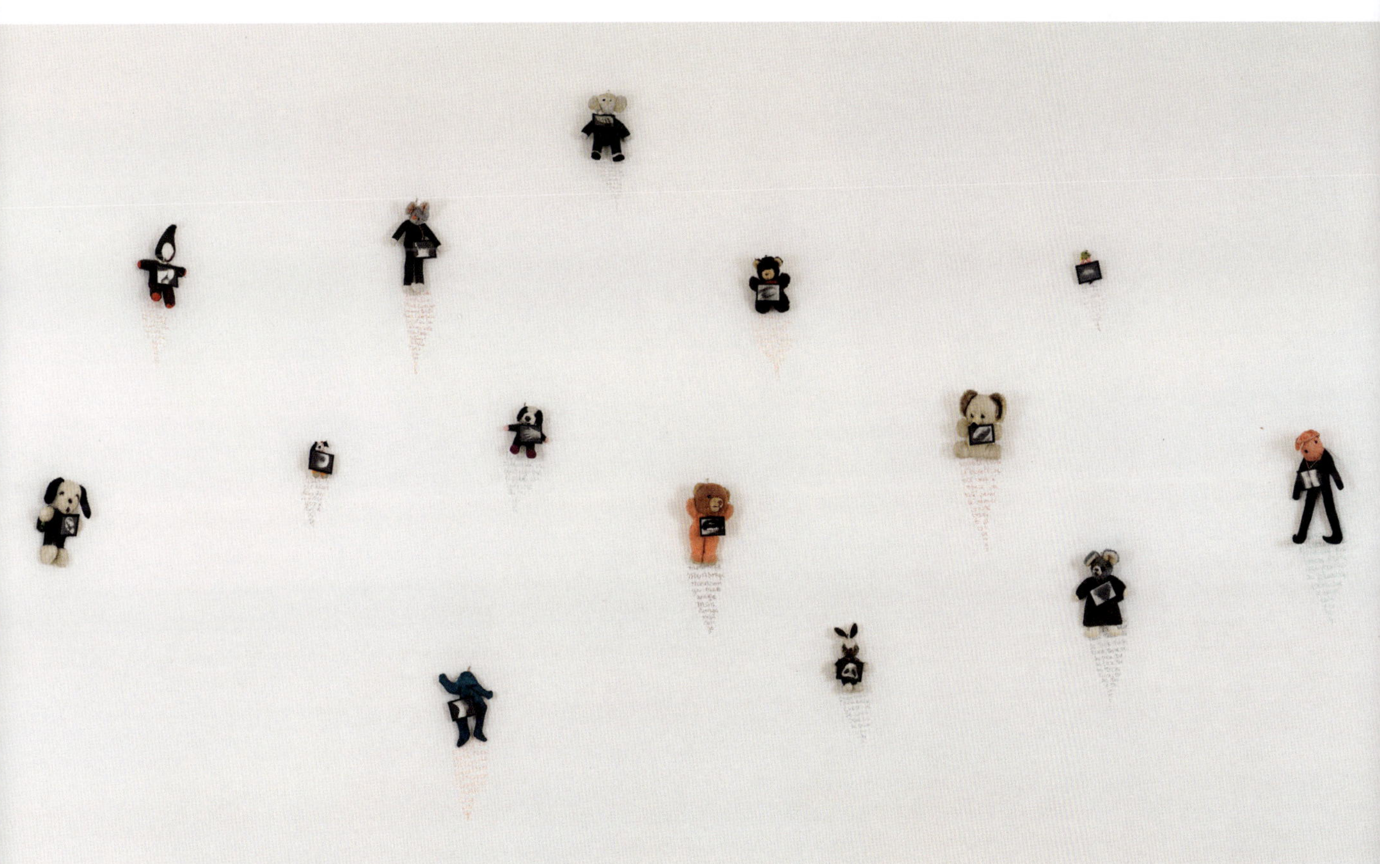

Mes petites effigies, 1988.
Installation of 13 stuffed animals and 1 fabric elf with framed black and white
photographs and writing on the wall.
Each framed photograph 6 × 8 cm (2⅜ × 3⅛ in), largest effigy 33 cm (13 In),
smallest effigy 11 cm (4⅜ in).

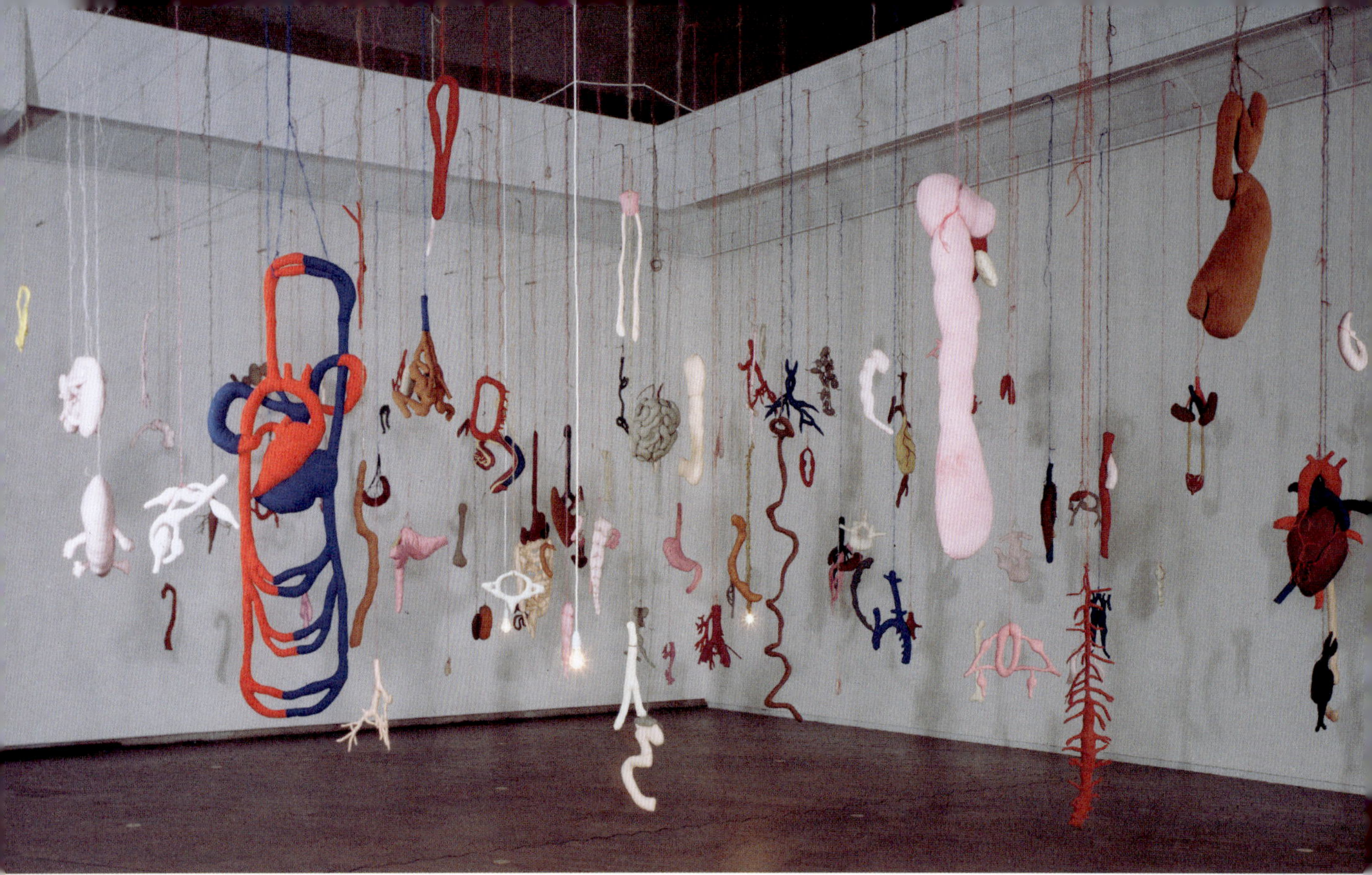

Pénétration, 1993–94.
Cotton stuffed with polyester, angora wool, nylon, electric lights.
500 x 500 x 1100 cm (196⅞ x 196⅞ x 433 in).

and museums available to her in the city – perhaps a little too much so, because she was eventually asked to leave school due to poor attendance.

In 1971, Messager was invited to exhibit in a show themed around wool. She answered the call by creating a sweet little knitted sweater to outfit an unusual model: a dead sparrow. This idea grew into a series of similar sculptures titled 'The Boarders', in which she posed taxidermy birds in assorted positions. There's a childlike quality to this act of dressing tiny creatures and posing them like little dolls. Each one dons their own knitted sweater, which has been designed to accommodate the shape of their body. The clothing gives an initial innocence to the vignettes that is quickly undercut by the overarching awareness of death. Laid out on a surface and frozen in motion, the stuffed birds capture a moment in time as a photograph would do. In this sense, these taxidermy works are a macabre cousin of Messager's photography practice.

'The Boarders' marked the beginning of Messager's use of taxidermy and stuffed animals in her work. The next major iteration of this idea came with her 1988 series 'My Little Effigies'. In these installations, she mounts small stuffed toys on a wall with framed black and white photographs hanging from their necks. Below each animal, a triangle of text hangs down like a pennant with a repeated word written in colour pencil. By incorporating everyday objects such as children's toys into the installation, Messager infuses the work with those items' social and emotional associations. This leaves the viewer having to reconcile the popular connotations of the objects with the unusual context in which Messager has presented them.

With her effigies, the materials immediately invoke ideas of childhood play before other darker ideas rise to the surface. The term 'effigy' suggests that these animals may be stand-ins for a person or people – perhaps in some sort of ritual capacity. This feeling is underscored by the close-up views of human body parts on the photo necklaces, which personalize each toy. Suddenly, the installation takes on a darker tone, wherein the viewer is left wondering about the relationship between animals and their respective photographs. One begins to wonder if the repeated word is some sort of incantation? Are the effigies imbued with the spiritual essence of the pictured human?

Messager's curiosity for the connections between spirituality and the body can be traced back to her interest in Catholicism – first stoked by early church visits with her father, and later by exposure to *ex votos* during the competition prize trip in which she visited churches in Greece and Italy. *Ex votos* are paintings or objects placed in Christian churches as offerings of thanks or to make a wishful prayer. These votives can often take the form of an object related to the prayer; for example, hanging wax or wooden body parts to represent a wish to heal afflictions in those areas.

Messager plays off of this idea in her installation *Penetration* (1993–94), wherein she suspends soft sculptures representing parts of the body in a gallery space, as an *ex voto* might do in a church. A viewer's first impression of the installation is likely the opposite to the initial cuteness of 'My Little Effigies'. The sewn and stuffed intestines in *Penetration* immediately stand out and, casting an eye around the room, one can discern a heart and other recognizable shapes like lungs. It becomes apparent the 'penetration' that has taken place may have been the cuts to extract these body parts. It's a grim thought, but through the bright colours and illustrative depiction of these organs, we are reminded that they are just stuffed sculptures, after all – only effigies of the real thing and as innocuous as a child's plush toy. She deftly walks the line between contradicting ideas with the installation, and rather than coming across a grotesque scene, the sculptures offer a surreal and playful look at the human body. Messager previously explored a similar concept in her two-dimensional work *My Vows:*

Messager's work defies succinct summary – perhaps this is why she has given herself so many elusive titles over the decades. Collector, Trickster, Peddler, Artist. The unconstrained breadth of her practice is what gives it such a timelessness.

Circle – Triangle (1990), wherein she hangs close-up photographs of body parts on a wall in a circle. In this piece, Messager's use of the word 'vows' in the title is another clue to the work's spiritual kinship with *ex votos*.

Messager's work defies succinct summary – perhaps this is why she has given herself so many elusive titles over the decades. Collector, Trickster, Peddler, Artist. The unconstrained breadth of her practice is what gives it such a timelessness, which is a quality of outsider art (that of children, untrained artists, etc.) that draws her to it most. Her receipt of the Golden Lion award at the 2005 Venice Biennale is a credit to her mastery of bringing the 'outside' in and her ability to successfully utilize marginalized practices and materials in the global arena.

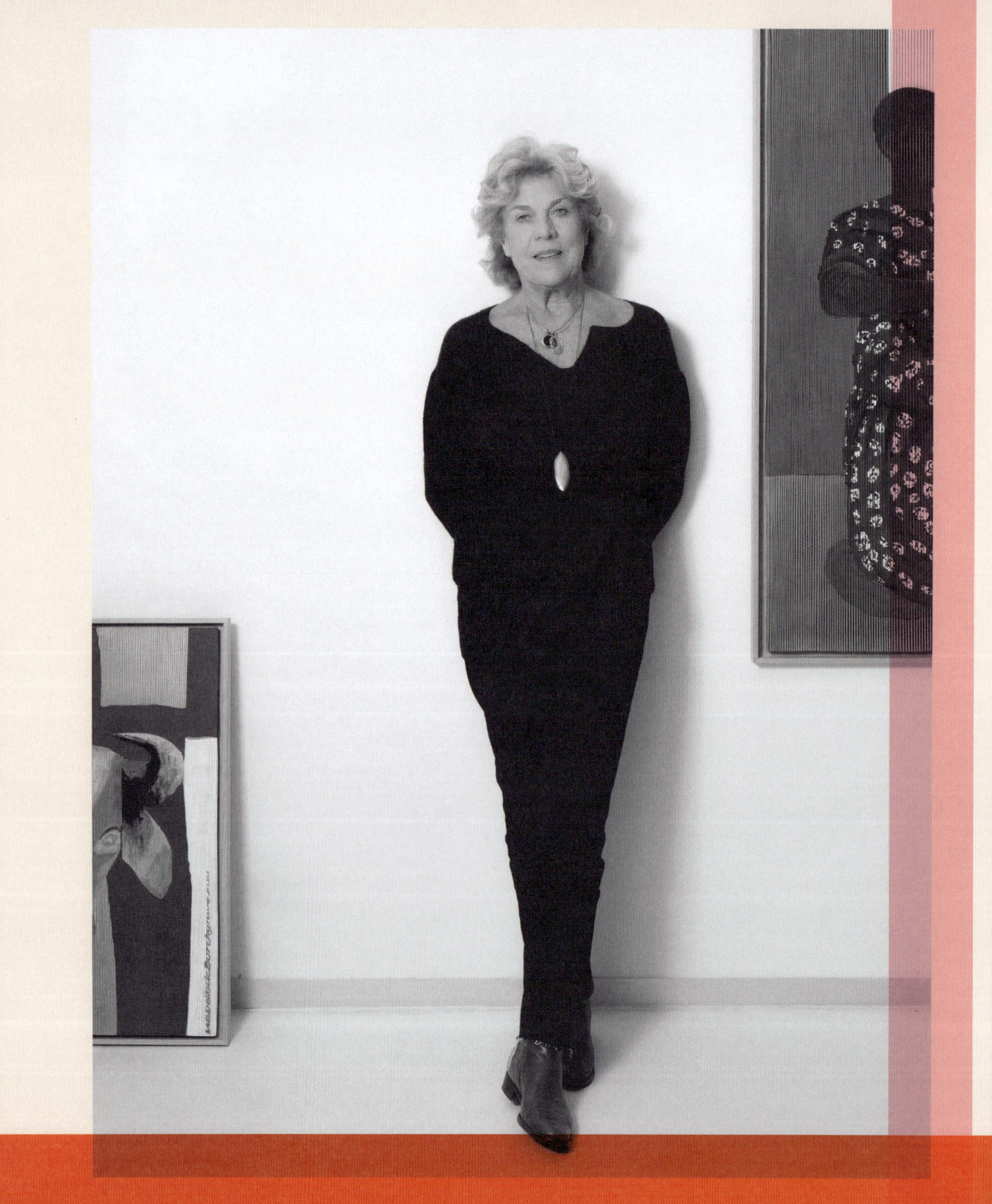

Isabelle de Borchgrave

(b.1946)

Wearable art

There's a saying in fashion for people who look good in whatever they wear that they'd 'even look good in a paper bag'. Whoever coined that expression clearly never imagined the incredible fashions that could be made with paper. Isabelle de Borchgrave may not work with bags, but she does use a range of papers – chocolate wrappers, for example – to make stunning painted recreations of some of the most intricate dresses in fashion history.

De Borchgrave – born Isabelle Jacobs in Brussels – spent her childhood roaming through nature and drawing as much as she could. Her family were very accommodating to her artistic interests, taking her to visit museums and allowing her to draw all over their walls. When she filled a wall up with images, they simply painted it over and she would fill it again. Her joy for drawing and painting was only matched in intensity by how little she enjoyed school. She sat in the back of her classes drawing to pass the days, but by the age of fourteen she'd had enough. With the support of her parents, she changed schools to study drawing at the Centre de Arts Décoratifs before continuing her education at the Royal Academy of Fine Arts in Brussels when she was seventeen.

After graduating, she rented a studio where she worked on freelance design projects and taught art lessons to children. Around this time in Brussels, there were several balls held per week, where people would gather and socialize in lavish attire. Teaching provided the money de Borchgrave needed for her studio space, but not for additional extravagances, like ballgowns, so she decided to make them herself. The garment construction was simple, but she painted the fabrics with beautiful landscapes, flowers, birds and patterns. Soon,

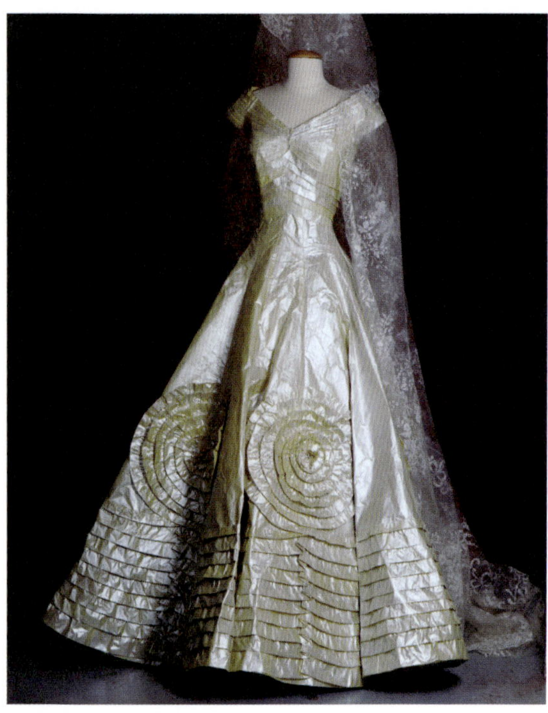

Paper Replica of Jacqueline Bouvier's Wedding Dress, 2004.
Mixed media.

fellow ballgoers were clamouring to have their own hand-painted dresses. Her business grew until she was able to open a shop, La Tour de Bébelle (Bébelle is a nickname for Isabelle). It was a five-story house with a shop on the ground floor. Different levels accommodated an apartment and dedicated areas for printing fabrics, designing and sewing.

Over the years, De Borchgrave's business expanded to include textile and furniture design, but the next big shift in her design practice came after a 1994 trip to New York. While visiting the city, she was hugely inspired by an exhibition on eighteenth-century dresses at the Metropolitan Museum of Art and a retrospective on Yves Saint Laurent at the Guggenheim. When she returned home, she began to create elaborate trompe l'oeil paper masterpieces from periods ranging from the Renaissance to the mid-twentieth century. Many of

these garments had already been a feat to construct in their original fabrics, and the painstaking process of hand painting, folding and moulding them from paper added another layer of difficulty.

De Borchgrave hasn't shied away from recreating some of the most iconic garments ever made. One impressive example is her rendition of Jacqueline Kennedy's wedding dress, originally designed by the woefully under-celebrated Black American designer Ann Lowe. De Borchgrave painted and treated the paper to mimic the shimmery effect of the ivory silk, and the result is practically pearlescent. After the painting process, her frequent collaborator Rita Brown constructed the gown, complete with layers of pleating and massive rosettes adorning the skirt. The paper dress was originally commissioned for Marshall Field's department store in Chicago before it was donated to the John F. Kennedy Library and Museum. The museum exhibits de Borchgrave's paper version in lieu of Lowe's original dress, which is too fragile to have on permanent display.

She was able to visit the original Kennedy wedding dress to plan her paper version, but for many of her historical dresses she relies on paintings for visual clues. She looked to a luxurious Rococo painting by François Boucher to create her version of a of a gown worn by the eighteenth-century French style maven Madame de Pompadour. Boucher's painting is an exhibition of excess, embodied in part by the yards and yards of silk worn by Pompadour. De Borchgrave didn't attempt to faithfully recreate the design but offers a close interpretation of the bodice covered in tiers of pink bows, roses trailing the hems of the overcoat and skirt and even uses paper mimicking the sheened look of the expensive fabric. Her knowledge of paper and paints shines in the uncanny realism of the design.

Another way of reimagining fashions from art history can be seen in her 'Les Ballets Russes' collection. In the early twentieth century, the founder of the Ballets Russes, Serge Diaghilev, commissioned cutting-edge artists, like Sonia Delaunay, Pablo Picasso and Henri Matisse, to design captivating costumes and sets for his

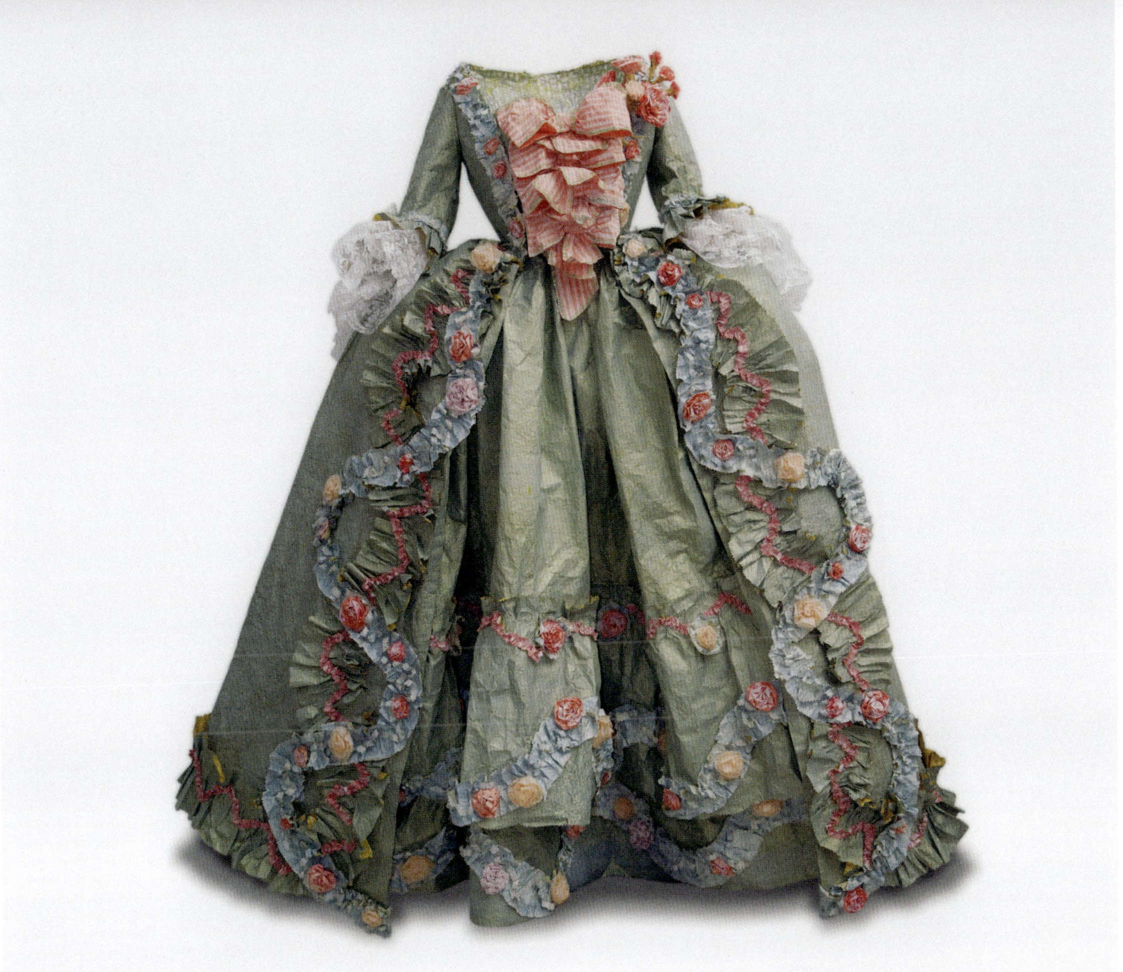

Madame de Pompadour Dress, 2011.
Paper, cut, folded, and molded with acrylic paint, ink, metallic
powder and adhesive, mounted on dress form.

company. De Borchgrave's collection pays tribute to the playful outfits these artists created. She once again looked to two-dimensional works for visual cues, taking her greatest inspiration from sketches she found in books.

The connection between her creations and the artists' sketches is especially clear in her interpretation of the 1922 'La Péri' costume, designed by artist Léon Bakst. The figure wears layers of boldly patterned fabrics, sheer bell sleeves and balloon trousers that droop around him. To display the Ballets Russes collection, de Borchgrave used iron wire to pose the figures in dynamic positions that convey movement. Her 'La Péri' figure strikes a similar pose to Bakst's illustration, and she brings the drawing to life through details like the ripples in the billowing fabric around the ankles. As with her other paper fashions, she takes artistic license in the execution, painting her own version of the ikat print fabric and making her sleeves comparatively more opaque (a limitation of paper), but the garments are thoughtful tributes to the originals.

De Borchgrave's works provide a transportive and immersive opportunity to engage with hundreds of years of avant-garde fashion. It's easy to be distracted by the fun and wonder of seeing the opulent clothing from paintings and history given new life, but it's important not to lose sight of the incredible skill and creativity required to execute these paper garments. Her work is a brilliant amalgamation of fashion history, art history and unmatched skill with paints and paper.

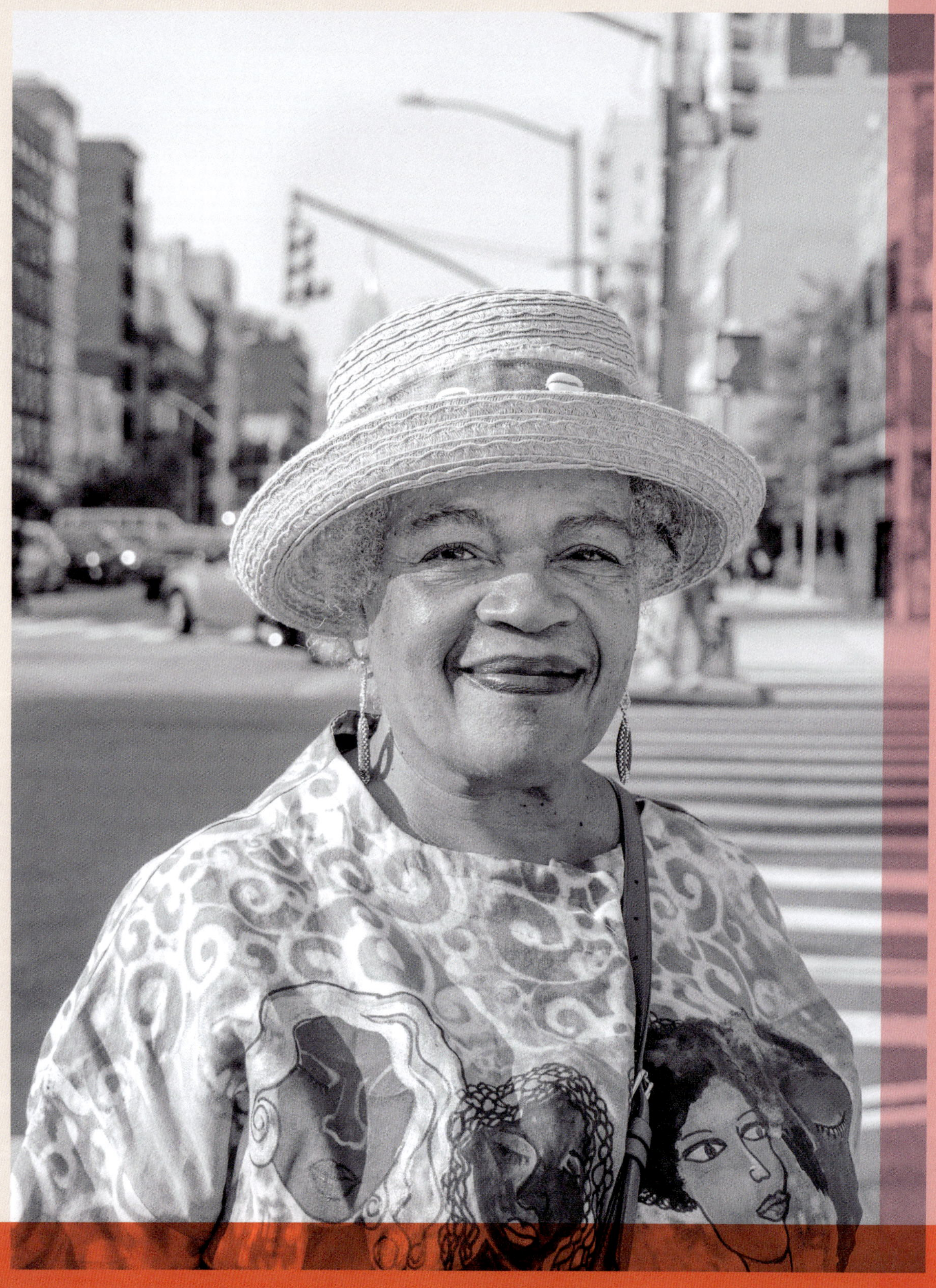

Dindga McCannon

(b.1947)

Quilting

Dindga McCannon learned and flourished through cultivating a creative community with other likeminded artists. She is drawn to celebrating the stories of Black women through her mixed-media artworks, and her vibrant textile works spotlight their incredible histories while drawing inspiration from traditional art forms.

McCannon declared she wanted to become an artist at the age of ten, and everyone thought it was an impossible dream. She grew up in a close-knit neighbourhood in Harlem, and no one in her circle knew of a professional artist on which she could model a career. Nevertheless, she knew she loved to draw and paint from her time spent copying comic book pictures and painting with a little tempura set. No matter what people said, that's what she intended to do with her life.

For high school, she wanted to go to a specialized school for art, but her mother would only acquiesce so far as to allow her to attend the High School of Fashion Industries. The women in her family were adept at sewing and needlework, and McCannon already had some experience helping her grandmother sew aprons to earn extra cash. Thus, her mother felt fashion was a reasonable compromise between creativity and stability. McCannon was among the first group of Black students allowed into the fashion design course at the school but was forced to leave after a year-and-a-half when she was met with a lack of support after failing a course. She went on to graduate from a traditional high school that, unfortunately, had no art programme.

After graduating at the age of seventeen, McCannon landed a volunteer job working as a teacher in Harlem while attending night classes at City College. During this period, she found out about a group of artists who were part of the growing Black Arts Movement, making

Portrait of Dindga McCannon

art for and about Black people. She immediately became associated with a group within this movement, Twentieth Creator Art Creators, who split in 1966. She and some of the other members of the group went on to form the Weusi Artists Collective, where the support she received was far more nurturing than what she was receiving at college. They even helped her with basic fundamentals like where to get art supplies and how to stretch a canvas. Only a few hours after turning eighteen (hello, adulthood), McCannon left her family home to make her way in the world as an artist, uninhibited. Out from under her mother's edifying eye, McCannon was able to join Civil Rights groups like the Congress of Racial Equality (CORE), attend protests and soak up the stories and artistic output of figures like Nina Simone and Miriam Makeba.

McCannon attended City College for nearly two years but didn't feel the teachers understood her needs and goals as an artist, so she left. From 1970 to 1972, she returned to her studies, this time taking courses at the Art Students League in Manhattan. There, she was able to choose her own teachers and she studied under artists she greatly admired, including Jacob Lawrence and Richard Mayhew. Her paintings during this period reflected messages of Black Power and equal rights, and aesthetically could have sat comfortably alongside the work of Lawrence.

Around this same time, she was once again putting her sewing skills to good use to support herself. One of the popular fashions among young Black activists at this time was the *dashiki*, which was associated with Afrocentrism, and she made and sold these garments for $5 each. These were an early precursor to the wearable art pieces she would make a little later in her career, and helped provide regular income between selling larger artworks.

By the 1970s, McCannon was a single mother and had been navigating the art world for several years. She came to realize that while there were many shared issues among the Black artists in her circle, her experiences as a Black *woman* were different from that of her male counterparts. She had to defend her right to make art as a woman, she had to defend her freedoms as a Black American, and she had to struggle to make ends meet as a single mother. It was a tiring and often thankless battle. She took these thoughts to fellow artists Kay Brown and Faith Ringgold, and in 1971, they started the collective Where We At, Black Women Artists. This developed into a sisterhood of women who exhibited together, taught workshops and even babysat for each other. The same year they founded the collective, Brown's mother died. She asked McCannon if she could make a memorial art piece from a collection of her mother's belongings, and this became McCannon's art quilt.

'One of my major focuses is on the history of African American women … I usually choose to do works about people whose lives are very interesting – women especially who have overcome all kinds of obstacles to succeed in whatever field that they succeeded in … They're things that people don't necessarily know, so I'm educating and just putting out our history.'

Although McCannon created her first quilt in the 1970s, painting and printmaking were her primary modes of expression through the late 1990s. She had a growing interest in producing textile works during the 1980s but was discouraged by the cold reception galleries still gave the medium. In 1998, she exhibited her first quilt in a museum as part of the *Spirit of the Cloth: Contemporary African American Quilts* show at the American Craft Museum in New York. She was buoyed to see that perceptions around quiltmaking in the art world were broadening, and her own quilt practice expanded. Her piece for the exhibition was *The Wedding Party: The History of Our Nation is Really the Story of Families*, depicting the complex social dynamics that take place at family events.

Most of the figures look out of the picture plane, while a woman on the left stares intently towards

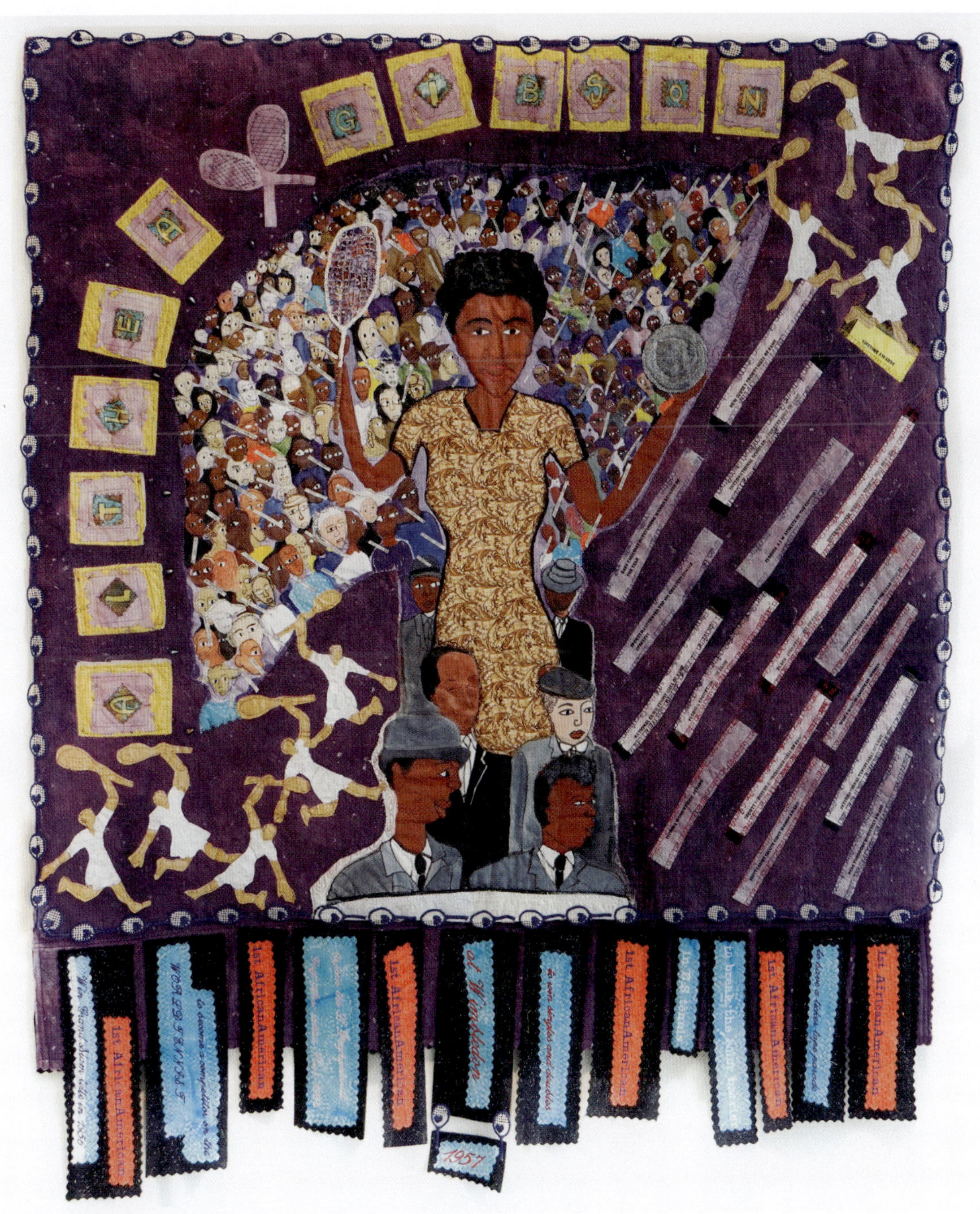

Althea Gibson, First African American to Win Wimbledon 1957, 2012.
Mixed media quilt. 142.2 × 121.9 cm (56 × 48 in).

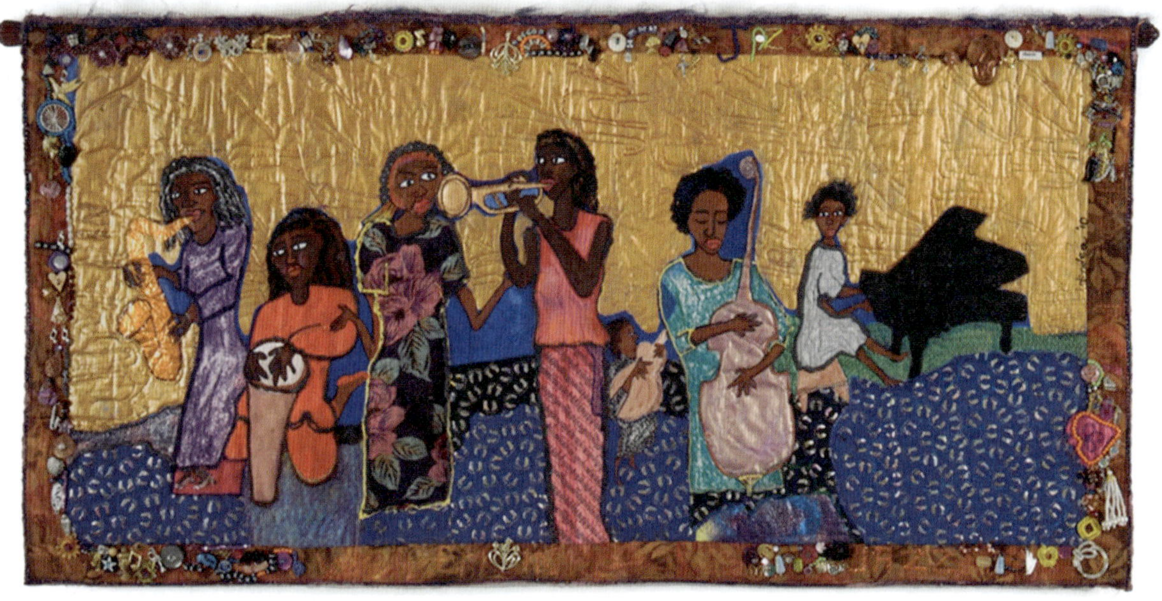

Art Quilt from 'The Women in Jazz' series.
Painting and appliqué over-dyed cotton batting, hand-dyed
cottons, vintage jewelry, charms and other objects.
81.3 × 114.3 cm (32 × 45in).

the group. It's unclear where she is looking, but her wide-eyed expression is familiar to anyone who's ever been quietly shushed by an elder during church service. To the back, two older women smile and look knowingly at each other, as if sharing a secret. The quilt, made through a combination of sewing and painting, represents a relatable image of a family coming together and the interactions that often play out at gatherings.

One mustn't get too comfortable with a straightforward label of 'quilts' when it comes to McCannon's work, because she experiments with collage and unusual objects as a part of these pieces. All materials are fair game for use and, in her 2012 piece, *Althea Gibson*, she even puts the batting used inside of quilts on display. Gibson was the first Black American to win tennis' Grand Slam title, facing challenges of racial discrimination

throughout her career. McCannon's image shows the champion lifting up a Wimbledon trophy and racket while, behind her, eight figures swing rackets in the air as if diving for balls they'll never hit. In the making of this piece, McCannon incorporated glass beads, acrylic paint, metal charms and even paper grocery bags from Trader Joes.

Community has been a major theme across McCannon's life and work. The Black women in her life have been instrumental in her development as an artist and, in turn, she has put her efforts into uplifting other Black women. When she couldn't find the support she craved from her male counterparts, she created a sisterhood. When she wanted better representation of Black stories in art, she painted them. She co-opts the tools once used to try to tame her artistic longings to express herself in a fearless blend of materials.

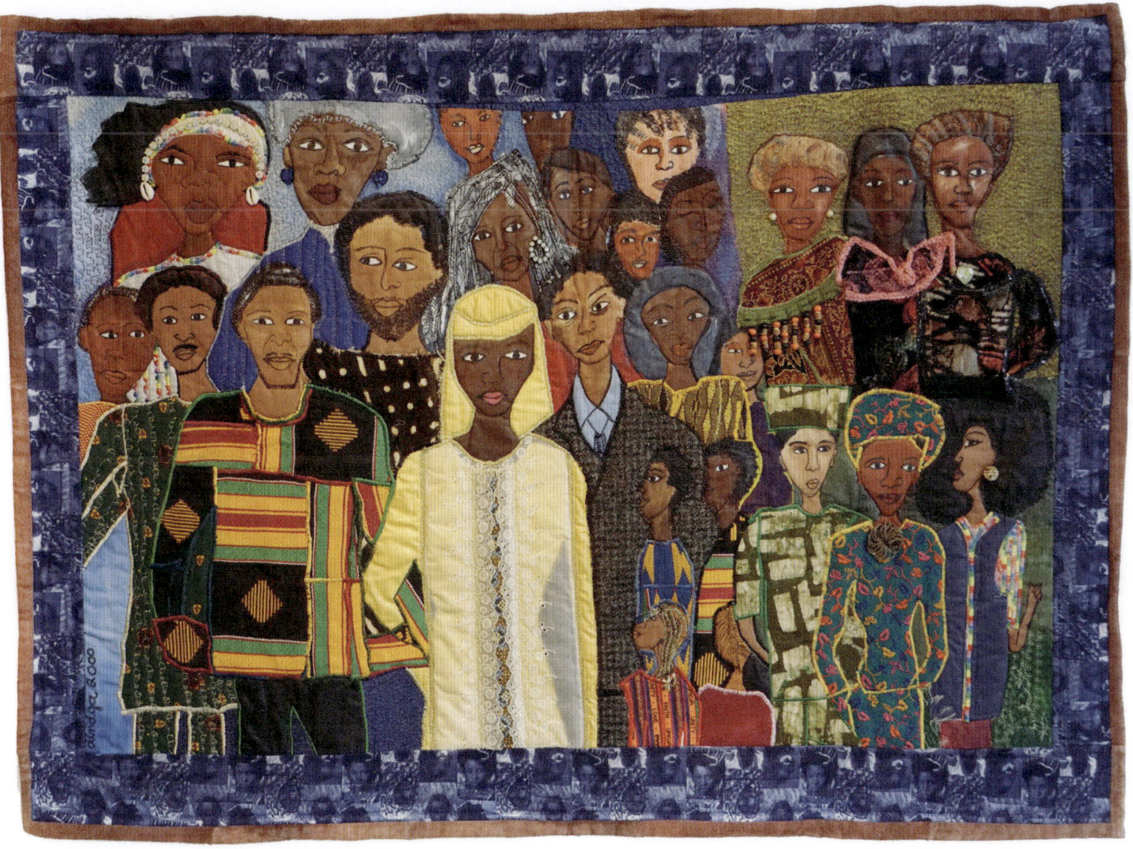

The Wedding Party: The Wedding Party #2, The History of Our nation is Really the Story of Families, 2000. Mixed media quilt. 88.9 × 116.8 cm (35 × 46 in).

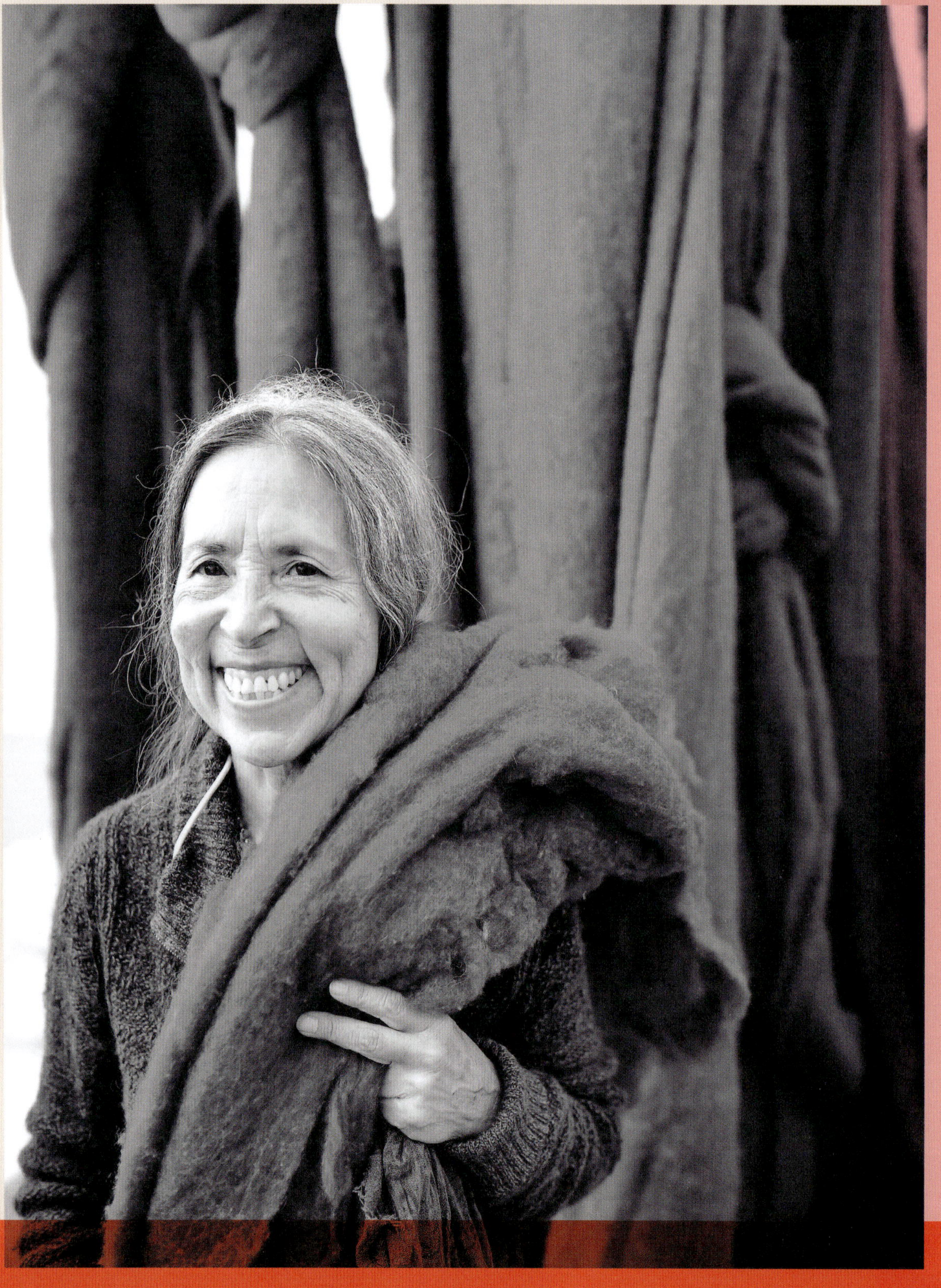

Cecilia Vicuña

(b.1948)

Fibre art

A surprising amount of information can be wrapped in a knot. Cecilia Vicuña's artworks draw on historical South American record-keeping methods and modern fibre art to engage with concepts of memory and its fragility. In the latter part of her career, she has become known for her colourful installations made with soft wool strips, but don't let the downy materials fool you. These are rebellious works that tackle tough issues, including South America's colonial legacy, the environment and more.

Vicuña's great-grandfather and grandmother were both sculptors, and one of her grandfathers was a writer. Not only was she born into a creative family, she grew up in a home filled with art books. When she wasn't engrossed in reading, she loved to write and draw, and when she was sixteen, her father gave her a supportive boost by building a studio for her in their garden in La Florida, Chile. With the space and freedom that came with having her own workroom, she began to create large abstract paintings.

After graduating high school, she enrolled in the architectural programme at University of Chile in Santiago, but later switched to the fine arts department. Even as early as her university years, Vicuña was producing remarkably sophisticated work. She created a series of assemblages from found objects called *basuritas* (garbages) and made the first in a long-running series of precarious sculptures (*precarios*) from natural and delicate materials. The latter are designed to deteriorate or be otherwise dismantled by nature over time. She was first struck with inspiration for the idea after a walk on a beach wherein she reflected on how all things are connected and impact one another.

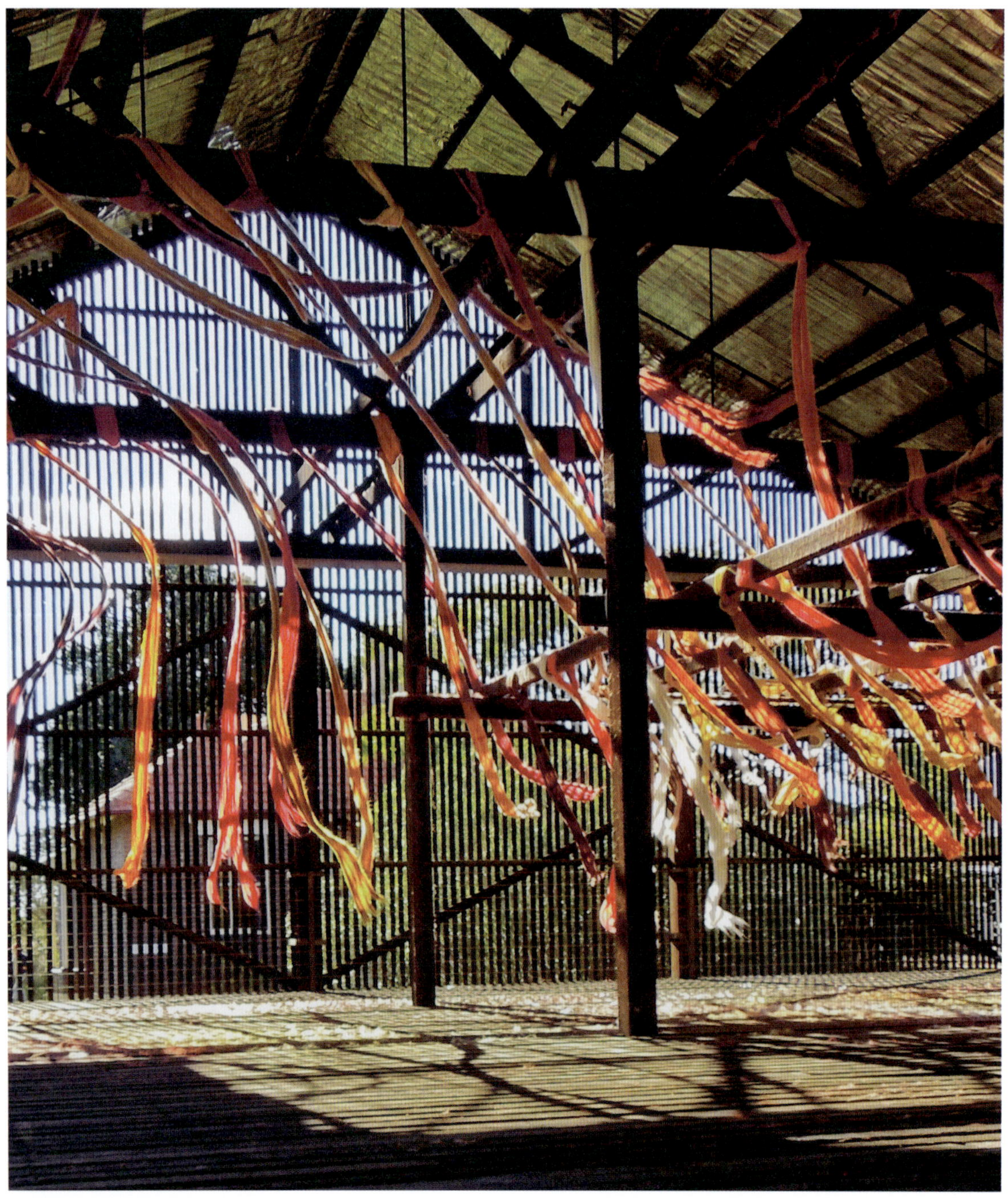

Quipu Austral, 2012.
Installation with wool strips, eighteenth Biennale of Sydney.

One of her first *precarios* was inspired by the Andean tradition of *quipus*, which are a system of knotted strings historically used to record and communicate data and stories. Vicuña's conceptual take on these devices was *Quipu That Remembers Nothing* (c.1966), in which she used an unknotted string to represent a *quipu* that bore no discernible information. Knowing the purpose of this string as a *quipu*, the viewer is left wondering what mysterious story it fails to tell and what information has been lost.

Concurrent with her visual art practice during this period, Vicuña founded a collective of artists and writers called Tribu No and wrote the group's manifesto. They would perform happenings throughout Santiago and publish poetry and other writings. Maintaining these three threads of writing, performance and visual art would be a continual theme throughout her life.

She went on to complete her MFA at the University of Chile in 1971 and held her first two solo exhibitions at the National Museum of Fine Arts, Santiago, that same year. Off the back of her strong portfolio, she earned a scholarship from the British Council to study painting at the Slade School of Fine Art in London. During her time there, her life was forever changed when the president of Chile, Salvador Allende, was ousted in a military coup – she has lived in exile from her home country ever since. She co-founded Artists for Democracy in 1974 to draw attention to the political crisis in Chile and began creating works that engage with those issues. In the years that followed, Vicuña moved to Bogotá, Colombia, and travelled throughout South America before eventually settling in New York.

Throughout the 1970s and 1980s, Vicuña periodically revisited the concept of *quipus*, albeit on a much smaller scale than the installations she would eventually create. A photograph of her 1989 piece, *Quipu in the Gutter,* depicts a mass of knotted yellow, pink and red fibres splayed along the edge of a New York sidewalk. The documentation of works like these is important to their preservation, as they are knowingly subjected to damage from

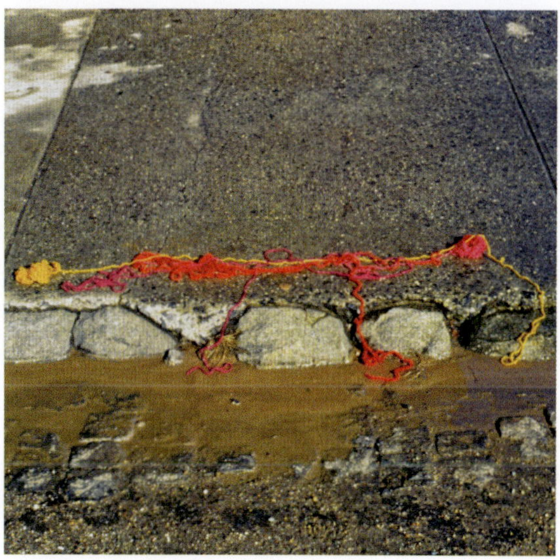

Quipu in the gutter, 1989.
Street installation with thread, New York.

the elements and – in this case – passers-by. Once again, where a traditional *quipu* should provide information, Vicuña's raises questions around what story the knots are intended to tell and how it came to be in a gutter. Memories – such as those contained within the knots of a *quipu* – are only as potent as someone's ability to remember them, pass them along and understand them.

In the 2000s, the scale of Vicuña's *quipus* grew considerably, and her works often tackled social or political issues. She created *Quipu Menstrual* (2006) at the foot of the Cerro el Plomo Glacier near Santiago as a way of symbolically voting in the 2005 Chilean presidential election. On voting day, she climbed the glacier and laid long, red wool fibres in support of the female candidate, Michelle Bachelet. As the title suggests, the red is a symbol of blood – her placement of the fibres next to the glaciers was intended to draw connections between blood and water as life forces, and to urge the government not to sell the glaciers to commercial entities.

Vicuña stages installations in a variety of environments, but she has increasingly become

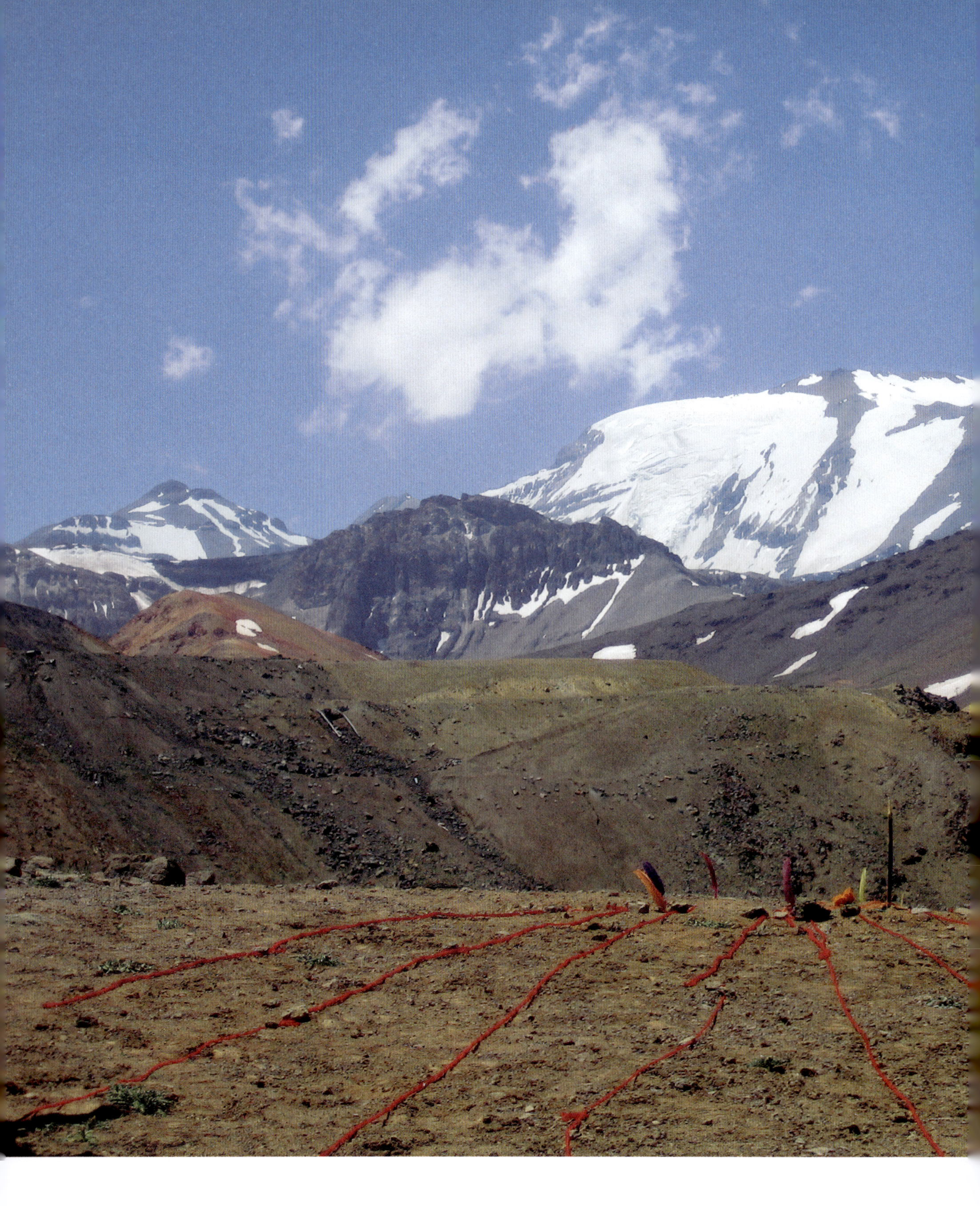

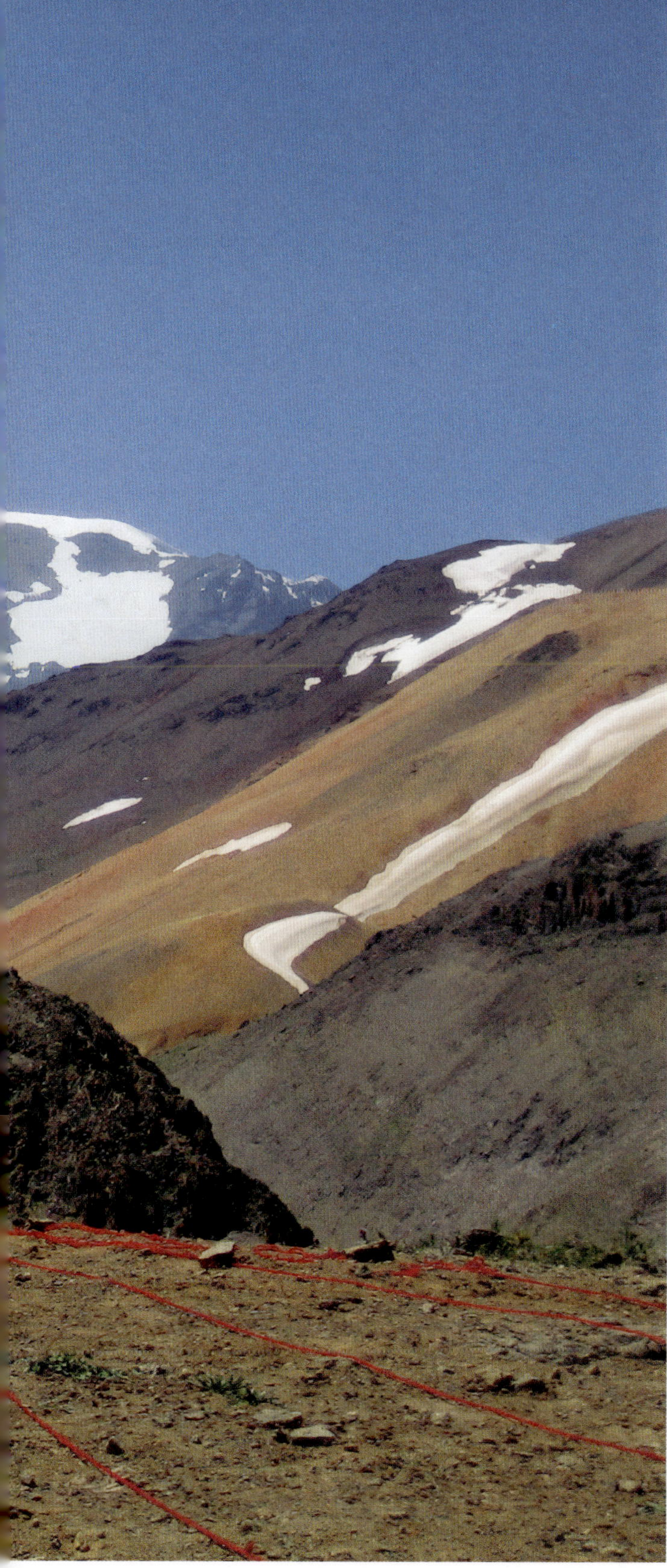

known for her large indoor installations. For these works she hangs long unspun wool from the ceiling and allows them to softly pool on the floor. Many are set in pristine gallery spaces, but in 2012, she created *Quipu Austral* for the eighteenth Biennale of Sydney in an old timber drying facility. Perhaps calling this an 'indoor' installation isn't totally accurate, as the building in which it was installed had no walls. The wool strips swayed in the breeze as a recording of Vicuña reciting her poetry played over a loudspeaker, elegantly blending her multidisciplinary interests in performance, writing and visual art.

The term 'austral', which appears in the title, refers to the Southern Hemisphere. In creating this work, Vicuña reflected on connections between the indigenous peoples of Australia and South America who were tragically impacted by colonization. *Quipus* are an example of the type of traditions that were lost or hindered by these interactions. *Quipu Austral* functions as both a form of rebellion against that suppression and a love letter to the art form. Vicuña was intrigued by Aboriginal stories and beliefs she encountered in Australia, and the similarities that can be found across indigenous austral peoples. In that way, installing this work in Australia was also about recognizing a shared experience. The fibres are left unknotted and unspun, as if in a state of readiness to receive information – the visitors are the carriers of the memories as they move through the space.

Vicuña's work addresses a breadth of issues with an equally diverse arsenal of creative tools. Outside of her fibre works and *precarios*, her paintings from the 1960s and 1970s depict fantastical scenes that engage with the multicultural influences that have shaped modern South American cultures, and she has published over twenty art and poetry books.

Quipu Menstrual (El Plomo), 2006.
Installation with wool fibre, Cerro el Plomo Glacier.

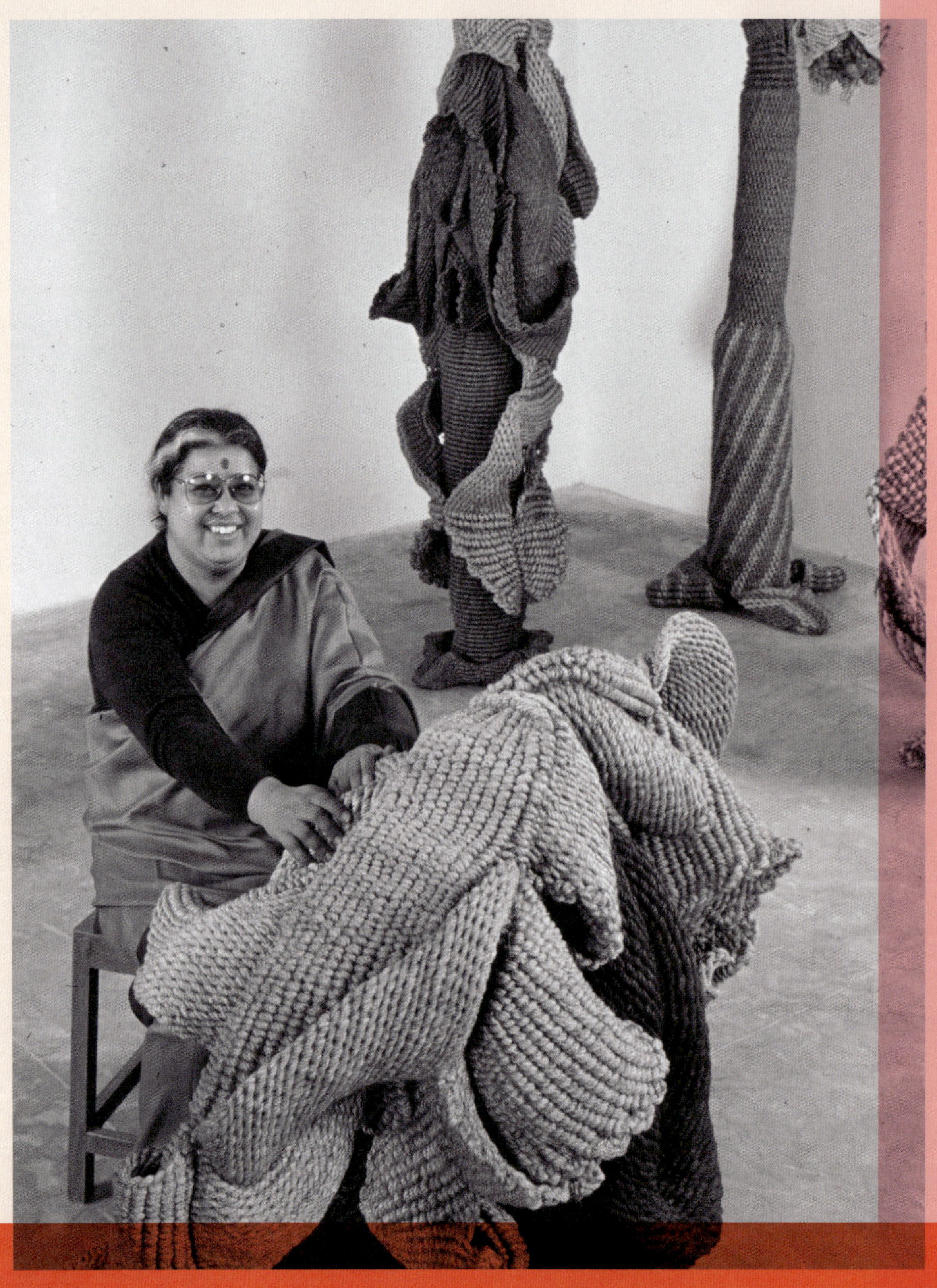

Mrinalini Mukherjee

(1949–2015)

Fibre art, Soft sculpture, Ceramics

Mrinalini Mukherjee combined imagery from nature, religion, and the body to create towering sculptures from natural fibres and clay. Drawing on modern and traditional Indian art, she created a pantheon of imagined deities and enchanting plant-like forms that are unlike anything else.

Artistic parents don't necessarily have artistic children, but in the case of sculptor Leela Mukherjee and muralist Benode Behari Mukherjee, they most certainly did. It didn't always appear that it would be this way, however, for Mrinalini Mukherjee. Born in Mumbai, she grew up splitting her time between the picturesque hillside city of Dehradun, in Uttarakhand, and the cultural hub of Santiniktetan, in west Bengal, where her father taught other artists. She attended the Welham Girls' School, and the extent of her art practice at this time consisted of making drawings for her biology class. Initially, she thought she'd like to become a doctor or accountant, which seemed like practical career options after witnessing her parents struggle financially as artists, but when the time came to select a career, she chose art. At the age of sixteen, she made this choice believing that studying art would enable her to continue living at home with her parents. Instead, her father sent her to study at Maharaja Sayajirao University in Baroda (now Vadodara) – there went that plan!

At university, Mukherjee focused on painting and mural design under the mentorship of K.G. Subramanyan, a former student of her father. Both men were part of a wave of artists working towards creating a modern art aesthetic that reflected a newly independent India (India had gained independence from Britain in 1947). As part of his artistic philosophy, Subramanyan encouraged Mukherjee to engage with traditional Indian art forms and unconventional materials. This guidance led her to experimenting with rope and macramé. In the 1960s and 1970s, macramé crafts were gaining popularity among hippies and housewives in the United States, and instructional materials were making their way over to India as well.

Using locally sourced jute and hemp fibres, Mukherjee began creating her own knotted designs outside of prescribed patterns, which she then showed at student art fairs. It wasn't long before Mukherjee's hangings took on increasingly three-dimensional forms and more complex configurations. For several of her early pieces, she was inspired by the verdant environments in the towns in which she grew up. The shapes and colours of these works resemble walls of vegetation, with sections folding outwards and looping back on to themselves. Her final examination submission was *Bougainvillea* (1972), a lush wall hanging made from dyed hemp, jute, cotton and wool, with moss-like loops and knots of bright pink fibres cascading down.

After graduating, Mukherjee moved to New Delhi – specifically, the artsy Nizamuddin East neighbourhood. She moved in a circle of hip artists, architects and designers, and was able to secure much-needed commissioned work through her friendships. Success begot further success, and she had a steady stream of work throughout the 1970s, with many hangings taking her one to two years to complete. Some pieces, like her 1976 commission for the Mahatma Gandhi Institute in Mauritius, were so large that she had to enlist the help of studio assistants. When complete, this mural was a staggering 80 ft (24.4 m) high. At the same time, Mukherjee was also creating pieces that stood or hung away from the wall – a choice that placed her work more firmly within the realm of sculpture.

By the 1980s, Mukherjee had exhibited in India to great acclaim and spent a year living in the UK on a scholarship from the British Council. When she was once again settled in New Delhi, her sculptures entered a new phase – her vegetal, biomorphic forms were now anthropomorphic and otherworldly.

Mukherjee's choice to create representational figures in the round places her practice in its own category of fibre sculpture. Combinations of nature, divinity and the body were prevailing themes for the rest of her career.

She drew inspiration from sculptures of Hindu deities and laboriously created her own versions of towering gods and goddesses from knotted fibres. Some pieces look as though a divine being has just shed their skin after a hard day's work and hung it up to be donned in some future godly activity. They were relig-*ish*, but not religious – Mukherjee invented her own mythology, vaguely alluding to existing deities and charging works with sexual energy through depicting phallic and vulval forms. Her 1994 sculpture *Vanshri* stands independent of wall or ceiling supports, with a plum-coloured goddess nesting in a tree-like structure. As with some of her previous pieces, she depicts the figure's breasts and labia, but it's the clearly distinguishable facial features that counts it as one of her most distinctly humanoid works.

Mukherjee's choice to create representational figures in the round (and even some tableaux with multiple elements) places her practice in its own category of fibre sculpture. Combinations of nature, divinity and the body were prevailing themes for the rest of her career, although her work with fibre declined from the mid-1990s as her preferred materials became scarcer.

Mukherjee discovered her next medium of choice – cermaics – at an art workshop organized

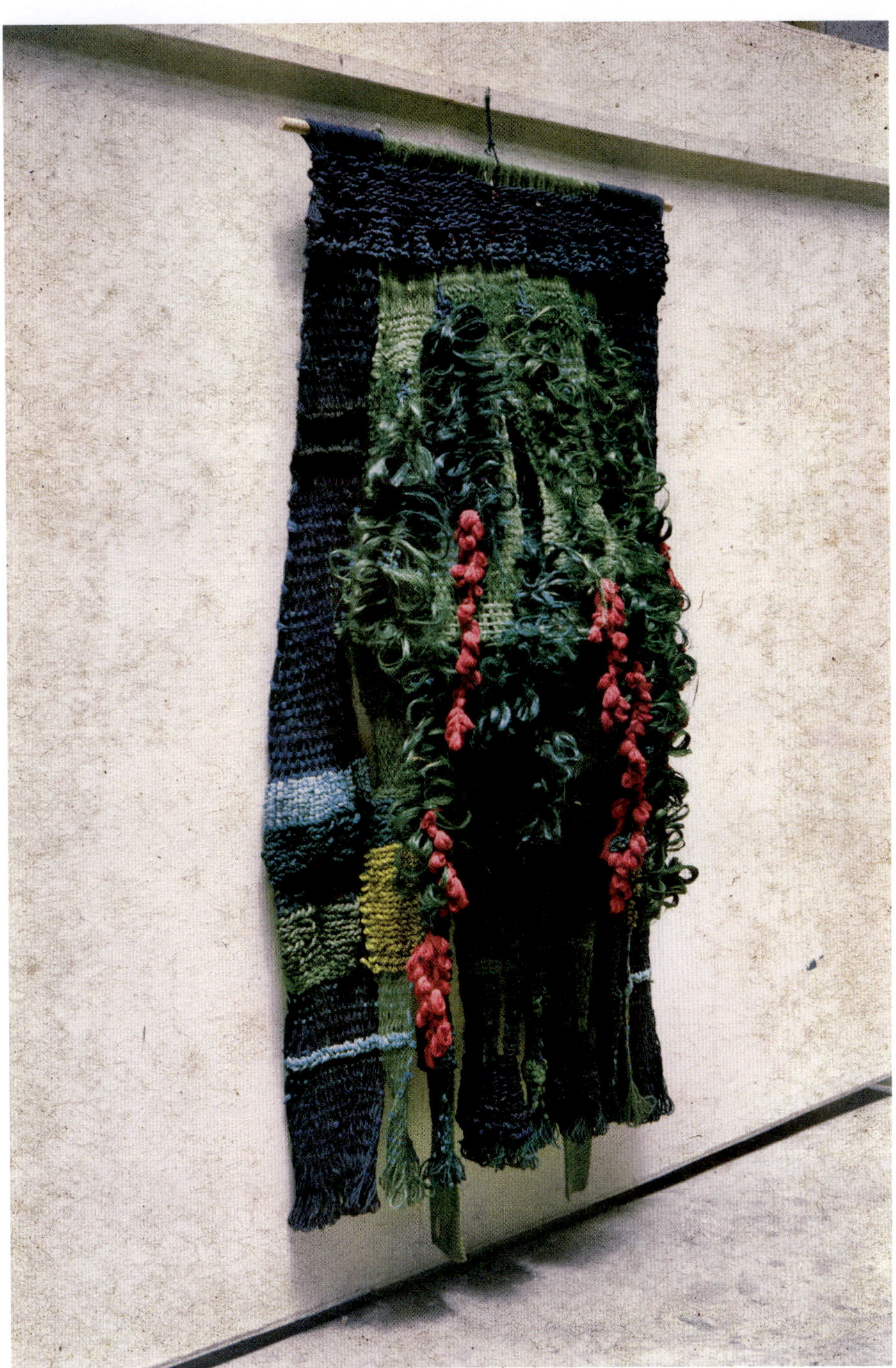

Bougainvillea, 1972.
Fibre.

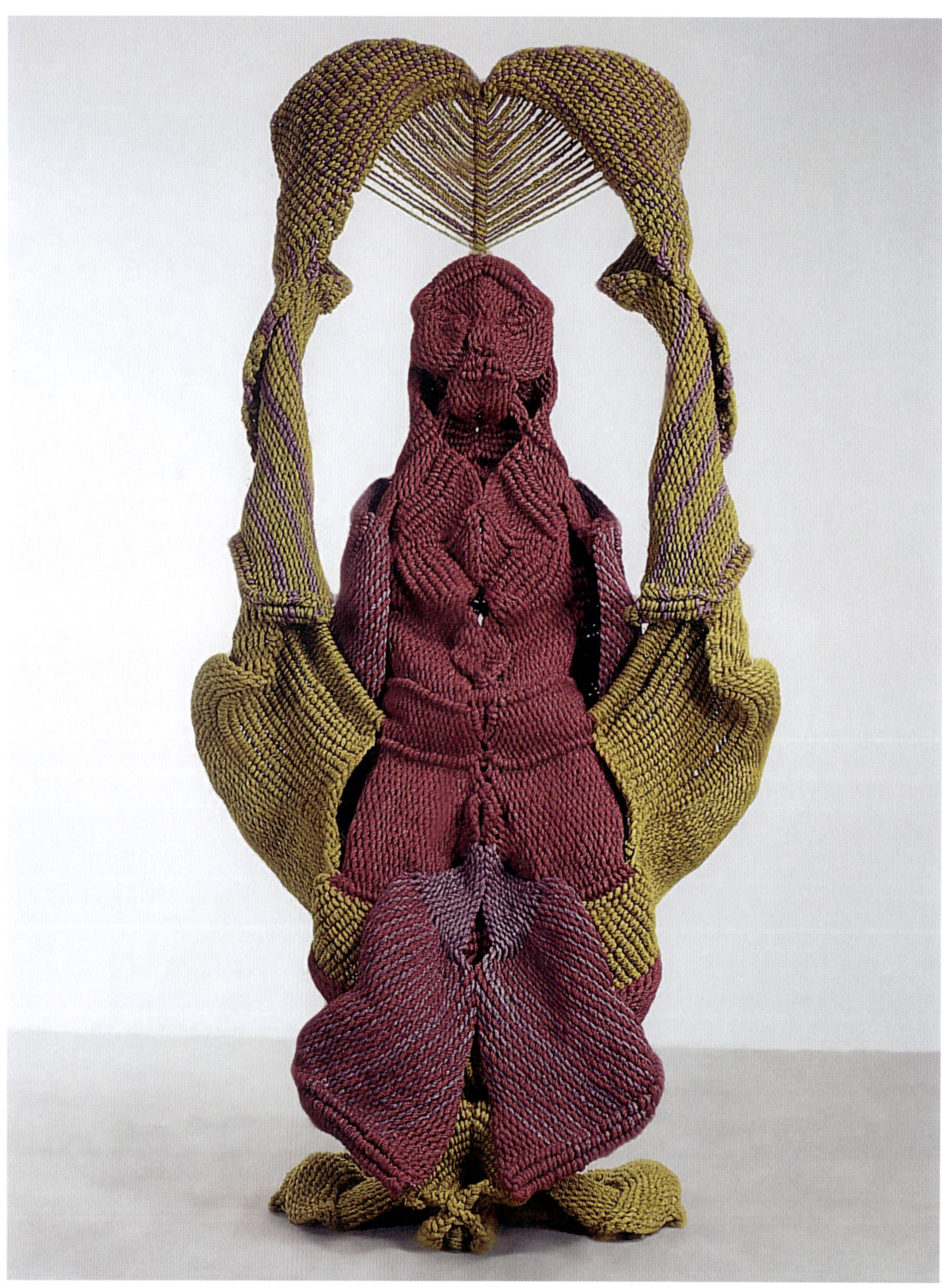

Vanshree, 1994.
Hemp. 250 × 130 × 90 cm (98½ × 51⅛ × 35½ in).

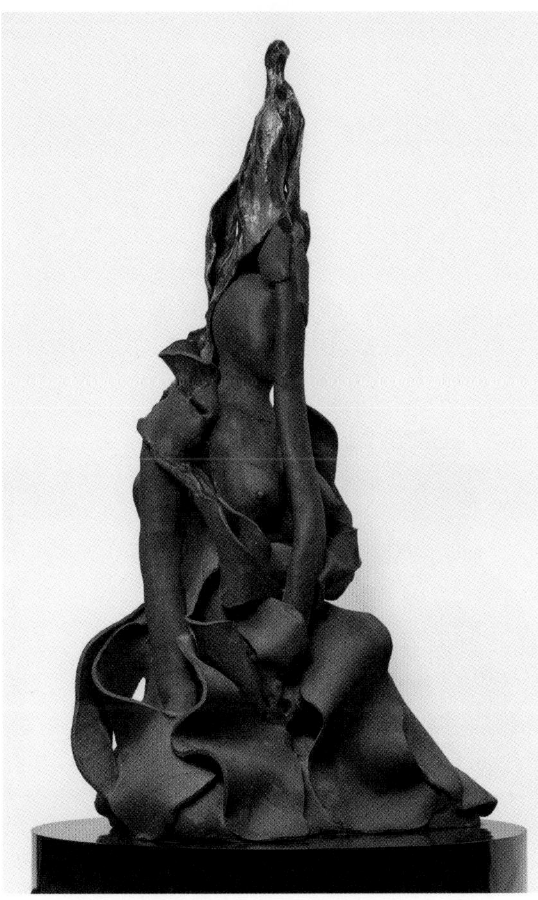

Night Bloom VI : 1999–2000.
Ceramic. 145 × 7 × 610 cm (57 × 2¾ × 240⅛ in).

by the Foundation of Indian Artists and Sanskriti Pratishthan in 1995. Following the event, she experimented with creating terracotta forms in a rudimentary outdoor kiln. One of her earliest works was a collection of thirteen domed pieces entitled *Lotus Pond*. Here, again, she blended imagery of nature and the body, with many of the lotus flowers possessing petals in the shape of sexual organs. In 1996, she did a residency at the European Ceramics Work Centre, where she was able to expand her technical abilities and experiment with glazes.

With experience, Mukherjee grew the scale of her ceramic pieces. In *Night Bloom VI* (1999–2000), she created another goddess figure, but this time from a mountain of clay. She sculpted the shape of the head and upper torso clearly, but the majority of the sculpture is constructed from rippling strips of clay. Her treatment of the material, with flowing ribbons and sheets wrapped into three-dimensional forms, shows that Mukherjee approached the material in a similar way to her fibre works. Works of this scale were easiest for her to carry out during her residencies abroad, but at home in Delhi, she didn't have access to large kilns. This is one reason she worked in bronze in the latter stages of her career.

Mukherjee died unexpectedly in 2015, one week after the opening of her retrospective at the National Gallery of Modern Art in New Delhi – she was only sixty-five. More than four decades of her career reveal an artist with a consistent and fearless vision. She didn't have contemporaries in India working with fibres in the same way, but she forged ahead to develop a style that merged India's natural materials, landscape and religious iconography with a modern, adventurous aesthetic. Her work is stunning challenge to traditional conceptions of sculpture and a triumph for the possibilities of fibre materials.

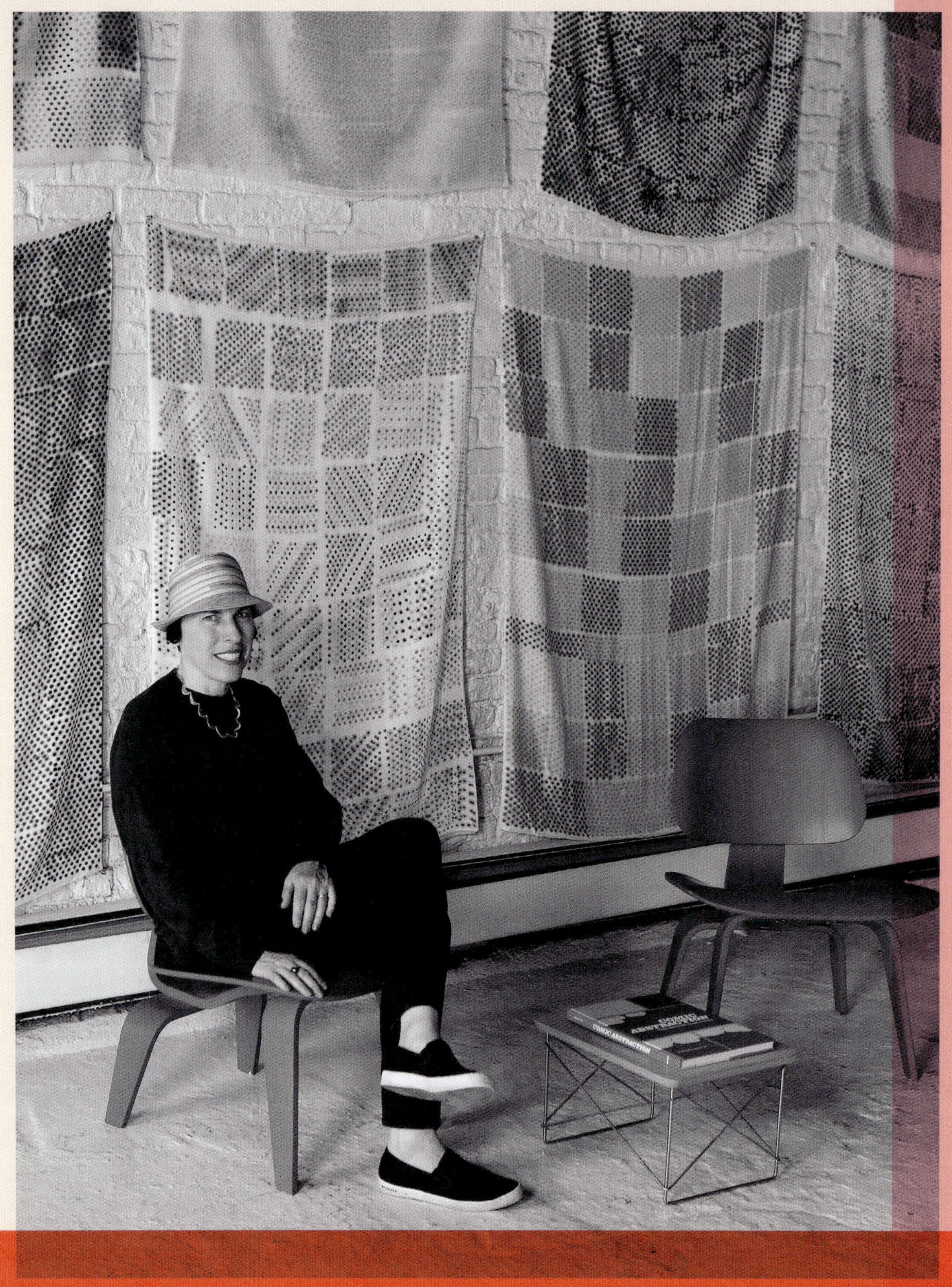

Polly Apfelbaum

(b.1955)

Ceramics, Textile art

Familiarity and fluidity are key concepts in the work of Polly Apfelbaum. She draws from a wide range of imagery – both modern and traditional art forms – to remix familiar ideas in new and irreverent ways. She is best known for her vivid fallen paintings displayed on the ground, but her endless curiosity has inspired her to explore weaving, ceramics, sculpture and more. Apfelbaum takes a flexible approach to her practice that is threaded together by her excellent command of colour and her willingness to be bold.

Apfelbaum can't remember a time when she didn't want to be an artist. Growing up in Abington Township, Pennsylvania, she and her family visited Pennsylvania German auctions and the Barnes Foundation in Philadelphia, where they would take in artworks ranging from Matisse paintings to traditional quilts and tapestries. At the auctions, her parents purchased drawings, ceramics and other folk art pieces, filling their home with the objects they collected. As a child, Apfelbaum loved to sit on her own and draw, and in high school she was able to try other mediums, like ceramics, as well. She cites her dyslexia as one possible reason she was particularly enamoured with drawing. Having always been surrounded by art, the prospect of becoming an artist seemed perfectly attainable, so when the time came to go to university, she chose an art school.

Initially, Apfelbaum enrolled in SUNY Purchase, a recently established school for the arts that she recalls being a great environment, if not 'a little too sophisticated' for her. She eventually decided to transfer to Tyler School of Art, which was a better fit and a convenient ten minutes away from where she grew up. During her junior year, she ventured very far from home for a year, studying abroad in Rome before returning to finish her final year at Tyler. It was her first taste of living in a big city and, after graduating in 1978, she moved to another metropolis: New York.

During her studies, Apfelbaum studied printmaking, but in New York she became increasingly interested in painting. At this time, the Pattern and Decoration movement was in full swing (see Miriam Schapiro, page 68) and artists were also still continuing in abstract expressionist and minimalist styles. All of these movements swirled around her mind as she tried to develop and hone her own artistic perspective.

After struggling to find art opportunities in New York, she moved to Madrid for a year and created a new body of work. When she returned, she immersed herself in the cool, artistic East Village scene. She phoned a small gallery on 10th Street who agreed to look at slides of her work, and in 1986 she mounted her first solo show.

'I think the education I had was looking at art in New York, and living in New York, and trying to figure out how you bring all of these influences and interests together,' she says. 'At a certain point, yes, I was interested in drawing. Yes, I was interested in colour. Yes, I was interested in form. Yes, I was interested in abstraction and meaning and narrative, but how do you simplify this? With the early work, I always say it was like a group show by one person because I was just so excited by all this. I just was pulling it in. It was [like] school.'

In the 1990s, Apfelbaum had the idea to create what she calls 'fallen paintings'. These are fabric works displayed on the ground. As a burgeoning artist, this was a bold and genius move because, in a group show with paintings mounted on the wall, her work occupied space in the centre of the room. These works demand that viewers physically engage with them in the same way they would a sculpture, but minus the verticality. Apfelbaum liked the fluidity and changeability of fabrics, and enjoyed that they related to everyday imagery,

Apfelbaum thought of the pieces as being 'anti-monumental'. Monuments can often be tall, phallic structures and she wanted to create works in opposition to those masculine conventions.

like clothes piled on the floor. She thought of the pieces as being 'anti-monumental', and there were other women artists creating horizontal works around this time with the same concept in mind. Monuments can often be tall, phallic structures and these artists wanted to create works in opposition to those masculine conventions.

Apfelbaum also experimented with staining fabrics, drawing inspiration from abstract artists like Helen Frankenthaler. She poured colour directly on to fabrics and allowed the dye to spread organically, creating dots and circles in a variety of brilliant hues. In some paintings, the dot motif played on popular references, such as her 1996 painting *Wonderbread*, which visually references the blue, yellow and red dots of Wonder Bread packaging. She was taking inspiration from all over – the popular culture references of pop artists, staining and splashing of Abstract Minimalism, and the paired back forms of Minimalism.

She was also looking to more traditional art forms. She explored how she could lay patches of stained fabrics together in quilt-like configurations and made wall pieces of glittery flowers mounted in circular mandala-like designs (mandalas are sacred geometric symbols associated with some Eastern religions). These ideas later coalesced in her 'Powerpuff' series (2000) inspired by the *Powerpuff Girls* cartoon.

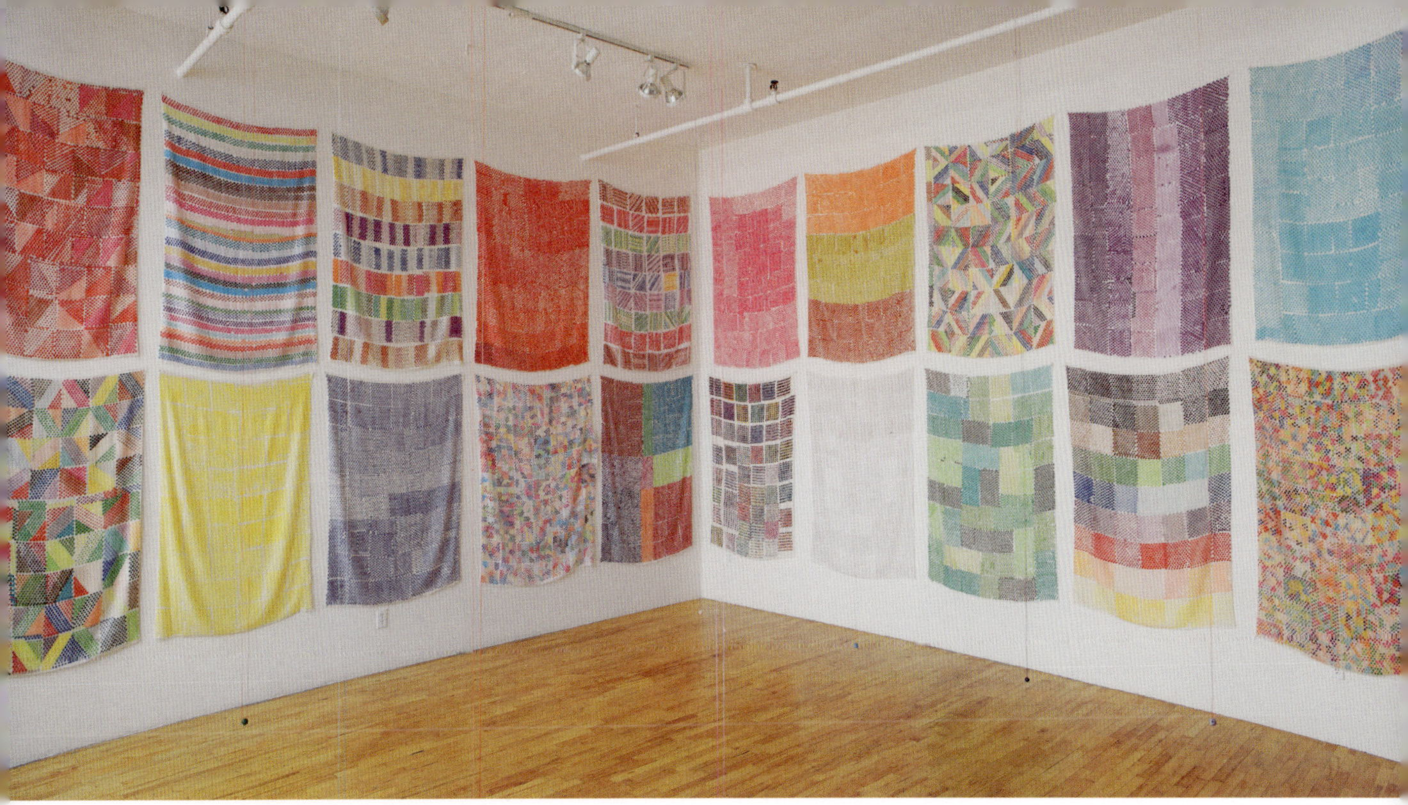

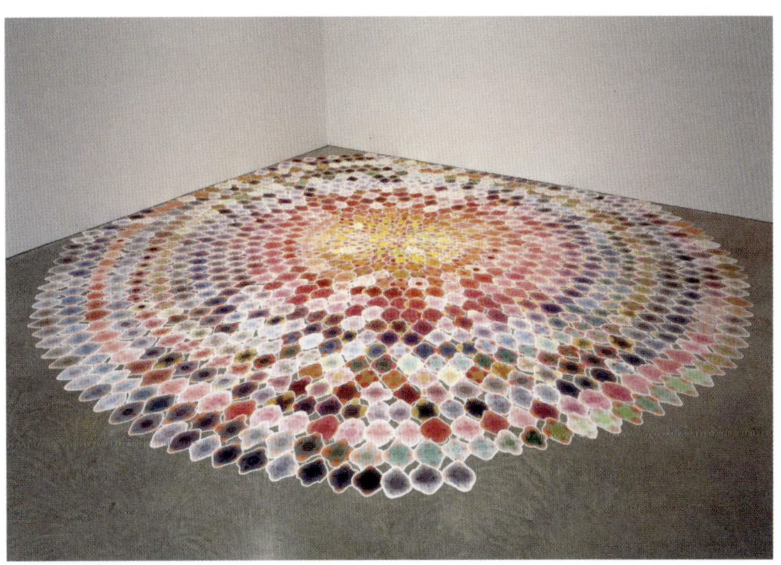

Hand weavers, 2014.
Marker on synthetic rayon, 50 sections.
Each approximately 142 × 91.5 × 1 cm (55⅞ x 36 x ⅜ in).

Blossom, 2000.
Synthetic velvet and fabric dye.
548.6 cm (216 in) in diameter.

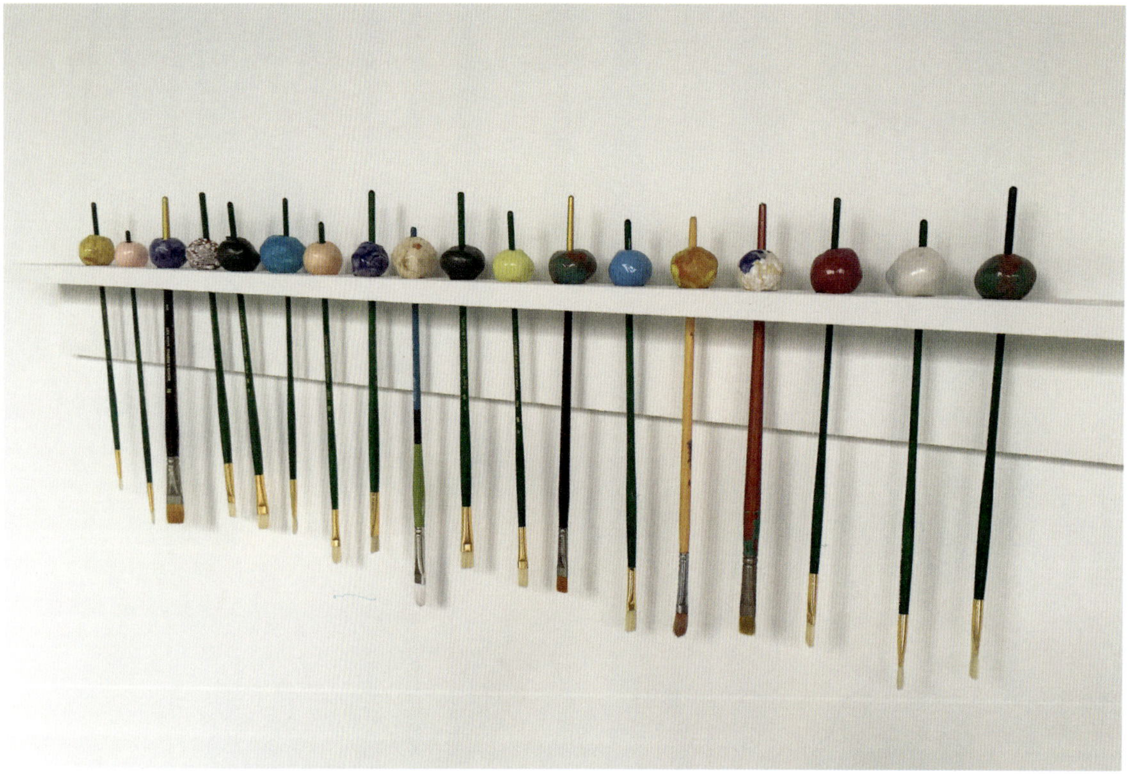

Apfelbaum stained diamond-shaped patches of synthetic velvet – one of her preferred materials – in colours matching each of the cartoon's three superheroines. She lays the patches in an overlapping spiral, forming an abstract portrait in the form of a mandala.

> 'I was aware of the history [of craft] and love the history, but also aware that it won't get visibility if it was stuck in the craft world, or stuck in different worlds … I was truly interested in all of this and making a hybrid language. I was lucky that was a dialogue people were interested in because I remember years ago, I gave a talk to a group of women textile artists, and they said, "How are you getting away with this?" I thought, "Oh, that so sad they're saying that."'

Over Apfelbaum's career, folk and decorative art techniques have come to the fore in her work. At times, she's thought back to the Pennsylvania German quilts she saw as a kid and has been curious to engage with other mediums, like weaving and ceramics. In 2014, she created a series of wall hangings inspired by the 1950 book *A Handweaver's Pattern Book* by Marguerite Porter Davidson. Rather than weaving the pieces, however, Apfelbaum used a plastic punch card and markers to replicate weaving patterns over lush white velvet in colourful dots. It's a collection with brilliantly layered points of inspiration. Punched cards were actually used in nineteenth-century jacquard weaving machines, so their use in these hangings is not out of place. The circles she stencils on velvet share a clear kinship with her early fallen paintings, but overlapping areas are also reminiscent of Ben-Day dots used in

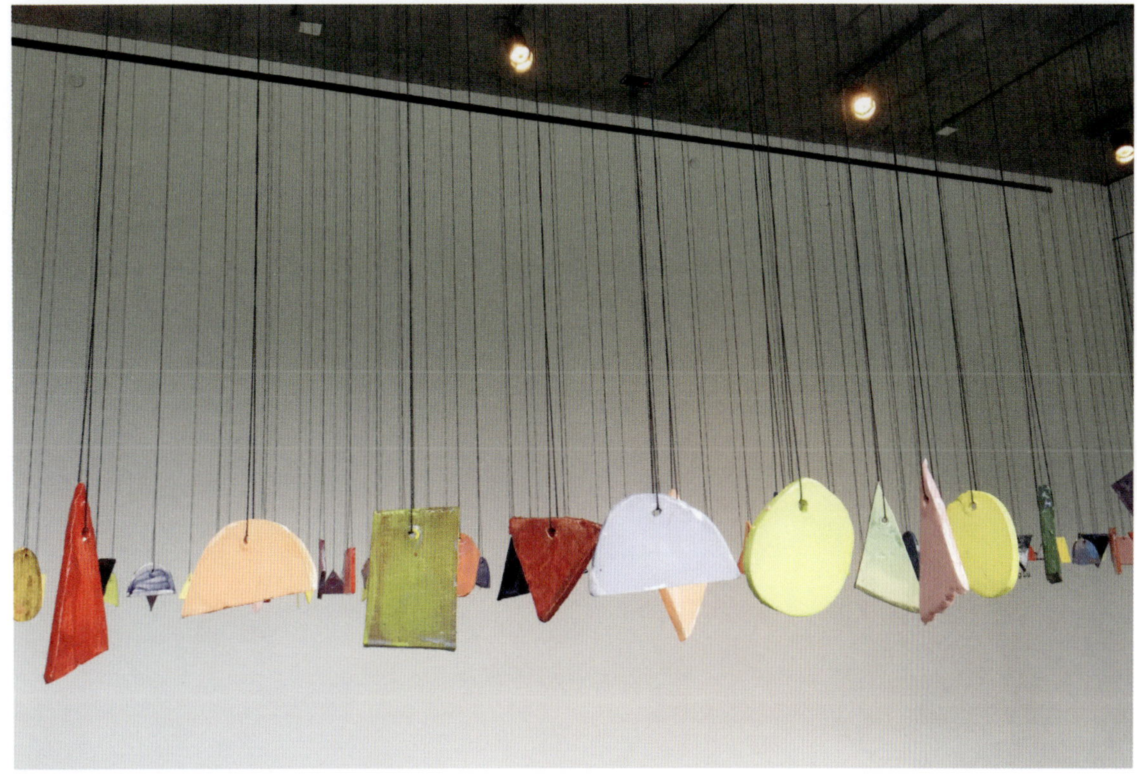

Above and opposite: *The Sound of Ceramics* 2016.
Ceramic, string, brushes. Dimensions variable.
Cohen Gallery, Perry and Marty Granoff Center for the Arts,
Brown University, Providence, RI, September 30 – October 24, 2016.

the printing process of some nineteenth-century newspapers and comics. Roy Lichtenstein famously co-opted this look for his comic-like paintings, and Apfelbaum's dotted weavings similarly create a 'pop'-ified version of the weaving patterns.

We've looked to the floor, we've looked to the walls, but we mustn't forget to look up to find Apfelbaum's work as well. For her installation *The Sound of Ceramics*, she collaborated with composer Wang Lu to create whimsical ceramic pieces she calls 'shape-notes'. Each geometric piece is handmade and suspended from the ceiling by strings. There are seven design variations that are intended to be struck with a small ceramic mallet to produce a unique musical note. The term

'shape-notes' originally refers to a popular system of music notation used to easily learn songs for social singing in nineteenth-century America. Likewise, visitors who engage with Apfelbaum's installation can swiftly learn the shape-note system as they tap the various shapes.

Apfelbaum's work is a multi-disciplinary amalgamation of ideas that is aware of the histories of art and craft without allowing those traditions to place constraints on her work. Before a viewer can feel too comfortable moving down a particular line of thought with her work, they may be upended by its placement on the floor, its pop culture references, captivating concepts, or any combination thereof.

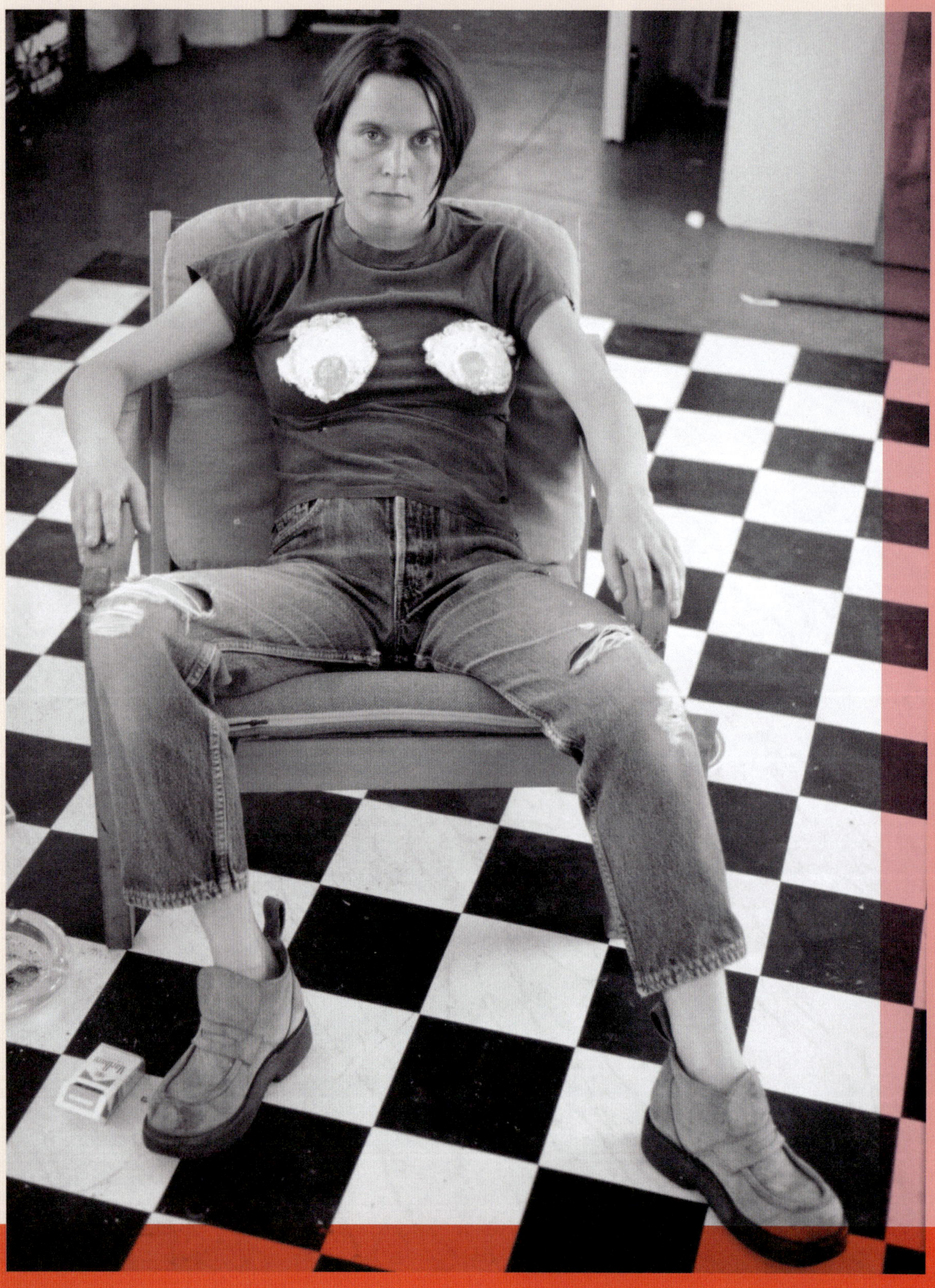

Sarah Lucas

(b.1962)

Soft sculpture

In the press, Sarah Lucas's work has been called 'rude' and 'punk' – labels often levied at artists with strong, irreverent points of view. But these terms oversimplify her practice. Lucas's career has been a constant exhibition of gutsy willpower, where she has asserted her artistic voice in a male-dominated space. Her installations and soft sculptures may appear playful, but Lucas is engaging with sexuality and gender in a thoughtful and provocative way.

Lucas was raised on a council estate in north London, where she played with the boys in her neighbourhood and learned how to curse without a true grasp of the impact of the words. She had no aspirations to become an artist at a young age and wasn't encouraged to devote too much energy to her schoolwork either. Lucas said her mother didn't allow her to do homework because she felt children did enough work during school hours. Thus, when she finished with mandatory education at sixteen, she left school to get a sense of what else life had to offer. She travelled around and was working at a children's centre for a brief stint when someone recommended that she try an art course. Lucas took an evening art class at the Working Men's College before enrolling at the London College of Printing and eventually graduating from Goldsmith's College in 1987.

The Goldsmith's art programme was awash with talent during Lucas's time there. Counted among the cohorts just behind her were other future art stars, including Damien Hirst, Gillian Wearing and Gary Hume. These burgeoning artists were an ambitious group who weren't afraid to promote themselves and put on their own exhibitions. Their

Self-Portrait with Fried Eggs, 1996.

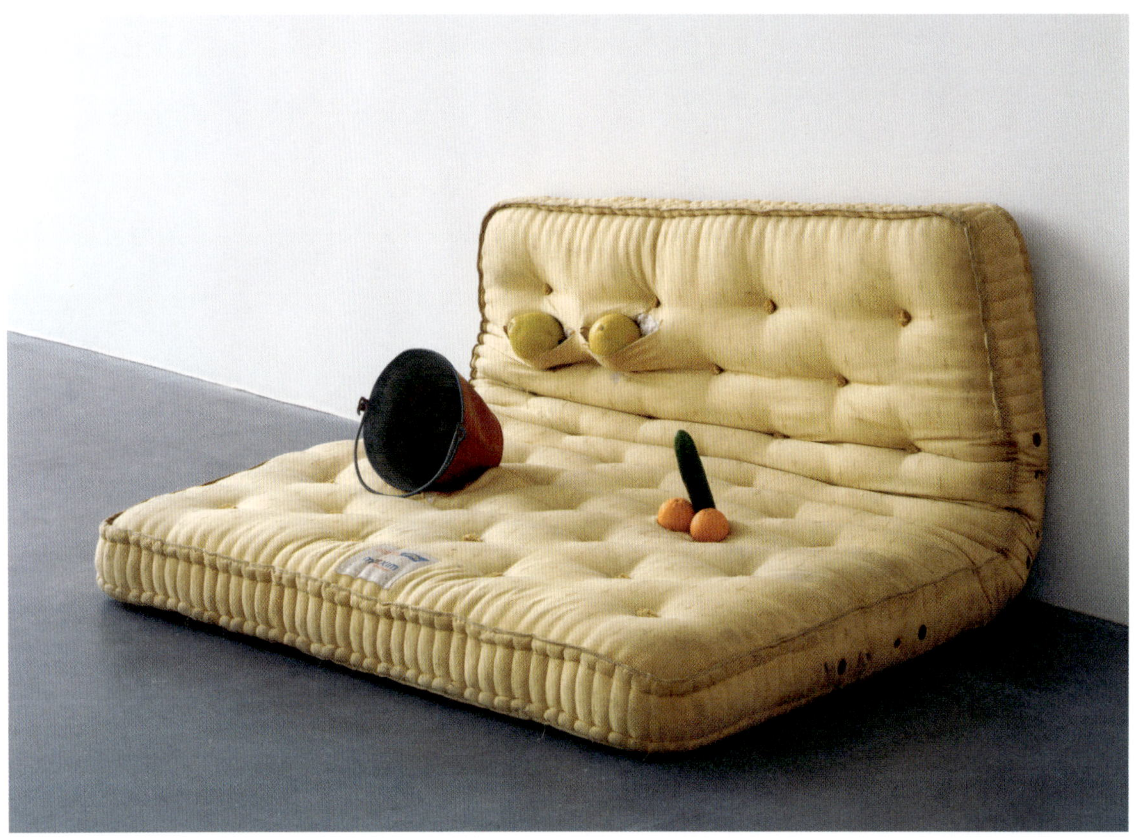

Au Naturel, 1994,
mattress, melons, oranges, cucumber, water bucket.
84 × 168 × 145 cm (33⅛ × 66 × 57 in).

first show was Freeze, organized by Hirst in 1988. A couple of years later, more followed, including *East Country Yard Show*, which was organized by Lucas and Henry Bond in 1990. Moneyed advertising businessman Charles Saatchi took an interest in the group's work and threw his financial support behind them. In 1992, Saatchi organized a series of group exhibitions called *Young British Art* and, thus, Lucas became associated with the nebulous band of artists that came to be known as the Young British Artists (YBAs). They were rebellious and oh-so cool.

This all sounds very exciting, but the attention the group garnered came with a sting in the tail. The male artists in the YBAs received preferential treatment from galleries and the press, while Lucas was often invited to events as a 'plus one' for Hume, who she was dating at the time. She was frustrated by this inequity, so for six months in 1992, she collaborated with fellow YBA Tracey Emin to open The Shop in Bethnal Green, London. The duo created and sold small objects alongside slogan shirts painted with edgy phrases like 'Complete Arsehole' or 'Have you wanked over me yet?'. The latter phrase may be shocking to some, but it boldly confronted the sexist attitudes they were facing in the art community. Lucas also started to read more books about feminism and sexuality during this time, expanding her views on these topics. Her

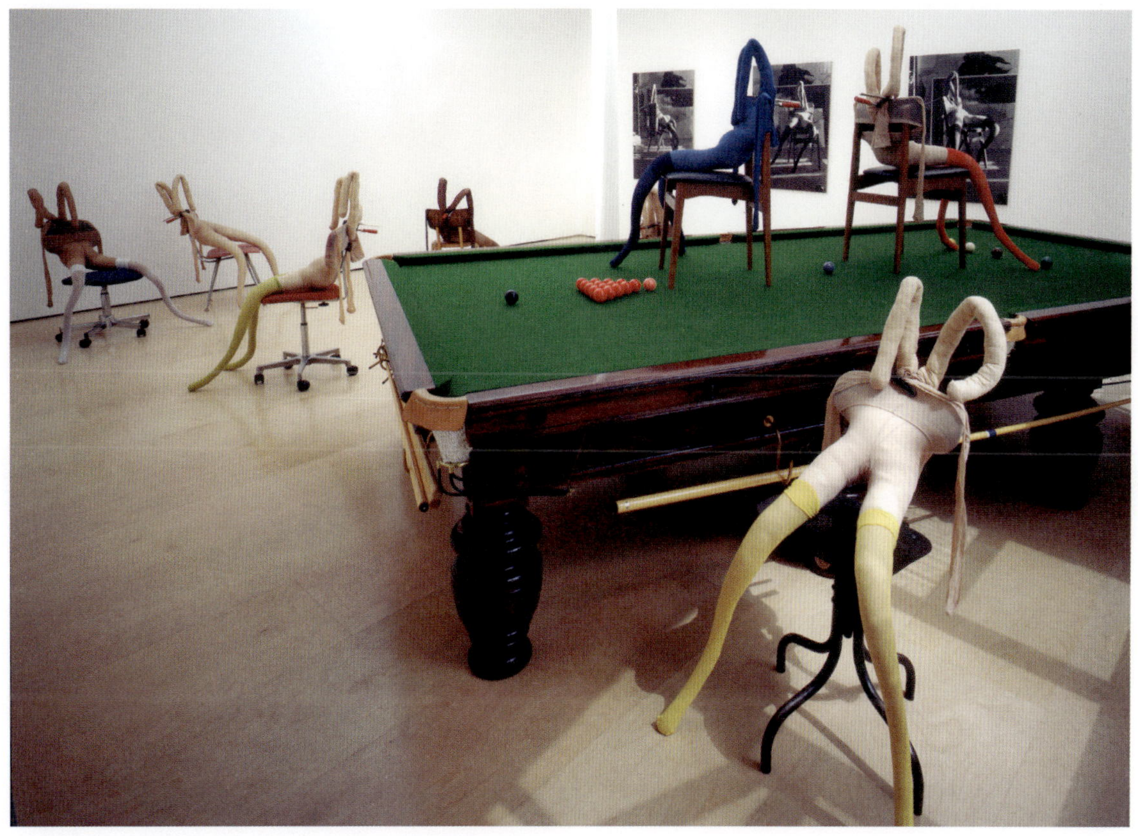

Bunny Gets Snookered, Sadie Coles HQ, London, 12 May–20 June 1997).
Wooden chair, vinyl seat, tights, kapok, metal wire, stockings and
metal clamp.
95 × 64 × 90 cm (37½ x 25⅛ x 35½ in).

thoughts and feelings swirled together and came to the fore in her work as she began to use found objects to create sexually charged assemblages that packed punch.

Lucas's 1994 installation *Au Naturel* combines food with a dirty tan mattress to create a comically sexual image. On one side, two slits are cut into the casing, creating pockets to hold two melons. Just beneath them, a bucket is placed on its side. To the right of the bucket, a cucumber is propped up against two oranges. Given their arrangement, the viewer may assume that the melons are breasts, the bucket is a vagina, and the cucumber and oranges are a penis. This assumption is validated by the title of the work, which is a euphemism for nudity. It's a double entendre that translates from French to 'of nature', which could also refer to the fresh fruit in the work. The used and slumped mattress in the scene is deeply unsexy, yet the arrangement of these objects on its surface certainly allude to sex. One could argue that the work is 'rude', but we all share culpability in that rudeness by interpreting the work's bawdy subtext. And what's so rude about sex, anyway? After all, it's natural.

Lucas's 1997 installation, *Bunny Gets Snookered,* displays a snooker table with coloured balls positioned for a game. Office chairs surround the table, and two wooden chairs sit on top, each with stuffed bunny figures slouching in the seat. The figures are constructed from stuffed women's stockings with coloured thigh-high tights worn over top. All but a blue bunny seated on top of the table are in nude skin tones, and their coloured tights correspond to the coloured balls of the game. Lucas said she was first drawn to work with tights because they're sexy, and there *is* an odd sexiness to the installation. The bunny figures are skin toned, which implies nakedness, and they are slumped down in the chairs with their legs parted. Lucas is contrasting the femininity of the stockinged figures with ideas of masculinity that can be associated with a snooker game. Within the game, to 'get snookered' is to be blocked from scoring. The installation works well as a metaphor for situations where women have been 'snookered' in their efforts within male-dominated spaces and systems.

Lucas has continued to experiment with stuffed stocking forms with her 'NUDS' soft sculptures. Unlike her 'bunnies' which depict recognizable body parts, these pieces are amorphous, tangled forms. The nude tone of the stockings stuffed with Kapok gives them the appearance of a living organism with skin and veins. The twisted shape could allude to entangled bodies, curving around each other in the act of lovemaking, or it could also look like a hideous creature curling on to itself (a decidedly less sexy thought).

There's humour and playfulness in Lucas's work, yes, but that doesn't mean it shouldn't be taken seriously. She puts a challenge to the viewer to see past the initial veneer of sexual imagery and bodies to the real substance. If a viewer is uncomfortable or finds something crude, they should ask themselves why. Once you're asking questions, then you're *really* seeing the work.

NUD CYCLADIC 16, 2010.
Tights, fluff, wire. 30 × 49 × 33 cm (11¾ × 19¼ × 13 in).

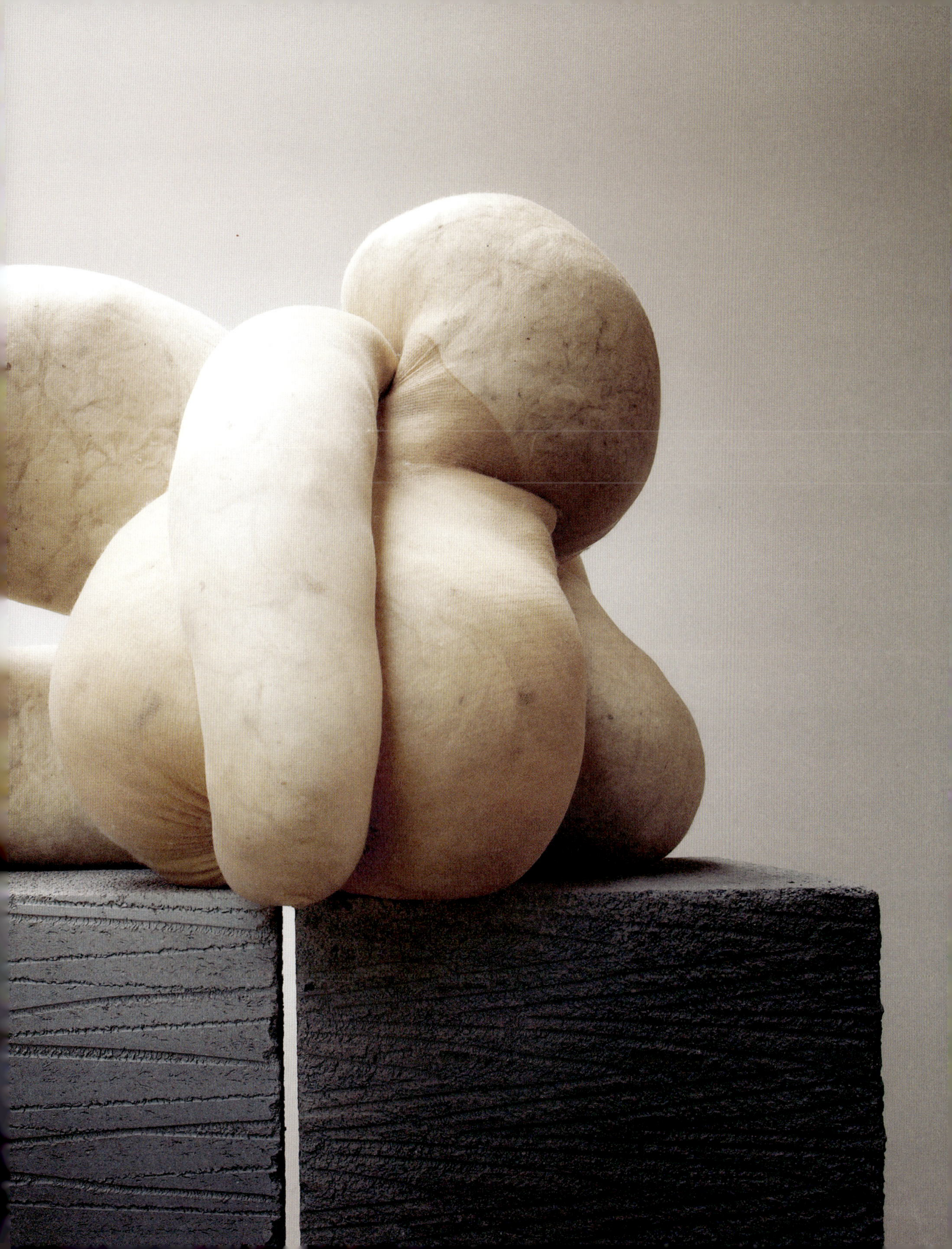

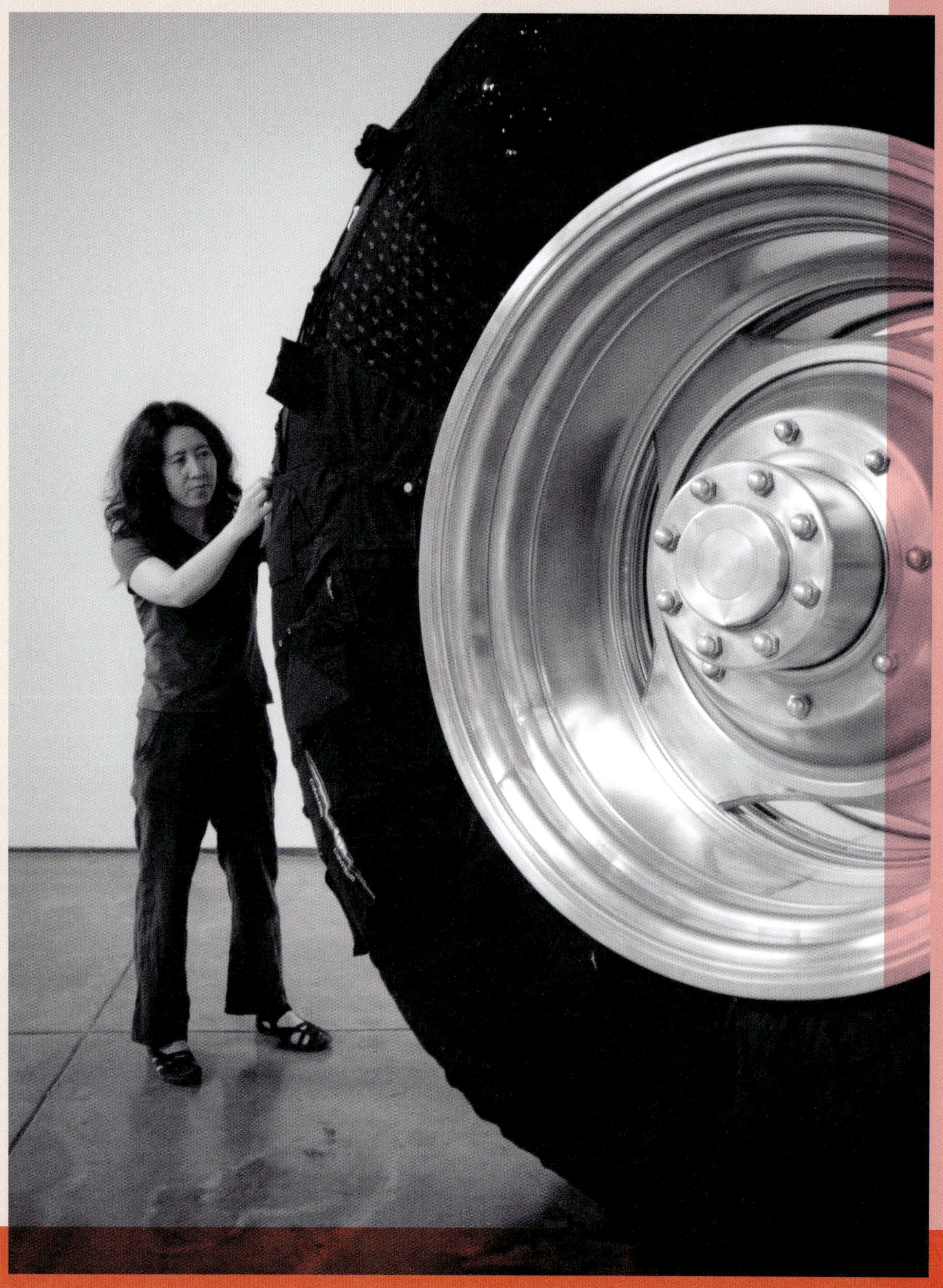

Yin Xiuzhen

(b.1963)

Soft sculpture, Textile art

Experiencing a smell, taste or even hearing a song can serve as a sensory transport to another place in time. They can be little triggers that set off a stream of memories and emotions. Yin Xuizhen has observed a similar connection in clothing. She describes clothes as a 'second skin' that is with us throughout most of the moments of our lives. In her soft sculptures incorporating second-hand clothing, Xuizhen gives a new life to found materials to explore ideas around memory and global identities.

Xiuzhen was born three years before the start of the Cultural Revolution (1966–76) in China. As the government enacted policies to consolidate power, the nation was steered aggressively in the direction of collectivity and uniformity. These principles were evident in the politics at the time, but Xiuzhen also observed this in the way people dressed and how they lived. She was particularly attuned to this phenomenon as it relates to clothing because her mother worked in a garment factory. She enjoyed watching her mother make and patch clothes, eventually learning from her how to do this herself. Getting new clothes was a rare occurrence, so items were often kept for years.

Xiuzhen was introduced to art by another woman in her life: her sister. To develop the preferred socialist aesthetics and philosophies within the visual arts during this time, the government sent many artists to the countryside to work alongside peasants. Xiuzhen's older sister was one such artist. After visiting her sister's commune during primary school, Xiuzhen became immediately enamoured with painting. She decided she'd also like to become an artist but when she entered high school, she was assigned to study maths and science.

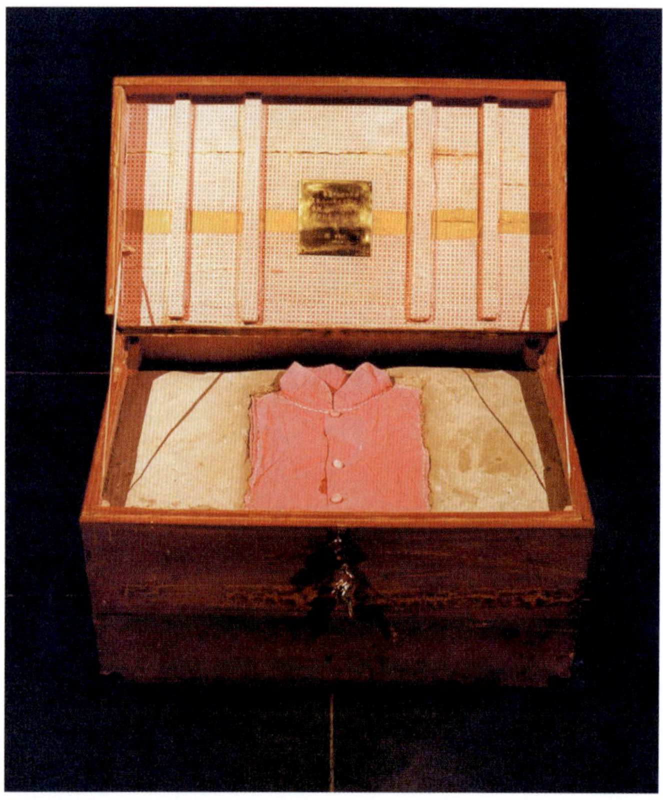

Dress Box, 1995. Wooden trunk lined with paper, clothes, cement, bronze plaque and single-channel VHS tape transferred to digital video.
38 × 67.5 × 44.5 cm (15 × 26½ x 17½in)

At this time, students were either placed on a humanities or science track, so she was forced to leave painting behind. Fortunately for her – although it may not have felt so at the time – she failed her science college entrance exam after high school. She discovered that she could sit exams for humanities with some additional study and, in 1985, was accepted into the oil painting department at the Capital Normal University (then called Beijing Normal Academy).

The preferred academic painting style at this time was Socialist Realism, but in the years since the end of the Cultural Revolution, groups of avant-garde artists were springing up around China. This movement came to be known as the '85 Art New Wave (it lasted from roughly 1985 to 1989). Their fresh approach to art was not taught in academies, but art students like Xiuzhen were inspired to innovate as much as they could independently. Her time at school was bookended by the 1985 Robert Rauschenberg and 1989 *China/Avant-Garde* exhibitions held at Beijing's National Art Museum. In each show, she was moved by the experimental possibilities of art. The China/Avant-Garde exhibition was closed after only two hours, when the artist Xiao Lu shot her own artwork. Xiuzhen

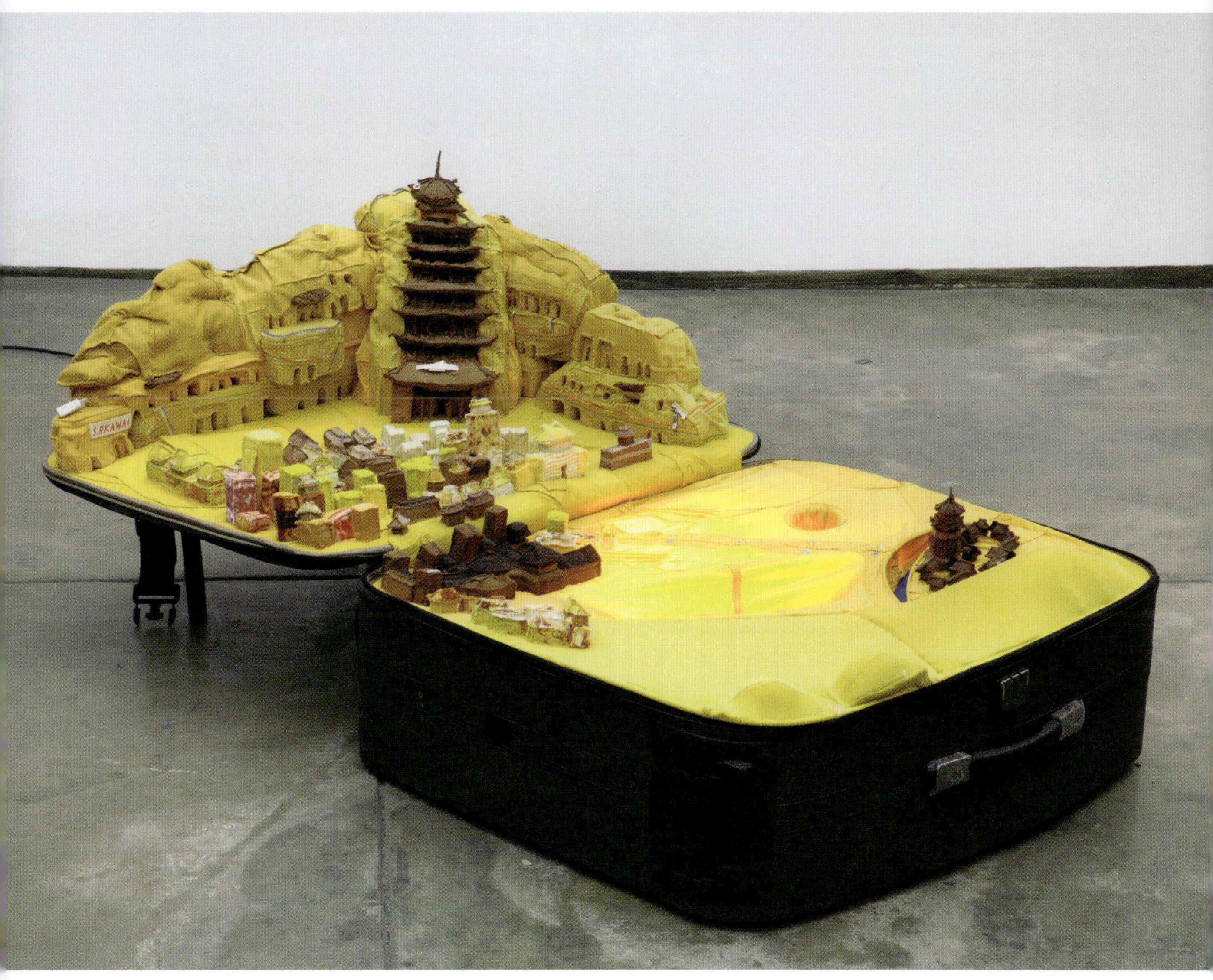

Portable City: Dunhuang, 2010.
Suitcase, used clothes, magnifying glass, map, sound
and CD player.
85 × 28 × 78.5 cm (33 $^7/_{16}$ × 11 × 30⅞ in).

felt a shift in the art climate, and worked as a high school painting teacher for the next few years.

By 1992, the contemporary art scene was once again beginning to bubble with new energy. In the years after finishing university, Xiuzhen gradually left painting behind in favour of performance and installation pieces. Her career as an artist began to blossom around 1994 and, by 1995, her installation *Dress Box* was already engaging with themes and materials that would become central to her long-term art practice. Xiuzhen placed a folded pink dress from her childhood into an old wooden chest her father had made for her years earlier. She then filled it with cement, sealing the garment in position on top. She neatly placed other clothes she'd worn throughout her life on the floor surrounding the suitcase. Having worn these items over the course of her life – some for many years – the garments had become associated with various memories and experiences, as they had been worn across time.

Dress Box is part installation, part performance. When Xiuzhen initially installed the piece, she unpacked and folded the garments neatly before sewing them closed and laying them in a grid. It was a ritualistic and cathartic act, as if she was closing out the various chapters of her life the clothing items embodied.

Xiuzhen once again employed suitcases and clothing as materials in her 'Portable Cities' series beginning in 2001. As she travelled more and more, spending time lugging bags through airports, she felt that her home was contained in a suitcase. This was the inspiration for the first *Portable City of Beijing*. Over time, Xiuzhen has used found suitcases as a base for sewn miniature recreations of more city skylines and buildings, selectively depicting identifiable landmarks. The materials for each piece are used clothes sourced from the city or region it represents. As the clothes in *Dress Box* can stand in for different stages of Xiuzhen's life, the garments in each *Portable City* are charged with the essence of their origin cities through their connection to authentic residents. By depicting so many cities from around the world, the series becomes an

As the clothes in *Dress Box* can stand in for different stages of Xiuzhen's life, the garments in each *Portable City* are charged with the essence of their origin cities.

interesting way to explore globalization and the things that connect and distinguish societies.

Xiuzhen has made other series that incorporate suitcases, second-hand clothes, and the mixing thereof, but many of her works are far too mammoth to enclose in baggage. At the 2007 Venice Biennale, Xiuzhen transformed everyday items, such as pots, pans and clothing into weapons – perhaps the works from this series could more appropriately be called an 'arsenal'. The visual of 210 sharp-tipped projectiles (the version in the Tate Modern collection includes thirty) suspended from the ceiling invokes menacing thoughts of missiles zooming towards a target. But there is a second interpretation of these pointy forms. Xiuzhen has shaped the weapons like the National Radio and TV Tower in Beijing, which speaks to a different way of wielding power through media. Representing these weapons in soft sculpture is an interesting play on the ideas of hard and soft power – in this case, missiles and media, respectively.

In a way, Xiuzhen's work is as much about the process as it is about the resulting work. Would a viewer know by looking that the clothes used in her 'Portable Cities' come from their respective locations or that Xiuzhen has worn the clothes in *Dress Box*? Not necessarily. But the act of her gathering those materials for the pieces and conveying those stories injects the works with deeper layers of meaning. This is what makes her approach to soft sculpture so clever and impactful.

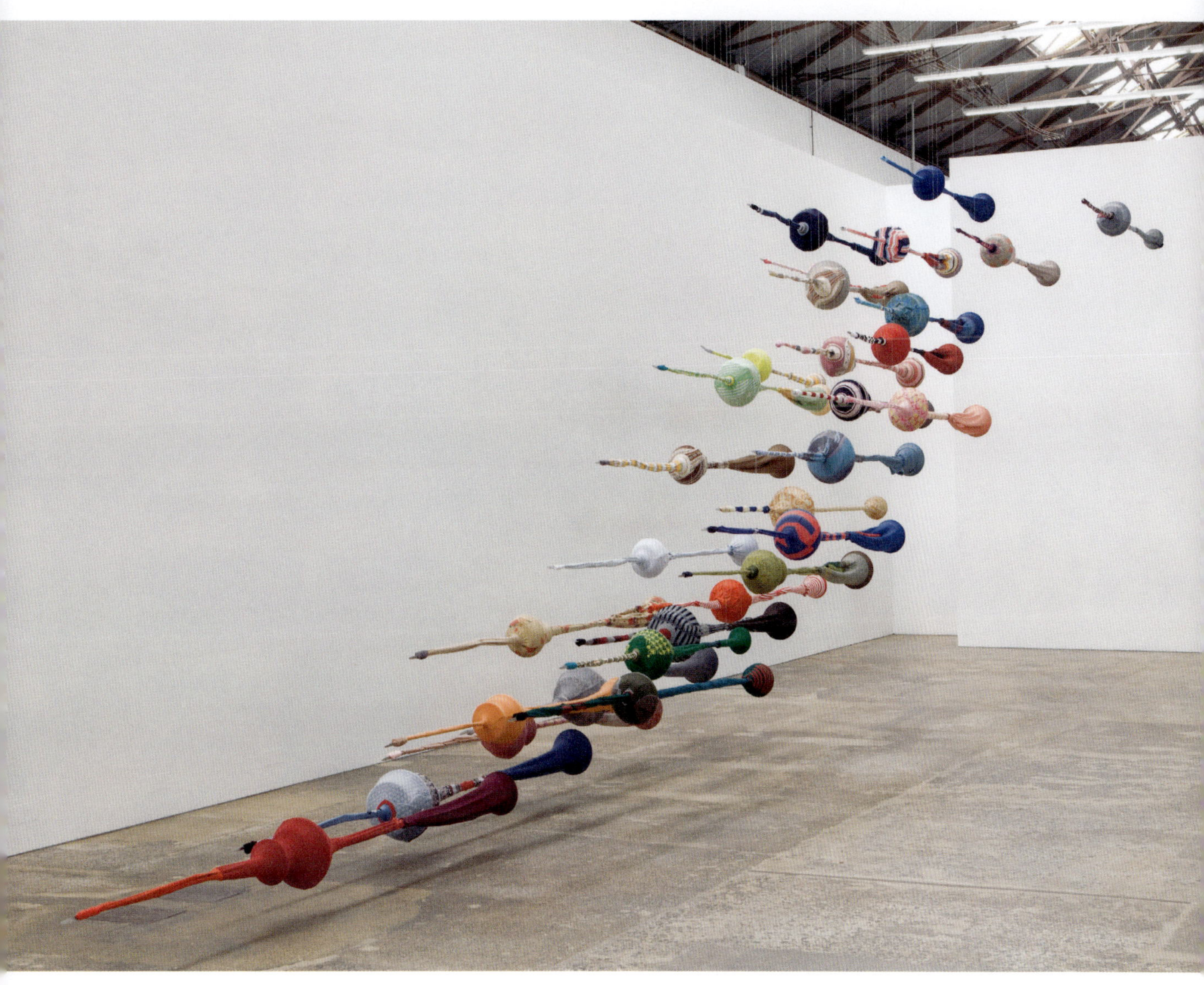

Weapon, 2003–2007.
Used clothes and daily-life items. Each piece 300–400 cm
(118⅛–157½ in) × 30–70 cm (11¾–27½ in).

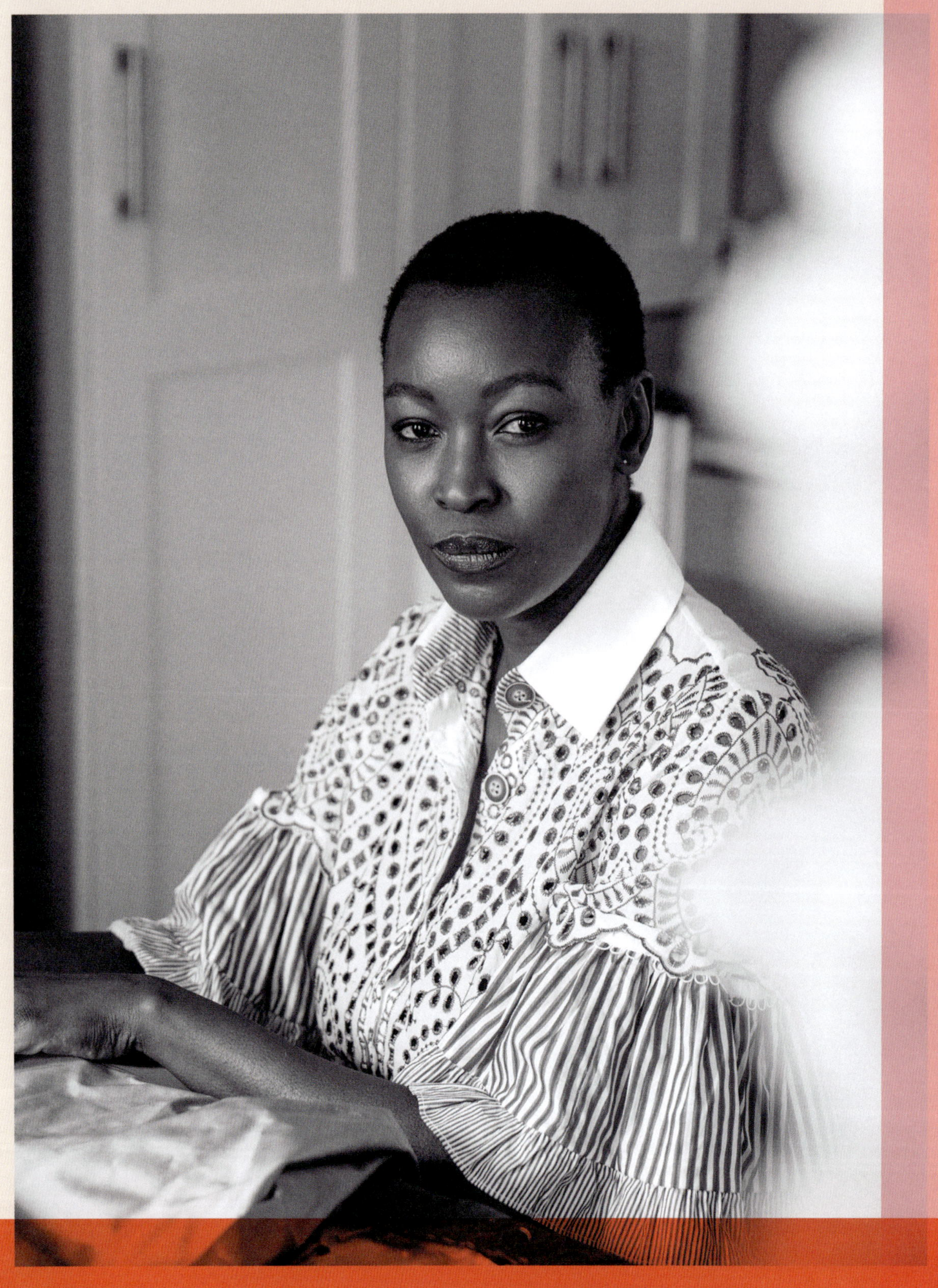

Billie Zangewa

(b.1973)

Tapestries

Sewing tapestries has become a therapeutic experience for Billie Zangewa. They provide a mechanism for self-expression and self-love. Just as the silk she uses is created through the transformative processes of insects, Zangewa views her tapestries as the by-product of transformations, wherein she turns her thoughts, emotions and experiences into tangible works of art.

The early years of Zangewa's life were spent having carefree adventures with other children in Malawi. After rainstorms, when the clay was soft, she would go outside, scoop up heaping mounds and form little earthen dolls. At around the age of six, Zangewa and her family moved to Zimbabwe for two years before settling in Botswana. It was there that she met her childhood best friend, Phillipa, who subsequently introduced her to her life's calling. Phillipa showed her a drawing she'd made of Diana, Princess of Wales, and from that moment, Zangewa knew she wanted to make art too.

In the years that followed, her parents pretended not to notice when Zangewa spent every evening drawing after dinner. Her mother had grown up poor in apartheid South Africa and her father was also raised with very little in Malawi, so they worried that encouraging her art interests might send her down an impoverished path. Undeterred, Zangewa carried on drawing. She recalls that she didn't have exceptional talent, but her high school art teacher noticed her commitment and mentored her. One day, when he noticed her struggling with a colour pencil portrait, he suggested she experiment with creating the image using coloured collage paper. She cut out the silhouette of a head and filled in the forms in layers of solid colour. This was the beginning of the graphic style that she would later develop.

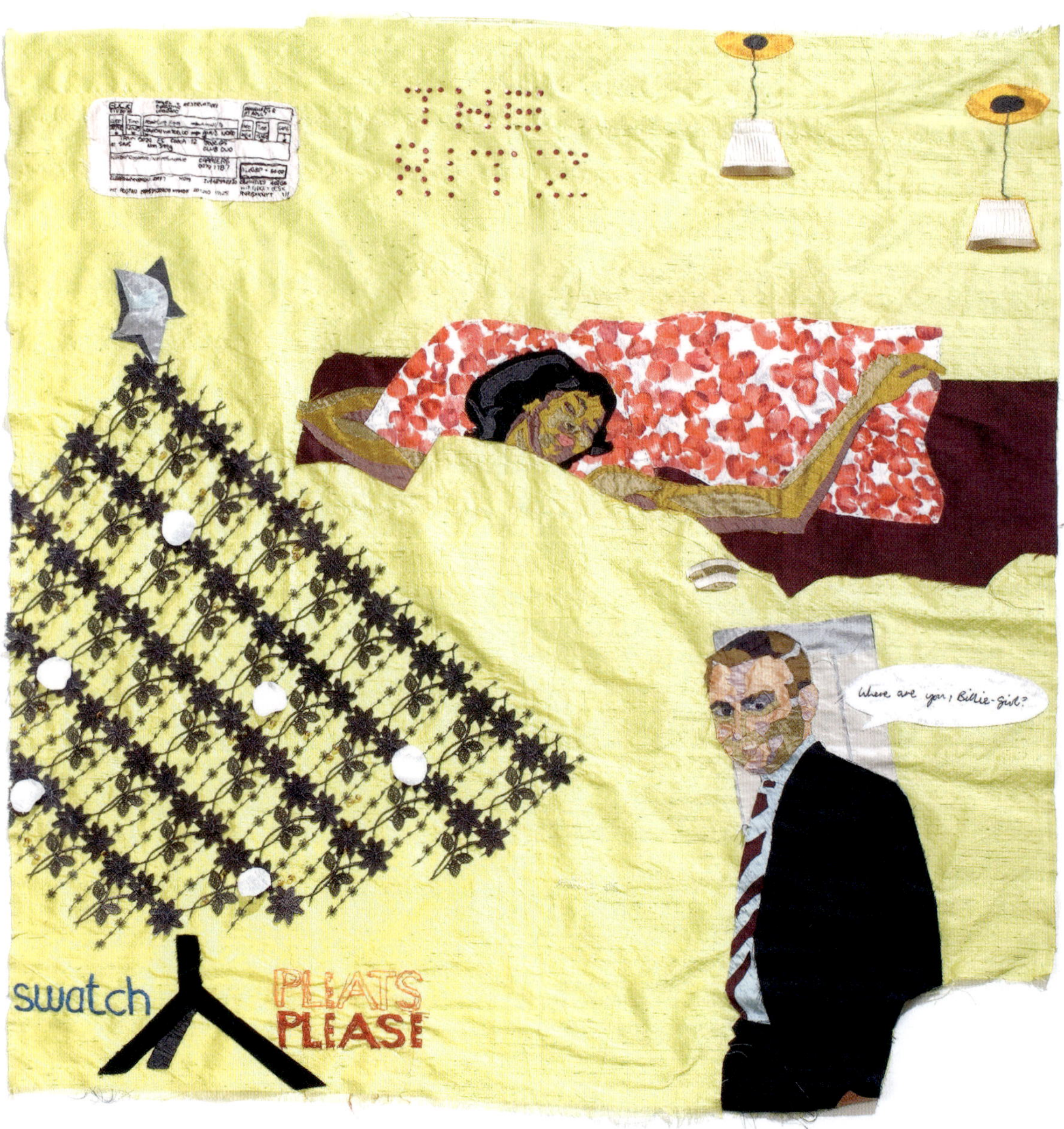

Christmas at the Ritz, 2006.
Silk tapestry. 120 × 111 cm (47¼ × 43¾ in).

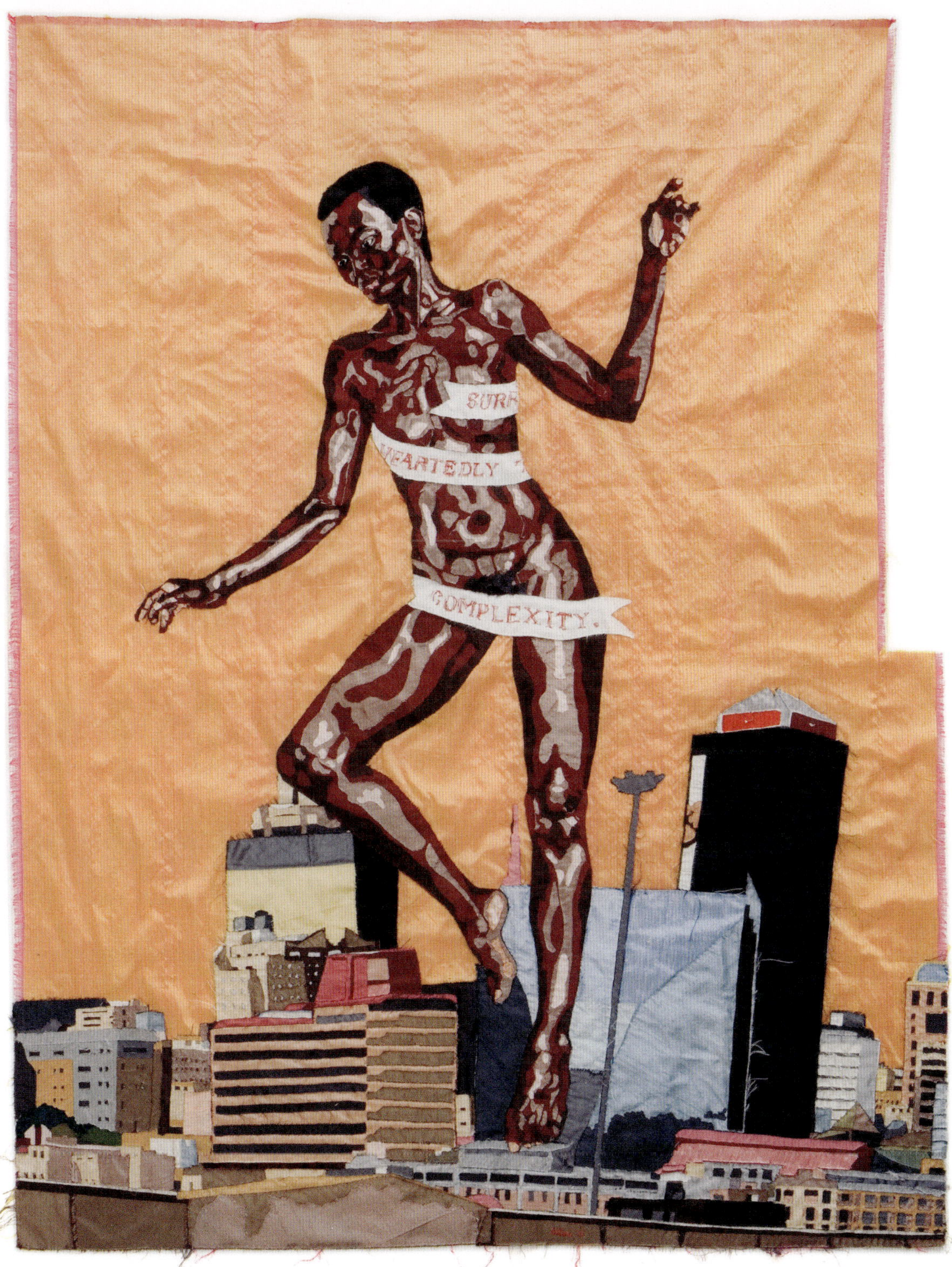

The Rebirth of the Black Venus, 2010.
Silk tapestry. 127 × 130 cm (50 × 51¼ in).

After high school, Zangewa earned her BA at Rhodes University in South Africa. She specialized in graphics and printmaking because she felt the structure of the printmaking programme allowed for more creative experimentation than the more traditional still lifes, portraits and landscapes coming out of the painting department. The only problem was that after graduating, she realized printmaking equipment was far too expensive for her to carry on working in the medium. Painting also wasn't an option. She lived back home with her parents at this time, and there was no way her father would allow her to have oil paints strewn about the house. Instead, she had the idea to work with textiles, which was easy to transport and tidy up. It was a choice born of practical needs.

In her early textile works, Zangewa used scrap fabrics to create pieces that reflected her surroundings. While home in Botswana, she depicted the animals and plant life she observed around her. After struggling to find an art scene large enough to support her work, she eventually moved to Johannesburg, South Africa. Inspired by her energetic new environment, she created a blend of cityscapes and self-portraits. Zangewa probed her relationship experiences in lush silk textiles overlaid with appliqué forms. The objects in her images are typically flat, solid colours, giving them a two-dimensional appearance, while figures have different fields of colour placed next to each other to produce an abbreviated gradient. It's similar in concept to the collage technique she first explored in high school. Another form of abbreviation – a term she uses – comes in the pared back details of the scenes. She is selective about how much detail she fills in, which gives her work a bold graphic quality and helps focus viewers' attention on the figures.

As Zangewa started to depict more of her relationship experiences in her work, she became concerned that the focus was too much on the way others – particularly men – saw her rather than her own perspective and perceptions of herself. She began to create self-portraits that showed herself in a more dominant posture, rather than as the object of the male gaze. In the 2010 tapestry, *The Rebirth of Black Venus*, her nude self-portrait hovers over the city of Johannesburg like a goddess presiding over her domain. The title and composition draw comparisons with Botticelli's *The Birth of Venus*, but Zangewa's Venus has open body language. Her Black Venus does not feel compelled to cover herself because she is a woman in full command of her body and presence. The partially obscured text of the ribbon surrounding her reads, 'Surrender whole-heartedly to your complexity.' It's a message of self-love and self-acceptance.

After Zangewa became a mother, a new main character was introduced to her tapestries – her son, Mika. She's created several pieces that show her interacting with her son and navigating the multiple roles of mother, artist and individual. Pieces such as *Temporary Reprieve* (2017), which shows her sleeping son lying next to his pacifier, represent the quiet moments of motherhood when one can lovingly look upon their sleeping child. In speaking about the themes that she continues to revisit, Zangawa says that moments such as this are a key component of her work. She explains, 'It's really shared humanity, the universal experience of daily life. That's pretty much my obsession to make everyday and the mundane extraordinary and special, and just see the value of it.'

Zangewa depicts domestic, everyday scenes to highlight the beauty that can be found in the quotidian. Her 2020 solo show, *Soldier of Love,* and her tapestry of the same title depict these ideas of daily personal actions as political acts of feminism and love. The way that a mother cares for her family and how women come together to uphold communities are radical, powerful acts of love, and love is a cause worthy of a fight.

Zangewa draws on personal experiences to celebrate the everyday woman as a feminist icon, and by using her own image, provides much needed representation of Black women full of joy and everyday concerns.

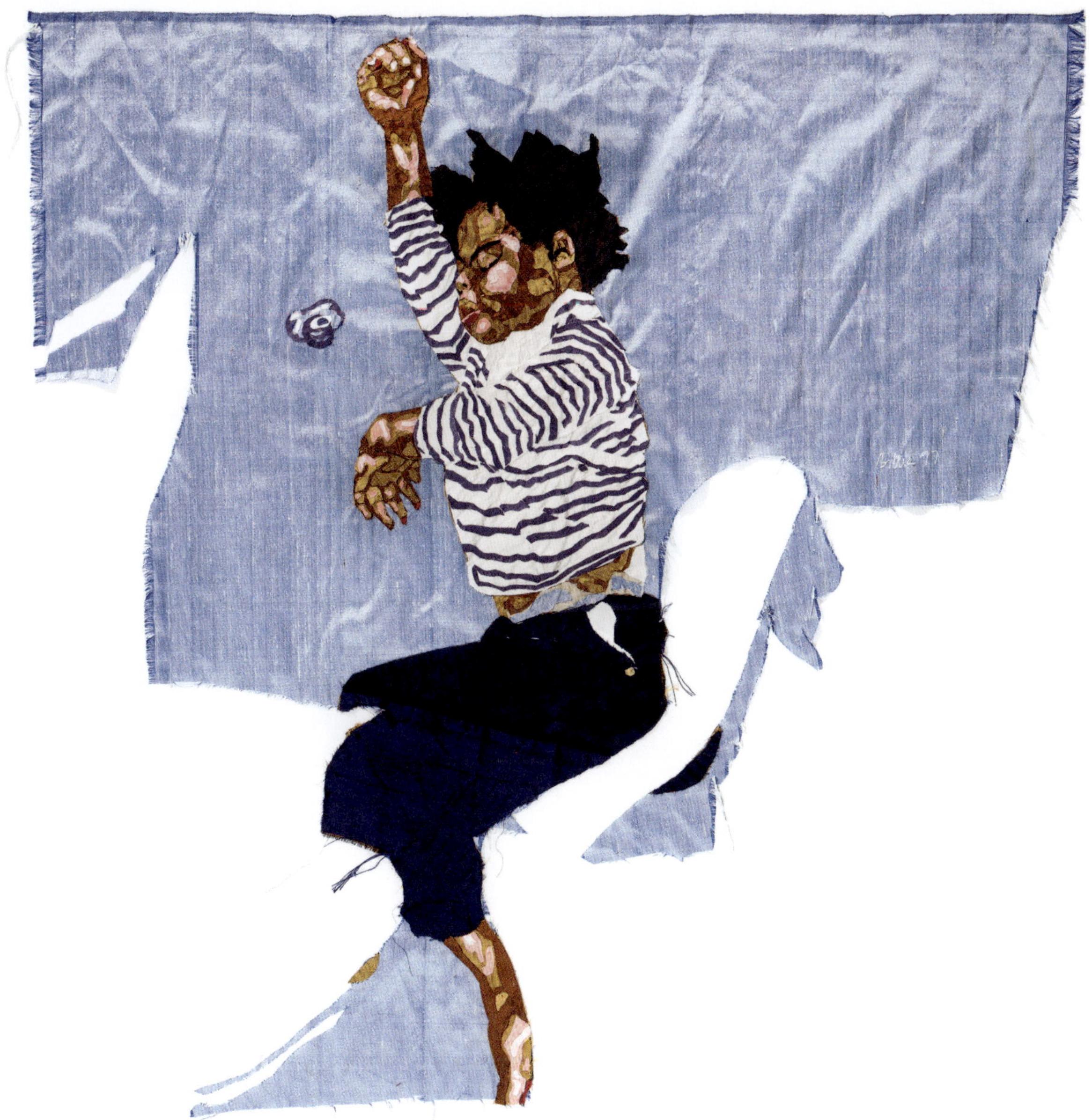

Temporary Reprieve, 2017.
Hand-stitched silk collage. 102 × 104 cm (40⅛ × 40⅞ in).

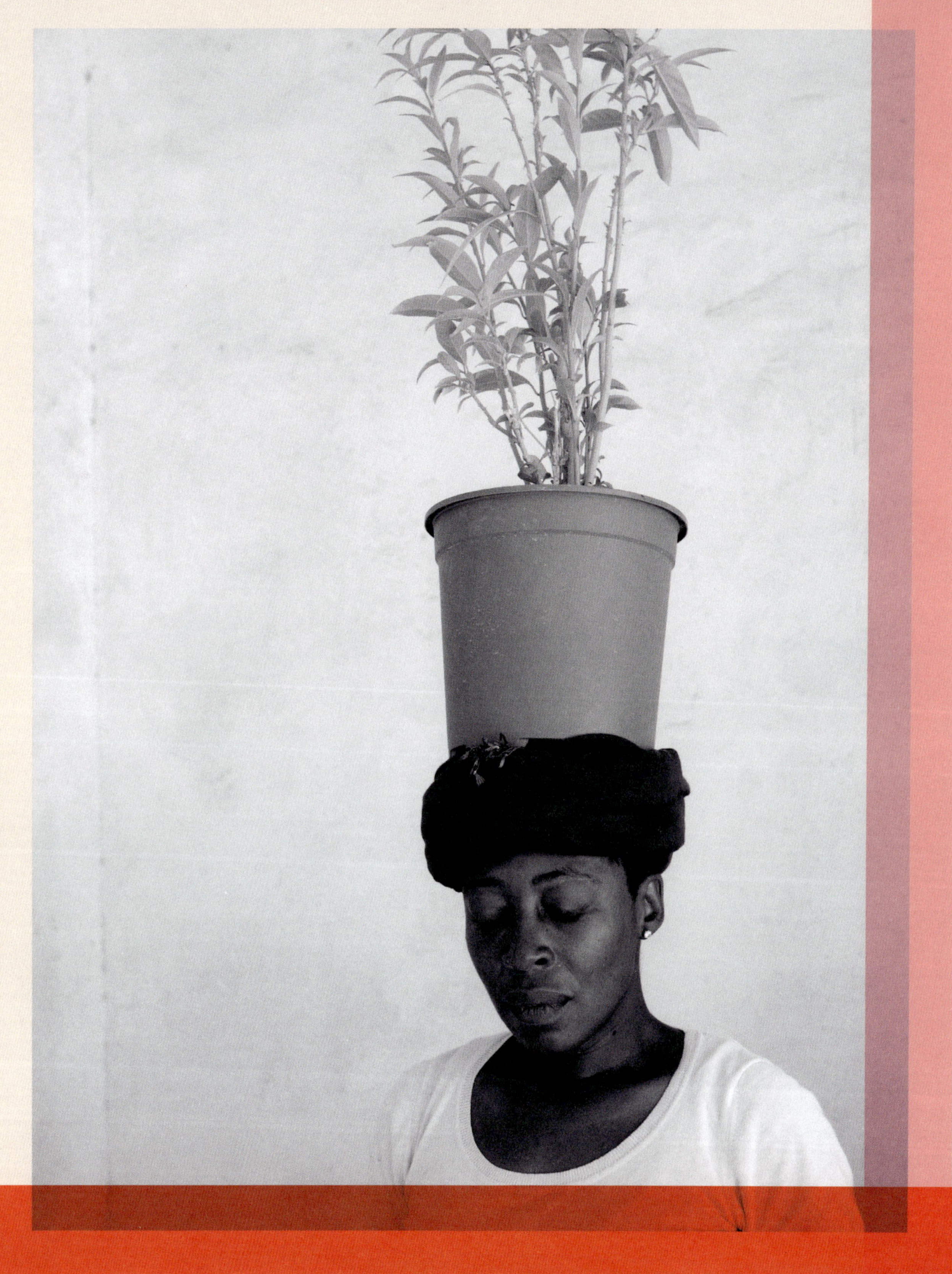

Otobong Nkanga

(b.1974)

Tapestries

Otobong Nkanga's work explores connections. Some connections are thematic – perhaps investigating the ways in which two cultures have engaged with each other over time or how humans interact with their environments. But she also explores a more subtle form of connectivity via her multi-disciplinary practice, threading elements of performance, drawing, photography, weaving and sculpture together across her incredible body of work.

Nkanga was born in Kano, Nigeria, and her family moved across the country to Lagos when she was around three years old. Her mother worked as a teacher at a polytechnic and the family lived on campus for a period before moving into their own home in a large block of flats. There she was exposed to diverse languages, foods and lifestyles, developing an early awareness of how different kinds of people share space and interact in the world. She also experienced her first major loss around this time when her father died when she was only seven. It was then up to her mother to look after Nkanga, her two brothers and her sister alone.

When Nkanga was young she loved to draw, but she didn't think of it in terms of creating 'art'. She simply enjoyed the quiet moments by herself where she could probe her thoughts in sibling-free peace. At the age of eleven, however, her art interests received a stimulating jolt when her family moved to Paris. Her mother was offered a diplomatic position through the Ministry of Education and Nkanga and her siblings were enrolled into the British School of Paris. Her class would take trips to art museums and she was entranced by the artworks she encountered. She would go back to school and spend her lunch breaks drawing as much

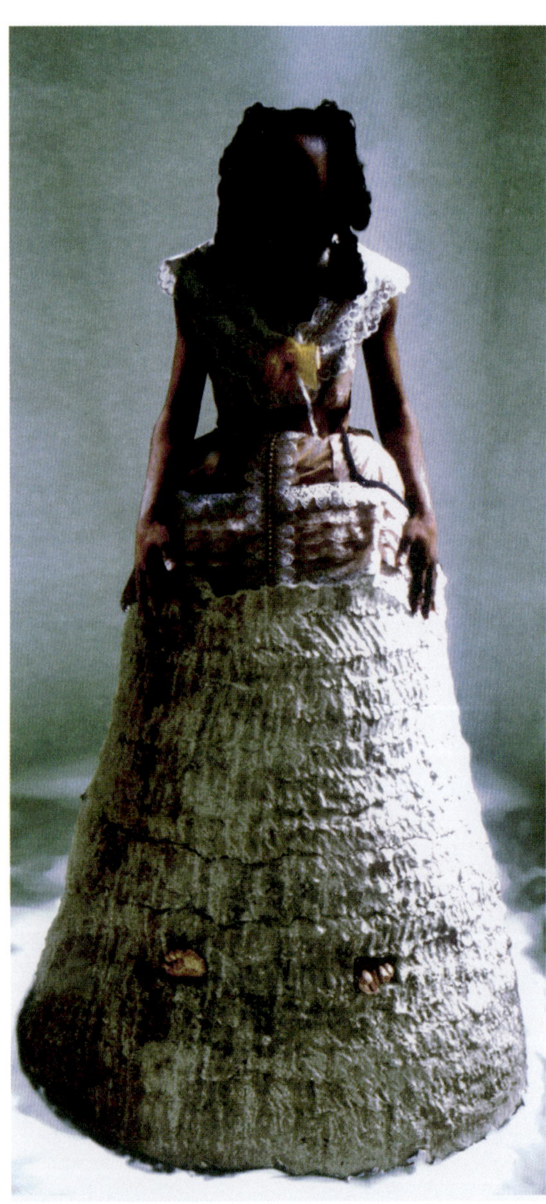

Fattening Room, 1999.
C-type photographic print.
180 × 85 cm (70⅞ x 33½ in).

as she could. Her art teacher, Diana Schöps, was so impressed by Nkanga's talent that when the time came for her family to return to Nigeria, Schöps offered to look after her so that she could continue her education in Paris. Her mother promptly replied that she *came* to Paris with four kids and would be *leaving* with four kids.

Back in Nigeria, Nkanga continued her art studies throughout secondary school. She also helped her mother earn extra income by making batik fabrics – a process of drawing designs on material in wax before dyeing them. Through taking trips to buy fabric with her mother and helping dye them, she gained a good understanding of the qualities of different materials that would come in handy in her later tapestry work. When the time came to apply to university, she considered studying architecture because she thought it would be a stable career, but her mother encouraged her to pursue her fine art dreams. She followed the advice and chose to study art at the University of Ife.

Sadly, around the time she started university studies, her mother died in a car accident. For the next two years, Nkanga employed the batik-making skills she learned from her mother to help support herself during school. She'd stayed in touch with her old art teacher from Paris all this time and, in 1994, took Schöps up on an offer to visit Paris for a while. Schöps encouraged Nkanga to apply to French art schools and after she was accepted into the Ecole Nationale Supérieure des Beaux-Arts, there was no way she could turn down the opportunity to study at one of the most prestigious art schools in France.

Her six years at the Beaux-Arts de Paris were spent training with master artists of different disciplines. She spent three of those years working in clay sculpture and was fully engrossed in exploring the medium. During this period, she created *Fattening Room* (1999), which is part sculpture, performance piece and wearable art. The sculptural element of this work functions as a clay skirt that Nkanga wore in a ceremony. The inspiration comes from the Ibibio people's tradition of preparing brides for marriage in a special room

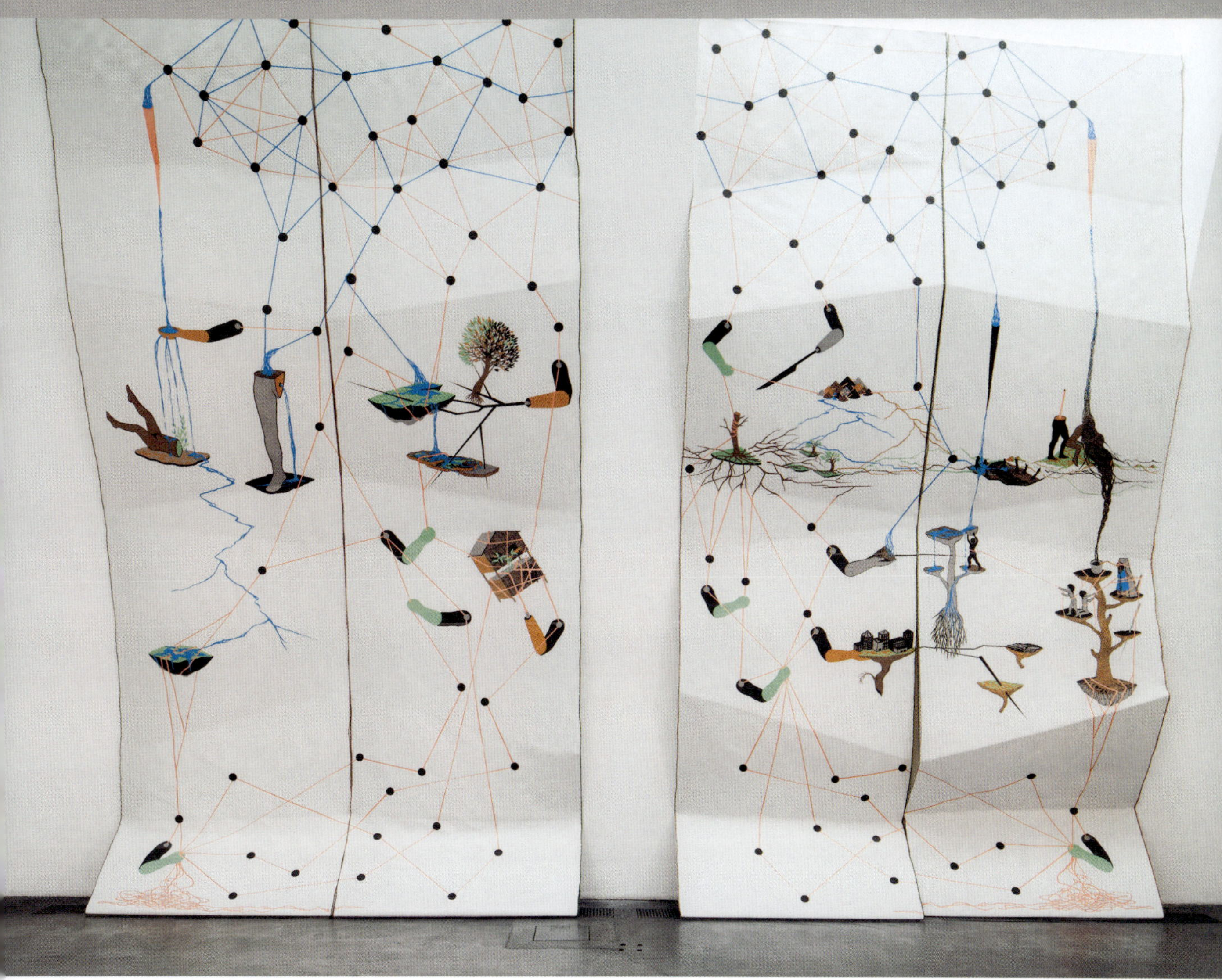

Fragiolologist's Predicament, 2011.
Double weave tapestry.
600 × 330 cm (236¼ x 130 in).

or house called a 'fattening room' in the months leading up to their wedding. During the ceremonies after the brides emerged, they would sometimes wear garments that are partially influenced by old Victorian fashions – a holdover from colonial times. Nkanga worked with a seamstress to design the lacy Victorian-style top of her fattening room dress and spent a year building up the conical walls of her skirt – this act of constructing is also part of the performative aspect of the work. When the top and skirt were complete, she donned her wearable fattening room and invited an audience to watch her stand in her own glorious womanhood.

After graduating, she left Paris for Amsterdam in 2002, where she was an artist-in-residence at the Rijksakademie van beeldende kunsten (that's a big deal). This was a period of exploration for Nkanga when she experimented with different materials and methods of making and performing. She was also travelling back and forth to Nigeria, photographing its shifting landscapes and architecture. During these trips, she saw examples of how ideas have moved from place to place – for example, the influence of Brazilian architecture on some Yoruba styles – and her practice was increasingly informed by her interest in the way people connect with one another.

Nkanga understands that exploring connections with other people and environments – whether through art or in life – is a powerful foundation for empathy.

'I think that connectedness is something that is so crucial in even understanding the ways in which we think about life itself, about the ways we're dealing with colonialism, with regards to economy, with regards to … rethinking structures that are in place. I think that the idea of connectedness instead of division is the way I understand the complexities of things.'

This concept of connectivity can be seen in Nkanga's first tapestry *Fragiologist Predicament* (2010). The large diptych shows black dots, natural resources and fragments of the human body connected by lines like a map of a constellation. In making this piece, she reflected on the environmental changes she'd observed in Nigeria over the years and the ways people had been affected by those changes. The motifs of lines and dots and the themes of nature and the environment span her oeuvre across mediums.

One can also observe interesting links between tapestry and performance in *Fragiologist Predicament*. Nkanga depicts isolated body parts, such as floating arms and legs, which are only included to carry out actions in the work. Any unnecessary extremities are not depicted, so as to maintain focus on the performance of that body part. Additionally, with most of her tapestry work, Nkanga carefully considers the scale in relation to the viewer and how people will interact with pieces within a space. This draws the viewer into a sort of unconscious performance through the act of engaging with each piece.

Her complex tapestries would take years to do by hand, so Nkanga collaborates with a cutting-edge TextielLab in Tilburg, The Netherlands to find new ways of innovating with unusual materials and textures. Her 2016 tapestry, *Steel to Rust – Corrosion*, is one such example wherein she soaked the piece in crystals that grew over the top of the work. The process and aesthetic mimic the visual of rust spreading across steel and relates to the idea of decay. Within this work, the strong material of steel functions as a metaphor for powerful institutions. As soon as a country, business or person gains power, they are in a constant fight to keep it, just as steel is in a battle against oxidization from the moment it is cast.

Nkanga has deservedly gained increased international recognition, exhibiting at biennials around the world and receiving multiple awards including the first *Lise Wilhelmsen Art Award* and the *Special Mention Award* of the 58th International Art Exhibition of La Biennale di Venezi in 2019. Her ability to confidently navigate the world through her travels and work speaks to her desire to connect with other people and environments. She understands that exploring those connections – whether through art or in life – is a powerful foundation for empathy.

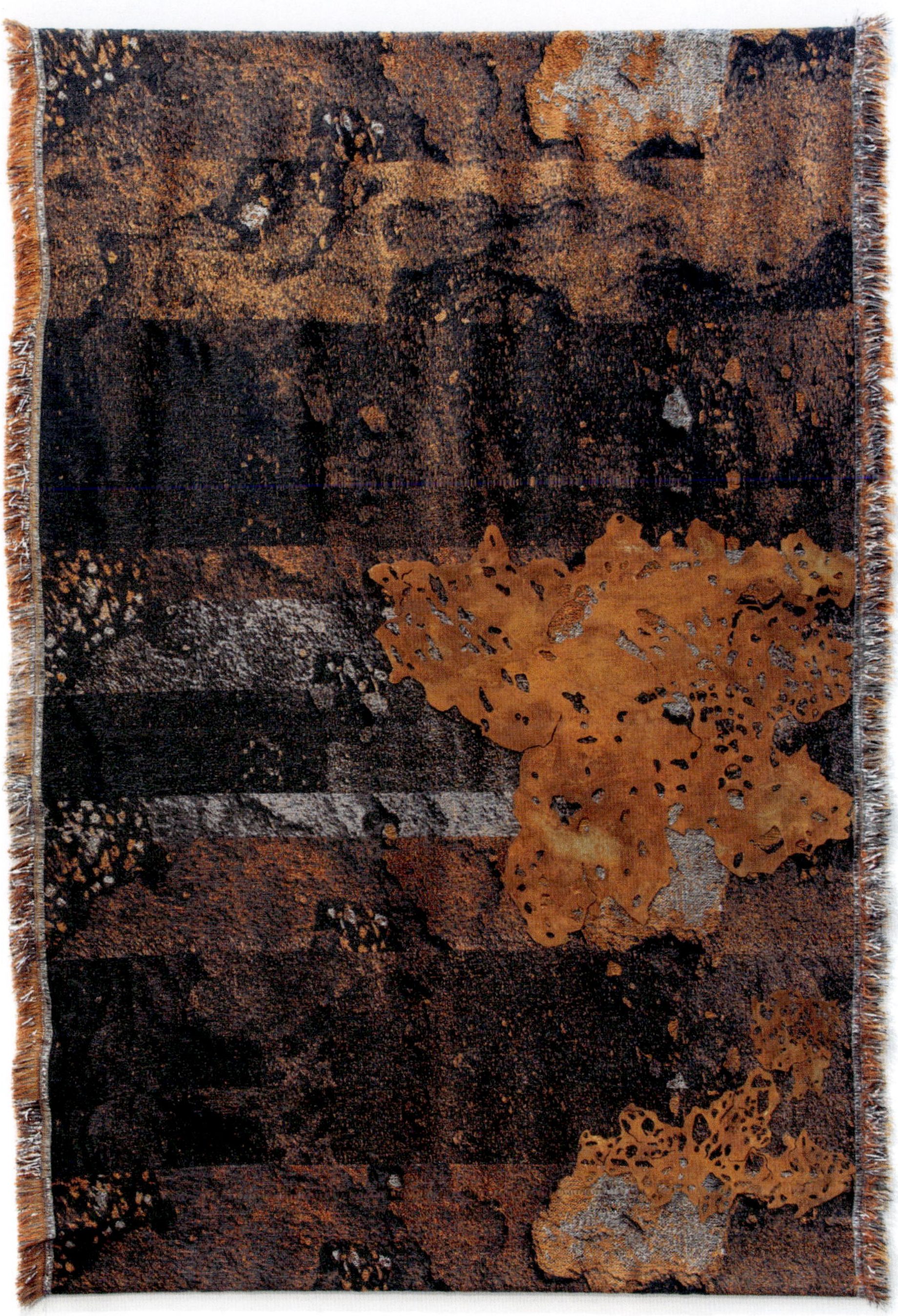

Steel to Rust – Corrosion, 2016.
Woven tapestry with lasercut metal rusted plates.
250 × 176 cm (98½ × 69¼ in).

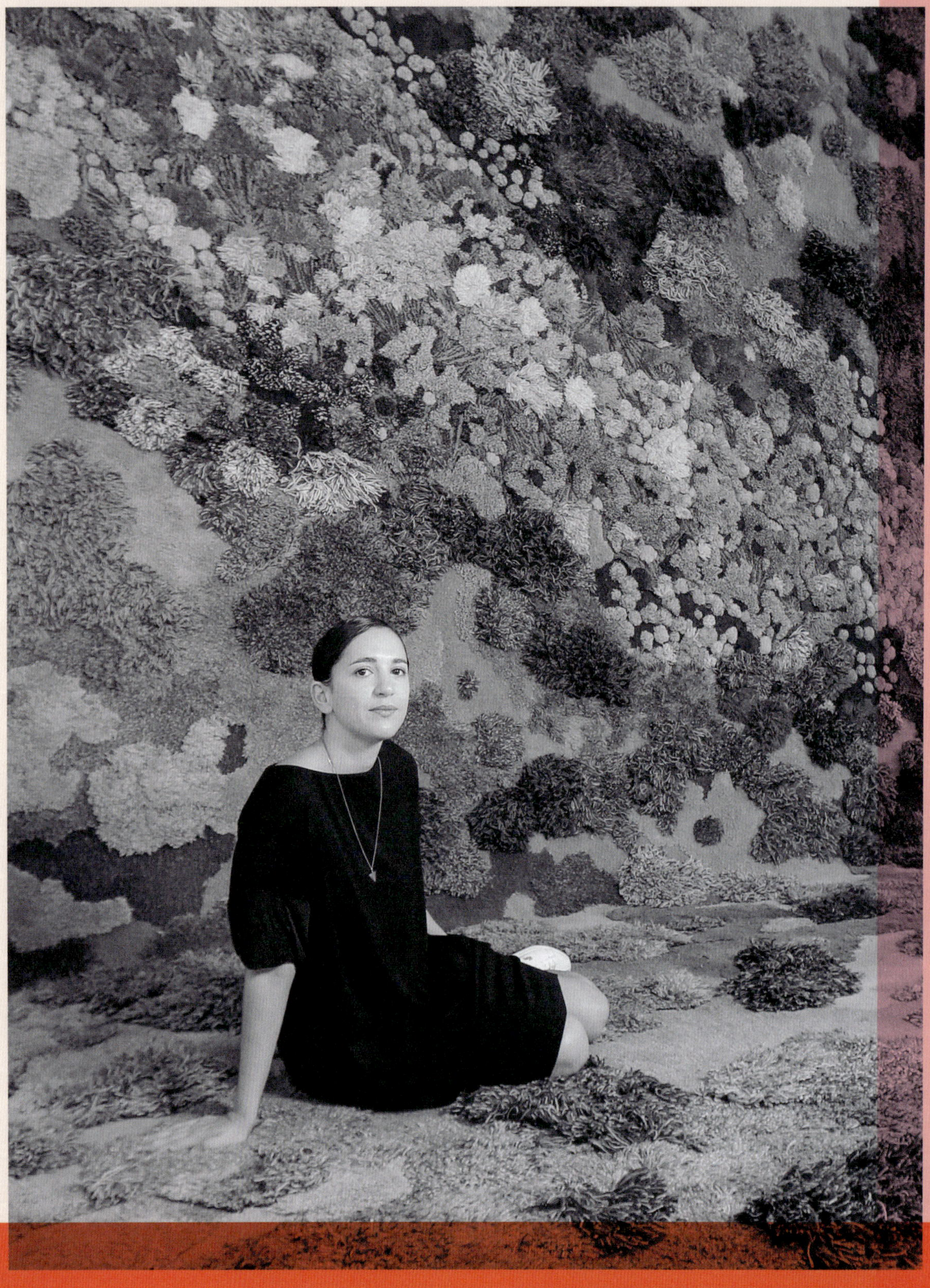

Alexandra Kehayoglou

(b.1982)

Tapestries, Carpets

There is something magical about Alexandra Kehayoglou's textile works. Stepping in front of – or on to – one of her massive installations is like being transported into the wilderness. Some of her carpet tapestries give a God's-eye view of miles-long stretches of land, while others depict intimate vignettes of tiny parcels of earth. Her works raise concerns about environmental issues, but they also connect viewers with the divine beauty and power that can be found in nature.

Looking back at Kehayoglou's childhood, it seems that her future as a landscape textile artist was written in the stars. Born in Buenos Aires, Kehayoglou grew up immersed in nature and playing in the huge, wooded area near her house. Her grandparents had emigrated to Argentina from Greece to flee war in the 1920s and later, in 1956, established a business producing hand-tufted carpets. By the time Kehayoglou was tagging along with her father to visit the factory, their operation was industrial and mainly carried out by machines. As part of a traditional family, she was expected to go into the carpet business, but she was determined to create her own path. Having taken art workshops and classes for much of her childhood, she decided to pursue those interests at the National University of the Arts in Buenos Aires.

During her studies, Kehayoglou specialized in painting and experimented with photography and sculptural mediums as well. Many of her paintings from this period were of Argentine *pastizales* (pastures). She was also drawn to studying sculpture alongside her two-dimensional work because she wanted to find a better way of representing space within her landscapes. After university, she began creating miniature rooms in boxes that placed tiny furniture in outdoor settings like grasslands or the beach. These were an early predecessor of her large-scale installations to come, but before Kehayoglou would create the lush room-sized tapestries for which she is now known, she had to first discover her love for carpet.

'I needed to represent space and time in a way that I could not do with painting, photography or video. I achieved that with carpet and that's when I realized this is something I want to work on because my interest for landscape – for nature in general – it's been always with me.'

After years of avoiding it, in 2007 Kehayoglou found herself working for the family business after all. While designing carpets for the company, she discovered she could create interesting textures by varying the length of the wool and she began to experiment with scrap materials in her free time. By the following year, she carved out a studio space for herself within the factory where she used a hand-tufting gun to create topographical landscapes. From then, she developed a blend of tapestry and carpets that occupy large floor areas and sometimes even climb walls.

Many of Kehayoglou's landscapes are based on real places she's visited but she experiments with their scale. Some carpets represent miles upon miles of land, and others may be based on very small patches that have been scaled up to provide a more intimate view. The way she alters the colours and pile height of the wool provides realistic recreations of geographical features, including rocks, trees, sand, water, grass and even glaciers.

Kehayoglou steadily shared her work on Instagram and her first major opportunity came in 2014, when the Belgian fashion designer Dries Van Noten came across her landscapes online. In the

month leading up to his Paris Fashion Week show, his team reached out to Kehayoglou to commission a 144-sqm catwalk for the event. Working day and night, with the help of friends, Kehayoglou was able to realize the 50 m long carpet the designer wanted. The design is inspired by John Everett Millais' hyper-detailed painting *Ophelia* (1851–52), and just as Millais' work showcases green and brown foliage of varying textures, Kehayoglou juxtaposed assorted hues and pile heights to create a verdant pathway for the models. Most interestingly, there's a clever duality to the scale of the piece – it could just as easily be viewed as a stretch of mossy forest floor as it could be seen as a bird's eye view of a forest canopy. She would later do another fashion collaboration with iconic Hermès brand, designing a series of dreamy window installations that looked like scenes from a fantastical garden.

Over time, Kehayoglou became more attuned to a spiritual component within her work. In viewing the natural themes within her tapestries and carpets, concepts around conservation and the environment are immediately apparent, but she is also engaging with the relationship between God, man and nature.

'I made this work called *No Longer Creek*. It depicts this place that I used to go running. They started to destroy this very pristine creek that went up to the riverbed. I remember having my runs, seeing this place, and feeling, "Wow, God is here." We're in the city, but God is here because of the animals and the fish – you could see everything. It's revealed.'

Kehayoglou's work has increasingly reflected on how humans interact with nature, how God can be found in nature, and how can humans experience God through nature. One of the best examples of this combination of spirituality and the environmentalism came in 2016, when she was invited to Melbourne, Australia to produce a

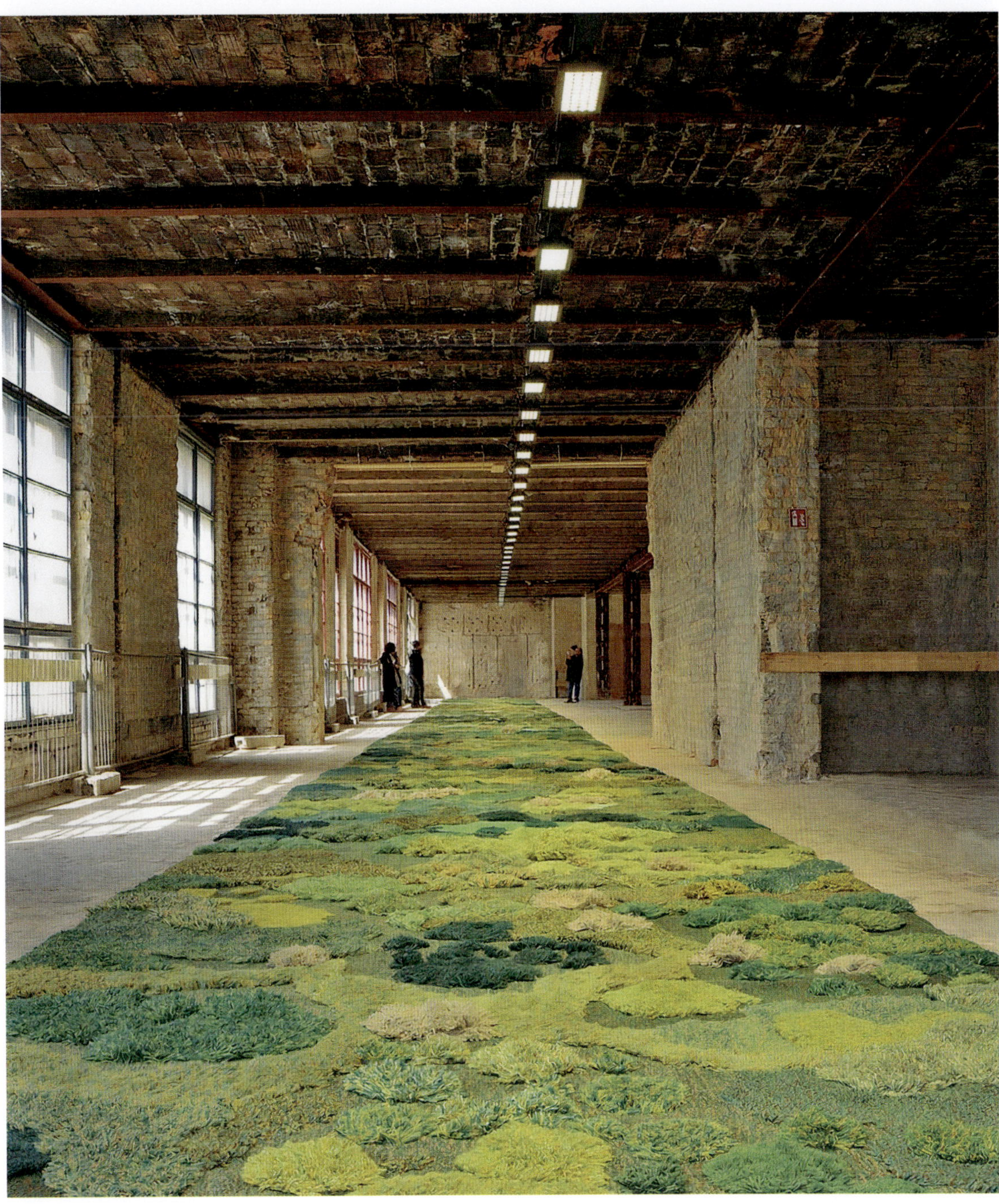

Pastizal DVN, 2014.
Textile tapestry (handtuft system), wool.
50 × 3 m (164 × 9¾ ft).

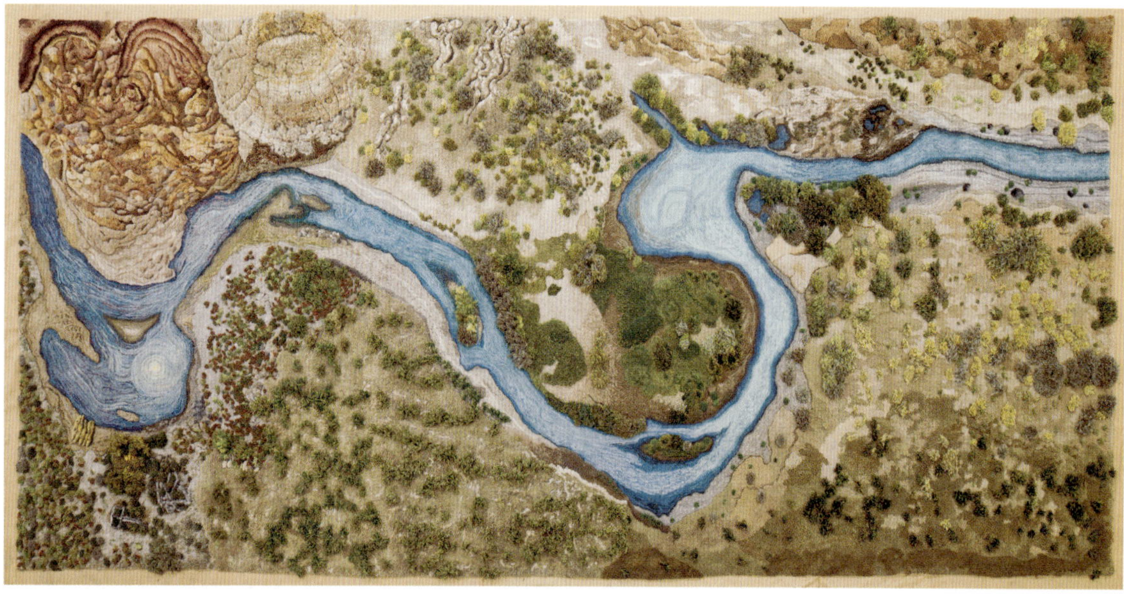

Santa Cruz River, 2016–2017.
Textile tapestry (handtuft system), wool.
980 × 420 cm (385¾ × 165¼ in).

work for the National Gallery of Victoria Triennial. She was asked to present a work relating to any water-related crisis within the world and she created *Santa Cruz River* (2016–17) to document Argentina's last free-flowing river. At this time, there were two proposals to build hydroelectric dams in the river, which would have drastically altered the surrounding landscape. She kayaked through the area for one week, taking notes and photographs of areas that would be flooded by a potential dam. She began to see the river as a spiritual entity, and felt that through visiting and documenting this area, she was connecting with the divine through the majesty of nature.

This experience inspired Kehayoglou to simultaneously work on a series of 'prayer rugs' depicting small patches of the riverbank. Her works are interactive, with viewers often standing and laying across her creations. In creating the prayer rugs, she thought about how the act of kneeling physically connects a person to the ground. She views the rugs as a way to facilitate a physical and symbolic connection to the earth, and therefore to the Supreme.

As her career has progressed, Kehayoglou has learned to trust her intuition and follow the concepts and opportunities that speak to her, spiritually. Her carpets and tapestries continue to reflect natural landscapes, but she experiments with depicting different points of view and diverse geographies that transform interiors into immersive and awe-inspiring wonderlands. Her works serve as a reminder that, however stunning her carpets are, they are inspired by the splendour found in nature, and it's our job to cherish and protect it.

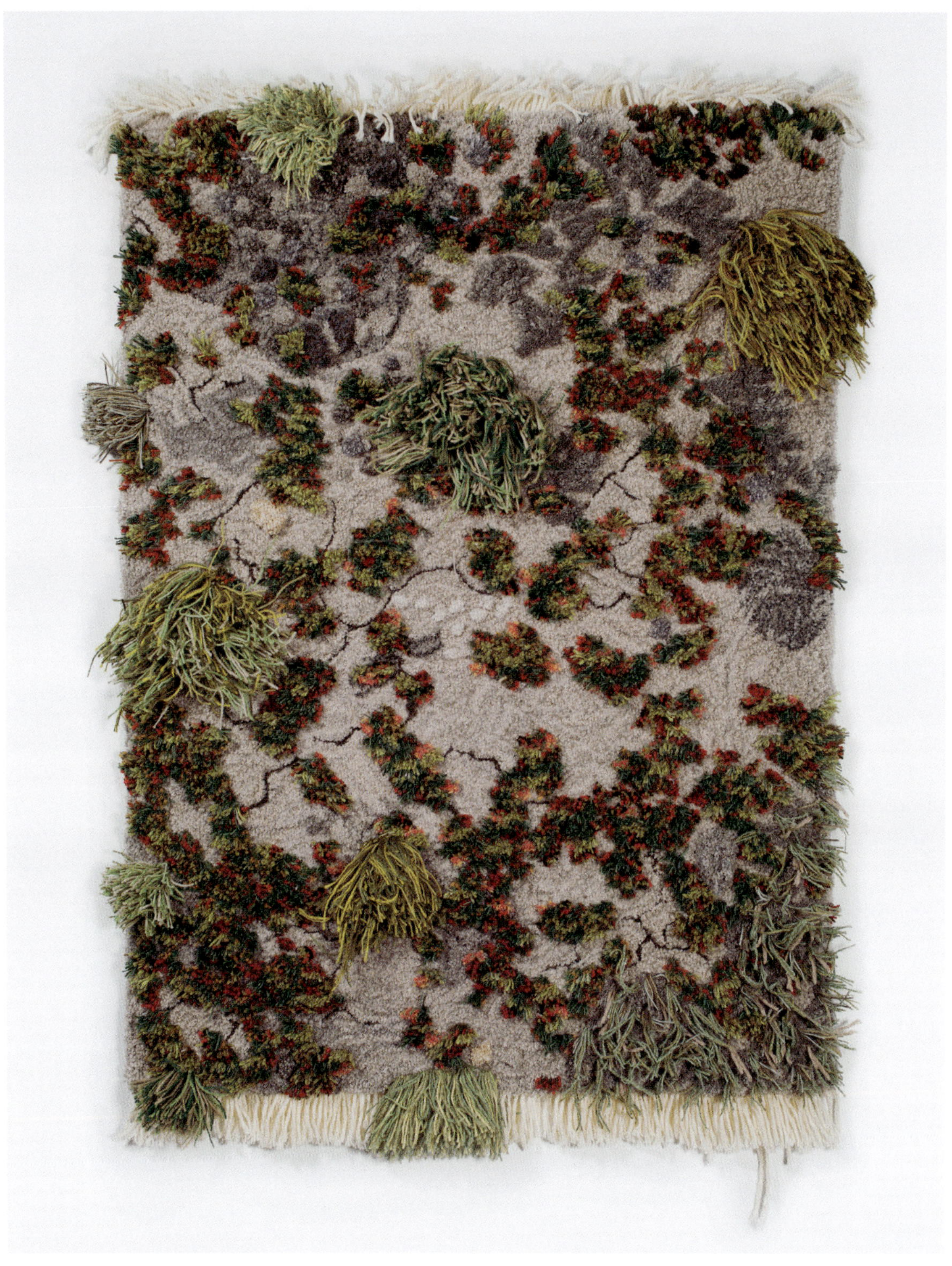

Prayer Rug, Santa Cruz series, 2018.
Textile tapestry (handtuft system), wool.
50 × 90 cm (19½ x 35½ in).

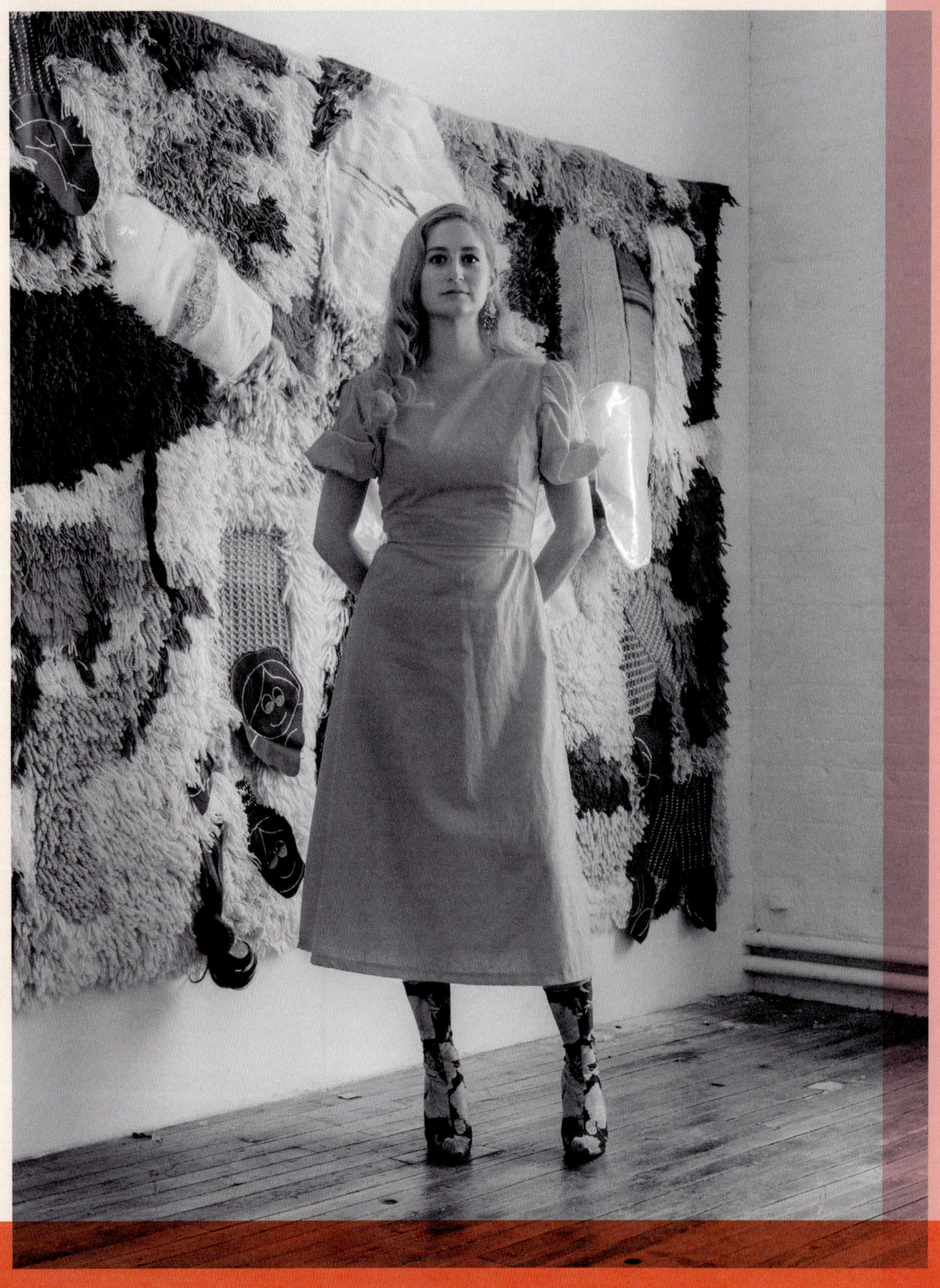

Sarah Zapata

(b.1988)

Fibre art, Soft sculpture, Weaving

Spirituality, sexuality and tradition converge in Sarah Zapata's deeply personal textile works. She uses mediums connected with her family's cultural heritage to explore where the elements of her identity intersect to ignite feelings of pride, guilt and rebellion. Through her practice, she undergoes processes of self-discovery and is able to better understand how to live authentically and joyfully.

Zapata and her two siblings grew up surrounded by tradition – some from their Peruvian father, and some from their mother, who comes from an evangelical Christian background. She was born in Corpus Christi, Texas, and the family eventually moved across the state to Plano. She saw less of her father's side of the family as a child, as most of them lived in Peru, but her family made frequent trips back to Corpus Christi to visit her maternal grandparents. From a young age, Zapata's grandparents on both sides had a formative impact on her interests. She heard stories about how her Peruvian grandfather owned a fabric store and her maternal grandmother often sewed clothes for Zapata and her sister. Eventually, she took to making her own garments, creating edgy alternatives to the expensive fashions available in stores. Zapata's high school sculpture teacher also allowed her to explore her textile interests in class and, by the time she graduated, she had decided to continue her art education by majoring in fibres at the University of North Texas.

At Zapata's university, fibre art students also took courses in sculpture and painting. She was developing artistically, but she was also learning more about herself, including exploring her queer identity. Coming from an evangelical background, she experienced deep feelings of guilt in connection to her sexuality and this manifested in her exploring the idea of control in her work as a way to process her thoughts and emotions. In one series created during her studies, she incorporated telephone book pages into weavings in a manner that she now reflects on as being 'overworked' – perhaps a result of her need for control at that time. She would cut the pages into strips and place them into the warp to create sculptural landscapes. She thought of the creation process for these works as having 'continuous mechanical motions', and felt that the lack of colour in the work mercifully reduced the number of decisions she had to make. These early works show a self-imposed restraint that she later lifted as Zapata began to further engage with the many aspects of her identity and interests.

Towards the end of her studies, Zapata's professors encouraged her to apply for grants and she was awarded funding from the Dallas Museum of Art, which enabled her to buy her own loom. After graduating in 2011, she worked in Austin over the summer and saved enough money to move to New York that autumn. She quickly found work at a boutique and an art fair, which led to her securing an internship with textile artists Steven and William Ladd. They taught her how to do bead weaving, helped her buy her first bobbin winder and encouraged her to understand that an artist's practice doesn't always have to be perfect.

Zapata had lugged telephone books with her from Texas to New York, thinking that would be the continued direction for her work, but she was soon drawn to other ideas. She began to write lesbian foot erotica to help contend with her feelings of guilt surrounding her sexuality and to explore the intersection of her queer identity and her religious upbringing. Zapata states that she was interested in feet because they 'are common in the Bible to talk about your relationship to Christ, they're a sign of humility and your trajectory through life, but contrastingly from a biological standpoint, they're really what defines us as humans from an evolutionary standpoint. We're the only full-time bipedal mammals.'

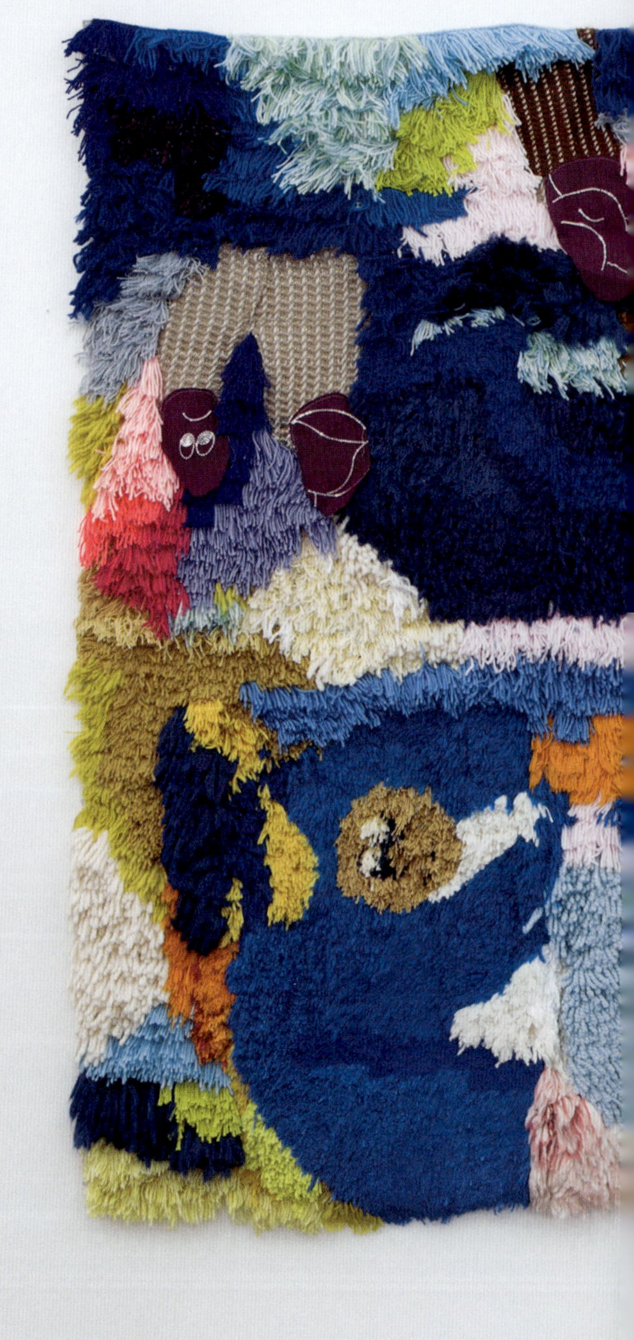

Siempre X, 2015–2016.
Natural and synthetic fibre, handwoven cloth, denim, vinyl and rhinestone transfer.
1.8 × 3 m (6 × 10 ft).

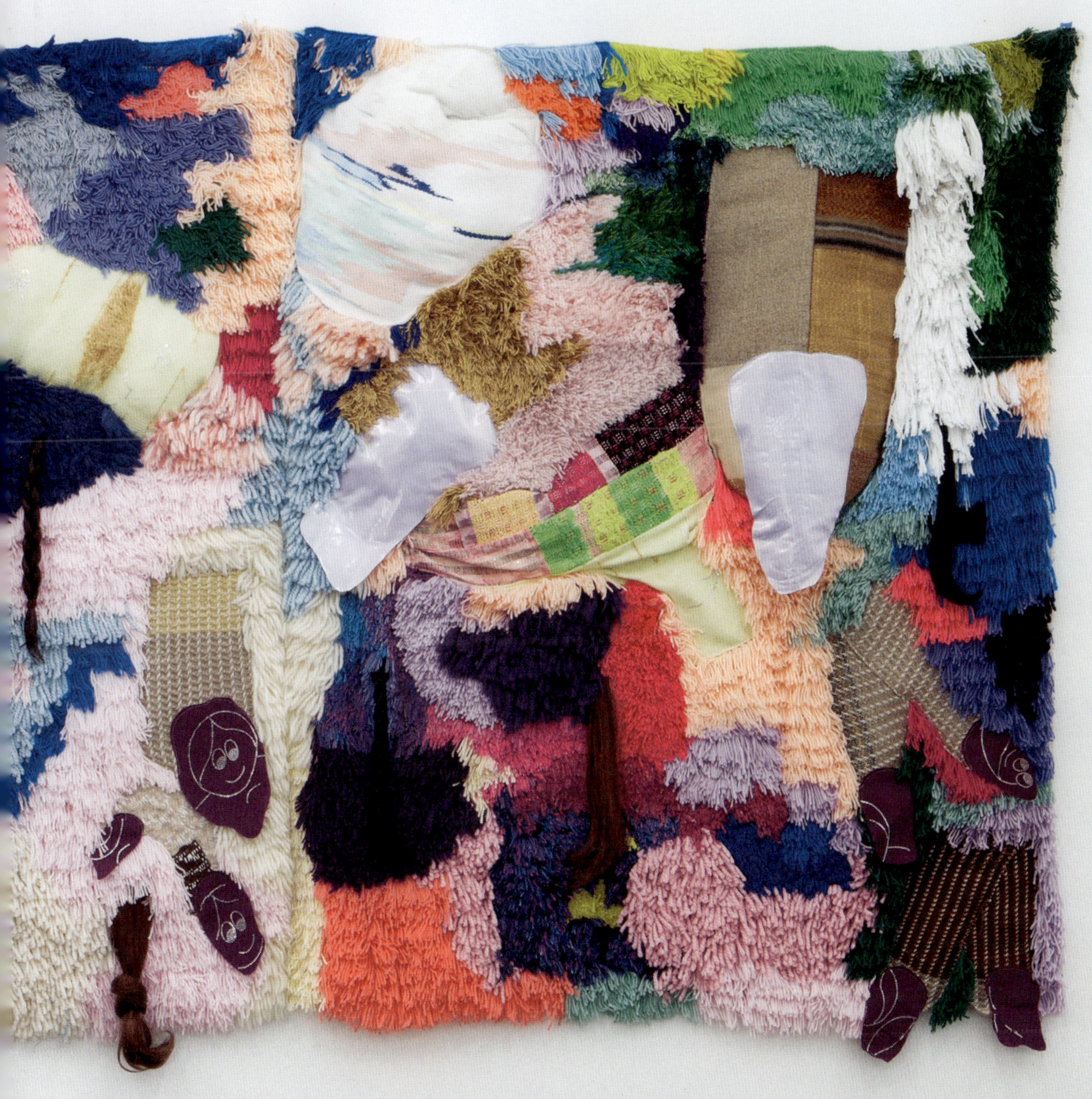

Feet have become a recurring motif in Zapata's work as a way to explore ideas of spirituality and worship. The first pieces she created around this concept were rugs, and some of her installations encourage visitors to remove their shoes and walk over the textiles. She has also developed a series of sculptures depicting coiled baskets and ceramics with feet that emerge to engage with her rugs in a self-interactive way.

From the end of 2012, Zapata has worked for a yarn company, assisting with administrative tasks and small knitting and crochet projects. There are often large amounts of excess yarn left over, so Zapata began to use the materials in her work. At first, she continued to shy away from colour and plucked out the more muted tones, but the availability of vivid hues pushed her to experiment. She enjoyed the rebellious act of employing these yarns – which were intended for craft use – within her work, as it challenged hierarchical views of 'high' and 'low' art.

Further developments in her practice came in 2015, when she took the first of many pilgrimages to Peru to visit family and learn more about the culture. Over many visits, she has taken weaving classes, travelled to cities and visited collections of pre-Hispanic textiles and ceramics – all of which has informed her practice. After her first visit to Peru, El Museo del Barrio commissioned Zapata to create *Siempre X* (2015–16). 'Siempre' means 'always' in Spanish and the 'X' is intended to serve as an open-ended placeholder. Zapata describes the work as 'overtly feminine' and images the 'X' could be replaced with labels associated with femininity.

Siempre X is inspired, in part, by textiles in Peru that employ a multitude of techniques within a single work. She chose to use a mixture of materials, including yarn, hair extensions and rhinestones, while also using several techniques, such as latch hooking, sewing and handweaving. The design is also informed by *arpilleras*, which are Chilean narrative textile works that were made primarily by women to address political issues in the 1970s and 80s. The abstract design draws on these textile traditions to create a large-scale work

that leans into ideas surrounding femininity while boldly challenging traditional notions that textile works by women should be useful and demure.

Since 2021, in the period after the onset of the Covid-19 pandemic, Zapata began a series of soft sculptures called 'Gargoyles'. The title refers to the stone figures that adorn some European churches to ward off evil spirits. She chose to weave striped material for the sculpture as a reference to the way striped patterns have historically been associated with social outcasts or untrustworthy people, particularly in some Biblical texts and in medieval Europe. Where some of her earlier works encourage viewers to engage and connect, the Gargoyles are mounted in corners out of reach. At a time when many were having to isolate or meet outdoors, Zapata looked to outside architecture for inspiration because she said the outdoors felt safe. The works simultaneously project the idea of being something to stay away from, while also functioning as symbols of protection.

Zapata's practice has developed to include immersive installations that incorporate rugs, wall hangings and sculptural works. As she continues to explore her identity and experiences, new ideas and aesthetics will likely emerge. Her work is as much about process and personal investigations as it is about the finished pieces. This is what makes her work so open-hearted and so unique.

> **"I think I was really struggling how to define myself within tradition and I wanted it to be on my terms. I think that's what led me to study textiles."**

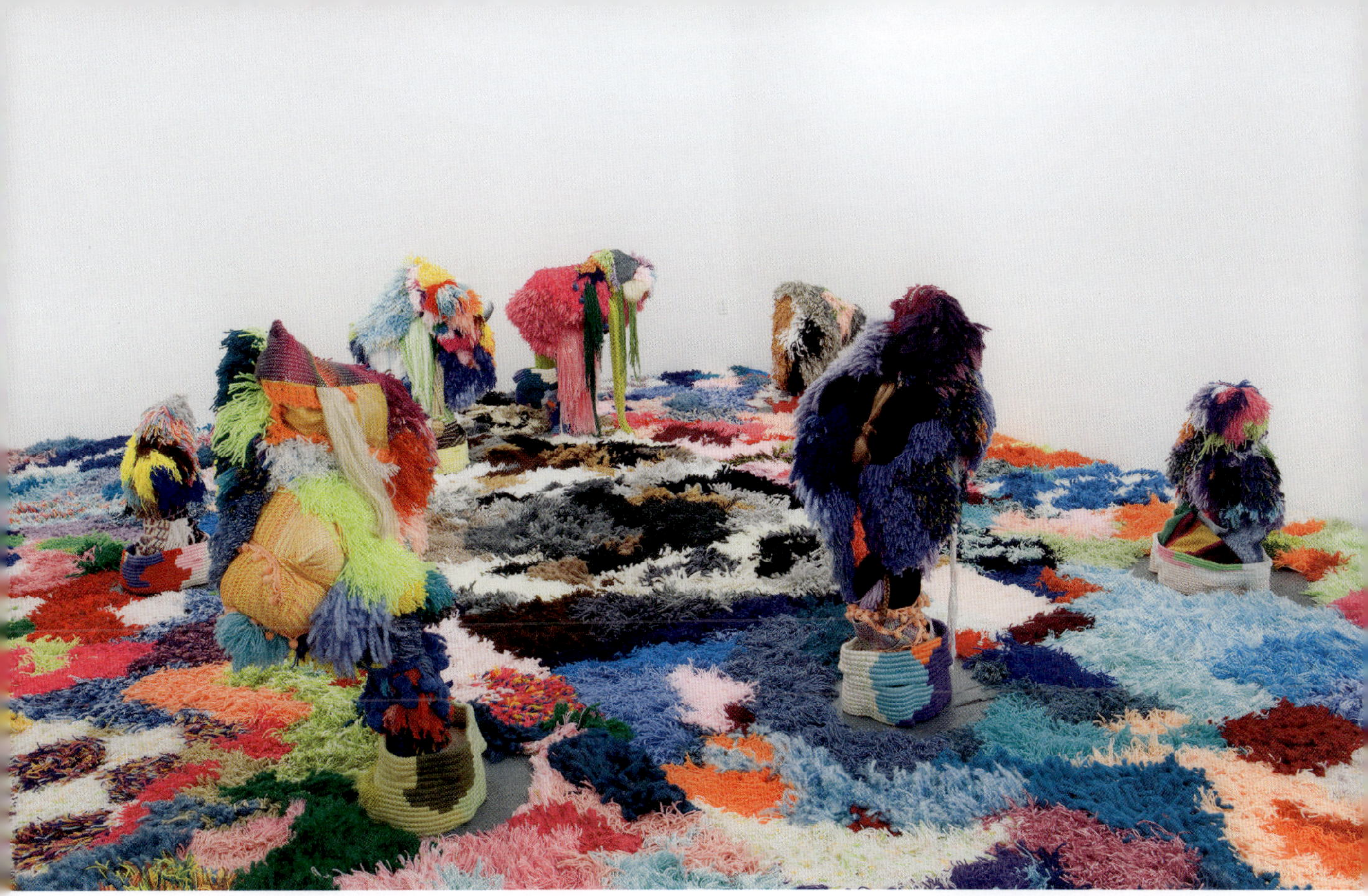

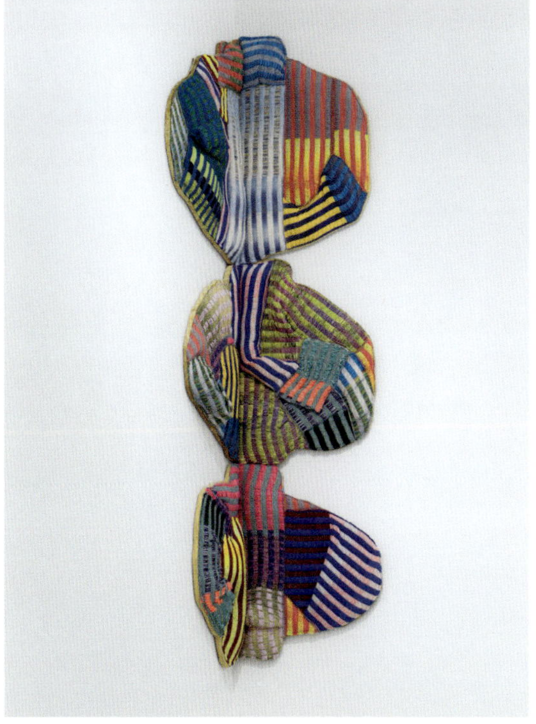

Above: *If I Could images*, 2017.
Natural and synthetic fiber, handwoven cloth, cement, steel.
Dimensions variable.
Right: *Living in Our Own Time (3 gargoyles)*, 2021.
Handwoven cloth stuffed and sewn on panels.
Dimensions variable.

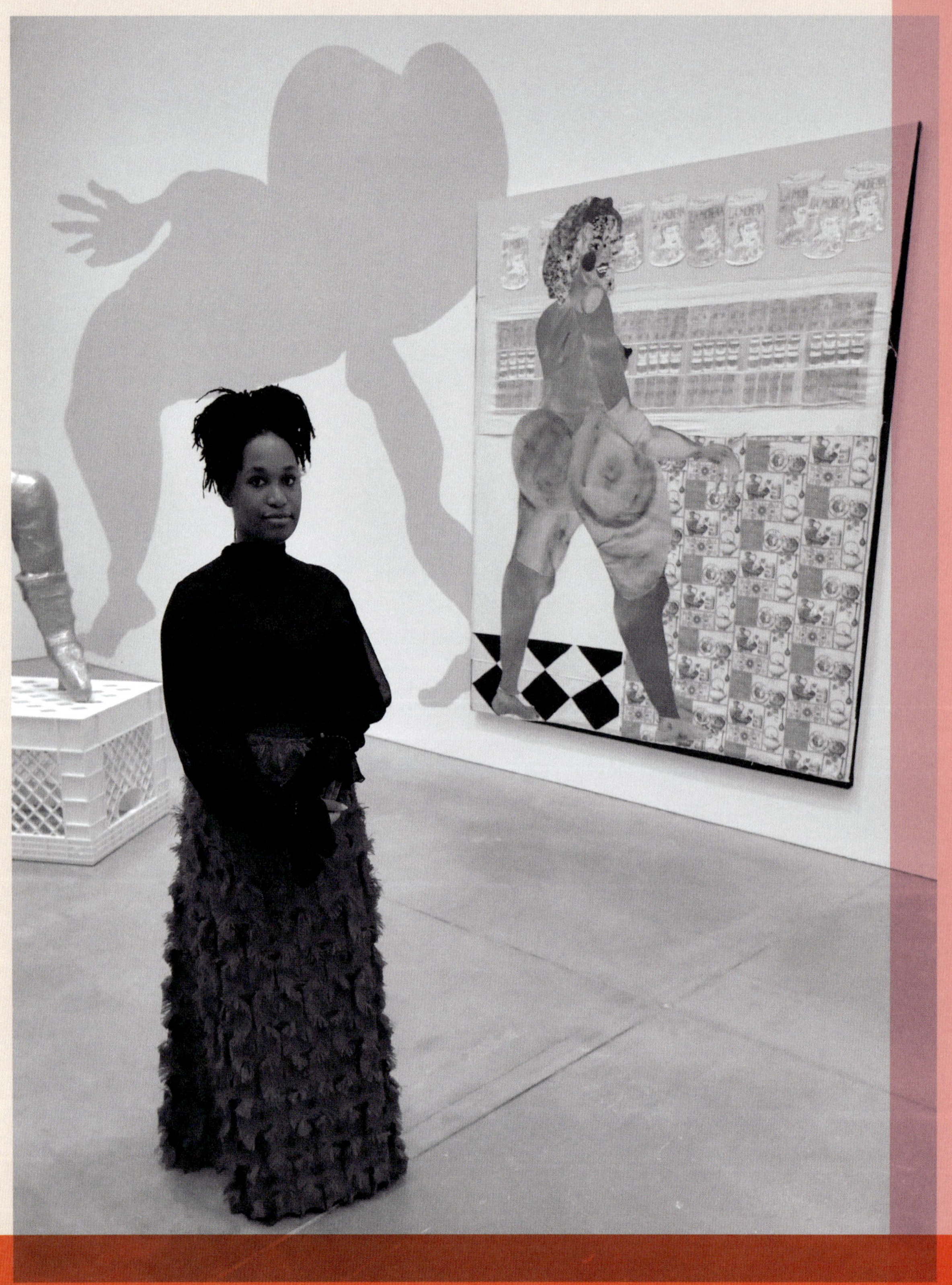

Tschabalala Self

(b.1990)

Appliqué

Many fabrics and materials come together to reflect equally complex identities in the work of Tschabalala Self. Her work navigates layers of race, sexuality and gender to understand how Black women are perceived in contemporary culture and shake up stagnant and uniform perceptions of 'Blackness'.

Self was born in Harlem as the youngest of five siblings. And not the youngest by a small margin – her closest sibling in age is twelve-years older. Her parents were well-travelled, well-educated and culturally switched on. This manifested in the names they bestowed on their children (Tschabalala is a South African name, and her other siblings have Arabic, Aztec and East African names) and in the interests they cultivated within them.

Creative exposure came at a young age. Self's father was a writer and her mother often bought or made interesting decor for their home, but her first real introduction to creating art came from time spent with her childhood babysitter, Miss Ella Robinson. She introduced Self to the very basics, like how to draw a stick figure, but she also planted an important seed about the power of representation. Miss Robinson would hunt for dolls with her in thrift stores and, if the pair couldn't find a Black doll, they would buy one of the available options and paint her. When Self eventually expressed interest in art, her mother insisted that if she wanted to be an artist, she should pursue a solid art education to develop her skills. In middle school, she earned a merit scholarship to take painting classes at the prestigious Harlem School of the Arts, and in high school she attended an all-girls' school with a strong art programme.

As a teen, Self found the art world alluring and mysterious. She knew she'd like a life connected to art but was unclear on the professional options available to her. To learn more, she did internships at a friend's parents' gallery and at the Metropolitan Museum of Art. As time approached to apply to universities, her high school best friend suggested that she attend an information session for Bard College. The friend pitched it to her as a place where artists go (indeed, people like Roy Lichtenstein and Toni Morrison are associated with the school), and it turned out to be the perfect place for Self to spend the next phase of her education.

At Bard, Self specialized in printmaking. She was particularly drawn to the mechanical processes of the medium, which she felt extended what she could create beyond the use of her two hands.

'It's a different way of working when you're using some kind of machine like a printing press, sewing machine – artists that deal a lot with fabrication would understand. It does introduce a different element into your practice … There are a lot of potentially political or social implications in working this that way as well. You're almost conceding to the fact that the work is meant for consumption because you are not solely involved in its production.'

As she approached graduation, she was firm in her desire to be an artist, but less sure on what she should do next. One of her professors strongly advised that she go to grad school, while another told her not to bother. She decided to head back to New York after finishing school to see if she could make her way as an artist. She ended up getting a less-than-satisfying job with a salt and olive oil company that, if nothing else, propelled her towards applying to graduate school. Her next step was an MFA in painting and printmaking from the Yale School of Art.

Self had a difficult start to grad school, when her mother died unexpectedly during her first year.

Her grief was immense, but with the support of her siblings, she carried on with her studies. She continued exploring the printmaking medium and discovered that she was more interested in the process and creativity that went into making printing plates than the act of transferring images to paper. She started to think of the plates as artworks in themselves and experimented with sewing them on to a canvas substrate before pivoting to making impressions of the plates on canvas. She would then cut out these impressions and sew them on to another canvas. Through this process, canvas became an active part of her materials, rather than just a surface, and this breakthrough was a prototype for her later use of appliqué.

Back home after graduating, Self no longer had access to printing materials and facilities but what she did have were piles of fabric that had belonged to her mother. Working with these materials provided a meaningful way for Self to connect with memories of her mother, and also inspired a revised way of working wherein she incorporated sewn fabrics alongside painting in her work. In her 2015 piece, *Out of Body*, she self-depicts female figures in a vibrant combination of appliquéd fabric. The body parts of the figures are broken up into different colours and materials, much as she might have split the parts across different plates during her printmaking process.

'How does one become a person? How does one form their personality, their persona, even? Imagining that maybe one's identity is not something that's inherent but a little more like something that is composed through a lifetime of various interactions and experiences. Ultimately, an individual is a singular construct but they are made of many different parts. It's important for me to have the work reflect this idea. That's why the figures are literally constructed from scraps and pieces that unite to create a whole.'

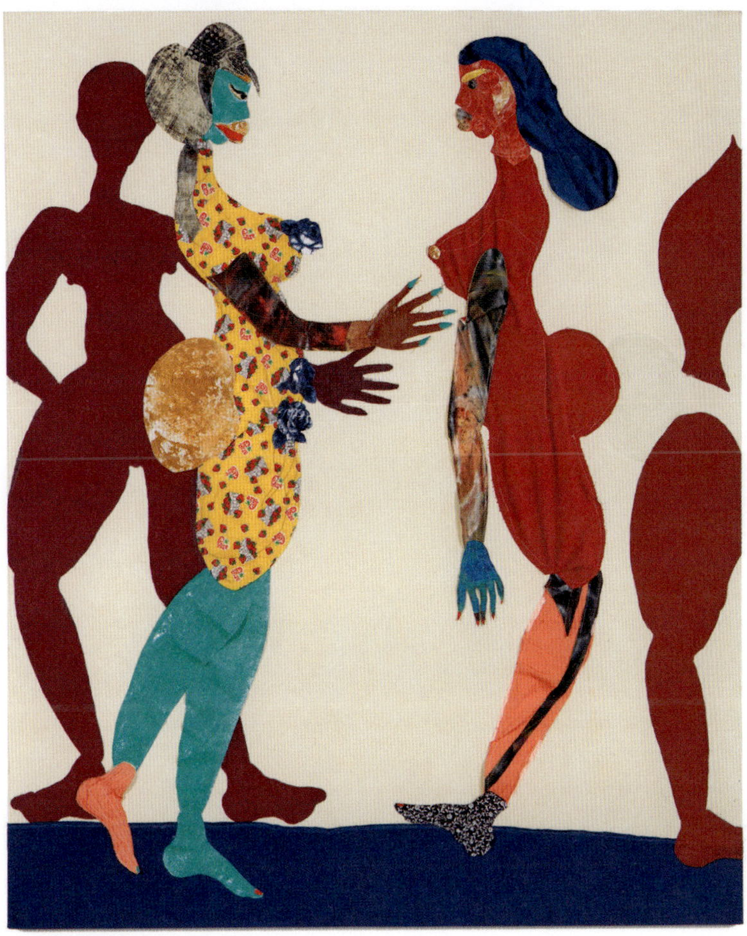

Out of Body, 2015.
Oil and fabric collage on canvas.
182.9 × 152.4 cm (72 × 60 in).

Some areas of the women's bodies are exaggerated in scale, relating to Self's experiences and observations of how Black women are received and depicted within society and popular culture. Across her work, Self often depicts Black women, aiming to represent them in ways that provide them space to be nuanced, complex beings. She's particularly keen to avoid playing into mythologies that support monoliths of what it means to be a Black woman. One can think of her work as displaying radical normality, wherein her figures are free to have a range of human experiences, irrespective of societal expectations. Self says, 'I'm obviously aware of all the societal beliefs and issues that are projected on to [the figures in my work], but I'm trying to make space for them to also just be spiritual beings or to be human beings that can have a narrative that exists outside of the general narrative surrounding this flattened idea of "Blackness" – this idea that "Blackness" needs to be either "this" or "that".'

Self's career trajectory has been that of a wunderkind, with the artist securing international solo shows within a couple years of graduating Yale. In her 'Bodega Run' series, exhibited in London, Shanghai, and New York, Self reflected on her roots in Harlem to depict scenes of everyday life within a predominantly Black, city environment. New York bodegas were originally established in the mid-twentieth century in Hispanic communities as hubs where people purchase goods; today they're found throughout many of New York's Black and Hispanic neighbourhoods. Self is fascinated by the complex and contrasting themes that play out in these shops, such as the way stores provide much-needed supplies to communities, but owners sometimes separate themselves from their patrons with plexiglass and by using surveillance to monitor their actions.

For a 2018 installation of *Bodega Run*, Self wallpapered a room with repeating images of products, as though they were lining a shelf. Her assemblage *Bayo* hangs on the wall, depicting a woman in a matching red crop top and shorts shopping in a bodega for pickled jalapeños. The blue and red chequered floor in combination with the concave mirror mounted in a corner, transports the viewer to a store environment and connects them to the woman on the canvas. The experience offers a Warholian look at consumerism and identity, but from the perspective of a Black metropolitan community.

There's freedom in Self's work, wherein she gives the characters she creates agency to embody myriad qualities and perspectives. She's inspired by her personal experiences and real people she encounters to reflect the multiplicity of the Black community – particularly Black women – that is not always portrayed in wider culture. It's celebratory, it's interesting and it's so, so needed.

Bodega Run, 2017.
Acrylic, watercolour, flashe, crayon, coloured pencil, hand-coloured photocopy, coloured photocopy, hand-coloured canvas on canvas. 243.8 × 213.4 cm (96 × 84 in).

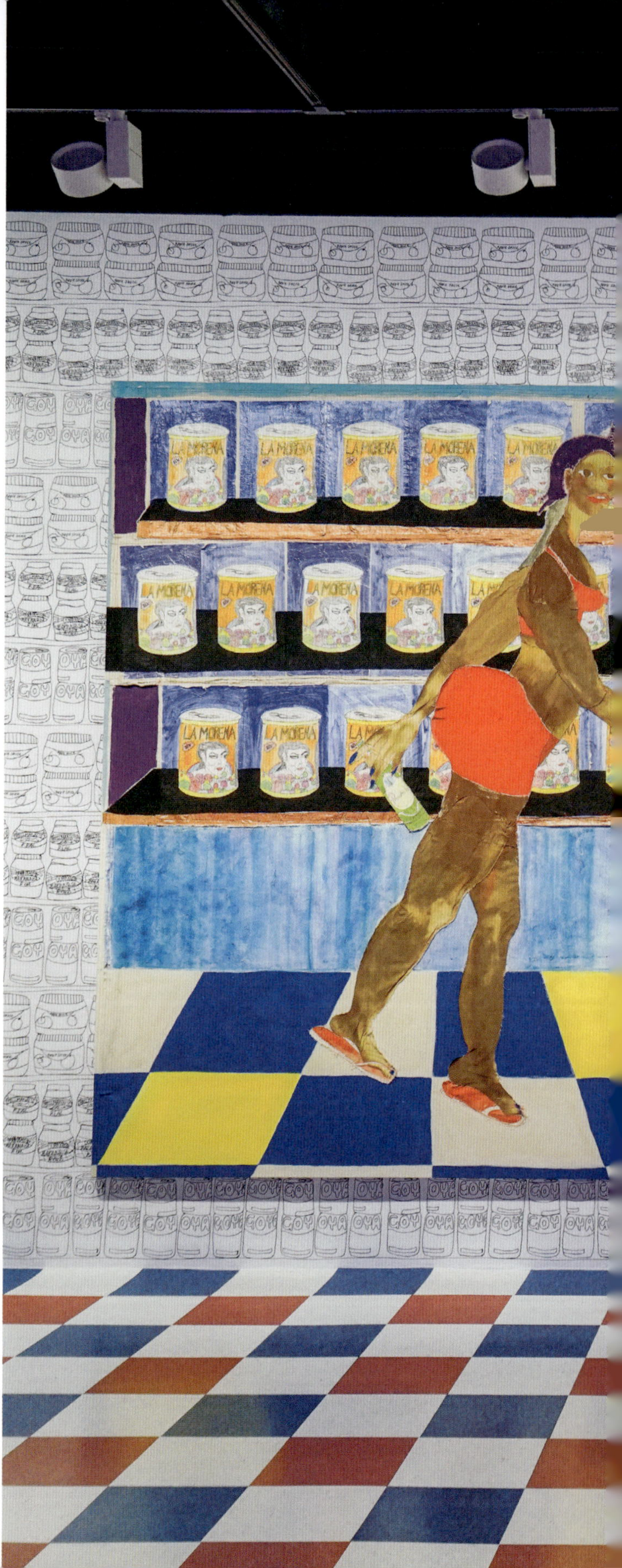

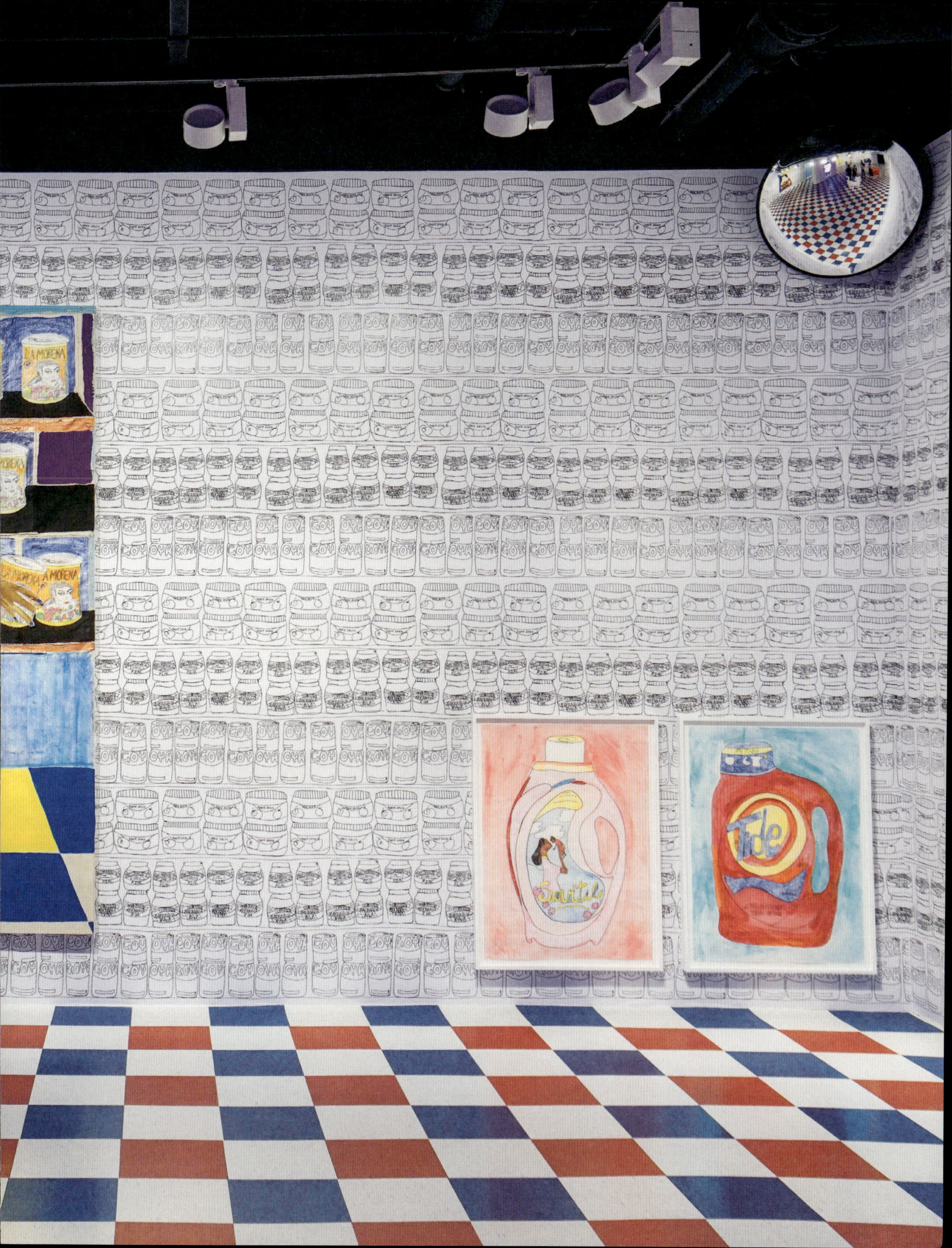

GOYA
LA MORENA
Tide

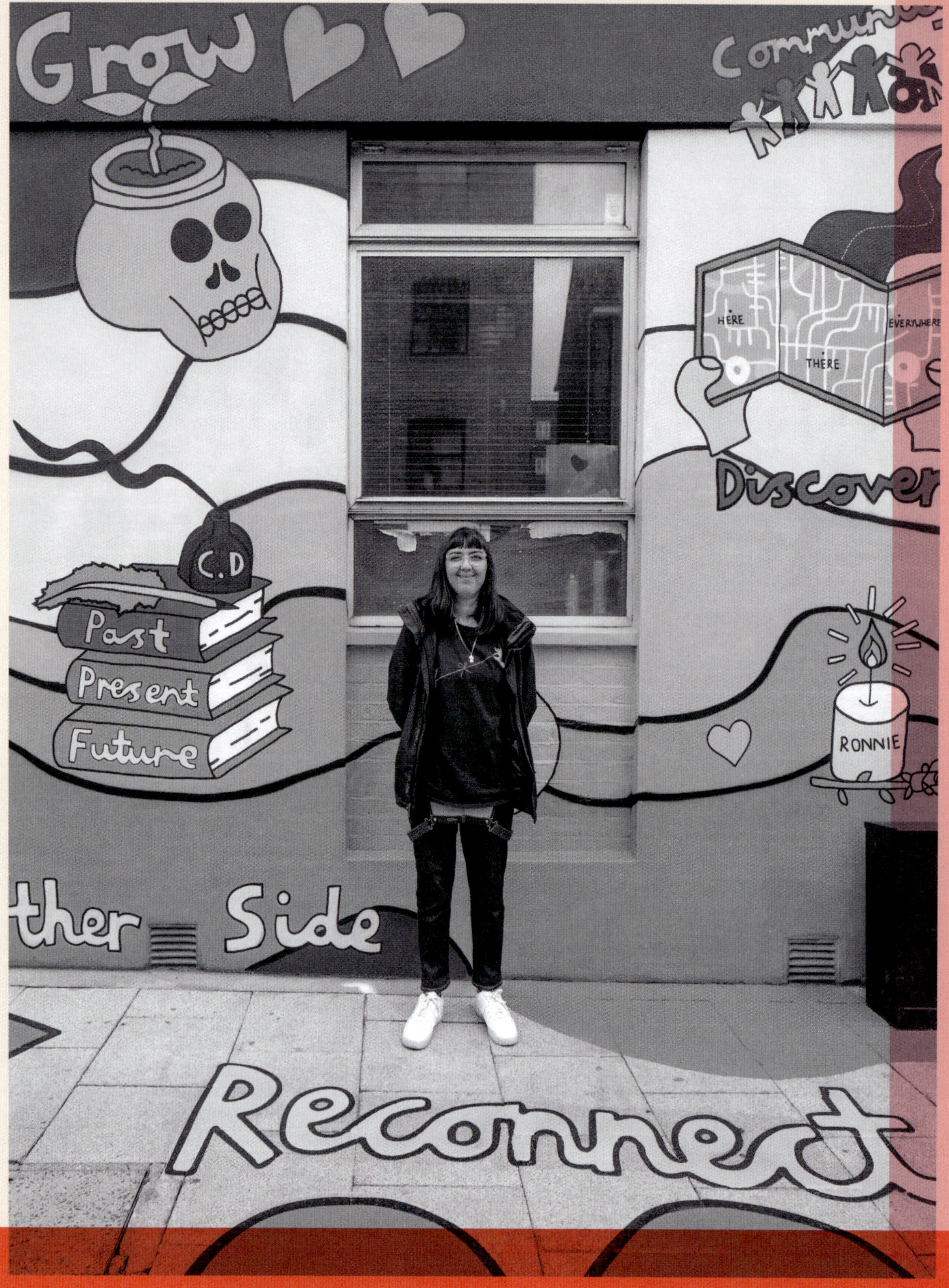

Grow
Community
Past
Present
Future
C.D
HERE
THERE
EVERYWHERE
Discover
RONNIE
ther Side
Reconnect

Hannah Hill

(b.1994)

Embroidery

On the list of the things considered 'radical' or 'bad-ass' embroidery may not initially rank very high for many people, but Hannah Hill has something to say about that. For Hill, embroidery is another form of mark-making that is as potent as any other medium. She puts needle to fabric to explore layers of her identity, to plumb her emotions and as a form of activism for social causes.

Hill was raised in a small family in north London, where her earliest exposure to textile art came from watching her mother sew and do craft projects. Her mum often made clothes, curtains and other items for the house, and told Hill stories about how her grandmother made dresses back in her mum's native home in Guyana. She also had a close relationship with her paternal grandparents from the moment she was born. They both worked as architects and would take her on walks, pointing out architectural features and generally stimulating her creative interests. They did such a good job of it that, for a time, Hill thought she'd like to become an architect as well.

As she entered her teens, she began to have issues with her mental health that eventually necessitated a break from school. When she returned after a couple of months, she focused on completing the core subjects of English and mathematics before entering a vocational course to study art and design. During this time, she worked across a range of mediums before finding her niche. When she took a class in surface design, her mother's skills with a needle came in handy as she was able to ask her for advice on techniques. From that point she was smitten – embroidery was her path forward.

Hill's mother had another set of skills that became a useful aid around this same time. Hill was producing and selling small Positivity Patches

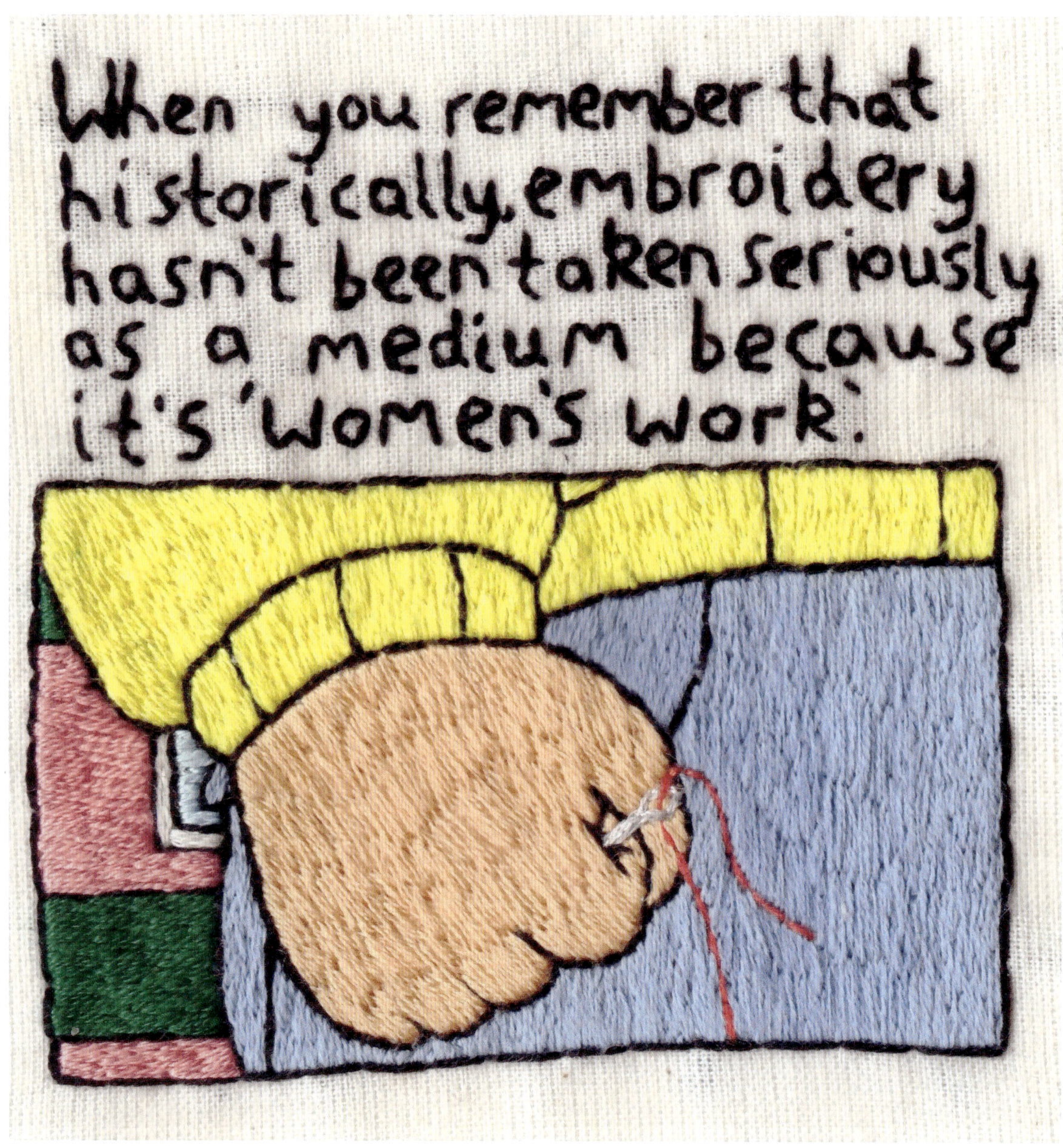

Arthur Meme, 2016.
Calico with cotton embroidery thread.
7 × 7 cm (2¾ x 2¾ in).

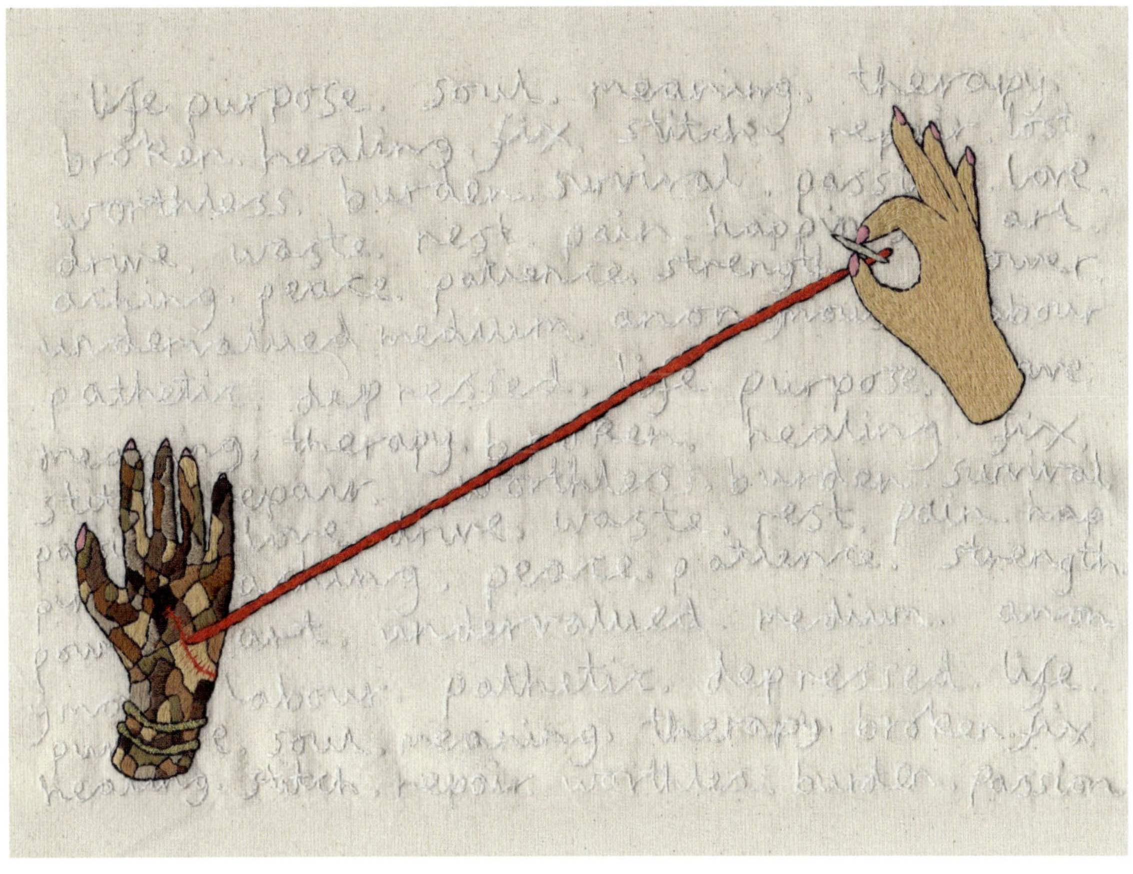

Healing Hands, 2019.
Calico with cotton embroidery thread.
36 × 25 cm (14⅛ x 9⅞ in).

with plucky phrases like, 'I took my meds today' and 'I showered'. They were small, embroidered patches on a felt background that people could wear like a merit badge to reward and encourage themselves. As they grew in popularity, she received word that three major retailers had plagiarized her designs for T-shirts. As her mother worked in Trading Standards for a London council, she was able to assist Hill in challenging these companies for using her work without permission, eventually settling the dispute out of court. Hill's bravery in standing up to big brands is impressive, especially considering she was nineteen years old at the time.

After finishing the vocational art course, Hill enrolled into Birmingham City University to study textile design with an emphasis on embroidery. At first, she thought she'd like to go down an interior or textile design career path, but a year of study brought on the realization that she decidedly did *not* want to do that. In search of an artistic, rather than commercial, route she switched to the fine art department. Her embroidery from this period often depicts outlined motifs floating in negative space in a style that could sit happily alongside the tattoo art of Sailor Jerry.

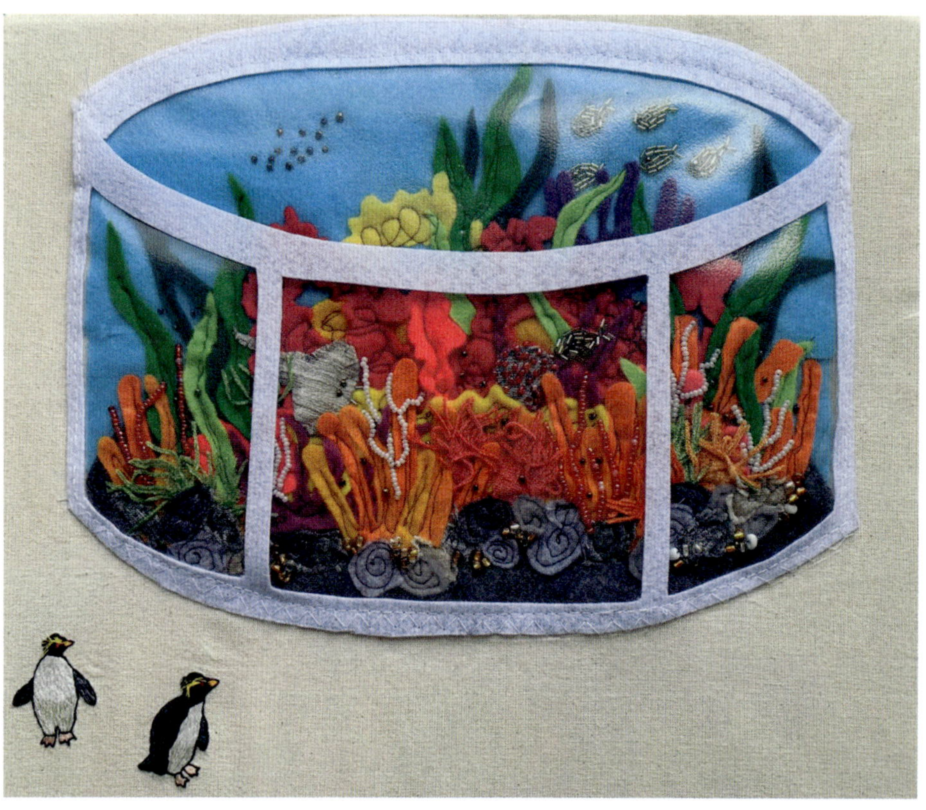

Pandemic Penguin Parade, 2020.
Calico, paint, felt, beads, plastic sheet and cotton embroidery
thread. 33 × 28 cm (13 × 11 in).

Alongside her formal university studies, Hill was receiving another form of education via social media, where she was reading and learning about feminism and other social causes. Sites like Twitter, Instagram and Tumblr also provided a platform for her to share images of her embroidery work, which would have been much more difficult for her to exhibit through more traditional means at that time. These channels continue to provided opportunities for Hill to engage with likeminded people, and this practice of creating work as part of a community has long been a part of many textile traditions.

'The communal side of textiles is important to me. As much as I say I'm sewing in my room and I'm happy just by myself, the communal history of textiles – quilting, working around the same thing, and completing it for warmth or to sell it – it's human history,' Hill explains. 'Especially when dealing with depression, embroidery is something that gave me a voice, gave me confidence. It's connected me with so many people.'

In 2016, she posted an embroidery interpretation of a meme from the children's cartoon *Arthur*. By the time she went to sleep and woke up the next day, her tweet of the piece had been shared more than 35,000 times. The meme in question shows an image of the character Arthur as he clenches his fist in frustration. It's often employed to convey quiet, simmering rage and accompanied by a caption. Hill subtly inserts a sewing needle into Arthur's hand (or is it a paw?) and sews text above commenting on her irritation with embroidery being dismissed as 'women's work', in a flippant manner. Appropriating a meme in this way is as powerful as the Pop artists' use of popular brands and media in the 1960s and 1970s; viewers who are au fait with the image can immediately contextualize what is happening and inject deeper connotations into the work.

After two more years in Birmingham, Hill moved back to London to finish her degree at City and Guilds London Art School. It was there that she was encouraged to delve deeper into her art history and activist interests through her work. From this time, her compositions took on more complex forms to address themes relating to feminism, identity and other social justice issues. In her final year of school, Hill began to experience severe hand cramps that continue to disrupt her ability to work. The year after she graduated, she was only able to produce one piece, entitled *Healing Hands*.

The image shows a solid-coloured right hand stitching a wound closed on a left hand composed of a patchwork of various shades of brown; the two hands are connected by a thick red thread. There's a notion of self-care and self-love in the piece, as the depiction of a left and right hand suggest they belong to the same body. In the background, Hill embroidered white text relating to her feelings about her hands and embroidery. Some words are positive, like 'peace' and 'love', but others are sorrowful, such as 'broken' and 'worthless'. The text is almost indiscernible from the background at a distance. This connects poetically to Hill's struggles with chronic pain and mental health, which can be invisible illnesses or challenges not easily observable by others.

In the period since Hill has not been able to embroider as often, she has looked to other mediums to express herself. In 2020, she created a felt piece titled *Pandemic Penguin Parade*, with her mother, inspired by photographs of penguins roaming free in aquariums that were closed during

"The communal side of textiles is important to me. As much as I say I'm sewing in my room and I'm happy just by myself, the communal history of textiles – quilting, working around the the same thing, and completing it for warmth or to sell it – it's human history."

the lockdowns following the global outbreak of Covid-19. The piece was featured in Grayson Perry's television series *Grayson's Art Club* and an associated exhibition at the Manchester Art Gallery that same year.

Hill also works to broaden the audiences engaging with embroidery through producing starter kits and colouring books. Her art practice is personal and self-exploratory, but it is also generous and deeply relatable. Hill encourages viewers to be kind to themselves and others, while celebrating the beauty and creativity of a challenging and versatile medium.

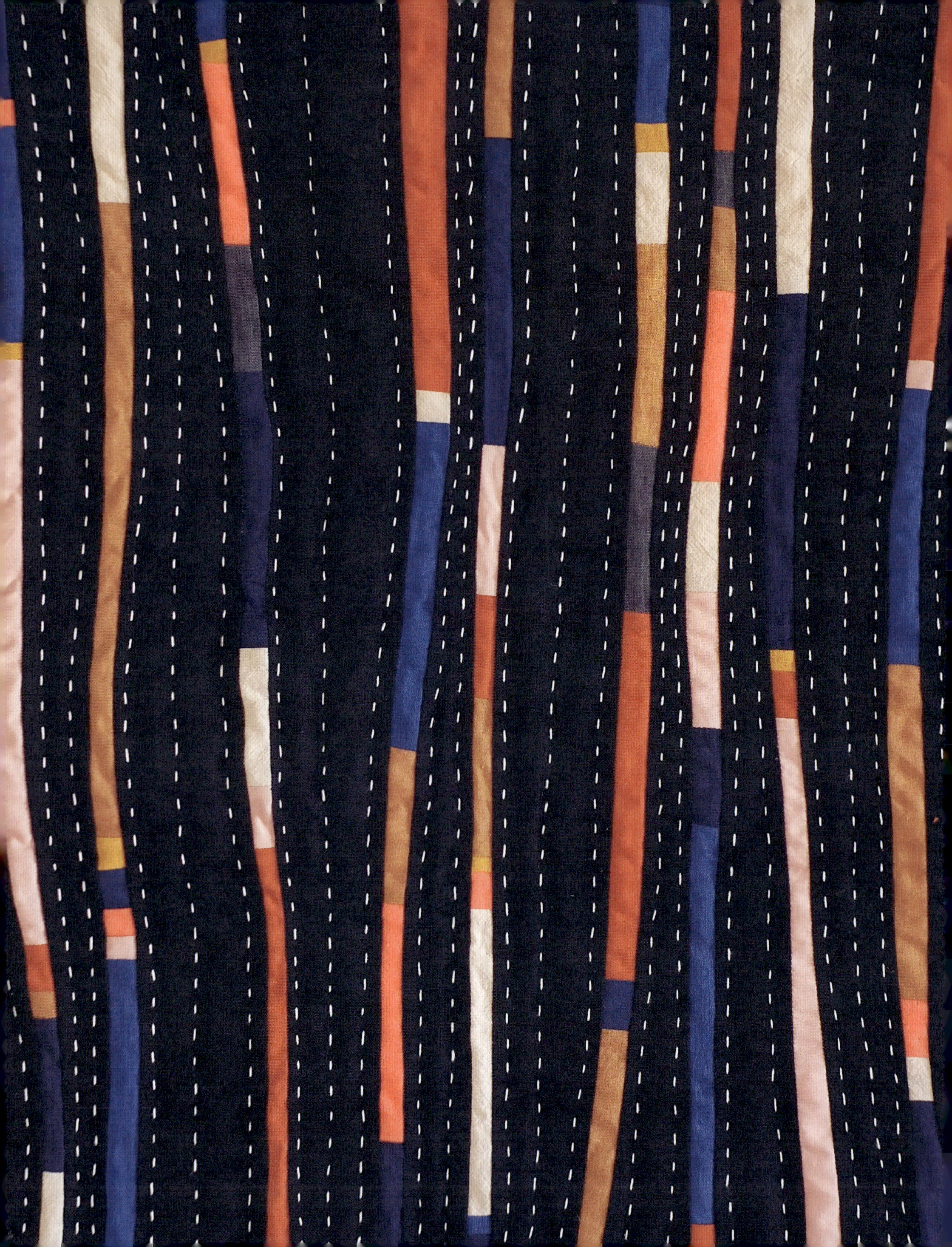

More artists to explore

Adelaide Alsop Robineau	Ceramics
Alison Britton	Ceramics
Ana Teresa Barboza	Embroidery
Anna Brown Ehlers	Weaving
Anna Dumitriu	Textile art
Beatrice Wood	Ceramics
Betty Woodman	Ceramics
Bisa Butler	Quilting
Bodil Manz	Ceramics
Britta Marakatt-Labba	Embroidery
Carol McNicoll	Ceramics
Cayce Zavaglia	Embroidery
Chiharu Shiota	Fibre Art
Constance Howard	Embroidery
Diana Scherer	Weaving
Edith Heath	Ceramics
Edith Meusnier	Fibre art
Elizabeth Fritsch	Ceramics
Elizabeth Morisette	Fibre art
Emilie Flöge	Wearable Art
Eva Zeisel	Ceramics
Faith Wilding	Weaving, Fibre art
Frances MacDonald	Textile design
Ghada Amer	Embroidery
Gillian Lowndes	Ceramics
Gina Adams	Quilting
Greer Lankton	Soft sculpture
Gunta Stölzl	Weaving
Harmony Hammond	Soft sculpture, Textile art
Harriet Powers	Quilting
Hillary Waters Fayle	Embroidery
Hoda Zarbaf	Soft sculpture
Ipnot	Embroidery
Irem Yazici	Embroidery
Iris van Herpen	Wearable Art

Jae Jarrell	Wearable Art
Jahnavi Innis	Quilting
Jane Morris	Embroidery
Jeongmoon Choi	Fibre art
Jessica So Ren Tang	Embroidery
Jessie Newberry	Embroidery
Joana Vasconcelos	Soft sculpture
Joyce Kolzoff	Textile art
Juno Birch	Ceramics
Kaarina Kaikkonen	Textile Art
Karen Karnes	Ceramics
Karine Jollet	Soft sculpture
Kiki Smith	Tapestries
Kimiyo Mishima	Ceramics
Kimsooja	Soft sculpture, Textile art
Klara Kristalova	Ceramics
Ladi Kwali	Ceramics
Léa Donnan	Soft sculpture
Lea McComas	Quilting
Lin Tianmiao	Fibre art
Lisa Larson	Ceramics
Lucy Sparrow	Soft sculpture
Magda Sayeg	Fibre art
Magdalene Odundo	Ceramics
Maija Grotell	Ceramics
Margaret MacDonald	Textile design
Marguerite Wildenhain	Ceramics
Marilyn Levine	Ceramics
Marion Tuu'luq	Embroidery, Textile art
Mary Louise McLaughlin	Ceramics
Mary Sibande	Soft sculpture
Mata Aho Collective	Fibre art
May Morris	Embroidery
Melissa Cody	Weaving
Meret Oppenheim	Soft Sculpture
Michelle Kingdom	Embroidery
Natalie Baxter	Soft sculpture
Nike Davies-Okundaye	Textile design
Olek	Fibre art
Orly Cogan	Fibre art, Embroidery
Rebecca Crompton	Embroidery
Rei Kawakubo	Wearable art
Rivane Neuenschwander	Textile art
Rose Cabat	Ceramics
Rose Eken	Ceramics
Roxanne Jackson	Ceramics
Ruth Asawa	Weaving
Ruth Duckworth	Ceramics
Sandra Chung Nga-shan	Soft sculpture
Sara Rahbar	Textile art
Senga Nengudi	Soft sculpture
Shary Boyle	Ceramics
Sheena Liam	Embroidery
Shio Kusaka	Ceramics
Simcha Even Chen	Ceramics
Simone Leigh	Ceramics
Sonia Delaunay	Wearable art, Textile art
Sonya Clark	Fibre art
Sophia Narrett	Embroidery, Fibre art
Sophie Taeuber-Arp	Weaving, Textile art
Susie Cooper	Ceramics
Susie Freeman	Textile art
Teresa Lim	Embroidery
Toshiko Takaezu	Ceramics
Tracey Emin	Embroidery, Applique
Vanessa Barragão	Fibre art
Vanessa Bell	Textile art, Ceramics
Victoria Udondian	Weaving, Textile art
Viola Frey	Ceramics
Xao Yang Lee	Embroidery
Yoshimi Futamura	Ceramics

Bibliography

'2015 Sarah Lucas.' Venice Biennale. British Council, 2015. https://venicebiennale.britishcouncil.org/history/2010s/2015-sarah-lucas.

'About Faith.' Faith Ringgold, n.d. https://www.faithringgold.com/about-faith/.

Ainley, Nathaniel. 'Embroidery Artist Weaves Memes with Modern Feminism.' *Vice*, April 10, 2016.

Albers, Anni. Oral history interview with Anni Albers, 1968 July 5. Interview by Sevim Fesci. *Archives of American Art, Smithsonian Institution*, July 5, 1968.

'Alexandra Kehayoglou.' Alexandra Kehayoglou, n.d. https://alexandrakehayoglou.com/.

Als, Hilton, Sadie Coles, Pauline Daly, Tracey Emin, Sarah Lucas, Gregor Muir, and Cerith Wyn Evans. 'Remembering Tracey Emin and Sarah Lucas's "the Shop".' Frieze, June 9, 2021.

Angeleti, Gabriella. 'Cecilia Vicuña: Tales of Text and Texture.' *The Art Newspaper*, December 6, 2019.

'Annette Messager at MoMA Web Site.' MoMA. The Museum of Modern Art, 1995. https://www.moma.org/interactives/exhibitions/1995/messager/index.html.

Apfelbaum, Polly. Interview by Ferren Gipson, December 11, 2020.

Barger, Michelle. 'Thoughts on Replication and the Work of Eva Hesse.' *Tate Papers*, no. 8 (2007).

Barnett, Laura. 'Monir Farmanfarmaian: "in Iran, Life Models Wear Pants."' *The Guardian*, July 12, 2011.

Bennetts, Leslie. 'JUDY CHICAGO: WOMEN'S LIVES and ART.' *The New York Times*, April 8, 1985, sec. Style.

Bent, Siobhan. 'INDIAN SCULPTOR MRINALINI MUKHERJEE DIES at 65.' *ArtAsiaPacific*, February 5, 2015.

'Biography.' Judy Chicago. Accessed June 1, 2021. https://www.judychicago.com/about/biography/.

'Biography – Billie Zangewa.' Lehmann Maupin. Accessed April 29, 2021. https://www.lehmannmaupin.com/artists/billie-zangewa/biography.

'Biography – Yayoi Kusama.' Yayoi Kusama, n.d. http://yayoi-kusama.jp/e/biography/index.html.

Bonét, Sasha. 'An Individual Is Made of Many Parts: Tschabalala Self Interviewed by Sasha Bonét - BOMB Magazine.' *Bomb Magazine*, November 20, 2018.

Borrelli-Persson, Laird. 'For Artist Isabelle de Borchgrave, the Future of Fashion Is in Paper.' *Vogue*, November 13, 2019.

Borzutzky, Daniel. 'Cecilia Vicuña: The Colour of Compassion.' *Ocula*, March 31, 2021.

Brenson, Michael. 'Magdalena Abakanowicz's "Abakans".' *Art Journal* 54, no. 1 (1995): 56–61.

Buck, Louisa. 'Tschabalala Self: "What Information Is Needed for One's Body to Become Gendered and Racialised?"' *The Art Newspaper*, February 7, 2020.

Budick, Ariella. 'Where Prayer Hall Meets Disco Ball.' *The Financial Times*, April 10, 2015.

Budick, Ariella. 'Miriam Schapiro, a Visionary, National Academy Museum, New York – 'Belated Homage to a Feminist Icon.' *Financial Times*, February 23, 2016.

Camhi, Leslie. 'A Career Woven from Life.' *The New York Times*, March 31, 2011, sec. Arts.

'Cecilia Vicuña.' Cecilia Vicuña, n.d. http://www.ceciliavicuna.com.

Chave, Anna C. 'Sculpture, Gender, and the Value of Labor.' *American Art* 24, no. 1 (March 2010): 26–30.

Chicago, Judy. Oral history interview with Judy Chicago, 2009 August 7-8. Interview by Judith O. Richards. *Archives of American Art, Smithsonian Institution*, August 7, 2009.

Clair, Kassia St. 'Elsa Schiaparelli and the Eternal Power of Shocking Pink.' *ELLE Decoration*, September 16, 2020.

Cliff, Aimee. 'Get to Know the Feminist Embroiderer behind the Best Arthur Meme on the Internet.' *The FADER*, October 7, 2016.

Clugston, Hannah. 'Polly Apfelbaum Review – a Trip into a Technicolour Dreamscape.' *The Guardian*, September 20, 2018.

Collins, Hattie. 'Hannah Hill Sews Powerful Statements through Embroidery.' *i-D*, December 6, 2016.

Constantine, Mildred. *Wall Hangings*. New York: The Museum of Modern Art, 1969.

Cooks, Bridget R. *Exhibiting Blackness : African Americans and the American Art Museum*. Amherst: University Of Massachusetts Press, 2011.

Cooper, Emmanuel. 'OBITUARIES Dame Lucie Rie.' *The Independent*, April 2, 1995.

Cotter, Holland. 'Lenore Tawney, an Innovator in Weaving, Dies at 100.' *The New York Times*, September 28, 2007, sec. Arts.

———. 'Louise Bourgeois, Influential Sculptor, Dies at 98.' *The New York Times*, May 31, 2010, sec. Arts.

———. 'Sculpture, Both Botanical and Bestial, Awe at the Met Breuer.' *The New York Times*, July 11, 2019, sec. Arts.

———. 'Silence Wrapped in Eloquent Cocoons.' *The New York Times*, December 4, 2014, sec. Arts.

———. 'Vivid Hallucinations from a Fragile Life.' *The New York Times*, July 12, 2012, sec. Arts.

D'Mello, Rosalyn. 'Lives of the Artists Mrinalini Mukherjee.' *Tate Etc*, no. 41 (October 29, 2017).

Das, Jareh. 'Billie Zangewa: Soldier of Love.' *Ocula*, April 24, 2020.

———. 'Tschabalala Self: "We Must Abandon the Lies and Mistruths We Have Been Told."' *Ocula*, November 25, 2020.

———. 'Dindga McCannon.' Shades of Noir Creative Database. Accessed April 26, 2021. https://www.shadesofnoir.org.uk/creatives/portfolio/dindga-mccannon/.

'Dindga McCannon.' Dindga McCannon. Accessed April 26, 2021. https://dindgamccannon.world/.

'Dorothea Tanning.' Dorothea Tanning, n.d. https://www.dorotheatanning.org/.

Duguid, Rosalind. 'Billie Zangewa on Her Sociopolitical Silk Works.' *ELEPHANT*, June 18, 2018.

Edemariam, Aida. 'The Saturday Interview: Sarah Lucas.' *The Guardian*. May 27, 2011.

Elderton, Louisa. 'Meet the Artist Examining the Colors and Queerness of the Gay Pride Flag.' *Garage*, September 26, 2018.

Elkin, Lauren. 'Dorothea Tanning: The Shape-Shifter.' *Tate Etc* Spring 2019, no. 45 (February 26, 2019).

Emin, Tracey, and Kate Abbot. 'Tracey Emin and Sarah Lucas: How We Made the Shop.' *The Guardian*, August 12, 2013.

'Eva Hesse Chronology.' The Jewish Museum, May 4, 2012.

Feigel, Lara. 'Dangerous Appetites: The Weird, Wild World of Dorothea Tanning.' *The Guardian*, February 8, 2019.

Ficpatrik, Milja. 'Miriam Schapiro.' Widewalls, May 16, 2015. https://www.widewalls.ch/artists/miriam-schapiro.

'Form and Fiber: Olga de Amaral's Textiles Weave Craft with Abstraction.' *Phillips*, May 18, 2016.

Freeman, Roland L. *A Communion of the Spirits : African-American Quilters, Preservers, and Their Stories*. Nashville, Tenn.: Rutledge Hill Press, 1996.

Gardner, Andrew. 'Mrinalini Mukherjee: Textile to Sculpture.' Post. The Museum of Modern Art, December 11, 2019. https://post.moma.org/mrinalini-mukherjee-textile-to-sculpture/.

———. 'Sheila Hicks.' MoMA. The Museum of Modern Art, n.d. https://www.moma.org/artists/2631.

'Gee's Bend Quilters.' Souls Grown Deep, n.d. https://www.soulsgrowndeep.org/gees-bend-quiltmakers.

Glueck, Grace. 'Dorothea Tanning, Surrealist Painter, Dies at 101.' *The New York Times*, February 2, 2012, sec. Arts.

Gouma-Peterson, Thalia. *Miriam Schapiro : Shaping the Fragments of Art and Life*. New York: Harry N. Abrams Publishers, 1999.

Greenhalgh, Paul. *Ceramic Art and Civilisation*. London ; New York: Bloomsbury Visual Arts, 2021.

Grimes, William. 'Magdalena Abakanowicz, Sculptor of Brooding Forms, Dies at 86.' *The New York Times*, April 21, 2017, sec. Arts.

———. 'Miriam Schapiro, 91, a Feminist Artist Who Harnessed Craft and Pattern, Dies (Published 2015).' *The New York Times*, June 25, 2015, sec. Arts.

Gupta, Trisha. 'Secular Deities, Enchanted Plants: Mrinalini Mukherjee at the NGMA.' *The Wire*, May 23, 2015.

Hazel, Tempestt. 'The Vessels That Marva Made: An Interview with Members of Sapphire & Crystals.' *Sixty Inches From Center*, December 18, 2018.

Hicks, Sheila. Oral history interview with Sheila Hicks, 2004 February 3-March 11. Interview by Monique Lévi-Strauss. *Archives of American Art, Smithsonian Institution*, February 3, 2004.

Hill, Hannah. 'About Hanecdote.' Hanecdote. Accessed July 19, 2021. http://www.hanecdote.co.uk/home/.

———. Interview by Ferren Gipson, January 25, 2021.

Hill, Hannah, and Kate Rolison. Artist Meets Hannah Hill x Kate Rolison. Interview by Tate Collective. *Tate*, December 10, 2018.

Holton, Curlee Raven. *Faith Ringgold : A View from the Studio*. Boston: Bunker Hill Pub. In Association With Allentown Art Museum, 2004.

Hoptman, Laura. 'Yayoi Kusama's Return to MoMA.' *Inside/Out* (blog), October 9, 2012.

Hou, Hanru, Stephanie Rosenthal, and Wu Hung. *Yin Xiuzhen*. London: Phaidon Press, Cop, 2015.

'Isabelle.' Isabelle de Borchgrave. Accessed March 2021. https://isabelledeborchgrave.com/pages/biography.

'It's All about ME, Not You.' Mattress Factory, n.d. https://mattress.org/works/its-all-about-me-not-you/.

Jhaveri, Shanay, ed. *Mrinalini Mukherjee*. Mumbia: Shoestring Publisher, 2019.

Johnson, Jameson. 'Weaving with the Thread of Time: In Conversation with Cecilia Vicuña.' *Boston Art Review*, May 14, 2019.

Joyce Wallace Scott. *ENTWINED : Sisters and Secrets in the Silent World of Artist Judith Scott.* Beacon, 2017.

'Judith Scott.' Judith & Joyce Scott. Accessed May 24, 2021.

'Judith Scott (Alum).' Creative Growth, n.d. https://creativegrowth.org/judith-scott.

Kahla, Harri. 'Bryk, Rut (1916 - 1999).' Henkilöhistoria, April 22, 1998. https://kansallisbiografia.fi/kansallisbiografia/henkilo/4803.

Kazanjian, Dodie. 'Artist Tschabalala Self Upends Our Perception of the Female Form.' *Vogue*, April 13, 2020.

Kehayoglou, Alexandra. Interview by Ferren Gipson, January 19, 2021.

Kennedy, Randy. 'Monir Farmanfarmaian, Iranian and Nonagenarian, Celebrates a New York Museum First.' *The New York Times*, March 20, 2015, sec. Arts.

Kent, Rachel. 'Annette Messager: Life Enlarged.' MCA Australia, July 24, 2014.

Knight, Christopher. 'Review: Polly Apfelbaum's Fallen Paintings and Beads of Devotion in Her Secular Chapel of Abstract Art.' *Los Angeles Times*, October 15, 2016.

Knott, Becky. 'Lucie Rie: A Secret Life of Buttons.' *V&A Blog* (blog), April 24, 2017.

Lauf, Cornelia. 'Dries van Noten and Ms Kehayoglou: Carpets and Bridges to Bring Diversities Closer.' *Lampoon*, March 31, 2021.

Levin, Gail. *Becoming Judy Chicago. A Biography of the Artist.* Berkeley: University Of California Press, 2019.

Levi-Strauss, Monique. 'Dorothea Tanning: Soft Sculptures.' *American Fabrics and Fashions*, no. 108 (1976): 68–69.

Lin, Xiaoping. *Children of Marx and Coca-Cola : Chinese Avant-Garde Art and Independent Cinema*. Honolulu: University Of Hawai'i Press, 2010.

'Louise Bourgeois: The Fabric Works.' Hauser & Wirth, n.d. https://www.hauserwirth.com/hauser-wirth-exhibitions/3595-louise-bourgeois-the-fabric-works.

Manchester, Elizabeth. ''Pauline Bunny', Sarah Lucas, 1997.' Tate, 2000. https://www.tate.org.uk/art/artworks/lucas-pauline-bunny-t07437.

'Marva Lee Pitchford-Jolly.' Art & Design in Chicago. WTTW Chicago, n.d. https://interactive.wttw.com/art-design-chicago/marva-lee-pitchford-jolly.

"Marva Pitchford Jolly." Woman Made Gallery, n.d. https://womanmade.org/artwork/marva-pitchford-jolly-2/.

Masters, Christopher. 'Magdalena Abakanowicz Obituary.' *The Guardian*, April 24, 2017.

McCannon, Dindga. In Conversation. Interview by Lowery Sims. *Phillips*, November 16, 2020.

———. Oral History Project. Interview by Phillip Glahn. *BOMB Magazine*, August 3, 2020.

———. Interview by Ferren Gipson, December 8, 2020.

McDermott, Emily. 'Billie Zangewa – the Fierce Feminine.' Art Basel, n.d. https://www.artbasel.com/news/billie-zangewa-the-fierce-feminine-art-basel-miami-beach-2018.

Mcdonald, Robin, and Valerie Pope Burnes. *Visions of the Black Belt : A Cultural Survey of the Heart of Alabama*. Tuscaloosa, Al: The University Alabama Press, 2015.

McNay, Michael. 'Louise Bourgeois Obituary.' *The Guardian*, May 31, 2010, sec. Art and design.

Messager, Annette. Interview by Natasha Leoff. *Journal of Contemporary Art*. Accessed April 2021.

———. Interview by Bernard Marcade. *BOMB Magazine*, 1989.

Milofsky, Leslie. 'Magdalena Abakanowicz.' *Feminist Studies* 13, no. 2 (1987): 363–78.

'Miriam Schapiro.' West by Midwest. MCA Chicago, n.d. https://mcachicago.org/Publications/Websites/West-By-Midwest/Research/Artists/Miriam-Schapiro.

'Monir Shahroudy Farmanfarmaian.' Monir Shahroudy Farmanfarmaian, n.d. https://www.monirff.com/.

Morris, Bob. 'Faith Ringgold Will Keep Fighting Back.' *The New York Times*, June 11, 2020, sec. Arts.

Morris, Catherine. 'Biography Is Complicated.' *Art21*, October 30, 2018. https://art21.org/read/biography-is-complicated/.

'Mrinalini Mukherjee during the Preparation for the Fine Arts Fair, 1969.' Asia Art Archive, n.d. https://aaa.org.hk/en/collections/search/archive/jyoti-bhatt-archive-fine-arts-fair-1969/object/mrinalini-mukherjee-during-the-preparation-for-the-fine-arts-fair-1969.

Nemser, Cindy. 'An Interview with Eva Hesse.' *Artforum* 7, no. 9 (May 1970): 59–63.

Neyroz, Christine-Aurore. Letter to Ferren Gipson. 'Your Book (Questions for Isabelle de Borchgrave).' March 1, 2021.

Nkanga, Otobong. Interview with Otobong Nkanga. *The White Review*, October 2014.

———. Interview by Ferren Gipson, April 7, 2021.

Nochlin, Linda. *Women Artists : The Linda Nochlin Reader*. Edited by Maura Reilly. London: Thames & Hudson, 2020.

O'Neill-Butler, Lauren. 'Lauren O'Neill-Butler on Polly Apfelbaum.' *Artforum*, August 2014.

'Olga de Amaral.' Smith Davidson Gallery. Accessed June 7, 2021.

'Olga de Amaral / About.' Olga de Amaral, n.d. https://olgadeamaral.art/about.html.

Ologundudu, Folasade. 'Tschabalala Self Presents the Beauty of Black Women in Her Own Terms.' *Cultured Magazine*, April 12, 2021.

'Opening Conversation with Isabelle de Borchgrave.' YouTube. Dixon Gallery and Gardens, October 19, 2017. https://www.youtube.com/watch?v=1N2xgj1XB_k&t=1126s.

'Otobong Nkanga | Visual Artist.' Otobong Nkanga, n.d. https://www.otobong-nkanga.com/.

'Otobong Nkanga: From Where I Stand – Exhibition at Tate St Ives.' Tate, n.d. https://www.tate.org.uk/whats-on/tate-st-ives/exhibition/otobong-nkanga.

Parker, Rozsika. *The Subversive Stitch : Embroidery and the Making of the Feminine*. London: Bloomsbury Visual Arts, 2019.

Perennès, Marie. 'Olga de Amaral.' AWARE. Archives of Women Artists Research & Exhibitions, n.d. https://awarewomenartists.com/en/artiste/olga-de-amaral/.

Pettway, Mary Margaret. Interview by Ferren Gipson, December 10, 2020.

Phaidon Editors, ed. *Great Women Artists*. London ; New York, Ny: Phaidon, 2019.

Pilling, David. 'The World according to Yayoi Kusama.' *Financial Times*. January 20, 2012.

Pitchford-Jolly, Marva Lee. Interview by The HistoryMakers. *The HistoryMakers*, July 15, 2008.

'Plushy Terrorism and Cities in Suitcases: Artist Yin Xiuzhen on How to Challenge Society with Its Own Refuse.' *Artspace*, January 14, 2017.

Pogrebin, Robin. 'With New Show, Tschabalala Self Explores Black American Identity.' *New York Times*, November 2, 2020.

'Polly Apfelbaum.' Institute of Contemporary Art - Philadelphia, PA, 2003. https://icaphila.org/exhibitions/polly-apfelbaum-2/.

'Polly Apfelbaum.' Polly Apfelbaum. Accessed May 2021. http://www.pollyapfelbaum.com/.

'Polly Apfelbaum. Blossom. 2000.' MoMA. The Museum of Modern Art. Accessed May 2021. https://www.moma.org/collection/works/86477.

Potts, Alex. 'Louise Bourgeois Sculptural Confrontations.' *Oxford Art Journal* 22, no. 2 (January 1, 1999): 37–53.

Rapoport, Marianna. 'Catwalk Carpet: Alexandra Kehayoglou Weaves Together Art and Fashion for Dries van Noten's S/S 2015 Showscape.' *Wallpaper**, February 2, 2015.

Raza, Nada. '"Jauba", Mrinalini Mukherjee, 2000.' Tate, January 2013. https://www.tate.org.uk/art/artworks/mukherjee-jauba-t14458.

Reif, Rita. 'ARTS/ARTIFACTS;Artistry and Invention Seamlessly Joined.' *The New York Times*, November 26, 1995, sec. Arts.

Reynolds, Pamela. 'At the ICA, "out of Body" Explores Color and Texture of Black Life in Harlem.' *WBUR*, January 16, 2020.

Riding, Alan. 'Annette Messager: A Bold Messenger for Feminist Art.' *The New York Times*, June 26, 2007, sec. Arts.

Ringgold, Faith. *We Flew over the Bridge : The Memoirs of Faith Ringgold*. Durham, N.C.: Duke University Press, 2005.

Ringgold, Faith, and Dan Cameron. *Dancing at the Louvre : Faith Ringgold's French Collection and Other Story Quilts*. Berkeley, Calif.: University Of California Press, 1998.

Ringgold, Faith, and Josephine Withers. 'Faith Ringgold: Art.' *Feminist Studies* 6, no. 1 (1980): 207.

Rose, Barbara. *Magdalena Abakanowicz*. New York: Harry N. Abrams, 1994.

'Rut Bryk.' Tapio Wirkklala Rut Bryk Foundation, n.d. http://www.

wirkkalabryk.fi/rb/Rut_Bryk_ENG/Rut_Bryk.html.

Salus, Carol. 'Miriam Schapiro.' Jewish Women's Archive, n.d. https://jwa.org/encyclopedia/article/schapiro-miriam.

Schapiro, Miriam. Oral history interview with Miriam Schapiro, 1989 September 10. Interview by Ruth Bowman. *Archives of American Art, Smithsonian Institution*, September 10, 1989.

Schiaparelli, Elsa. *Shocking Life : The Autobiography of Elsa Schiaparelli.* London: V&A Publishing, 2018.

Self, Tschabalala. Interview by Ferren Gipson, January 13, 2021.

Shaikh, Nageen. 'Exploring Sexuality and Myth through Fiber and Other Types of Sculpture.' *Hyperallergic*, September 3, 2019.

Shattuck, Kathryn. 'In the Woof and Warp of Miniatures, Interlocking Metaphors and Journeys.' *The New York Times*, September 4, 2006, sec. Arts.

Sierzputowski, Kate. 'New One-of-a-Kind Landscape Rugs by Alexandra Kehayoglou.' *Colossal*, September 9, 2016.

Simms, Molly. 'These Carpets Will Turn Your Home into a Lush Woodland.' Oprah.com. Accessed July 19, 2021. https://www.oprah.com/inspiration/alexandra-kehayoglou-nature-inspired-carpets.

Singh, Devika. 'Mrinalini Mukherjee.' *Frieze*, March 16, 2015.

Smith, Nia I'man. 'Teaching Resource: Special Exhibition, Judith Scott – Bound and Unbound.' Brooklyn Museum. Accessed May 10, 2021. https://d1lfxha3ugu3d4.cloudfront.net/education/docs/Judith_Scott_Teacher_Packet.pdf.

Smith, Roberta. 'Sarah Lucas, Unmasked: From Perverse to Profound.' *The New York Times*, September 5, 2018.

Starewicz, Artur. 'About Magdalena Abakanowicz.' Magdalena Abakanowicz, n.d. https://www.abakanowicz.art.pl/about/-about.php.html.

Stein, Donna. 'Monir Shahroudy Farmanfarmaian: Empowered by American Art: An Artist's Journey.' *Woman's Art Journal* 33, no. 1 (2012): 3.

Stevens, Kyes. 'Gee's Bend.' *Encyclopedia of Alabama*, March 9, 2007. http://encyclopediaofalabama.org/article/h-1094.

Sussman, Elisabeth. *Eva Hesse - Sculpture.* New Haven: Yale University Press, 2006.

Takac, Balasz. 'Inside Womanhouse, a Beacon of Feminist Art.' Widewalls, June 2, 2019. https://www.widewalls.ch/magazine/judy-chicago-womanhouse.

'Talking Textiles with Billie Zangewa.' Phaidon, March 13, 2019. https://www.phaidon.com/agenda/art/articles/2019/march/13/talking-textiles-with-billie-zangewa/.

Tanning, Dorothea. *Between Lives : An Artist and Her World.* Evanston, Ill.: Northwestern University Press, 2004.

Tapta. 'Soft Sculpture: Textiles in Architectural Space.' *Leonardo* 18, no. 3 (1985): 161.

Tawney, Lenore. Oral history interview with Lenore Tawney, 1971 June 23. Interview by Paul Cummings. *Archives of American Art, Smithsonian Institution*, June 23, 1971.

Terracciano, Emilia. 'On Being Crafty: Mrinalini Mukherjee's Sleight of Hand and the Politics of Fibre Art (1977–94).' *Oxford Art Journal* 43, no. 1 (March 1, 2020): 1–23.

'The Art of Louise Bourgeois – Look Closer.' Tate, n.d. https://www.tate.org.uk/art/artists/louise-bourgeois-2351/art-louise-bourgeois.

The Editors of Encyclopaedia Britannica. 'Dame Lucie Rie.' In *Encyclopædia Britannica*, 1998.

———. 'Elsa Schiaparelli.' In *Encyclopædia Britannica*, November 9, 2018.

The Josef and Anni Albers Foundation. 'Biographies.' The Josef and Anni Albers Foundation, n.d. https://albersfoundation.org/artists/biographies/.

'The Lenore G. Tawney Foundation.' The Lenore G. Tawney Foundation, n.d. https://lenoretawney.org/.

Thill, Vanessa. 'At the Borderline of Uncontrollability: Six Lessons from Eva Hesse.' Art in America. *Art News*, August 8, 2017.

'Timeline.' Judy Chicago. Accessed June 1, 2021. https://www.judychicago.com/.

'TSCHABALALA SELF.' Tschabalala Self, n.d. https://tschabalalaself.com/.

'Tschabalala Self: Bodega Run.' Yuz Museum Shanghai, 2018. http://www.yuzmshanghai.org/tschabalala-self-bodega-run/?lang=en.

Turner, Grady T. 'Yayoi Kusama by Grady T. Turner - BOMB Magazine.' BOMB Magazine, January 1, 1999.

Victoria and Albert Museum. 'Cravat, Elsa Schiaparelli.' , December 15, 1999. https://collections.vam.ac.uk/item/O15655/cravat-jumper-elsa-schiaparelli/.

———. 'Evening Coat, Elsa Schiaparelli and Jean Cocteau.' , October 28, 2005. https://collections.vam.ac.uk/item/O117953/evening-coat-schiaparelli-elsa/.

———. 'The Tears Dress | Dali, Salvador | Schiaparelli, Elsa | V&a Explore the Collections.' , September 24, 2003. https://collections.vam.ac.uk/item/O84418/the-tears-dress-evening-ensemble-dress-schiaparelli-elsa/.

'Wall Hangings (Press Release).' *MoMA*. The Museum of Modern Art, February 25, 1969.

Wallach, Amei. 'Fabric of Their Lives.' *Smithsonian Magazine*, October 2006.

Wan, Katy. "Weapon', Yin Xiuzhen, 2003–7.' Tate, July 2017. https://www.tate.org.uk/art/artworks/yin-weapon-t15249.

Weber, Nicholas Fox, and Pandora Tabatabai Asbaghi. *Anni Albers.* New York, N.Y.: Guggenheim Museum Publications, 1999.

Weiss, Sasha. 'Judy Chicago, the Godmother.' *The New York Times*, February 7, 2018, sec. T Magazine.

'Yayoi Kusama. Accumulation No. 1. 1962.' MoMA. The Museum of Modern Art, 2019. https://www.moma.org/collection/works/163826.

'Yin Xiuzhen.' Pace Gallery. Accessed April 2021. https://www.pacegallery.com/artists/yin-xiuzhen/.

Zangewa, Billie. Billie Zangewa: The Ultimate Act of Resistance is Self-Love. *Tate*, February 21, 2020.

———. Interview by Ferren Gipson, December 15, 2020.

Zapata, Sarah. Interview by Ferren Gipson, October 22, 2021.

Index

Page numbers in *italics* refer to illustrations

A

Abakanowicz, Magdalena 8, 86–91, 94
   Abakan Red 88–9, 90
   Embryology 90, *91*
   Heads (14 pieces) 90, *91*
Abrams, Willie 'Ma Willie', *'Roman Stripes' Variation 16*, 17
Abstract Expressionism 71, 106
Abstract Minimalism 156
Academy of Fine Arts, Warsaw 89
Albers, Anni 9, 28–33, 94, 101
   Untitled (1969) *33*
   Wall hanging 32
Albers, Josef 30, 101, 106
Allende, Salvador 145
Alvarez, Lili de 27
Amaral, Olga de 92–7
   Alchemy 50 96
   Entrelazado en rojo y negro 94, *95*
   Lienzo ceremonial 14 97, *97*
Apfelbaum, Polly 154–9
   Blossom 157
   Hand weavers 157, 158
   The Sound of Ceramics 158, 159, *159*
appliqué, Tschabalala Self 196–201
Arnett, William 17
Artists for Democracy 145
Artists Union 89
The Arts Council Gallery 37
Arts and Crafts 7
Awanyu 20

B

Bachelet, Michelle 145
Bakst, Léon 135
Balanchine, George 47, *47*
Bard College 198
Bass, Saul 17
Bauhaus 29–30, 41, 58, 93, 101
Bell, Vanessa 116
Bendolph, Louisiana P, *My Way 15*
Biennale of Sydney (2012) *144*, 147
Black Arts Movement 137–8
Black Mountain College 30, 93

Bonwit Teller 64, 65
Borchgrave, Isabelle de 132–5
   Madame de Pompadour Dress 134, *135*
   Paper Replica of Jacqueline Bouvier's Wedding Dress 134, *134*
Botticelli, Sandro 176
Boucher, François 134
Bourgeois, Louise 48, 50–5, 109
   The Destruction of the Father 52, *52*, 54
   Fragile Goddess 53, 54
   Untitled 55
Brach, Paul 71
Brandenburg, Martin 29
Brown, Kay 138
Bryk, Rut 56–61
   Jaipur 58, *60*
   Song of a Migratory Bird 58, 61, *61*
   Venetian palace: figures in a window 58, *59*
Buffet-Picabia, Gabrièle 24

C

California Institute of the Arts 72, 116
carpets, Alexandra Kehayoglou 184–9
ceramics 9
   Judy Chicago 114–19
   Lucie Rie 34–7
   Maria Martinez 18–21
   Marva Lee Pitchford-Jolly 110–13
   Mrinalini Mukherjee 148–53
   Polly Apfelbaum 154–9
   Rut Bryk 56–61
Chanel, Coco 23
Chicago, Judy 72, 114–19
   Birth Hood 116, *117*
   Birth Tear 117, 119, *119*
   The Dinner Party 116, 117
Chicago Institute of Design 41
City and Guilds London Art School 207
Cocteau, Jean, *Evening Coat 25*, 27
College Art Association 73
Coper, Hans 36
Cowan, Audrey 117
Cranbrook Academy of Art 93–4
Creative Growth Art Centre 122, 125
Cubism 82

D

Dada 8, 109
Dalí, Salvador 27, 46
de Kooning, Willem 64
Diaghilev, Serge 134–5
Duchamp, Marcel 24, 125

E

Ecole Nationale Supérieure des Beaux-Arts 127, 180

Ehrman, Marli 41
'85 Art New Wave 168
embroidery, Hannah Hill 202–7
Emin, Tracey 162
Ernst, Max 46, 47
Expressionism 82

F
Farmanfarmaian, Abolbashar 65
Farmanfarmaian, Monir Shahroudy 62–7
  Heartache No. 22 65, 67
  Shopping Bag, Bonwit Teller 64
  Third Family Hexagon 66
Feminist Art Movement 115
fibre art
  Cecilia Vicuña 142–7
  Eva Hesse 104–9
  Judith Scott 120–5
  Lenore Tawney 38–43
  Mrinalini Mukherjee 148–53
  Olga de Amaral 92–7
  Sarah Zapata 190–5
  Sheila Hicks 98–103
Foundation of Indian Artists 153
Frankenthaler, Helen 89, 156
Freedom Quilting Bee 17
Friends of Finnish Handicrafts 57

G
Gee, Joseph 13
Gee's Bend 12–17
Goldsmith's College 161
Goldwater, Robert 52
Guggenheim, Peggy 46
Guggenheim Museum, New York 67, 134
Gwathmey, Robert 82

H
Hepworth, Barbara 41
Hermès 186
Hesse, Eva 8, 78, 104–9
  Contingent 108, 109
  No Title 109
  Ringaround Rosie 106
Hicks, Sheila 94, 98–103, 106
  Greta Weaving No. 55 100
  Palitos con Bolas 103
  The Silk Rainforest 102, *102*
Hill, Hannah 202–7
  Arthur Meme 204, 206–7
  Healing Hands 205, 207
  Pandemic Penguin Parade 206, 207
Hirst, Damien 161, 162
Hoffman, Josef 35

J
Johns, Jasper 41
Judd, Donald 78, 106

K
Kahlo, Frida 46, 73, *73*, 116
Kaipiainen, Birger 57
Kehayoglou, Alexandra 184–9
  Pastizal DVN 186, *187*
  Prayer Rug 188, *189*
  Santa Cruz River 188, *188*
Kelly, Ellsworth 41
Kerlor, Wilhem de 24
Klee, Paul 17, 30, 58
Knoll 101
Kokoschka, Oskar 29
Kusama, Yayoi 8, 74–9, 106, 109
  Accumulation No. 1 8, *77*, 78
  All the Eternal Love I Have for the Pumpkins 79
  Infinity Mirror Room – Phalli's Field 76, 78

L
Ladd, Steven and William 192
Lampl, Fritz 36
Larsen, Jack Lenor 94
Lasansky, Mauricio 71
Laszkiewicz, Maria 89
Lawrence, Jacob 82, 138
Léger, Fernand 51
Levy, Julien 46
LeWitt, Sol 106, *107*
Liberty 36
Lichtenstein, Roy 159, 198
Louis Vuitton 79
Lucas, Sarah 8, 48, 160–5
  Au Naturel 162, *163*
  Bunny Gets Snookered 163–4, *163*
  NUD CYCLADIC 16 164, *164–5*
  Self-Portrait with Fried Eggs 160

M
McCannon, Dindga 136–41
  Althea Gibson, First African American to Win Wimbledon 139, 140
  Art Quilt from 'The Women in Jazz' series *140*
  Wedding Party: The History of Our Nation is Really the Story of Families 138, 140, *141*
Macdonald, Margaret and Frances 7
Martinez, Julian 20
  Black-on-Black Jar 21
Martinez, Maria 18–21
  Black-on-Black Jar 21
  Feather Bowl 20, *20*
Martinez, Santana Roybal 20
  Feather Bowl 20, *20*

Matisse, Henri 134, 155
Messager, Annette 7, 126–31
  Les Pensionnaires 128
  Mes petites effigies 129
  Pénétration 130, 131
Metropolitan Museum of Art, New York 134, 198
Millais, John Everett 186
Mimbres culture 20
Minimalism 156
Modernism 72
Moholy-Nagy, László 41
Monir Museum, Tehran 67
Morris, May 7
mosaics, Monir Shahroudy Farmanfarmaian 62–7
Mucha, Patty 8
Mud People's Black Women's Resource Sharing Workshop 113
Mukherjee, Benode Behari 149
Mukherjee, Leela 149
Mukherjee, Mrinalini 9, 148–53
  Bougainvillea 150, *151*
  Night Bloom VI 153, *153*
  Vanshri 150, *152*
Museum of Modern Art, New York 46, 106
  'Anni Albers Textiles' 30, *31*
  Judith Scott 125
  Louise Bourgeois 55
  Miriam Schapiro 69
  Sheila Hicks 101
  Wall Hangings (1969) 94

N
National Academy Museum, New York 72
National Endowment for the Arts 21
Nkanga, Otobong 178–83
  Fattening Room 180–1, *180*
  Fragiologist's Predicament 181, *182*
  Steel to Rust – Corrosion 182, *183*

O
O'Keeffe, Georgia 116
Oldenburg, Claes 8, 78, 106
Op Art 31
Oppenheim, Méret 27, 125
  Object (Le Déjeuner en fourrure) 8
Orplid 36

P
Parsons New School for Design 64
Pattern and Decoration (P&D) movement 72–3, 156
Perry, Grayson 207
Pettway, Mary Margaret 16
Picasso, Pablo 45, 82, 134
Pitchford-Jolly, Marva Lee 110–13

  Action Studio 112, 113
  Matilda and Mattie 113, *113*
Pop Art 78, 207
post-Modernism 72
Preston, Felicia Grant 113
Pueblo Native Americans 19–21

Q
quilting 9
  Faith Ringgold 80–5
  Judy Chicago 114–19
  Miriam Schapiro 68–73
  women of Gee's Bend 12–17

R
Rauschenberg, Robert 168
Ray, Man 24, 47
Rie, Lucie 9, 34–7, 94
  Footed bowl 36–7, 36
  Twisted rope buttons 36, *37*
Riley, Bridget 31
Ringgold, Faith 9, 80–5, 138
  Dinner at Gertrude Stein's (The French Collection, Part II: #9)
    83, 85, *85*
  Faith (The Family of Women) 83
  We Meet the Monster 84
Robinson, Miss Ella 197

S
Saatchi, Charles 162
Sanskriti Pratishthan 153
Sapphire & Crystals 113
Schapiro, Miriam 9, 68–73
  Barcelona Fan 72
  Big Ox 70–1, 72
  Conservatory (Portrait of Frida Kahlo) 73, *73*
Schiaparelli, Elsa 22–7
  Evening Coat 25
  The Tears Dress 26, 27
  Woman's Sweater 24, *24*, 27
Schöps, Diana 180
Scott, Judith 120–5
  Untitled (1994) 122, *122–3*, 125
  Untitled (2003–2004) *124*
  Untitled (JS 62) 122, *125*
sculpture *see* soft sculpture
Self, Tschabalala 196–201
  Bodega Run 200, *200–1*
  Out of Body 198, *199*
Shapiro, Miriam 116
The Shop 162
Simpson, Wallis 27
Slade School of Fine Art 145

Socialist Realism 168
soft sculpture 8
  Annette Messager 126–31
  Dorothea Tanning 44–9
  Eva Hesse 104–9
  Faith Ringgold 80–5
  Judith Scott 120–5
  Louise Bourgeois 48, 50–5
  Magdalena Abakanowicz 86–91
  Mrinalini Mukherjee 148–53
  Sarah Lucas 160–5
  Sarah Zapata 190–5
  Sheila Hicks 98–103
  Yayoi Kusama 74–9
  Yin Xiuzhen 166–71
Stein, Gertrude 83, 85
Stella, Frank 58, 67
Stölzl, Gunta 30
Subramanyan, K.G. 149–50
Surrealism 8, 27
  Dorothea Tanning 45, 46, 47, 48

T
Taipale, Martta 41
Tanning, Dorothea 44–9
  Eine Kleine Nachtmusik 46–7, *46*, 48
  A Guest 47, *47*
  Hôtel du Pavot, Chambre 202 48, *48–9*
tapestries
  Alexandra Kehayoglou 184–9
  Billie Zangewa 172–7
  Otobong Nkanga 178–83
Tawney, George 39
Tawney, Lenore 9, 38–43, 94
  Box of Falling Stars 43
  Dark River Wall Hanging 42
  Landscape 40, 41
textile art 9
  Judy Chicago 114–19
  Miriam Schapiro 68–73
  Polly Apfelbaum 154–9
  Rut Bryk 56–61
  Yin Xiuzhen 166–71
Thompson, Jane Gaddie 117, 119, *119*
Tribu No 145
Tubman, Harriet 82, 85
Twentieth Creator Art Creators 138

V
Van Noten, Dries 186
Vicuña, Cecilia 142–7
  Quipu Austral 144, 147
  Quipu in the gutter 145, *145*

Quipu Menstrual 145, *146–7*
Vienna Secession style 35, 36
Viennese Modernism 35

W
Wang Lu 159
Warhol, Andy 64, 78, 200
wearable art
  Dorothea Tanning 44–9
  Elsa Schiaparelli 23–7
  Isabelle de Borchgrave 132–5
  Olga de Amaral 92–7
weaving
  Anni Albers 28–33
  Lenore Tawney 38–43
  Louise Bourgeois 50–5
  Magdalena Abakanowicz 86–91
  Olga de Amaral 92–7
  Sarah Zapata 190–5
  Sheila Hicks 98–103
Webb, Aileen Osborn 94
West, Mae 27
Weusi Artists Collective 138
Where We At, Black Women Artists 138
Whitney Museum of American Art, New York 77, 109
World Crafts Council (WCC) 94

X
Xiao Lu 168
Xiuzhen, Yin 166–71
  Dress Box 168, 170
  Portable City: Dunhuang 169, 170
  Weapon 171

Y
Yale School of Art 101, 106, 198
Young, Annie Mae, *Work-clothes Quilt with Centre Medallion of Strips 14*, 17
Young British Artists (YBAs) 162

Z
Zangewa, Billie 172–7
  Christmas at the Ritz 174
  The Rebirth of the Black Venus 175, 176
  Temporary Reprieve 176, *177*
Zapata, Sarah 9, 190–5
  If I Could images 195
  Living in Our Own Time (3 gargoyles) 195
  Siempre X 192–3, 194

Picture credits

cover, pp.11, 209 Jessie Cutts.
pp.2, 199, 200–201 Courtesy of the artists and Pilar Corrias, London / Galerie Eva Presenhuber, New York / Zurich.
p.12 Photo Chronicle/Alamy Stock Photo.
p.14 © Louisiana Bendolph / ARS, NY and DACS, London 2021. Photo by Steve Pitkin, © ARS, NY.
p.15 Photo by Steve Pitkin, © ARS, NY.
p.16 © Estate of Willie "Ma Willie" Abrams / DACS 2021. Photo by Steve Pitkin, © ARS, NY.
P.18 Photo © CORBIS/Corbis via Getty Images.
p.20 © The Metropolitan Museum of Art/Art Resource/Scala, Florence.
p.21 © Cooper-Hewitt, Smithsonian Design Museum/Art Resource, NY/Scala, Florence.
p.22 Courtesy of Photo12/Universal Images Group via Getty Images
p.24 Photo © Philadelphia Museum of Art / Gift of Mme Elsa Schiaparelli, 1969 / Bridgeman Images.
pp.25, 26 Photo © Victoria and Albert Museum, London.
p.28 Photo courtesy of the Western Regional Archives, State Archives of North Carolina.
p.31 The Museum of Modern Art Archives, New York. Photographer: Soichi Sunami. Cat.: IN421.4. © 2021. Digital image, The Museum of Modern Art, New York/Scala, Florence © The Josef and Anni Albers Foundation / Artists Rights Society (ARS), New York and DACS, London.
p.32 Purchase, Everfast Fabrics Inc. and Edward C. Moore Jr. Gift, 1969 (69.134). © 2021. Image © The Metropolitan Museum of Art/Art Resource/Scala, Florence.
© The Josef and Anni Albers Foundation / Artists Rights Society (ARS), New York and DACS, London.
p.33 Courtesy of the National Museum of Women in the Arts, Gift of Wallace and Wilhelmina Holladay. © The Josef and Anni Albers Foundation / Artists Rights Society (ARS), New York and DACS, London.
p.34 Photo Tony Evans/Getty Images.
p.36 Photo Byron Slater Photography.
p.37 Photo by Phill Sayer. Coutesy of The Anthony Shaw Collection / York Museums Trust (York Art Gallery) & Phil Sayer.
p.38 Photo David Attie/Getty Images.
p.40 © Lenore G. Tawney Foundation. Alexander Demond Fund inv no. 1981.37. Chicago (IL), Art Institute of Chicago. Photo © 2021 The Art Institute of Chicago / Art Resource, NY/ Scala, Florence.
p.42 © Lenore G. Tawney Foundation. Greta Daniel Design Fund. Acc. no.: 133.1963. Photo © 2021 The Museum of Modern Art, New York/Scala, Florence.
p.43 © Lenore G. Tawney Foundation. Museum purchase through the Smithsonian Institution Collections Acquisition Program (1992.83). Washington DC, Smithsonian American Art Museum. Photo © 2021 Smithsonian American Art Museum/Art Resource/ Scala, Florence.
p.44 Photo Michael Ochs Archives/Getty Images.
p.46 © ADAGP, Paris and DACS, London. Photo Tate.
p.47 © ADAGP, Paris and DACS, London. Photo courtesy of The Dorothea Tanning Foundation.
pp.48–49 © ADAGP, Paris and DACS, London. Inv.: AM1977-204. Photographer Georges Meguerditchian. Paris, Musee National d'Art Moderne - Centre Pompidou. Photo © RMN-Grand Palais / Dist. /SCALA, Florence.
p.50 Alamy Stock Photo.
p.52 Collection Glenstone Foundation, © The Easton Foundation/ VAGA at ARS, NY and DACS, London 2021. Photo: Ron Amstutz.
pp.53, 55 © The Easton Foundation/VAGA at ARS, NY and DACS, London. Photo Christopher Burke.
p.56 © Maaria Wirkkala.
pp.59, 60 Tapio Wirkkala Rut Bryk Foundation Collection/EMMA – Espoo Museum of Modern Art. © Ari Karttunen/EMMA.
p.61 HAM Helsinki Art Museum. © Ari Karttunen/EMMA.
p.62 Photo by Ebrahim Safi. Courtesy of The Estate of Monir Shahroudy Farmanfarmaian.
p.64 Gift of Unknown Donor (2000-26-13). Photo © Smithsonian Institution. Cooper-Hewitt, Smithsonian Design Museum/Art Resource, NY/Scala, Florence.
p.65 Courtesy of The Estate of Monir Shahroudy Farmanfarmaian.
p.66 Courtesy of The Estate of Monir Shahroudy Farmanfarmaian and James Cohan, New York.
p.68 Photo © Lee Boltin / Bridgeman Images.
p.70–71 © Estate of Miriam Schapiro / ARS, NY and DACS, London.
p.72 The Metropolitan Museum of Art, New York. Gift of Steven M. Jacobson and Howard Kalka, 1993 (1993.408). Photo: The Metropolitan Museum of Art/Art Resource/Scala, Florence. © Estate of Miriam Schapiro / ARS, NY and DACS, London.
p.73 © Estate of Miriam Schapiro / ARS, NY and DACS, London. Image courtesy of Miami University Art Museum, Oxford, Ohio.
p.74 Photo M. Sobreira/Alamy
p.76, 79 © YAYOI KUSAMA.
p.77 above: Photo J. Countess/Getty Images; below: Purchase. Acc. n.:1182.2012. © 2021. Digital image, The Museum of Modern Art, New York/Scala, Florence.
p.80 Photo: Anthony Barboza/Getty Images.
pp. 83, 84, 85 © Faith Ringgold / ARS, NY and DACS, London, Courtesy ACA Galleries, New York 2021.
p.86 Photo: Artur Starewicz/East News.

Acknowledgements

I'd first like to thank the team at Frances Lincoln for their wonderful support on this project. Thank you to Nicki Davis for trusting me with this idea and to Charlotte Frost for your hard work throughout. It was wonderful to work with you both.

In writing this book, it was extremely important to me to reflect the lives and works of the artists in an accurate and thoughtful way. Working towards that aim, I interviewed nearly half of the living artists represented in the book, and there were several other artists and estates who provided further feedback and information, for which I'm very thankful. I'm immensely grateful to Polly Apfelbaum, Hannah Hill, Alexandra Kehayoglou, Dindga McCannon, Otobong Nkanga, Mary Margaret Pettway, Tschabalala Self, Billie Zangewa and Sarah Zapata, who kindly made time to have conversations with me and trusted me to share a small piece of each of your incredible stories.

One unexpected result of writing this book is that it inspired me to teach myself how to quilt (with some helpful beginner tips from fellow art historian Jess Bailey). I found myself thinking about the textile work of the women in my family—my paternal and maternal grandmothers, as well as my mother-in-law—and how special their talents are/were. Talents they used to clothe their children or keep them warm with blankets and quilts. I noticed how several artists in this book were first introduced to the textile medium through the women in their families as well. I wanted to explore that maternal connection in a tangible way, and I'm glad that I've been able to do that.

To my husband, Tom Lloyd, who has patiently listened to me think out loud throughout this writing project (and several others): bless you. Thank you for being there for me, for being my best friend, and for being a great dad to our son. I love you and Winter very much.

Finally, thank you to those of you who have taken the time to watch any of my videos, read my books, listen to my podcast, or come to one of my talks. You could do anything in the world, and you choose to occasionally spend some time with me—I think that's pretty cool.

The publisher would like to thank all of the artists, galleries and estates who helped make the book possible. In particular, Cristina Seghi at Scala for her patience and help in tracking down numerous artworks, and also Felicia Preston and Rose Blouin for their help in assembling the entry covering Marva Lee Pitchford-Jolly.

Quarto

© 2022 Quarto Publishing plc
Text © 2022 Ferren Gipson

First published in 2022 by Frances Lincoln Publishing
an imprint of The Quarto Group.
1 Triptych Place,
London, SE1 9SH
United Kingdom
www.Quarto.com

A catalogue record for this book is available from the British Library.

ISBN 978 0 7112 6465 6
Ebook ISBN 978 0 7112 8046 5

10 9 8 7 6 5 4

Design by Mariana Sameiro
Quilt featured on the cover and p.11 by Jessie Cutts: https://www.cuttsandsons.com

Printed in China